HUMAN SERVICES TECHNOLOGY

HUMAN SERVICES TECHNOLOGY

✻

RONALD F. HOLLER

Director, Mental Health Technology,
Arizona State Hospital and Maricopa Technical College,
Phoenix, Arizona

GEORGE M. DeLONG

Arizona State Hospital and Maricopa Technical College,
Phoenix, Arizona

THE C. V. MOSBY COMPANY

SAINT LOUIS   1973

Library of Congress Cataloging in Publication Data

Holler, Ronald F   1938-
   Human services technology.

   Bibliography: p.
   1. Mental hygiene. 2. Psychotherapy. 3. Mental
health personnel. I. DeLong, George M., 1947-
II. Title. [DNLM: 1. Behavior. 2. Mental health
services. 3. Mental disorders. WM 30 H737h 1973]
RA790.H54   362'.0425   73-1441
ISBN 0-8016-2227-1

In vain the sage, with retrospective eye,
Would from the apparent what conclude the why,
Infer the motive from the deed, and show
That what we chanced was what we meant to do.

Alexander Pope
Moral Essays

PREFACE

❦

This book is designed as an introductory text for those who have completed their secondary education and plan to pursue a career in the mental health field or one of the helping services at the college level. It will also provide a background for students who are studying or who may later obtain more advanced degrees in counseling, psychology, social work, special education, nursing, or other related disciplines.

Foremost in our thoughts have been several facts about the nature of human problems of living and the utilization and delivery of mental health services. As has always been the case, there is a dire shortage of personnel who have received sufficient training to enable them to relate therapeutically with other individuals, whether in an institutional or community setting. There has been a trend toward increasing the number of students in fields such as social work and clinical psychology, but several sobering factors suggest that highly trained doctoral or master's level personnel will not solve the manpower shortage in the mental health field.

One factor that was a determining influence for the preparation of this book was the recent findings of various researchers on psychotherapy that indicate individuals from a variety of educational, socioeconomic, and ethnic backgrounds can be rapidly trained to work therapeutically with individuals in distress. Second, the amount of time required and the attrition rates associated with professional education limit the number of the highest educated persons available to perform this type of work. An often overlooked but very important factor is the economic requirements of the professional in mental health. In order to meet the demands of society for mental health services, it would be economically difficult or impossible to employ the large number of master's or doctoral level people necessary. These facts indicate both the need for and the feasibility of training programs designed specifically to produce a human service worker/mental health generalist at the college level.

Thus, *Human Services Technology* has been written to fulfill the need for a basic textbook in this area, which we realized as a result of our work in a training program for human services personnel. We have attempted to provide an introductory perspective of human behavior and to describe the manner in which the technological discoveries of behavioral scientists may be applied to serving various human needs in relatively diverse agencies responsible for assessing and helping people with behavior problems. We have also examined the numerous roles an individual may play in serving others. Finally, but most important to us, we have attempted to present a broad and comprehensive introduction to the principles and skills required for successful service to others in the mental health field.

Instructors and students using this textbook will note that Appendix A contains a relatively more scientific and mathematical account of principles for assessing and understanding human behavior. This was not placed in the body of the text in order to avoid interference with the steady flow of verbal content.

We gratefully acknowledge the assistance and important influence of colleagues and helpers who contributed to the development of this book. In particular, a few of them are Willis H. Bower, M.D., Director of the Arizona State Hospital, whose vision and support have been of immeasurable consequence; T. E. Newland, Ph.D., University of Illinois, who provided the senior author with an original, sustaining impetus; Barbara Levy, Ph.D., Arizona State University and State of Arizona Health Department; and, at Maricopa Technical College, Norbert Bruemmer, Executive Dean; Floretta Awe, Chairman of Allied Health; and James B. Sutton, Ph.D. Our colleagues who broadened our perspective are Thomas A. Newhall, Ray Cohen, Mary Baker, Peggy Cronin, Mary Lou LeGrand, and Ron Roesch. Linda Call, Janis Jordan, and Joann Kroll, who prepared the final manuscript, deserve special commendation. Our greatest debt is to our wives, Lois and Elizabeth, who unfailingly encourage us.

Ronald F. Holler
George M. DeLong

CONTENTS

4. THE PERSON AND GROUP MEMBERSHIP, 60

5. METHODS OF BEHAVIOR ASSESSMENT, 85

HUMAN SERVICES TECHNOLOGY

1
INTRODUCTION

It is a fact of life that things do not always go as well as we would like. This idea is expressed in a famous poem that states "the best laid schemes o' mice and men gang aft a-gley." All people have difficulties in coping with the daily stresses and strains of living. Some find themselves in very unfortunate conditions and develop inappropriate, self-defeating, or very deviant behavior. Individuals with such extreme behavior are commonly referred to as being "mentally ill." We will have considerably more to say about the usage of the term "mental illness," although we will use it as a matter of convention. Primarily, "mental illness" simply refers to behavior that is considered abnormal or inappropriate by some person or group.

Abnormal behavior in American society causes people to be placed in penal or correctional institutions, mental hospitals, special education classrooms, alcoholic treatment programs, and a host of other agencies. Probably everyone knows someone in his immediate or extended family who has been considered mentally ill. Readers will note numerous behaviors in this book that pertain rather directly to themselves and that are classified as some type of mental disorder. Everyone is occasionally extremely upset or disturbed, and, on the other side of the coin, some severely disturbed persons are often quite rational, effective, and normal. In other words, the distinctions between normal and abnormal are often vague, shifting, and fine.

Many people have fears of becoming mentally ill. This apparently results from a misunderstanding of what mental illness really is. The term "mental illness" often gives a very inaccurate and false connotation of abnormal behavior. An old Quaker proverb sums up the way people view the behavior of others while defending their own actions and standards. The proverb states: "Everyone is queer save thee and me, and sometimes I think thee a bit queer too."

We tend to believe that our problems are unique, that no one else could possibly have any problems similar to our own. This is patently false, for people

1

have many more similarities than they do differences. Superficial appearances can be very deceiving.

Another problem in the human services field relates to the disgrace people feel in regard to their personal problems. Although they will consult medical specialists in regard to medical problems and educators in regard to educational problems, people continue to believe they are weak or "sinful" when they find they cannot cope with the problems of life. They tend to avoid seeking help and sometimes develop more severe disorders as a result. They are not aware of or refuse to attend to another important fact, which is that everyone's be-

Fig. 1. Problem-solving huddle. (EPA Newsphoto, Editorial Photocolor Archives.)

havioral effectiveness can be increased. By no means is this improvement considered a cure, for people must continue to cope with their problems as long as they are alive.

One of the greatest problems facing modern society is the delivery of adequate and effective human services. There is a manpower shortage that results from numerous interacting factors, including the rapid shift of population to the cities and the relatively recent development of sophisticated and effective methods of understanding and controlling deviant behavior. This book provides knowledge and skills at an introductory level to increase the effectiveness of human services manpower. The term "human services" broadly subsumes mental health, corrections, welfare, education, and others. Although "mental health" is used most commonly, the reader can substitute the term most relevant to him, and the content largely will remain of comparable meaning.

HISTORICAL PERSPECTIVE OF MENTAL HEALTH AND DEVIANT BEHAVIOR

History is replete with accounts of disordered behavior exhibited by famous persons. The Bible reports behavior by numerous individuals that would be termed abnormal, at least in the sense of being very deviant, cruel, criminal, or sexually inappropriate. Many ancient people also report unusual behavior and their understanding and treatment of it. Human skulls from the Stone Age have been found with rather large circular areas of the bone cut away. This early form of brain surgery was done to allow evil spirits, which were thought to cause unusual behavior, to escape from the person. Some individuals actually may have survived these crude operations.

There is much in literature that would suggest that some men of all times had an unusual ability to understand and modify abnormal behavior by methods that have some parallels today. However, their theories, techniques, and ability to evaluate the effects of their treatment have certainly undergone extensive improvement throughout the ages. A major theme regarding the cause of mental illness has been the concept of demons or evil spirits, and this conception resulted in very unfortunate and inhumane methods of changing the person. A parallel still exists among many otherwise intelligent people both within and outside the mental health professions today. This parallel involves the conception that mental illness is indeed an illness, rather than a categorization of behavior. In effect, what has occurred is a substitution of the word "demon" with "mental illness." There are, of course, people who have a much more adequate understanding of people and their problems. At a recent conference on mental health one of the speakers was asked how his particular techniques could be used with schizophrenics. He replied: "I would use them with schizophrenics in the same manner as I would use them with witches." The speaker was questioning the actual existence of people categorized as schizophrenics in the same way he questioned the existence of witches. There are no witches and there are no schizophrenics, at least not to him.

During the Middle Ages the epidemic known as the black death killed millions of people and forever altered numerous social organizations. People who behaved strangely during this disruptive period were often tortured or executed in a most barbarous fashion. They were burned, hanged, decapitated, drawn and quartered (pulled apart by four horses), and mutilated in uncountable ways. They were whipped, starved, immersed in scalding water, and set upon by killer animals. Even children were not exempt from such punishment.

What could form the basis for such treatment to alter the behavior of people who were perceived as different from others? One basis for such tragic treatment was religious dogma, and the formal Christian religion was one that actively encouraged it. The reasoning was that people behave deviantly because they are possessed by the devil and/or are being punished by God for sins. The person was thought to be actually an agent of the devil or, in other words, a witch. This viewpoint had such an effect that pious persons only a few hundred years ago felt that their religious duty was to seek out, identify, and kill the witches. They cheered and felt self-satisfied as they watched a disturbed or retarded person being tortured and murdered. Picture a gathering by neighbors gleefully cheering the murder of another neighbor.

One Pope during the Middle Ages appointed two monks to write a manual that attempted to confirm the existence of witches. It noted that those who did not believe in them either were in honest error or were heretics. It described the behaviors or clinical symptoms that would help identify witches and provided the legal basis for examining and sentencing a witch. The accepted and certain way to gain a confession from a person, according to the manual, was to torture him until he admitted he was a witch. This manual was believed by many to be divinely inspired, and it emphasized the duty of all truly religious people to follow it closely.

A confession of being a witch could be obtained from anybody if the torture were made severe enough, for being put to death as a witch seemed preferable to painful mutilation. Furthermore, many disturbed people then, as today, will say the most outrageous and false things about themselves, such as being a disciple of the devil or a wolf in human disguise.

The exact number of people murdered as a result of such demonological concepts is unknown, although there were many thousands. It is reported that in Geneva, Switzerland, 500 persons were burned in the single year 1515. Nor was the horror of the witch hunt restricted to Europe. Salem, Massachusetts, is famous for witch trials, and the reader is encouraged to review the accounts to obtain an accurate indication of man's inhumanity to man. Cruelness is not restricted to the concentration camps of Nazi Germany but can and has occurred in the name of Christianity. It can also occur in the name of psychology, medicine, or any other discipline concerned with human life and the human condition.

DEVELOPMENT OF MAJOR MENTAL HEALTH INSTITUTIONS

The witchcraft and demonology participants began to receive opposition, including changing perspectives from the Christian churches. Monasteries often became havens for the disturbed and different, and in 1547 the monastery of St. Mary of Bethlehem at London became a mental hospital by decree of Henry VIII. The word "bedlam" was contracted from the name of this institution because of the chaotic and violent conditions existing there. Other institutions developed in France, the United States, and other countries. Although by today's standards they were very inhumane, moralistic, and authoritarian, they were far superior to receiving certain death at the hands of the witch hunters. Reforms then began to occur in such institutions, with Pinel of eighteenth-century France receiving fame for unchaining the inmates and generally providing them with treatment acceptable for human beings.

In the United States the movement to provide more humanitarian methods for the treatment of the mentally ill received impetus from Dorothea Dix. Miss Dix was a schoolteacher who began working with the disturbed in jails, hospitals, and other institutions during the 1840's. She aroused citizens to provide funds for the establishment of many mental hospitals, some of which are still in existence. Although at the time her work was perceived as an important reform movement, she has the distinction of leaving a heritage of many state mental hospitals with deplorable conditions. That is, what began as a reform movement eventually resulted in the warehousing of the misfits of contemporary society.

These early institutions were not viewed as medical, but gradually they became staffed by professionals trained in medicine. In 1844, thirteen of these superintendents formed the Association of Medical Superintendents of American Institutions for the Insane. This group formed the basis for today's American Psychiatric Association. Other groups involved with the behavioral effectiveness and abnormalities of people were not and are not medically oriented. Welfare organizations, public schools, halfway houses, adoption agencies, personnel departments in industry, and many others are staffed by people not trained primarily in medicine. The mental hospitals, both private and public, are the only major institutions in the general area of behavioral effectiveness that have a clear and definitive medical and biological orientation regarding their clients. The residents of such institutions usually are still called patients.

DEVELOPMENT OF MAJOR MENTAL HEALTH PROFESSIONS

Along with the emerging trend toward mental institutions and other agencies for the treatment of deviant or socially unacceptable behavior, there occurred a series of changing viewpoints, a diversification in skills of the personnel delivering services, and a formation of specialty professions. Psychosocial or behavioral science based–professions include psychology, social work, education, and rehabilitation. The biological science–based professions include psychiatry, neurology, general medicine, and nursing. Each of these has its own history of development, areas of expertise, conflicts within and with other professional groups, primary locations of work, and current status and potential.

Psychologists. Psychologists are generally recognized as the group especially well trained in the scientific research aspects of behavior. They are also highly trained in the areas of behavior assessment, counseling and psychotherapy, teaching and consultation, and other areas involving a rigorous application of behavioral science to human problems. There are many psychologists who are not primarily interested in making direct applications of their science but who are more involved in doing basic research and teaching academic subjects in universities.

Applied psychologists may be called clinical psychologists, counseling psychologists, school psychologists, and industrial psychologists. The adjectives primarily describe the location in which they work. Their training, experience, and focus of interest vary considerably, sometimes within each subspecialty as much as among them.

Usually the fully qualified psychologist has a doctoral degree, which may be the Doctor of Philosophy (Ph.D.), the Doctor of Psychology (Psy.D.), or the Doctor of Education (Ed.D). The typical doctoral level psychologist has completed 4 years of college for the bachelor's degree, 2 years for the master's degree, 3 years for the academic doctoral requirements, a master's thesis, a doctoral dissertation, and 1 or more year's internship. This lengthy program usually requires 11 or more years of study and research beyond high school, and most psychologists are around 30 years old before they have completed their doctoral degrees.

Since psychologists are not medically trained, they do not do physical examinations, make medical diagnosis of physical conditions, prescribe drugs, or perform surgery. The doctorate is a recognition of their abilities as scholars and behavioral scientists. There has been a rapid growth in the number of psychologists, although there are currently only 30,000 members of the American Psychological Association. Psychologists are increasingly offering their services to the public as individual professional practitioners.

Social workers. The fully qualified social worker usually has a Master of Social Work (M.S.W.) degree, which requires 2 years of graduate study beyond the bachelor's degree. The master's program is usually a third to a half experience in the field actually working with people. There are also many people at the bachelor's degree level performing social work tasks, and some social workers are now obtaining doctoral degrees. Doctoral level social workers tend to function as professors in university schools of social work.

The social worker is a key person in many settings, including mental hospitals, schools, community guidance centers, and various types of welfare agencies. Often the first person the patient or client sees is the social worker, who will obtain the background information and provide a preliminary understanding of the person's life difficulties. Social workers obtain histories, perform therapy and case work, and often serve as direct links from the agency to the total family. A few social workers are in private practice, often with psychologists and psychiatrists. A particular area of expertise is that of referring clients and coordinating services among community agencies.

Educators. Since many people are in need of information and an increase in academic and vocational skills, educators are employed in numerous agencies, and of course the major one is the public schools. Educators almost always have at least a bachelor's degree with training in educational methods and a background in at least one academic or vocational area that they teach. They may also have advanced training at the master's and/or doctoral level.

Their training includes courses on understanding and working with people with problems more significant than average. Through their experience they become highly aware of individual differences in abilities and disabilities. Educators probably lead all professional groups in continuing their education after being admitted to their profession. Graduate schools of education often have students in their middle and later years of life obtaining advanced instruction. Educators are the group to which other professions often make referrals for more direct behavior change services.

Rehabilitation therapists. Rehabilitation personnel include occupational therapists, rehabilitation counselors, recreation therapists, and personnel with similar titles. They have much in common with educators in general, but their training is focused more toward returning patients to their former levels of functioning with the use of less direct teaching methods. Rehabilitative personnel usually have 4 years of college and advanced supervised experience in working with disturbed and disabled people. Many have master's or doctoral degree in rehabilitation, psychology, or other areas. They help clients explore job possibilities, which may be more limited because of injuries or disabilities. They provide supervised experience in occupational training to help their clients learn new jobs, understand themselves, and obtain therapeutic benefits from recreational and creative activities, including arts and crafts. The rehabilitative therapists are quite diverse in their orientation and skills, and they are the recipient of referrals from other professional personnel. They tend to have an educational and psychosocial emphasis. They are probably somewhat more attuned to physical problems that interfere with the effectiveness of their clients' behavior than are psychologists and educators, for example.

Psychiatrists. Psychiatry is a medical specialty. The biologically and physically oriented medical doctorate is usually obtained after 4 years of college and 4 years of medical school, after which the person obtains the M.D. He then serves an internship and is qualified for general practice as a physician. Such physicians are often the first source of contact with people having psychosocial problems, and the physician makes proper referral for such patients.

If the physician desires to become a psychiatrist, he must serve a 3-year residency for that specialty. The residency involves study and supervised experience in the area of abnormal behavior. Unlike the psychologist, the psychiatrist is not strictly a behavioral scientist, but he is qualified to make medical and physical diagnoses, prescribe drugs, and perform surgery. Like the psychologist, the psychiatrist is trained to understand and help people who have behavioral difficulties, and he has the skills to assess persons' behavior with various techniques and do psychotherapy. In practice there is probably at least a 75% overlap between the actual roles and functions of psychologists and psychiatrists in most settings.

Psychiatrists work with many different kinds of agencies and institutions serving the disturbed. They are usually the professionals designated as being administratively responsible in mental hospitals. Many also offer their services privately.

Some medical schools have attempted to reduce the 12 years or so beyond high school usually required before becoming a psychiatrist, because the psychiatrist is usually around 30 years of age before he can assume his practice. One medical school has developed a program that allows the high school graduate to obtain a medical doctorate 6 years after entry. Those physicians who specialize in psychiatry may serve their residency in 3 years, with a total of 9 years elapsing before assuming psychiatric practice.

Nurses. There are several ways to become a nurse; one may obtain a diploma from a hospital school of nursing, a 4-year bachelor's degree from a university program, or an associate of arts (A.A.) degree from a 2-year community college. The training is similar in all three programs in terms of academic content and supervised experience. The title registered nurse (R.N.) is obtained after completing the basic requirements and passing a state board examination. Registered nurses do not necessarily have bachelor's degrees, but bachelor's degree programs may become more common in the future. Some nurses have master's and doctorate degrees and, like social workers, they are usually employed in universities training nurses.

Most people are familiar with the role and functions of the nurse in physical care settings. However, the public is generally less familiar with the functions of professional nurses in mental health settings. The psychiatric nurse has obtained advanced training through supervision and in-service programs, and the job duties may include psychotherapy, supervision of less trained personnel, and other functions in common with the other mental health personnel.

Mental health workers. This brief account of the major mental health professional groups indicates both similarities and differences among all the professions employed in mental health settings. There is research to clearly indicate a great need for increasing the number of personnel in all fields, and some of the traditional professions have attempted to alter their training programs to graduate more personnel.

The new mental health technicians or workers are increasingly receiving more adequate and specific training, and they are being recruited in larger numbers. Ultimately the new mental health workers may become recognized as the most numerous (and possibly most effective) group in the mental health field.

SOCIAL INFLUENCES ON CONCEPTIONS OF MENTAL HEALTH

The concepts of insanity and criminality are based on cultural standards of behavior. They are the historical results of political, economic, and religious influences, and they are rarely if ever acceptably defined for everyone within the culture. Hence they tend to be very much subject to conflicting viewpoints and change through the years. Social influences on the concepts of insanity and criminality are pervasive, but they are subtle and very complex.

It has been stated that one person's mental illness is another person's mental health. A person who behaves with great anger under particular circumstances may be viewed by some members of society as well within his rights. Another observer may believe the same person is overreacting and exhibiting a lack of adequate self-control and reason. Many white people view the behavior of blacks as deviant from the normal, whereas the black American may well have a very opposite perception. In contemporary Russia the intellectual who does not wholeheartedly accept communism may be placed in a mental institution for his deviant behavior. Russia has recently come under much criticism for institutionalizing citizens who criticize the political and economic systems. Lest we become too smug about our own rationality, we should be aware that university professors who denounce capitalism and obtain a measure of success in doing so stand a very high probability of being fired. Their statements are labeled as "weird, pinko communism," and they may ultimately be labeled paranoid or with some other word from the field of abnormal psychology. At least by implication they are being considered insane and unworthy of normal consideration. Some believe they should be placed outside the mainstream of life.

American citizens who are rich and powerful and who behave in unusual ways are often considered eccentric and humorous. They may avoid interaction with other people to a fantastic degree and practically throw away vast amounts of money. The public follows such activities in the newspapers and magazines with great interest. Since such people have the power and resources to obtain legal and social protection, they rarely end up in state mental institutions. On the other hand, if a very poor and illiterate person engages in such unusual behavior, he has a good chance of being committed to a mental institution. Poverty stricken and poorly educated persons are termed the "high-risk population," meaning they have a high probability of being labeled insane.

The degree to which religion influences public conceptions of insanity is evidenced by the differences between the Christian United States and the Hindu, Buddhist, and Moslem countries. Thomas Szasz (1970) has written a book entitled *The Manufacture of Madness: A Comparative Study of the Inquisition and the Mental Health Movement*. He compares the witch hunts of the Middle Ages with modern attempts to identify and commit to mental institutions citizens who behave in a manner significantly different from the majority of the people. Where the inquisitors of the Middle Ages were serving the religious authorities, mental health professionals of today are serving the political state. This extreme position of Szasz, which is at least partly unfair and inaccurate, has come under much criticism. Nevertheless, it is most certainly true that millions of Americans believe people who behave differently or in a way that upsets them should be categorized as disturbed. They desire to place them outside American society, perhaps preferably in a fenced and locked building outside their own living area.

Behavioral scientists believe that behavior, both normal and abnormal, is determined or caused. They must believe this in order to proceed about their business of scientifically studying the causes and maintainers of behavior. The concept of determinism, as contrasted with free will, sometimes comes into direct conflict with moral and legal authorities, at least according to those who assert that people are totally responsible for their own behavior. The place of psychologists and psychiatrists as expert witnesses in the courtroom and other functions in legal matters has been well publicized and often condemned.

Insanity is a legal term. The expert witness in the past was asked to testify whether or not a person was at the time of an illegal action unable to distinguish between right or wrong, which is known as the McNaghten Rule for insanity. This legal interpretation of insanity has been changed in some courts because it was considered insufficient. The Durham Rule is increasingly used, which holds that the defendant will not be held criminally responsible for his behavior if he has a mental illness or defect. At this time a third view, which is the idea of "irresistible impulse" to behave abnormally, is being considered. This indicates that defendants may have had their behavior caused and determined by events, thoughts, and feelings beyond their effective control.

THE AIDE CULTURE

As institutions and professions in mental health developed, mental hospitals in particular became very crowded. Although Miss Dix's original institutions were very treatment-oriented, humane, and rather effective, they soon became understaffed and overwhelmed with large numbers of inmates. Personnel with little or no training were hired to perform many of the required duties. They were responsible for most of the day-to-day care and services for the residents, and they began to develop a kind of in-group culture of their own in regard to the way in which they related to patients and other staff members. Many of the characteristics of state mental hospitals have been and remain strongly influenced by aides (Ullman and Krasner, 1969).

The aides began to take as their model of patient problems the medical and mental illness orientation of the physicians and nurses. They tended to view the residents as alien people who were sick, rather than viewing their difficulties as exaggerated problems of living. They were able to place a great distance between themselves and patients with the use of such protective methods.

Interestingly, these aides in mental hospitals had many characteristics in common with the patients. This included having few occupational skills, little formal education, a very low salary, poor working conditions, unpopular working hours, and an emotionally and physically draining job. Many of the aides were quite emotionally disturbed themselves, and sadistic, cruel treatment occurred occasionally. More often the poor treatment of the patients was a result of inattention and other subtle means. There are many aides in mental hospitals today who could be accurately described in this way, but some institutions have personnel who function at a much higher level. The new mental health worker career structures and educational programs are largely a result of attempts to correct this situation.

As a natural course of action aides sometimes attempted to improve themselves and their conditions, which unfortunately occurred to the detriment of the patients. Aides learned to keep patients clean, subdued, and passive in order to protect themselves and their method of earning a living. There was and perhaps still is less of a focus on teaching patients to behave more appropriately in order to leave the hospital. Aides rewarded patients for behaving in a manner that actually led to a chronic stage of withdrawal, which eventuated in the condition known as chronic schizophrenia. That is, people who have been residents of institutions for years often have been rewarded for behaving in ways that will keep them in the hospital. The aide culture resulted in the improvement and comfort of the aides' condition, rather than that of the patients.

In many if not most mental institutions the patient is admitted to the hospital and immediately deprived of privileges, clothing, respect, and other aspects of his humanity. He is dehumanized and made less than a person. He is told when he can get out of bed, eat, and go to the bathroom. He is told to take his medications whether he wants to or not. He is often deprived of the right to vote and other civil liberties. His clothing is taken away and he is given the standard garb of the institution, which is often baggy and otherwise demeaning. He is made to attend individual and group therapy sessions, regardless of appropriateness or his desire to do so. Sexual behavior is usually complete suppressed, and if the patient exhibits sexuality he is believed to be merely exhibiting a symptom of his illness. This occurs in spite of the fact that sexuality is quite normal and natural outside the institution. Often he is given very limited attention from anyone, unless he is behaving precisely in the ways that will cause prolonged institutionalization. He is the recipient of anger from the aides that may or may not be directly expressed. The person is taught how to behave as a sick patient, and if he does not he receives avoidance and perhaps punishment. The patient is supposed to calmly sit and wait for advances in medicine that will cure his mental illness. Psychotherapeutic methods are often considered minor techniques to keep the patients busy and quiet, rather than necessary and central methods for eliminating behavioral and emotional problems.

Not only is the patient not allowed personal possessions, he is often deprived of daily newspapers and magazines. The television blares continuously whether the patient desires it or not. There is little furniture, and what there is is often unattractive and uncomfortable. There is limited privacy in the restroom and sleeping areas.

A popular book by Kesey (1962), *One Flew Over the Cuckoo's Nest*, somewhat overdramatically portrays the conditions of many state hospitals and the behavioral interactions that transpire within them. A new patient arrives on a ward and is amazed at the conditions he finds. The patients are like weak, inadequate zombies with little remaining of their humanity. The new patient attempts to organize the chronic patients into groups and otherwise intervene in this systematic destruction of human personalities. He is different, does not want to become like them, and believes they can again become effective and truly alive men. However, he is confronted and harassed by the bureaucratic system and the ward personnel who find him very irritating and obnoxious. He refuses to be a "good patient." His chief antagonist is a nurse in charge of the ward, who is called the "Big Nurse." She is very masculine, controlling, and deceptively authoritarian and cruel. Although the new patient has a minor degree of success in the early stages of the confrontation, the fun and assertiveness aggravate the staff members so much that they find a way to destroy him. They finally perform brain surgery and turn the new patient into a working, breathing, but dead person. One of the other patients whom he had helped then carried the murder to its conclusion by suffocating him to put him out of his misery.

Although mental institutions may not be as bad as this picture indicates, there is certainly considerable dehumanization that continues to occur. Many people have attempted to alter these deplorable situations with some success. The problem is that changes are not occurring rapidly and pervasively enough. It is questioned whether people in many mental institutions would not be better off if they were simply discharged en masse from them. Unfortunately, these residents become so accustomed to their treatment and, in fact, so dependent upon it that a return to the community is often frightening, and they do what they can to appear mentally ill in order to remain in the institution. Furthermore, community mental health services are not sufficient to provide the guidance necessary for reentry into community living.

THE NEW MENTAL HEALTH WORKERS

Since more people are becoming aware of the highly significant role of aides, including their performance in mental hospitals, schools, child guidance clinics, alcoholic treatment groups, and numerous other agencies, there have been attempts made to provide adequate selection and training procedures for these personnel. Increasingly, they are referred to as mental health technicians, mental health workers, counselors, and other terms, instead of aide, which indicate a recognition of their importance. As the population has grown it has become obvious that traditional concepts of delivering mental health services are not feasible. There are simply too many people with too many problems to be housed in a custodial setting, and they are receiving insufficient treatment from the traditional mental health professions. The last 10 years has witnessed a significant growth in the area of out-patient and community mental health services. The importance of the school in regard to preventing and decreasing behavioral problems also is receiving new and proper attention.

The problem remains, however, of the economic feasibility of staffing these agencies with the specifically educated new mental health worker. The concept of the aide as a person who primarily does custodial chores has been closely re-examined in recent years. The new mental health technician is basically conceived of as an individual who has received specific mental health and behavioral effectiveness education at the associate of arts degree level. He has been trained as a generalist in mental health and is well versed in the technical skills that will enable him to assume many of the assessment, therapeutic, and coordinating duties previously held by the traditional mental health professions or not performed at all. The last chapter of this book will provide more detailed information about the selection, training, and functioning of the new mental health technician.

CLARIFICATION OF TECHNOLOGY IN MENTAL HEALTH

Along with the concept of the new mental health worker or technician has come an increasing emphasis on the application of the findings of research from the behavioral sciences to the solution of the complex problems faced by the individual in society. At present there is a large body of knowledge, which has been acquired over the years from research in psychiatry, psychology, sociology, and other disciplines, forming the basis for a technology that can be used effectively by the new mental health worker. Our current status of technological applications in mental health work is indicative of a very significant cultural lag. We know much more than we are using in the mental health field.

Lanyon (1971) has clearly identified and defined the major aspects of technology in mental health. The reminder of this section draws heavily upon his thinking, although some elaboration, extension, and alteration have been made in reference to the new mental health worker.

The term "technology" has many connotations and is often used in a very loose and vague fashion. Technology in business and industry refers to harnessing knowledge and skills in such a manner as to increase productivity, or the amount of useful work performed by each worker. Practical knowledge, in other words, is made available by the developers of such knowledge to personnel who are generally unaware of the research and theory on which that practical knowledge is based.

Technology has several characteristics in the work situation. Again drawing upon the analogy of the business and industrial setting, technology involves, first, an increasing division of labor. The parts of a task are broken down into small components and each component assigned to an individual or small group. Hence, workers often do not know the results of their performance or the total outcome. In industry this has created some problems that occasionally appear to be more significant than the problems they were meant to overcome. For example, automobile manufacturers have found workers on the assembly line who have a very high absentee rate and exhibit general dissatisfaction, regardless of the amount of money they are paid. Attempts have been made to form small groups whose function is to be responsible for the entire product. Workers in some Japanese automobile factories are now being formed into small groups and made responsible for production of entire automobiles, rather than individuals or small groups being responsible for producing parts of the automobile. Teachers, mental health technicians, and others usually have a limited number of clients, students, or patients for whom they are generally responsible.

Second, highly skilled manpower is replaced with less skilled workers or with fewer workers who are given better tools and/or more specific training. In the mental health field, institutions dependent upon public tax support are often required to proceed with their task with limited funds. They are also very much subject to having their financial support reduced, which means they sometimes must perform their task with the same amount of money while expenses are rising. To compensate for such financial difficulties, mental hospitals and schools have resorted to using mental health technicians and teacher aides rather than the more expensive professionals in the field of mental health and education. Furthermore, preservice and in-service training programs have been developed to specifically train these employees and place them on the job at a significant savings in personnel salaries.

Third, manual work tasks are facilitated by the use of machines, computers, and simplified methods of operation. The state hospitals often use behavior rating scales that are completed by mental health technicians, rather than the significantly more costly psychiatric and psychological assessments performed by professionals.

Finally, mass production becomes a goal with highly standardized procedures and work processes. Mental health workers have their tasks clearly outlined and their rules and regulations defined, sometimes unfortunately to the point of rigidity and tunnel vision. However, the scientific knowledge base has increased to the point that many of the traditional professionals in mental health have carefully analyzed the nature and organization of the work process and have increasingly begun to view the assembly line as a model with some applicability to mental health organizations.

IMPLEMENTING TECHNOLOGY IN MENTAL HEALTH

There are numerous difficulties involved in attempting to make mental health a truly technological area. It is highly questionable whether mental health technology should adapt industrial technology methods and, if so, to what degree.

Undoubtedly, complete adoption of such ideas will prove impossible, and the real question is to what extent the method and procedures of industrial technology can be appropriately adapted to mental health work.

The criticism may be made that this new technology is dehumanizing, providing a structure for both mental health technicians and their clients or patients that is not in the best interest of either and that may well make them less effective persons than they should be.

In regard to mental health technicians, although they are perceived as new mental health generalists, their status on the social, educational, and economic scales will be considerably less than that of the psychologist, social worker, or psychiatrist. They will be drawn more from the lower classes, have less general education, and make considerably less money. They may be viewed by some as the drones in mental health, but they will be viewed by others as the new wave. Whereas the traditional mental health professional is a craftsman who carries out the entire work process by himself, the mental health technician, even though discussed often as a generalist, will not be a high-level expert.

There are factors posing considerable resistance to the development of technicians. The prestige attached to the role of craftsman or practitioner will not be accorded the new user of technological knowledge, skills, and attitudes. The individual's pride and satisfaction in regard to successful performance may be significantly less. The technician will have many difficulties in developing his own new professional group and attending to all the problems associated with building a new profession.

The patient or client may also feel much less secure with the technician than with a craftsman whose skill has been learned from the traditional professional process. The craftsman has spent considerable time and energy under the direct supervision of a recognized professional from whom he can model his own professional behavior. The counterpoint to this difficulty will probably be having the new mental health technician become generally competent in working with the patient or client as a total functioning human being. Technology is currently available for a consideration of use in several areas.

Objectification of psychological assessment. Mental health technicians can use many standardized psychological assessment instruments that will give an objective description and understanding of the behavior of their clients or patients. Furthermore, they can be taught to make some interpretations of psychological test findings with the use of objective instructions and rules.

Automation of psychological assessment. After objective rules have been delineated for using standard psychological tests, the information can be fed into a computer, which will make higher level interpretations of the information. The computer may take the raw data from the mental health technician and rapidly produce a complex and highly meaningful written report. The use of the computer with its elaborate library of statements and methods of using the information frees the mental health technician from needing an extremely high level of specialized knowledge and skill. Instead of a computer, a traditional mental health professional may be consulted.

Automation of psychiatric classification. It is sometimes helpful to classify patients and clients on the basis of traditional psychiatric labels and categorizations. The computer, or the traditional professional, can also receive basic information from the mental health technician and assign patients traditional psychiatric diagnostic categories. This information may be useful for understanding the individual patient, doing research, or obtaining indications for therapy.

Decision-making technology. It often occurs that there are alternative actions the mental health technician can make in regard to the individual or groups of patients. Models from decision theory can help clarify the possible outcomes of alternate courses of action and help lead to more appropriate decisions.

Systems technology. Complex human organizations, such as hospitals, universities, schools, and community groups, are understood as systems. In a system every action has some reaction and in general influences the entire system. The technician is a part of the system and can have a central influence.

Machine-aided counseling and therapy. It is possible to use an automation approach to aid in doing counseling and therapy. Indeed, a number of attempts have been made to provide information on a standard and automated basis. Vocational and educational counseling is one area in which factual information can be provided to the client quite rapidly and accurately. Traditional psychotherapy has been attempted with the use of a computer, the therapist's questions and statements being programmed for appropriate response to the client's verbalizations.

Automation and psychiatric patient care. Nursing notes, case histories, and behavioral observations are very important bits of information that can be standardized and given to computers for categorization and general information processing. The result can be a highly increased efficiency leading to viewpoints and understandings that were formerly not readily available. It is important in this area, as well as others, not to exaggerate the actual positive benefits of such machinery.

Behavior modification technology. Behavior modification is almost totally derived from the scientific exploration of general principles of learning and reinforcement. To a meaningful degree the principles are relatively easy to learn by mental health technicians of whatever name and can be applied with less of a requirement for high-level conceptual ability and knowledge than most of the other techniques for changing behavior. In particular, in comparison with psychoanalytic therapy, behavior modification techniques are rather simple, at least on the surface. By no means does this indicate that behavior modification techniques are not to be supervised by those expert in the area. It is clear that although behavior modification techniques can be used on hospital wards and in schools without supervision on an hourly basis, the need for consultation by those with the expertise in the area is necessary.

THE GENERALIST IN MENTAL HEALTH

Although provided with technical skills at the level of the current technological development in mental health, the new mental health technician is also conceived as a generalist. His training and experience are sufficiently broad that he is not restricted to providing services in only one agency or with one group. That is, he does some of everything therapeutic that is needed for the patient or client and has a beginning professional level of responsibility. He relies on knowledge and skills of all the major professions, but this is a consulting rather than a strictly supervisory role for the psychologist, social worker, and others. The education of technicians is never complete but is a continuing process.

An analogy is sometimes made with the public school educator. The teacher is the duly authorized professional in the classroom. Teachers obtain consultation from many professions, including those outside the educational field, but the responsibility for performance and decision making remains with the teacher. There may be some incompatibility of elements in the concepts of technology and generalist, but in one sense the mental health technician is at least a generalist at a basic level.

REFERENCES AND SUGGESTED READINGS

Coleman, J. C. 1964. Abnormal psychology and modern life, ed. 3. Chicago, Scott, Foresman and Company.

Guerney, B. G., Jr., editor. 1969. Psychotherapeutic agents: new roles for nonprofessionals, parents, and teachers. New York, Holt, Rinehart and Winston, Inc.

Holler, R. F. 1971. Selecting and training associate of arts degree mental health workers. Presented at Western Psychological Association, San Francisco.

Kesey, K. 1962. One flew over the cuckoo's nest. New York, The New American Library Inc.

Lanyon, R. I. 1971. Mental health technology. American Psychologist **26**:1071-1076.

National Commission of Mental Health Manpower. 1968. Careers in psychiatry. New York, The Macmillan Company.

Szasz, T. S. 1970. The manufacture of madness: a comparative study of the inquisition and the mental health movement. New York, Harper & Row, Publishers.

Ullmann, L. P., and Krasner, L. 1969. A psychological approach to abnormal behavior. Englewood Cliffs, N. J., Prentice-Hall, Inc.

Wolman, B. B., editor. 1965. Handbook of clinical psychology. New York, McGraw-Hill Book Company.

Zilboorg, G., and Henry, G. W. 1941. A history of medical psychology. New York, W. W. Norton & Company, Inc.

2

UNDERSTANDING BEHAVIOR

The person as a biological organism

To understand the behavior of an individual, it sometimes is important to distinguish between the human physical organism and environmental influences. Although to some extent we will be discussing the human biological organism and the effects of the environment separately, we do so as a matter of convenience and for clarity of presentation. Separating biology and environmental influences in behavior does not indicate that these two systems do not interact. In fact, the only way we can be made aware of problems in either the environment or the biological organism is through behavior. If a person is physically ill we only become aware of it when he either tells us about it or begins to react to his environment in unusual ways. Similarly, environmental problems such as social deprivation, prolonged punishment, and negative parental or peer group relationships only become apparent when the person involved is able to tell us about his problems or begins to behave inappropriately as a result of them.

Both physical illnesses and environmental factors are important in determining behavior. In dealing with deviant or abnormal behavior, it is important that the technician be aware of the effects that physical/biological processes can have on behavior. Since the mental health worker is often the person who spends the greatest amount of time interacting and observing patients or clients, he is exposed to the greatest amount of information about them. Thus, the technician should be aware of certain biological systems that have the greatest effect on behavior, so that the services that he provides are of maximum benefit to the client.

The individual is an incredibly complex organism on the physical level. Just as each individual is unique in his behavior, thinking processes, and life experiences, so do we find a great deal of variability in the physical structures

18

of the body. Regardless of the many structural differences, there are certain common points of structure and many essential functions that must be provided by the body as a biological organism if man is to function normally in society.

The central nervous system and the endocrine system are prominent biological determinants of behavior. However, these two systems are not fully developed and functioning until adolescence or early adulthood. Prior to this time (from conception to adolescence and adulthood), the body as a whole is growing and developing largely in accordance with the genetic code transmitted to the individual from his ancestors.

GENETIC INFLUENCE

The individual begins to develop at conception, the moment at which the sperm cell of the father penetrates the ovum of the mother. The result of the union of the sperm and the ovum is known as a zygote. The sperm and the ovum are also known as germ cells.

Germ cells are quite different from the other cells that make up the body, since they have twenty-three chromosomes. In other body cells there are twenty-three pairs, or forty-six chromosomes. The chromosome is the carrier of the genes, the basic units controlling the reproduction of body cells. Genes exert their influence through the control of enzyme production. Enzymes are chemical compounds governing the speed of chemical reactions within the body.

Prior to conception the germ cells divide. Each of the two resulting cells contain exactly half the number of chromosomes (twenty-three) contained in the original cell (forty-six). The process is known as reduction division (Winchester, 1965) and is differentiated from normal cell division by the fact that when other body cells divide, the result is another cell containing twenty-three pairs, or forty-six chromosomes. Thus the germ cell does not duplicate itself when it divides, as do the other cells in the body.

The zygote contains twenty-three pairs of chromosomes, half of which are contributed by the mother and half by the father. It is from the zygote that the human being develops. Specific physical characteristics are in large part determined by the influence of the genes contributed by the mother and father.

However, not all of the genes express themselves. That is, not every gene in the original zygote will lead to the development of a specific physical characteristic. Some of the genes are dominant and others are recessive. For example, the genes that control eye color vary in dominance. Brown eyes are carried by a gene with dominant characteristics, whereas blue eyes are controlled by a recessive gene. This means that when a gene that controls brown eyes is present in the zygote, the individual will have brown eyes, even though a gene for blue eyes is also present. The only way an individual will develop blue eye color is if both genes for eye color have the blue characteristic. A number of other characteristics, including hair color, color vision, normalcy of sight, hearing, and blood composition are also controlled by dominant and recessive genes. Although abnormalities in sight and other bodily systems certainly may lead to behavioral problems for the individual, the dominant and recessive characteristics of the genes controlling these structures and functions do not exert a direct control over behavior. However, heredity can and does play an important role in determining behavior. One of the most obvious examples of this fact is the sex of the individual. This is determined solely by the genetic contribution of the father. The mother always contributes the same gene in determining the sex of the offspring.

Such characteristics as individual sex, eye and hair color (Morrison, Cornett, and Tether, 1959), and the presence or absence of diseases such as hemophilia (Knudson, 1965) are readily demonstrated to be the result of the action of specific genes. However, such traits as intelligence, athletic ability, and predisposition to behavior disorders are much less readily demonstrated to be closely associated with heredity. This difficulty in examining the relationship between heredity and various psychological and behavioral dimensions is primarily the result of the abstract nature of these concepts. That is, intelligence, aptitude, personality characteristics, and emotional disturbance describe particular patterns of behavior rather than actual physical structures within the body.

A number of researchers have made attempts to study the relationship between heredity and schizophrenia, personality, and intelligence. The method primarily used in this type of research is the study of identical twins. Identical twins are assumed to be genetically identical. This is based on the theory that identical twins result from the splitting of the fertilized zygote into two separate but identical zygotes, each of which develops simultaneously. This is not the case with fraternal twins, which are the result of the simultaneous fertilization of two ova by two sperm cells. Although fraternal twins develop simultaneously in the mother, they are assumed to be no more similar genetically than any other sibling pair.

Identical twins are always of the same sex, but fraternal twins may be of the same sex. Determination of zygosity cannot be made on the basis of the sex of the neonate alone, or even on the basis of similarity of physical characteristics in adolescence and adulthood. It is impossible to determine with a great degree of accuracy whether or not the twins resulted from the same zygote (monozygotic) or from different zygotes (dizygotic) simply on the basis of identical sex at birth and physical similarity. Until relatively recently there was no method for the determination of zygosity independent of sex at birth and physical similarity.

Scientists have studied the incidence of schizophrenia and the similarity of personality in twins in the absence of an independent method of zygosity determination. They have found that there is a much greater similarity in intelligence, personality, and probability of schizophrenia between identical twins than there is between fraternal twins. The earliest research in this area indicated an extremely high correlation in twins in these areas. Subsequent research has consistently found relationships that are not as high as initially reported. This difference is most probably a result of the availability of better methods of zygosity determination. Although there is undoubtedly a hereditary component in schizophrenia, intelligence, and personality, the effect of genetic factors is not as great as was initially hypothesized and cannot be thought of as the only factor influencing these dimensions of individual differences.

Thus, although genetic factors undoubtedly play some role in determination of behavioral characteristics, the most important influence that these factors have on future behavior lies in their control over the development of body systems that are directly linked with the control of behavior. The two body systems that have the most pervasive influence on behavior are the central nervous system and the endocrine system. Disease or dysfunction in either of these systems, whether the result of an inherited defect or environmental trauma, usually results in behavioral disturbance.

NERVOUS SYSTEM

The nervous system functions to coordinate all body activities and behavior by responding to both internal and external events (Jacob and Francone, 1965). This includes such functions as digestion, excretion, and respiration, as well as such activities as thinking, feeling, and speaking. There are three principal divisions of the nervous system. These are the peripheral nervous system, the autonomic nervous system, and the central nervous system. Although disease or injury in any of these systems is serious, there may be different effects on the regulation of body functioning. Damage in some areas is relatively minor, whereas dysfunction in others may be irreversible and/or fatal.

The basic unit of the nervous system is the neuron (Morrison, Cornett, and Tether, 1959). This is a type of body cell arranged in sequences or chains that conduct electrical impulses through chemical activity. The neurons are not directly connected with each other physically. Rather, the neural impulses are conducted from one neuron to another at points known as synapses. The neural impulse travels from one neuron to another through chemical activity in the space between two neurons (the synapse), not through a direct physical contact between the two cells themselves. Thus the nervous system consists of millions of tiny neurons joined together chemically at the synapses.

The neurons are not like the wires in a switchboard. Although they do transfer electrical impulses, they are not continuous strands like wires. Instead, they are discrete elements of transmission that work together through the chemical activity at the synapses but otherwise function independently of one another.

In terms of basic functioning, all the neurons of the body are similar, all transferring electrical activity through synapses. However, there are many different types of neurons, all of which represent specific adaptations to the type of function they perform in the body. Each nerve cell performs a specific function within the system of which it is a part. The neurons of the various subdivisions of the nervous system possess differing characteristics corresponding to the function that system performs.

Central nervous system

The central nervous system consists of the brain and the spinal cord (Kimble, 1966). This system is more highly developed in man than in any other creature. It is impossible for an individual to function in any way without involving some part of the central nervous system. For this reason, the central nervous system must be intact if man is to behave in a normal and effective manner.

The neurons of the central nervous system possess two qualities that differentiate them from the neurons in the other parts of the nervous system. First, they are covered with a layer of tissue known as a myelin sheath that serves to protect the neuron from trauma. Second, the nerves of the central nervous system are incapable of regeneration. Once severed or injured, they cannot repair themselves, and the function that they control is either lost or must be taken over by another part of the nervous system. This is not true of the neurons in the other parts of the nervous system. Although regeneration may be slow, unless the neural structures are completely destroyed or removed they may eventually regenerate and the functions that they control may be restored.

Spinal cord. The spinal cord extends from the base of the brain to the base of the back and is housed inside the vertebral column. It consists of millions of nerve cells grouped together in various structures covered by a myelin sheath. It functions to convey information in the form of neural impulses to and from the brain, and it controls many reflex actions of the body that do not involve the brain. The information that travels to and from the spinal cord goes through thirty-one pairs of nerves, which are known as the spinal nerves. They are part of the peripheral nervous system. These groups of neurons are of three types: sensory, motor, and mixed. The sensory nerves carry information to the spinal cord from the various body regions. The motor nerves carry information from the spinal cord to the body parts. The mixed nerves perform both sensory and motor functions.

Although the spinal cord functions largely as a carrier of information to and from the brain, it can and does control many body movements in the absence of influence from the brain. These movements, known as reflexes, can occur without our thinking about them as they happen. For example, the knee jerk reflex, often checked by physicians in the course of a physical examination, is one such reflex. When the knee is tapped in the appropriate place an impulse travels through one of the sensory spinal nerves to the spinal column. Immediately upon reaching the spinal cord, this impulse is relayed to one of the spinal motor nerves, conveying the impulse to the muscles of the leg and causing the leg to move forward. This action almost always takes place without any nerve impulses being relayed up the spinal cord to the brain.

Other actions, such as removing the hand from a hot object, are also reflexive, but they involve information being conveyed to the brain about the pain that is felt or the sensation of heat. One possible explanation for this difference is that many reflexes, such as the knee jerk, are unlearned. That is, they are built into the organism through the action of heredity. The individual need not experience a tap on the knee several times before he learns to move his leg forward in response to the tap. Other reflex actions, such as pulling the hand away from a hot stove, are learned. The individual must be told about or experience the heat and burning of touching a hot object before the movement away from heat becomes apparently reflexive.

The spinal cord and the spinal nerves provide the stimulation to the limbs and the many muscles in the body that result in movement. The coordination of these activities, in most cases other than the reflexes, takes place in the brain itself. However, if movement is to occur, the spinal cord and the spinal nerves involved must be intact. In the presence of severe damage to the spinal cord or a disease, such as poliomyelitis, resulting in the loss of functioning in part or all of the spinal cord, the information from the brain is not conveyed to the muscles involved and paralysis ensues. For example, if an individual were hit by an automobile and suffered a complete severance of the spinal cord in the middle of his back, he would be paralyzed from that point downward. He would not be able to voluntarily move any of the muscles controlled by the spinal cord below the point at which the nerves were severed, even though these muscles might respond reflexively to stimulation. Without the functioning of the spinal cord, the mediating influence of the brain has no way of affecting the muscles, and voluntary movement becomes impossible.

Brain. The brain occupies the cranial cavity and is almost completely encased in bone. It is one of the most well-protected organs of the body. An adult human brain usually weighs about 3 pounds and is composed of millions of highly specialized neurons grouped together in structures that coordinate and control all bodily functions.

Cortex. The outer covering of the brain is known as the cerebral cortex (Kimble, 1966). This outer layer of the brain is most highly developed in man and is one of the most important central nervous system structures differentiating man from the lower animals. For example, the brains of the frog, fish, and bird contain little, if any, cortical cover. It is only necessary to consider one side or hemisphere of the brain at a time, since each half of the brain is believed to be identical in structure. That is, the right half of the brain contains structures identical to those contained in the left side. The surface of the cerebral cortex contains a number of high and low points, or ridges and valleys, known as convolutions and fissures. The area between any two fissures is the convolution.

The cortex is divided into four lobes. The portion of the brain directly behind the forehead is the frontal lobe. It is more highly developed in man than in any other creature, and it primarily contains the centers controlling thinking and logical reasoning. The center portion of the brain underneath the top of the skull is the parietal lobe, which is divided by the fissure of Rolando. The portion of the parietal lobe that is toward the frontal area contains the motor areas of the cortex. These areas control the sending of nervous impulses to the face, tongue, and limbs. Immediately opposite the motor areas on the other side of the fissure of Rolando are the sensory areas of the cortex. They receive information from the various sense organs of the body. In the rear of the head, almost at the base of the skull, is the occipital lobe. This area of the brain is sometimes known as the visual projection area and is the point at which the nerves coming from the eyes terminate. It is thought that the experience of sight is localized in this area of the brain. Because of this, a blow to the head in this region will often result in the individual "seeing stars." Just below the fissure of Sylvius is the temporal lobe. This portion of the brain lies directly behind and above the ears and is of major importance in hearing. It should not be thought that these various areas of the cortex function independently of one another. Recent research in central nervous system functioning has indicated that the parietal, occipital, and temporal areas are linked in coordinating the activities of the body and storing and recalling information.

Earlier in this century an operation known as lobotomy (Coleman, 1964) became popular for use with mental patients. Simply stated, this operation involved severing neural connections between the frontal lobe and the rest of the brain. The results of this operation initially were very encouraging. It was found, for example, that patients who had undergone such surgery became calmer, often could return home, and presented fewer problems in management. In some cases the operation was thought to have "cured" the person, for he seemed to return to a normal pattern of living. However, subsequent research on the result of lobotomy indicates that this operation in many cases resulted in the individual being unable to adequately utilize information of an abstract nature. That is, patients who have undergone this form of surgery tend to think very concretely. In many cases they are unable to understand analogies or see similarities between various objects. These effects are often subtle and in most cases unpredictable. Prior to the operation it is impossible to predict the extent to which the individual will benefit from it in the sense that the deviant behavior he exhibits will be lessened, as opposed to the extent to which he will suffer a marked loss of intellectual functioning.

Other brain structures. Other major structures of the brain important in controlling behavior are the cerebellum, the thalamus, the hypothalamus, and the reticular activating system (Kimble, 1966). The cerebellum is located at the base of the brain at the top of the spinal cord. It is about the size of a baseball and is partially covered by the cortex at the back of the head. The major function of the cerebellum is coordination of body movements. This part of the brain operates to enable a person to walk or to move his arms, hands, fingers, legs, head, facial muscles, and neck in a smooth, graceful manner. Injury to this portion of the central nervous system most often results in spastic or unco-ordinated and jerky movement in the affected area.

The thalamus lies almost in the exact center of the brain. It is one part of the brain that receives information from both the spinal cord and the cerebral cortex. The thalamus serves as a relay station where information from all of the sense organs, except for the nose, arrives before traveling to the parts of the cortex controlling movement or action in that area. The information sent to the brain from the sense organs in the nose does not pass through the thalamus but goes directly to the cortex.

Immediately below the thalamus is the hypothalamus, a very small structure that is one of the main coordinators of emotional activity. The thalamus and the hypothalamus are essential to life and adequate behavioral functioning. A severe injury to the thalamus almost always results in death. A tumor or injury in the area of the hypothalamus will usually result in gross behavioral distur-bance characterized by loss of control over emotions.

The reticular activating system is located at the top of the spinal cord. Like the thalamus, the reticular activating system relays sensory information to the brain. The reticular activating system has been shown to be very important in the control of sleep cycles, and it is also necessary for body movement. Should the reticular activating system be destroyed or severely damaged, the person would be paralyzed and almost totally senseless. He would not only be unable to move but would be unable to receive any information through his senses.

Peripheral nervous system

The central nervous system mediates the reactions of the body to events in the environment. However, the functioning of the central nervous system as an organizer of behavior is dependent upon a portion of the nervous system that lies outside of it, the peripheral nervous system. Its main function is to provide the central nervous system with information about the environment. The peripheral nervous system is composed of the three forms of nerves—sensory, motor, and mixed—that were discussed previously. Aside from the thirty-one pairs of nerves originating from the spinal cord, the peripheral nervous system also includes twelve pairs of nerves originating in the brain, the cranial nerves. The nerves of the peripheral nervous system are connected to special sense organs (Morrison, Cornett, and Tether, 1959), including those that are respon-sible for sensing taste, smell, sound, touch, and sight. They are also referred to as receptor organs. They receive information about the environment and translate it into electrical activity that is processed by the central nervous system.

Taste. The receptor organs responsible for taste are taste buds located in the mouth and tongue. These special sensory organs are essentially exposed nerve cells that respond to the chemical composition of the substance with which they come in contact. The sensations we know as salty, sweet, sour, and bitter result from the chemical reaction that takes place when the substance in the mouth comes in contact with the taste bud.

Smell. The receptor organs responsible for the sense of smell are primarily located in the air passages of the nose. Like the receptors of taste located in the mouth and tongue, the receptor organs for smell are essentially exposed nerve cells. When air passes through the nose it must pass over and around these exposed receptor organs. The various chemical properties of the air that pass through the nose give rise to the sensation of smell when these substances come in contact with the nerve endings.

Sound. The organ responsible for sensing sound is the ear. This is an incredibly complex structure. Unlike the receptor organs in the mouth and nose, the ear must convert sound waves rather than chemical substances into nerve impulses. Sound waves are present in the environment in the form of molecular motion in the air. They are transformed into mechanical motion in the middle ear and into electrical activity in the inner ear.

The ear consists of three principal parts. The outer ear includes the auricle through which wave motion in the air is channeled inside the skull. The middle ear, through the action of several very tiny bone structures, transforms this molecular motion into mechanical or physical activity. The inner ear transforms the mechanical motion of the middle ear into electrical activity, further transferring it to the central nervous system. The peripheral nerve endings responsible for the sensation of sound are located in the inner ear. The middle ear and outer ear function primarily as transformers of sound into a form of energy that can be processed by the peripheral and central nervous systems. Thus, in order for an individual to hear properly, all three parts of the ear must be unobstructed and uninjured. If the outer ear is obstructed and the molecular motion cannot be admitted to the middle ear, or if the tiny bones and membrane within the middle ear are somehow injured and cannot transform the sound waves into mechanical energy, the person will be unable to hear. If for some reason the special receptor organs in the inner ear have been destroyed, for example by exposure to an extremely loud noise for a long period of time, the person will also be unable to hear normally.

Touch. The sense of touch involves many different types of receptor organs, including special neurons adapted to sense pressure on the skin. There are other types of receptor organs included under the heading of touch, which involve the sensing of pain, heat, and cold. All of these different types of receptor organs represent unique adaptations of the neuron to the needs of man for information concerning the objects with which he comes in contact. Some of these organs respond to the presence of certain chemicals on the skin, others to physical pressure, and still others to the presence of stimulation such as heat and cold. Therefore, the sense of touch cannot be thought of as a unitary sense, as is smell or taste for which the receptor organs respond to only one particular type of activity. The receptor organs involved in touch respond not only to chemical activity but to other forms of energy.

Sight. The special receptor organ responsible for sight is the eye, the only organ that transforms light waves into the electrical and chemical activity that is processed by the nervous system. There are two major structures in the eye. The first is the one that is apparent when we look at the eye and is composed of the pupil and the iris. The pupil is the dark opening in the center of the eye, and the iris is the band of colored material surrounding the pupil. The iris responds to changes in the intensity of light. When light is dim it enlarges, allowing more light to pass inside the eye. When light is bright the iris contracts and reduces the amount of light passing into the eye. These changes in the iris are controlled by sets of tiny muscles inside the eye. The movement of the eyeball itself is controlled by other sets of muscles outside the eye, which are attached to the bones surrounding the eye. The other major structure of the eye is the retina, which is located at the rear of the eyeball. It consists of millions of highly specialized nerve cells that transform the light admitted through the pupil into nerve impulses. These nerve cells are connected to the central nervous system through the optic nerve.

Summary. All of the information obtained through the special sense organs is transferred to the central nervous system. It should be noted that none of the senses functions independently of the others. In order to adequately utilize the information gained from the sense of sight, we also need to be able to use the sense of touch and hearing. The various senses influence each other in determining how we perceive our environment. For example, during the process of eating, all the senses play a part. If we sit down to a table and a large charcoal-broiled steak is placed in front of us, we see its shape and color, smell its aroma, touch it to feel whether it is warm or cold, and before tasting it may be told by the person serving us that it will taste good. However, if we took the same steak, covered it with green food coloring, sprayed a foul-smelling odor in the air, chilled it, and were told by the person serving it that it would taste horrible, it would be highly probable that when we took our first bite of the steak we would believe it tasted terrible. The green steak objectively possessed properties that were no different chemically from the one that tasted good. However, after subjecting the steak and the situation to a number of different sensory conditions, the taste of the steak would be experienced quite differently. In both cases the same chemical characteristics of the steak came into contact with the same receptor organs in the mouth, but in the latter case the experience of tasting the steak was unpleasant.

Similar types of experiences are common in individuals who suffer from some disorder or damage to any one sense organ. It is common knowledge, for example, that food does not taste as good when one has a cold. This is because the nasal passages are clogged and we are unable to smell the aroma of the food. Children who suffer from some imbalance in the muscles controlling eye movement may have great difficulty in learning to read and communicate with others and may complain of headaches. As a result they may exhibit various types of aggressive, antisocial behavior, such as fighting, or some form of withdrawal, such as a refusal to go to school or to communicate with their peers.

A person who lacks an accurate sense of touch or hearing or who is unable to speak effectively because of some physical problem may begin to exhibit abnormal types of behavior. These behavioral disturbances can be understood as the result of the person attempting to function in a world that he cannot perceive or experience accurately because of physical disability.

A person with some form of hearing loss may speak in an excessively loud tone of voice or much more softly than a normal person would. A person with a visual problem may stumble over or bump into objects, and he may have difficulty performing simple tasks. It should not be thought that disorders in the peripheral nervous system are limited in their effects to the experience of those qualities in the environment. Rather, it should be remembered that these special sense organs in the peripheral nervous system supply the central nervous system with the information with which the behavior of the individual is organized. If the peripheral nervous system is for some reason not functioning normally, the information received by the central nervous system will be inaccurate and will result in a greater or lesser degree of disorganized behavior.

We have noted that injury or malfunction in the central and/or peripheral nervous system can result in disordered behavior. However, the behavioral disturbances that accompany malfunction in the nervous system are often accompanied by an emotional or "affective" component. One who suffers from some central or peripheral neural handicap will often experience negative feelings as a result. Control over the biological components of emotion is regulated by a part of the nervous system.

Autonomic nervous system

The autonomic nervous system is often referred to as the involuntary nervous system (Morrison, Cornett, and Tether, 1959). The word "involuntary" is used to call attention to the fact that an individual usually has little conscious control over its activities. It responds to changes in the internal and external environment in a very rapid manner. This part of the nervous system controls heartbeat, movements of digestion in the stomach and intestines, regulation of temperature, and control of the bladder. In terms of physical correlates of emotion, the autonomic nervous system is responsible for the reaction of the body to emergency situations. The control of the internal environment and of responses to stress and emergency is divided in the autonomic nervous system into two parts, known as the sympathetic and the parasympathetic nervous systems.

Sympathetic nervous system. The structures of the sympathetic portion of the autonomic nervous system are responsible for the acceleration of heartbeat, the constriction of blood vessels in the skin, the inhibition of salivation and glandular secretion in the stomach and intestines, and the stimulation of adrenaline production by the adrenal glands. This system functions primarily in the mobilization of the body in a time of stress or emergency. Through constriction of the blood vessels in the skin a greater blood supply is diverted to muscles and other vital organs, and the stimulation of the adrenal glands results in the release of sugar from the liver for immediate use by the body.

There have been many cases in which individuals have exhibited phenomenal strength under periods of stress. An otherwise normal individual may find himself capable of lifting the weight of a small automobile in order to save the life of a person trapped underneath it. This unusual display of physical strength is a direct result of the action of the sympathetic portion of the autonomic nervous system. Through the production of adrenaline and the release of sugar, as well as the dilation of blood vessels in the muscles and heart, a great amount of chemical energy is placed at the disposal of the muscles for conversion into movement. The emotional or experiential correlates of mobilization of the sympathetic nervous system include such things as dryness of the mouth and a feeling of nervousness or tension.

It is important to note that this system exacts a heavy toll in wear and tear on the body when it is greatly aroused. It is impossible to live for any extended period of time in the presence of continued high arousal of the sympathetic nervous system. An individual who lives in a highly stressful environment will be prone to develop physical disabilities as a result of the continuing demands put on the body by the sympathetic nervous system.

Parasympathetic nervous system. The parasympathetic portion of the autonomic nervous system functions in antagonism with the sympathetic nervous system. The parasympathetic system is responsible for the deceleration or slowing down and maintenance of body functions. For example, following a period of severe stress and sympathetic nervous system arousal, it is the parasympathetic system that returns the body to a normal level of functioning. The parasympathetic system stimulates secretion in salivary glands, the dilation of the blood vessels in the skin, and the secretion of the glands in the digestive tract.

The autonomic nervous system is one of the most important systems in the body. Although it does not possess many receptor organs, it is the part of the nervous system that most directly controls the activities of organs such as the heart, stomach, and liver. The autonomic nervous system is dependent upon the accuracy of the information conveyed to it through the peripheral and central systems if it is to adequately regulate body functioning and emotional experience.

Summary

Although we have divided the nervous system into three separate parts (the central, the peripheral, and the autonomic), none of them functions independently of the others in determining behavior. All of these parts of the nervous system interact with and are dependent upon one another for accurate information. Essentially, this means that malfunction in any of the parts of the nervous system is not limited but is pervasive in its effect on behavior.

The nervous system as a whole should not be thought of as the only major determinant of behavior on a biological level. Just as the different parts of the nervous system interact with each other in controlling and organizing body functioning and behavior, other organs in the body influence the action of the nervous system. Other body structures that also have a pervasive effect upon behavior and that are not a part of the nervous system are the endocrine glands.

ENDOCRINE SYSTEM

The endocrine system consists of a number of structures called glands, which produce substances released into the body known as hormones. The word "hormone" is derived from the Greek and means "to arouse." Arousal accurately describes the action of many of these substances. The process of producing and releasing hormones into the body is secretion. When an abnormally large amount of a particular hormone is secreted, the condition is described with the prefix "hyper-" followed by the name of the gland. For example, if the thyroid gland is secreting an unusually large amount of its hormone, the condition is referred to as hyperthyroidism. In contrast, if a gland is producing an abnormally small amount of a particular hormone, it is indicated by the prefix "hypo-" followed by the name of the gland. Production of an extremely small amount of thyroid hormone would be referred to as hypothyroidism (Morrison, Cornett, and Tether, 1959).

The action of hormones secreted by the glands of the endocrine system is widespread in the body. The effects of the hormones produced by the glands are not limited to the area around the gland itself. Several of these glands empty their secretions directly into the bloodstream. They can have profound effects on the functioning of body structures that are physically far removed from the gland itself.

Much is known about the chemical composition of the substances produced by the glands of the endocrine system, although much remains to be learned. The thymus and the pineal glands, in particular, are not well understood at present. Scientists have not been able to determine exactly what function they perform in the body, but it is known that the thymus is somehow related to the immunity of the body to disease. None of the structures of the endocrine system functions independently of the others or of the nervous system, but for purposes of clarity we will discuss each of the endocrine glands individually.

Pituitary gland

The pituitary gland is very small, approximately the size of a cherry, and is located beneath the base of the rear of the forebrain. It is partially encased in bone and near other vital central nervous system structures, which makes it difficult to perform surgery on it with present techniques. The pituitary secretes several hormones (Morrison, Cornett, and Tether, 1959), two of which have profound effects on behavior. The first of these is known as the somatotropic hormone. This substance is directly related to the control of physical growth of the body. The most noticeable effect of this hormone is during the growth period between infancy and adulthood. Should the pituitary hypersecrete the somatotropic hormone during this period, the resultant condition is giantism, which is characterized by extreme growth of the body; the individual may reach a height of 7 to 9 feet. A condition known as dwarfism is caused by a deficiency of somatropic hormone during early life. The deficiency prevents normal body growth, and an individual may never attain a height of more than 2 or 3 feet. In adulthood the presence of an excessive amount of somato-tropic hormone is characterized by a condition known as acromegaly, which is manifested by a lengthening of the arms, hands, feet, and jaw and which reflects an increase in the growth of the bone structures in these portions of the body.

None of these conditions necessarily includes any deviations in intelligence or emotionality (Boyd, 1971; Coleman, 1964). An unusual amount of somatotropic hormone at any period in life does not by itself produce disordered behavior. This does not mean, however, that an individual afflicted with any of these conditions will not develop some pattern of deviant behavior. Abnormal be-havior in association with pituitary dysfunction of somatotropic hormone is the result of difficulties that the individual experiences in the environment because of his unusual physical appearance. If an individual is diagnosed as suffering from a pituitary dysfunction related to somatropic hormone production, synthetic substitutes for the hormone may be administered and the abnormalities in physical structure avoided. On the other hand, once the body structure has developed any of these conditions, the administration of a synthetic hormone will do nothing to correct the structural abnormality. It is most important that an abnormality in somatotropic hormone production be detected and treated as early as possible if physical abnormality is to be avoided.

The pituitary gland also secretes another hormone that can have a profound and most direct effect on behavior. The substance, known as thyrotropic hor-mone, controls the activity of the thyroid gland.

Thyroid gland

The thyroid gland is located on the windpipe approximately in the middle of the neck. It regulates the rate of body metabolism (Morrison, Cornett, and Tether, 1959). The word "metabolism" refers to the chemical process that takes place within the cells of the body. In very general terms, metabolism involves the rate at which the body expends the energy available to it. Ab-normality of the secretions of the thyroid gland can have far-reaching effects on behavior (Boyd, 1971; Coleman, 1964). Hypothyroidism in infancy results in a condition known as cretinism, which is characterized by lack of growth in physical body structures and limited development of intellectual functioning. Hypothyroidism in adulthood is known as myxedema and is manifested by obesity, puffy facial features, and generally sluggish behavior. An adult with myxedema will generally be overweight and have difficulty in efficiently performing simple tasks. He may report that he "just doesn't have enough energy to get anything done." Hyperthyroidism in adulthood results in a drastic acceleration of metabolism. This condition is characterized by tenseness, excitability, loss of weight, and tremors or uncontrollable movements of muscles in various parts of the body. In its advanced stage hyperthyroidism in adulthood may be accompanied by a very bizarre behavior, including the hearing and seeing of things that are not there (hallucinations) and/or holding beliefs that clearly have no basis in reality (delusions).

There are a number of potential causes of thyroid dysfunction, some of which can be corrected and some of which are not correctable. However, in most cases the symptoms of the abnormal secretion of the thyroid gland may be alleviated through the use of synthetic hormonal substances. As in the case of pituitary dysfunction, it is of utmost importance that the abnormality of secretion in the thyroid gland be discovered early. Once the individual reaches adulthood the effects of hypothyroidism in infancy cannot be corrected. If myxedema or hyperthyroidism is allowed to continue over a long period of time, it may have irreversible effects on body functioning and may even cause death.

Parathyroid gland

The parathyroid gland is located a short distance below the thyroid gland. It controls the metabolism of calcium and phosphorus (Morrison, Cornett, and Tether, 1959). A normal level of calcium and phosphorus in the blood is essential to the adequate development of the nervous system and the bones of the body. A disorder of the parathyroids during gestation or infancy may lead to abnormal nervous system development and/or abnormalities in bone structure in the infant. In adulthood the destruction or removal of the parathyroid gland results in a condition known as tetany, which is characterized by uncontrollable muscular twitches, tremors, cramps, and convulsions. The symptoms of tetany can be relieved by injections of substances extracted from the parathyroid gland and by increasing the calcium content of the diet. Dysfunction of the parathyroid must be identified as soon as possible, for any drastic drop in the level of calcium in the blood or any prolonged deficiency of these substances will always lead to disordered behavior or death (Boyd, 1971; Coleman, 1964).

Adrenal glands

There is one adrenal gland located on the top of each kidney (Morrison, Cornett, and Tether, 1959). The hormones secreted by these glands perform two principal functions. The first of these is the mobilization of the body in times of stress, the hormone adrenaline making extra energy available to the body for use in meeting emergencies. The other hormones secreted by the adrenal glands influence the development of secondary sex characteristics, which differentiate the appearance of men and women. For example, secondary sex characteristics of men include the growth of facial hair, broad shoulders, and narrow hips. Secondary sex characteristics for women include the absence of facial hair, enlargement of the breasts, and widening of the hips.

There are several disorders associated with abnormalities of the adrenal glands (Boyd, 1971; Coleman, 1964). One of the rarest of these is known as pubertas praecox, a disorder related to hypersecretion by the adrenal glands of hormones influencing the development of secondary sex characteristics during childhood. The result is premature sexual development and an aggressive interest in sexuality. Although the child with this disorder possesses a body that is physically mature sexually, his mental development proceeds at a normal rate. He is not capable of a realistic evaluation of his sexual drives. Addison's disease is related to hyposecretion of one of the adrenal hormones and results in fatigue, anemia, irritability, lack of appetite, and a darkening of the skin.

The severest condition associated with the adrenal glands is their complete failure to function. Failure of the adrenals is apparently a breakdown that follows a period of prolonged stress. This failure to produce the hormones needed by the body is the end point of a sequence of events known as the general adaptation syndrome, which describes how the body reacts to stress. When an emergency arises the body reacts with a mobilization of the sympathetic nervous system and a stimulation of the adrenal glands, further resulting in the secretion of adrenaline and other hormones releasing large amounts of energy for immediate use. The mobilization of the body to meet a crisis exacts a heavy toll on the body structure as a whole. It is impossible for the body to remain functional and at the same time be constantly emotionally mobilized for a long period of time. After a lengthy period of arousal the parasympathetic nervous system often will begin to slow down the body processes and reduce the general level of arousal and the secretion of such hormones as adrenaline. This reaction will occur in spite of the continuing presence of the situation initially causing the stress. If the stress continues the body will eventually remobilize and remain mobilized until the adrenal glands fail to function. When this occurs, death is imminent.

Gonads

The gonads in the male are the testicles and in the female the ovaries. They significantly influence the physiological aspects of the sex drive and control the development of secondary sex characteristics (Coleman, 1964). The hormones secreted by these glands differ for the male and female. The influence of the pituitary over these glands is through two different pituitary hormones. The two major disorders associated with dysfunction of the gonads are eunuchism and menopause. Eunuchism refers to castration of the male before puberty or to hyposecretion of the gonads during childhood. Castration before puberty usually leads to the development of female secondary sexual characteristics. Hyposecretion of the gonads during childhood may result in failure to develop secondary sex characteristics and a lack of sex drive or interest in sexual relationships. Menopause is characterized by a great reduction of the secretion of gonadal hormones in women during middle age. This is a natural transition in the female from the age during which she is capable of bearing children to the time that she is no longer fertile. The response of women to this condition is varied; some pass through this period with very few if any negative experiences. However, in many cases menopause is accompanied by irritability, restlessness, agitation, depression, and insomnia.

Pancreas

The islands of Langerhans in the pancreas are responsible for the production of a hormone known as insulin, which enables the body to convert sugar to a form that can be stored in the liver. It also plays an important function in the metabolism of other body substances (Morrison, Cornett, and Tether, 1959). Individuals who lack a sufficient amount of insulin have an abnormally large amount of sugar in the bloodstream, a condition known as diabetes mellitus. If the condition is not corrected through control of diet and the use of a drug that can replace insulin in the body, death will result.

When insulin is injected into the body of a diabetic individual, there is an immediate drop in the blood sugar level. The use of insulin in treating diabetes is sometimes dangerous because of the possibility that too much will be injected at one time. Should this happen the level of sugar in the blood drops rapidly, resulting in hypoglycemia. Convulsions and death may ensue because the central nervous system is deprived of the minimum amount of sugar necessary for functioning. When hypoglycemia occurs the individual must raise the sugar level in his blood as quickly as possible. For this reason many diabetics who use insulin carry with them a few pieces of candy or other sweet substances to offset the effect of hypoglycemia. Disordered behavior resembling intoxication, such as disorientation and staggering, will accompany hypoglycemia. Through proper exercise and diet the effects of a deficiency of the production of insulin by the islands of Langerhans can be overcome and the individual can lead a very normal life. Oral medications can be used in place of injected insulin by many diabetic individuals.

Summary

Treatment of hypo- or hyperactivity by any of the glands in the endocrine system is a medical matter and generally calls for the institution of a therapeutic program involving the substitution of a synthetic or animal hormone to correct the disturbance. Medical treatment of disorders of the endocrine system is often very effective in alleviating the imbalance of the hormones in the body.

However, it has been well documented that the behavioral disturbances that often accompany such disorders as hyperthyroidism or Addison's disease may not be removed once the hormonal balance of the body is restored.

It may be hypothesized that this behavior persists after the correction of the hormonal imbalance because it is maintained by the environment in which the individual functions. In essence then, the hormonal imbalance provides a situation in which the individual may learn to behave in bizarre or inappropriate ways. Once this behavior has been learned it becomes independent of the endocrine system and may not be affected by a return to physiological normalcy. In dealing with abnormal behavior caused by endocrine dysfunction the regulation of the hormone production of the endocrine system is only part of the problem of returning the individual to society. The other major part of the problem is making sure that the individual again learns to behave in a socially appropriate and acceptable manner following the medical treatment of his illness.

The nervous system and the endocrine system have been carefully researched, but scientists still have many puzzling questions that need to be answered. Some of the most interesting questions about the biological bases for behavior are raised by scientists who concern themselves with instinct and behavioral development.

INSTINCT, IMPRINTING, AND DEVELOPMENTAL UNFOLDING

The use of instinct as a concept and explanation for behavior is ancient. At one point during the early twentieth century behavioral scientists had postulated the existence of so many instincts that the concept became useless for understanding behavior and was abandoned. More recent behavioral scientists, especially those in the specialized field of ethology, have revived interests in instinct, and research has begun to be pursued again with vigor. In terms of an overall understanding of human behavior, instinct and imprinting can be subsumed under the concept "developmental unfolding." We will discuss the concepts of instinct and imprinting separately and then integrate them with the current knowledge regarding developmental unfolding of human behavior.

Instinct

Instinct refers to a behavior pattern that can be shown to be inherited and that is displayed by the organism in the absence of prior training or experience (Morgan, 1965; Morgan and King, 1966). One of the most often discussed examples of instinctive behavior is maternal behavior, which includes such activities as nest building and cleaning, feeding, and protecting the young. These behaviors in various animals are generally believed to be inherited because they characterize the behavior of an entire species. For example, in observing the maternal behavior of one particular type of rat, we would probably find that all rats of the same type displayed an almost identical pattern.

Through scientific control and experimentation it can also be shown that this maternal behavior occurs in the absence of any training or experience. If we isolate an animal immediately after birth and raise it in an environment in which is never allowed to see other animals engaging in maternal behavior, and in which we do not give the animal any training in maternal behavior, it will nevertheless display the maternal behavior characteristic of its species when it becomes pregnant.

Instinct theories for understanding human behavior once were almost completely abandoned, partly because it is extremely difficult, both technologically and ethically, to impose scientific conditions necessary for substantiating the presence of an instinctive behavior pattern in humans. Scientific ethics prohibit the experimental isolation of a child from its mother, and technology has not provided effective methods of controlling early experience. Researchers examining instinctual human behavior are required to rely upon rare cases in which for some reason a child has been isolated from its parents and other humans. These cases do not provide very suitable material for testing hypotheses about the development of instinctive behavior patterns in humans because the early experiences of the individual have not been controlled and are generally characterized by extreme deprivation and other unusual circumstances. It is quite tenuous to make inferences from these cases about the role of instinct in normal human behavior.

Imprinting

Imprinting describes a specific phenomenon that is the major focus of study in the field of ethology. Theories of imprinting differ from theories of instinct in a very substantial fashion. The idea of imprinting includes the concept of an optimum time for practice and behavioral expression. The major studies of imprinting have been done with animals, especially birds such as chickens, ducks, and geese. The most common finding is that certain behaviors appear at a critical time and become attached or associated with a specific stimulus. For example, ducklings will follow an object that shares some common characteristics with a mother duck. If the mother is removed from the ducklings during this critical period (Lorenz, 1952) and a human is placed in the situation and begins to make rhythmic sounds similar to those of a mother duck, the ducklings will follow the human being rather than the mother duck, even if at a later point in time the mother duck is replaced in the situation. The behavior of following the mother becomes imprinted or attached to the human being, and the ducklings will never, after this critical period, follow their mother. They will follow the human in the same fashion that other ducklings follow a mother duck.

The concept of imprinting is especially important in understanding human behavior because it introduces the idea that there may be critical periods in which specific types of learning or behavior change take place. Should learning not take place, because of such conditions as deprivation, or should it occur in the presence of an inappropriate stimulus, a deviant pattern of behavior may emerge. Although very little research has been done on imprinting in humans, primarily because of the same difficulties associated with studies of instinct, researchers who have studied human development have found that there are critical periods for the learning of some skills. Deviancy does not manifest itself immediately but becomes more apparent as the individual continues to develop through childhood and adolescence.

Developmental unfolding

The nervous system, endocrine system, and other structures are far from mature at birth and do not reach complete functional maturity until later in life. In association with this continuing development of the human as a biological organism, specific patterns of behavior develop in a somewhat predictable sequence. Although some individuals may develop more quickly or slowly than others, all proceed through the same sequence. Because of the incomplete development of his muscular and nervous systems, an infant begins crawling before he is able to stand alone and stands alone before he is able to walk. The same sequence holds for other types of behavior that are more social in nature. The infant begins communicating with others on a very primitive level before he is able to communicate his feelings and thoughts more precisely. The first communications of an infant include such behaviors as crying and grunting, which are not readily distinguished as referring to differing states within the infant. Subsequently, the infant begins to make different sounds that indicate different states such as hunger or pain. It is not until much later that the individual is able to use words in describing himself, and combining words into meaningful phrases and sentences occurs even later.

It has also been demonstrated that many characteristics of the individual's early environment may either facilitate or inhibit the development of effective communication skills. Early deprivation of body contact may have an adverse effect on future interpersonal behavior. A series of famous studies in this area was conducted by Harlow at the University of Wisconsin (Harlow and Harlow, 1962). Experiments on the effect of body contact and contact comfort were done with rhesus monkeys from infancy through adulthood. Immediately after birth the infant monkeys were placed in one of several experimental conditions.

Some of the monkeys were placed in isolation in the presence of a surrogate or substitute mother made of cloth, other monkeys were placed with a surrogate made of wire, and still other monkeys were left to develop normally with their natural mothers. The monkeys placed with a surrogate mother were fed through a bottle while clinging to the surrogate apparatus. This is similar to the manner in which a normal monkey feeds by clinging to its mother. Although there were many differences between the monkeys raised on the wire surrogates and cloth surrogates, the most impressive effects of raising these infants in the absence of a real living mother manifested themselves when the infants became adults. Monkeys who had developed in the presence of a mother surrogate were socially, emotionally, and sexually deviant in adulthood. They did not relate effectively to other adult monkeys and reacted to their environment inadequately. They rarely engaged in sexual intercourse, and when a female did become pregnant, she often abandoned the infant.

These experiments were done with monkeys and are certainly limited in the extent to which the results can be said to characterize the way humans would behave under similar developmental conditions. Nevertheless, there is considerable research available that indicates that human infants, when raised in an impersonal environment such as in some orphanages in which there is little

Fig. 2. Behavior is largely socially determined. (H. Armstrong Roberts.)

contact with other human beings, develop abnormal patterns of emotional behavior. Many show signs of intellectual impairment or deficit.

Although man can be clearly differentiated from animals in the degree to which his behavior can be understood with instinct and imprinting, it is apparent that there are critical points in the early life of an individual during which the learning of specific skills and the experience of interpersonal relationships are extremely important. These periods are so important that should the individual not be exposed to an adequate environment, he will likely develop abnormal patterns of behavior in adolescence and adulthood.

REFERENCES AND SUGGESTED READINGS

Boyd, W. 1971. An introduction to the study of disease. Philadelphia, Lea and Febiger.

Coleman, J. D. 1964. Abnormal psychology and modern life, ed. 3. Chicago, Scott, Foresman and Company.

Harlow, H. F., and Harlow, M. K. 1962. Social deprivation in monkeys. Scientific American 207(5):136.

Jacob, S. W., and Francone, C. 1965. Structure and function in man. Philadelphia, W. B. Saunders Co.

Kimble, D. P. 1966. Physiological psychology: a unit for introductory psychology. Reading, Mass., Addison-Wesley Publishing Co., Inc.

Knudson, A. G. 1965. Genetics and disease. New York, McGraw-Hill Book Company.

Lorenz, K. 1965. Evolution and modification of behavior. Chicago, University of Chicago Press.

Morgan, C. T. 1965. Physiological psychology. New York, McGraw-Hill Book Company.

Morgan, C. T., and King, R. A. 1966. Introduction to psychology. New York, McGraw-Hill Book Company.

Morrison, T. F., Cornett, F. D., and Tether, J. E. 1959. Human physiology. New York, Holt, Rinehart and Winston, Inc.

Winchester, A. M. 1965. Modern biological principles. Princeton, N. J., D. Van Nostrand Co.

3

UNDERSTANDING BEHAVIOR

The person as a behaving organism

The person as a behaving organism is described in terms drawn from the behavioral sciences. In the preceding chapter we discussed the biological bases of behavior, using terms common to the physical and biological sciences. In this chapter a number of new terms that are the products of years of research in the behavioral sciences will be introduced. They are used to describe behavior without direct reference to the individual as a biological organism. That is, we will be discussing the manner in which the behavior of an individual can be described, predicted, and controlled without reference to or manipulation of biological variables. We will be dealing with the manner in which external events affect an individual's behavior. The one area of study in the behavioral sciences that best describes and encompasses all of the effects of external events upon behavior is learning.

LEARNING, THEORY, AND BEHAVIOR

Probably no area of the behavioral sciences has received as much attention on the theoretical, experimental, and applied levels as learning. Some learning theorists have hypothesized the presence of various theoretical and physical structures inside humans to account for the manner in which people learn. B. F. Skinner (1953), in his book *Science and Human Behavior*, discusses at length the application of such inner causes to the behavioral sciences. He believes that relying on such inner states as explanations for behavior is of relatively little value and actually has negative effects. Because the structures said to be responsible for learning are located within the organism, they are not available for observation and manipulation. Theories and definitions of learning that hypothesize inner states of the organism as causes of behavior do not enable either the scientist or the therapist to influence, control, or manipulate the behavior of the individual. As an alternative to attempting to explain behavior in terms of inner causes, Skinner proposes that we deal with the prediction and control of behavior in terms of those events outside the organism that can be observed and manipulated. This approach has the distinct advantage of making available to the scientist and practitioner a means of modifying behavior. Behaviorism, a general name for this approach, refers to the examination of events in the environment and how they relate to behavior. Events in the environment should be conceptualized very broadly to include the various inanimate objects surrounding an individual, the behavior of others, and the behavior of the individual himself.

Learning defined

When we speak of learning in the present discussion we will be referring to the *acquisition* or *modification of a specified behavior,* rather than a process that goes on within the individual. The majority of rigorous laboratory research on the acquisition and modification of behavior has been undertaken by psychologists using both human and animal subjects. Experiments on learning done in the laboratory are often termed studies of conditioning, although the term "conditioning" is used scientifically in reference to the learning of only a particular kind of behavior.

Because much of the research on learning has been carried out on animals and has been labeled conditioning, much controversy has arisen in relation to the application of such laboratory-derived principles of learning to human beings. The application of learning principles for understanding human behavior has been criticized by some who feel that this is somehow demeaning and degrading to the individual. There are many reasons why studies of learning have been primarily carried out with animal subjects. These include the greater degree of control over the environment and interaction with other organisms. It is not ethical, and in many cases technologically impossible, to impose the types of experimental controls that are necessary for rigorous and meaningful scientific research when human beings are used as subjects. Therefore, animals must often replace men as subjects for studies of learning in the laboratory.

These facts hold true for research in other basic and applied areas of science, notably biology and medicine. Through the use of animals much useful information about the human as a biological organism has been inferred and later substantiated. Many valuable medical techniques that immeasurably increased the quality of human life have been discovered and refined. The same potential for increasing the quality of life is present in studies of behavior with animals. Principles of learning derived from the study of animals in the laboratory situation are certainly no more degrading or demeaning when applied to the understanding of human behavior than are the principles of medicine and biology derived from animal studies and applied to the understanding of the individual as a biological organism. In neither the biological nor the behavioral sciences does the researcher assume that men are no different than animals. Rather, he utilizes animals as experimental subjects out of convenience and ethical necessity in an effort to better understand the human organism. When the behavioral scientist suggests that principles of learning derived from the study of animals in a laboratory may be useful in understanding human behavior, he is not implying that humans are no different from animals. He is examining the possibility that the principles he has discovered in the laboratory may be useful in understanding the behavior of the individual human being and potentially useful for increasing the quality of human life.

PRINCIPLES OF LEARNING
Basic definitions

The study of the acquisition and modification of behavior requires knowledge of several descriptive terms that have come to be widely used.

Behavior. In the broadest sense of the word, behavior includes any bodily activity or movement. Bodily activity or movement includes everything an individual can be observed to do. Using this definition, feelings and thoughts can be included as behavior, for the individual engages in some activity or movement, such as speaking, crying, smiling, or walking, that one can observe.

Stimulus. Stimulus refers to any event that is consistently associated with behavior.

Response. Response refers to a small unit of behavior. A response can generally be thought of as any behavior that follows a specifiable stimulus. Importantly, not all behavior can be shown to follow a particular stimulus event.

Behavior chains. Behavior chains are a series of discrete responses arranged in some meaningful order. Another phrase that is similar to the idea of behavior chain is "pattern of behavior." An example of a behavior chain is the act of smoking. This can be broken down into many discrete responses, including opening a package of cigarettes, taking a cigarette out of the package, placing the cigarette in the mouth, opening a book of matches, lighting a match, placing the match at the end of the cigarette, and inhaling so as to ignite the tobacco. For this behavior chain, each response can be conceived as a stimulus for the next response. For example, holding the lighted match at the end of a cigarette is a stimulus event in the sense that it is followed by another response, inhaling to ignite the tobacco.

Generalization. Generalization refers to the extent to which similar stimuli and similar responses are found to be associated with each other. There are two types of generalization. "Stimulus generalization" refers to the frequency with which similar stimulus events are followed by a particular response. The 5 year old on his first day in school calls his teacher "mama," and the delinquent responds to all adult men as if they were cruel authoritarians. "Response generalization" refers to the frequency with which similar responses follow a specific stimulus. The 5 year old refers to his mother as mama, mudder, and mom. The extent of stimulus generalization is a crucial test in determining the effectiveness of attempts to modify human behavior. It is hoped, for example, that when an individual leaves a mental hospital after having learned to respond appropriately to the stimuli in the hospital, these more effective responses will generalize to stimuli outside the hospital, such as toward his family and employer. If significant stimulus generalization is not observed when the individual leaves the hospital, then the process of therapy can certainly be considered incomplete.

Three types of learning

As was noted previously, some scientists interested in the phenomena of learning have developed theories that hypothesize inner causes as explanations of behavior. Because different individuals have attributed different causes as explanations of learning, it sometimes appears that there is really only one type of learning and that only one theory of learning can be correct. However, examination of the results of studies of learning over many years indicates that there are at least three different types of learning. We will focus on the defining characteristics and controlling conditions for each type and not discuss theories that have been generated as explanations for them.

Respondent learning

The first scientist to examine respondent learning was the Russian physiologist Pavlov (Morgan and King, 1966). Respondent learning is also referred to as classical conditioning. The usage of the word "classical" is indicative of the wide respect accorded to the "classic" experiments of Pavlov in this area. Although the basic principles of respondent learning have not continued to play a major role in the development of behavioral theory in the United States, Pavlov's work has exerted a continuing and pervasive influence in Russia and is the basis of many techniques used in the Soviet Union in education, social engineering, and behavior modification.

Defining characteristics

Respondent behavior is elicited. A particular stimulus always elicits or leads to a specific response. The basis of the association between one stimulus and one response is believed to be reflexive. In other words, the relationship between a stimulus and the subsequent response is based in the nervous system. The association is similar to that in a primitive reflex, such as the knee jerk. The basic stimulus and response pattern in respondent behavior is thought to be primarily innate. For respondent learning these innate, reflexive patterns of behavior become associated with different stimuli.

A model of respondent learning. There are four basic terms used in describing respondent learning.

The *unconditioned stimulus* is any stimulus event that invariably elicits a particular response. The *unconditioned response* is that behavior that always follows the presence of an unconditioned stimulus. A common example of an unconditioned response is the forward movement of the leg following the un-conditioned stimulus of a tap on the knee.

The *conditioned stimulus* is any environmental event that, through associa-tion with an unconditioned stimulus, eventually begins to elicit a behavior similar to the unconditioned response. The *conditioned response* is that be-havior elicited by the conditioned stimulus. It is similar in nature to the un-conditioned response.

Examples of respondent learning. Probably the most widely known example of respondent learning is the elicitation of the salivary response in dogs follow-ing a conditioned stimulus. Pavlov used dogs as subjects in many of his initial studies of respondent behavior. In his experiments he found that the sight of food served as an unconditioned stimulus that always elicited salivation as an unconditioned response. By associating the sound of a bell with the sight of food many times, it was found that the bell eventually acquired the properties of a conditioned stimulus. That is, after many presentations of the bell in con-junction with the sight of food, ringing the bell alone without allowing the dog to see the food was sufficient to produce salivation. This salivation, when elicited by the bell or conditioned stimulus alone, was labeled the conditioned response and showed properties very similar to the salivary activity that always followed the unconditioned stimulus of the sight of food itself.

In understanding human behavior, respondent learning has often been used as a method of accounting for the acquisition of fear and many other emotional responses. For example, pain is an unconditioned stimulus that will always elicit fear as an unconditional response. If we were to analyze a person's fear of other people, we might find at some period during his life the individual ex-perienced pain (the unconditioned stimulus) in the presence of other individ-uals (the conditioned stimulus). As a result of the association between the un-conditioned stimulus of pain and the presence of other people, the sight of other people eventually acquired the properties of a conditioned stimulus and became sufficient to elicit a fear reaction, a conditioned response very similar to the original unconditioned fear response elicited by the unconditioned stim-ulus of pain.

Controlling conditions. The acquisition and maintenance of a conditioned response is governed by several factors (Reynolds, 1968).

Temporal order. The major factor determining the speed of acquisition and the similarity of the conditioned response to the unconditioned response is the relationship in time between the presentation of the conditioned stimulus and the unconditioned stimulus.

When the conditioned stimulus and unconditioned stimulus are presented simultaneously or closely (that is, the conditioned stimulus precedes the un-conditioned stimulus by no more that 5 seconds), respondent learning will be fastest and the conditioned response will be most similar to the unconditioned response.

When the conditioned stimulus is presented after the unconditioned stimulus, the learning will be less efficient, for it will take longer for the conditioned stimulus to begin to elicit the conditioned response, and the conditioned response will be less similar to the unconditioned response than in the simultaneous or close temporal method of presenting the conditioned and unconditioned stimuli.

Time itself may also serve as a conditioned stimulus. For example, if an animal is always fed at one specific time during the day, it can be shown that this point in time will become a conditioned stimulus for salivation even in the absence of food.

Habituation. Habituation is a factor controlling both acquisition and maintenance of respondent behavior. Habituation refers to the tendency of an unconditioned response to become less pronounced following repeated presentation of the unconditioned stimulus. The presence of certain chemical compounds in the air is an unconditioned stimulus for the experience of an unpleasant odor. However, when one remains for a lengthy period of time in the presence of these unconditioned chemical stimuli, the unconditioned response becomes weaker. Following a lengthy period of exposure to the unconditioned stimulus, the individual no longer experiences the sensation of an unpleasant odor, the unconditioned response. Similarly, if an animal is repeatedly shown a dish of food many times during the day, the unconditioned response of salivation will gradually diminish and eventually disappear. However, if the unconditioned stimulus is again presented after a sufficient time period following habituation, it will again elicit an unconditioned response equally as strong as that present before habituation took place.

Extinction. Extinction refers to the gradual weakening and eventual disappearance of the conditioned response following repeated presentation of the conditioned stimulus in the absence of the unconditioned stimulus. Extinction is differentiated from habituation by two facts. First, extinction refers to the disappearance of the conditioned response following presentation of the conditioned stimulus. Second, after extinction has taken place the conditioned stimulus will not elicit the conditioned response until the conditioned stimulus is again presented in association with the unconditioned stimulus. If the conditioned stimulus is ever to elicit the conditioned response again, the entire sequence of respondent learning (the pairing of the conditioned and unconditioned stimuli) must be repeated.

Operant learning

The major proponent and a most significant contributor to the research in the area of operant learning is B. F. Skinner. This type of learning can be used to understand the acquisition, maintenance, and modification of much more complex patterns of behavior in animals and men than respondent learning. Although research in respondent learning has indicated that it is possible for subjects to learn short sequences of responses through the pairing of conditioned and unconditioned stimuli, the characteristics of operant learning make it possible to understand the acquisition of entire systems of behavior (Reynolds, 1968).

Defining characteristics

Operant behavior is emitted. The major defining characteristic of operant learning is that it deals with the control of behavior that is emitted, rather than elicited, as is the case for respondent learning. The term "emitted" refers to behavior that is not elicited by any known specific stimulus event.

A model of operant learning. The basic model of operant learning includes only two elements, the emitted response, or operant, and the reinforcing stimulus. The reinforcing stimulus is any event that follows the emitted behavior and that has some effect on the probability that the emitted behavior will occur again. The terms "reinforcement" and "reinforcer" are commonly used to describe a reinforcing stimulus. There are two basic types of reinforcing stimuli. A positive reinforcer is any stimulus whose presence increases the probability that the emitted behavior will occur again. A negative or aversive reinforcer is any stimulus whose withdrawal increases the probability that the emitted behavior will occur again.

The relationship between an emitted response and a reinforcing stimulus is known as a contingency. Contingency refers to the fact that a particular behavior must be emitted before the reinforcing stimulus will occur. That is, reinforcement is contingent upon the presence of a specific behavior. Food for an animal in a laboratory study of operant learning may be made contingent upon specific responses, such as pressing a lever. In everyday life contingencies of reinforcement are often much more subtle and less apparent. However, one that all of us have or probably will experience at one point in our lives is that which governs the receipt of a paycheck. In order for the reinforcing stimulus event (receipt of a paycheck) to occur, we must emit specific behaviors during a defined period of time (work).

When a specific contingency is always present in a particular situation, the various environmental stimuli that are a part of that situation may eventually begin to exert some control over the emitted response. The first time a laboratory animal is placed in a cage and exposed to a contingency with food as a reinforcing stimulus, the probability that the animal will immediately engage in that behavior is relatively slight. However, after repeated presentation of the reinforcing stimulus, the emitted behavior begins to come under the control of the environmental stimuli present when that behavior is reinforced. That is, the probability of the specific behavior occurring is higher in the presence of those stimuli that have been associated with the reinforcement and lower in the absence of those stimuli.

Controlling stimulus events are often referred to as "discriminative stimuli." They do not elicit behavior, but a discriminative stimulus indicates the presence of conditions under which the emitted behavior has previously been reinforced. A particular day of the week may become a discriminative stimulus for requesting the paycheck from the supervisor because it is indicative of conditions under which asking for a paycheck will be reinforced by receiving the paycheck.

It is important to understand that the relationship between controlling stimuli and a particular operant is essentially a matter of probability. We can never state with certainty that a response will occur in the presence of stimuli that have been associated with reinforcement of that operant in the past. This is a significant point that differentiates respondent learning from operant learning. In respondent learning we can be certain that the unconditioned stimulus will always elicit the unconditioned response, whereas in operant learning we can never be positively assured that a particular response will be emitted in the presence of controlling stimuli.

Examples of operant learning. Pigeons and rats are some of the most frequently used animals in experiments studying operant learning. These animals are usually studied in a very special environment known as the Skinner Box (Reynolds, 1968). This experimental chamber is constructed to minimize the extent to which stimuli outside the chamber can be perceived by the animal. It provides for control of the dispensing of food and water and often includes various devices that make it possible to administer shocks to the animal. The chamber may also include mechanical devices that can be manipulated by the animal, as well as other mechanisms for the presentation of specific discriminative stimuli such as lights or sounds. With the use of the Skinner Box, experimental animals can be taught to perform remarkable sequences of behavior.

To teach an animal a very simple response requires the experimenter to wait for the animal to emit that response and then provide a reinforcing stimulus. For example, if the experimenter wished to train a pigeon to peck at a light on the side of the chamber, he would wait for the bird to emit this response and then provide a reinforcing stimulus such as food or water. Once the reinforcing stimulus event has occurred, the probability that the operant will occur again is greatly enhanced and the length of time between each succeeding emission of the operant will decrease following reinforcement. Thus, the measure of the effectiveness of a reinforcing stimulus is the rate of responding of the experimental subject. If there is no increase or decrease in the response rate following an event that is hypothesized to be a reinforcing stimulus, that event is by definition not a reinforcing stimulus, and the scientist will have to find another event to take its place as a reinforcer if response rate is to be increased.

Examples of operant conditioning are most clearly seen in the animal laboratory. This is because of the enormous amount of control possible over contingencies of reinforcement when an animal is in an experimental chamber such as a Skinner Box. An examination of the behavior of men in their natural environment, however, clearly indicates that it is much more difficult to observe and control contingencies of reinforcement. The effect of reinforcement on the rate of emission of a particular behavior of children is more often readily apparent. A child walking down the aisle of a grocery store holding on to his mother's skirt may begin to pull up and down on the skirt. If this emitted behavior is followed immediately by an event that serves as a positively reinforcing stimulus, such as a small piece of candy, a pat on the head, or some other sign of attention or affection, the probability that this behavior will occur again is greatly enhanced. In many cases when such behavior is initially emitted the parent feels that the appropriate thing to do is to pay attention to the child if he is to stop the bothersome behavior. Observation, however, clearly indicates that attending to a bothersome behavior, such as skirt pulling, serves as a reinforcing stimulus. Attending to such behavior simply serves to increase its rate of emission rather than eliminate it. This point is exceptionally significant in human service work, particularly schools and mental institutions. Regardless of the factual evidence, many staff members simply refuse to believe that their attempts to eliminate a particular behavior are actually reinforcing such behavior.

Controlling conditions. Research in the area of operant learning has indicated that there is a diverse number of conditions that can affect response rate. All of these conditions are in some way related to the type of reinforcing stimulus or the manner in which it is presented. The key concept is: behavior is a function of its consequences.

Positive and negative reinforcing stimuli. As was noted previously, a reinforcing stimulus may be either positive or negative. Negative reinforcement in the laboratory often takes the form of electric shocks that are delivered to the animal. These are usually administered in one of three ways. First, in escape training the removal of a shock or other aversive stimulus is made contingent upon the emission of a particular operant, perhaps running out of the Skinner Box. Second, avoidance training involves a contingency in which the emission of an operant allows the subject to avoid or postpone the presentation of the aversive stimulus, perhaps pushing a lever at a high rate to keep the electric shock circuit from closing. Punishment is a third type of operant procedure involving a negative reinforcer and is designed to reduce response rate. When punishment is used the emission of an operant is followed by the presentation of an aversive stimulus, such as the animal receiving a shock for drinking water.

The use of positive reinforcers is preferred in the acquisition and maintenance of human operant behavior. There are several reasons for this. Although negative reinforcers and punishment have been examined widely in animal research and their effects on behavior are well documented, the use of these methods for humans is generally a last resort. The use of punishment as a technique to eliminate a bothersome behavior in a child will generally be very effective as a suppressor of that behavior and, in fact, may eliminate the behavior entirely. Unfortunately, the delivery of punishment as a reinforcing stimulus also will elicit many respondent behaviors (Reynolds, 1968), such as fear, crying, or flight, which may be equally bothersome or socially inappropriate. Thus, although punishment is usually accompanied by a decrease in the rate of emission of the behavior that is punished, it may be accompanied by other undesirable behaviors. It does not provide any discriminative stimuli associated with positive reinforcement. Although the individual may cease emitting one particular bothersome response, he receives no information indicative of the manner in which positive reinforcement might be obtained in that situation. Thus, whenever possible it is preferable to use positive reinforcement in promoting the acquisition of appropriate behavior.

Shaping: the method of successive approximation. The process through which complex patterns of behavior are developed through operant learning is known as successive approximation or shaping. For the example cited previously in which the experimenter wished to train the pigeon to peck at a light on the side of a Skinner Box, he waited for the bird to emit that response before dispensing the reinforcement. In attempting to teach animals or individuals complex responses, it is often inefficient and sometimes impossible to wait for the operant to appear before dispensing the reinforcement. For example, if we wished to train a rat to pick up a marble, it is likely that either the experimenter or the animal would expire before such a behavior was emitted. The method of successive approximation refers to the delivery of reinforcement following responses that are increasingly closer approximations of the desired behavior. Shaping would involve initially providing a reinforcing stimulus each time the rat made some movement toward the marble. Once movement toward the marble was a well-established response, reinforcement would be made contingent upon another behavior, such as touching the marble with the paws, this being a closer approximation of the desired behavior. After many such small increments of behavior change, the rat would eventually pick up the marble in his paws.

When the presentation of a reinforcing stimulus is under the control of an experienced experimenter, the process of a successive approximation may proceed quite rapidly and result in the production of very unusual terminal behaviors. Pigeons have been taught to play ping-pong, chickens to play songs on miniature pianos, and raccoons to play basketball. One of the most startling and impressive examples of the power of the method of successive approximation is described by Skinner (1960) in his article *Pigeons in a Pelican,* in which he explains how pigeons were taught to function as guidance mechanisms for aerial bombs developed near the end of World War II.

Extinction and schedules of reinforcement. One assesses the effectiveness of a reinforcing stimulus by observing the response rate. The presence of a reinforcing stimulus will always lead to an increase in the rate of responding. However, there is an almost infinite number of possible ways in which reinforcement can be made contingent upon the presence of a specific operant. These different methods of presenting reinforcing stimuli are known as schedules of reinforcement, and each has predictable effects on both response rate and resistance to extinction.

The term "extinction" in operant learning refers to the effect upon response rate that is observed when reinforcement no longer follows an operant that has previously been reinforced. The removal of reinforcement in extinction has three different effects on the operant. The first and most general of these effects is a gradual decline in the rate of responding of the individual. Second, when extinction is first begun the rate of responding may briefly increase before beginning to decline and, third, the characteristics of the operant may become more variable. For example, if after shaping a rat to pick up a marble we no longer followed this operant behavior with reinforcement, the first apparent effects of extinction to be observed would include the rat picking up the marble more rapidly than he did immediately prior to extinction. This increase in response rate would then likely be followed by the appearance of new operants associated with picking up the marble, such as throwing it in the air or jumping up and down while holding it. Finally, if the extinction procedure is maintained, the behavior that we had shaped will gradually decline and eventually disappear.

When an operant is no longer emitted as a result of extinction, a very curious effect often occurs. This effect, known as spontaneous recovery (Reynolds, 1968), describes the reappearance of a previously extinguished operant when the subject is placed in the environment in which the operant had previously been reinforced. Spontaneous recovery may occur several times, but in the absence of reinforcement the operant will most probably eventually disappear again and spontaneous recovery will no longer occur.

The degree to which an operant is resistant to extinction depends primarily on the schedule that was used in the presentation of the reinforcing stimulus events. There are two basic ways in which reinforcement can be scheduled.

CONTINUOUS REINFORCEMENT. A continuous schedule of reinforcement means that each emission of the operant is followed by a reinforcing stimulus. A continuous schedule of reinforcement for the rat would be to dispense food as a reinforcer for each time it picked up the marble. Although the use of continuous reinforcement is clear and logical, its effect on response rate and resistance to extinction is not as profound as other methods of scheduling reinforcement. Following each operant with reinforcement is not the most efficient way to develop a very rapid response rate and does not produce behavior that is as resistant to extinction as do other schedules of reinforcement.

PARTIAL SCHEDULES OF REINFORCEMENT. In actuality, continuous schedules of reinforcement rarely exist in the environment. A carnivorous animal must often attempt to catch its prey many times before his operant stalking behavior is reinforced with food. Most individuals who hold jobs are not paid every hour or every day. Rather, they must emit work behavior many times before it is followed by reinforcement. When only some of the operant responses of an organism are reinforced, the term "partial" or "intermittent reinforcement" is used.

There are many possible combinations of partial reinforcement, only a few of which we will discuss. Whenever partial reinforcement is used as a scheduling device, an event known as the "partial reinforcement effect" occurs (Reynolds, 1968). This effect describes the relationship between continuous and partial schedules of reinforcement and resistance to extinction. Specifically, the partial reinforcement effect refers to the fact that whenever only some of the emitted operant responses are reinforced, these operants will show greater resistance to extinction than operants that have been continuously reinforced. That is, when a partial or intermittent schedule of reinforcement is used, it will take longer for the behavior to be extinguished than when a continuous schedule is employed.

The two basic types of partial schedules of reinforcement are interval schedules and ratio schedules. For interval schedules reinforcement occurs after the lapse of a specific period of time. For example, a simple interval schedule might dictate that every 5 minutes, regardless of the frequency of response, one reinforcement be dispersed. Salaries are on an interval schedule. In contrast, on a ratio schedule the subject must emit a certain specified number of responses before receiving a reinforcement. The amount of time elapsing between reinforcements under a ratio schedule is irrelevant. A simple ratio schedule of reinforcement might dictate that one reinforcement be dispensed following every 25 responses. The reinforcement may be dispensed on the average of every 25 responses rather than each twenty-fifth response. This is known as a variable ratio schedule and quite effectively maintains the behavior of salesmen, gamblers, and the disturbed.

In terms of acquisition rate of an operant response, ratio schedules generally lead to a higher rate of responding more quickly than interval schedules. Once an extinction procedure is instituted, ratio schedules maintain or will lead to greater resistance to extinction than interval schedules. There is an almost infinite number of possible combinations of schedules. They can be combined to produce unique effects, which differ from other schedules of reinforcement in both acquisition and resistance to extinction.

The concept of schedules of reinforcement is one of the most powerful tools for understanding behavior. Sophisticated analyses of human behavior in everyday life indicated that much of the stability of man's behavior results from highly complex schedules of reinforcement. Schedules of reinforcement can also be useful for understanding the development of abnormal behavior and educational problems. Reynolds (1968) points out that an increasing interlocking schedule of reinforcement may be operating in our public education system in the United States.

An increasing interlocking schedule involves the contingency that reinforcement occurs as an increasing function of the length of time that has passed since the previous reinforcement and the number of responses emitted since the previous reinforcement. Under an increasing interlocking schedule, it is possible that the subject may never receive reinforcement if he does not begin responding at a high enough rate. That is, since the requirement in terms of response rate increases as a function of time, the individual must begin emitting the appropriate responses relatively early or the passage of time will require such a high rate of responding that the individual may never be reinforced. When a group of subjects is faced with this type of schedule, their initial response rate results in a very rapid division into two separate groups. Those who initially responded at a high enough rate to obtain reinforcement continue to respond at a high rate. However, those subjects who did not respond fast enough initially to obtain reinforcement begin to respond more slowly and eventually cease responding entirely.

Cumulative educational systems, in which students are promoted from one grade or level of performance to another, contain contingencies of reinforcement remarkably similar to those described by an increasing interlocking schedule. In order to obtain reinforcement associated with successful performance in the eighth grade, one must have performed successfully in the earlier grades. It is extremely difficult for an individual to obtain reinforcement in the higher grades if very little was learned in the earlier grades. Thus, both response rate and time determine the availability of reinforcement to students in our educational system. If in his initial experiences with education the student learns very little (that is, he responds at a very low rate), it is likely that he will receive little if any reinforcement. His rate of responding will continue to decline, and he will eventually be labeled a failure.

An analysis of factors associated with school failure often leads to the inference that the difference between students who are successful and those who fail is predetermined by intellectual or personality traits. An analysis of the education system in terms of an increasing interlocking schedule of reinforcement would indicate that the major difference between successful students and those who fail may lie in the fact that the initial response rate of the failures was too low to gain any reinforcement to maintain behavior leading to school success.

Observational learning

Bandura (1969) has contributed much to our understanding of modeling or observational learning. Although considerable research has been done with animals, the most valuable work has been performed by Bandura and his associates on the observational learning of children.

Defining characteristics. Observational learning refers to an individual acquiring or modifying his behavior as a result of observing another's behavior and its consequences. It has been shown, for example, that a person can learn various emotional responses by watching the reactions of other people who are experiencing pain or pleasure. Fears can be eliminated simply through the observation of another individual interacting with feared objects.

The process of observational learning is differentiated from both respondent and operant learning in the following respects.

Absence of observable response. In acquiring or modifying a particular response through observation of another individual, the learner need do nothing more than watch what the model is doing. The learner may neither engage in nor emit operants at the time that learning takes place.

Absence of observable reinforcement. The learner is observing the behavior of the model. Not only are there no observable responses by the learner, but no observable reinforcement is necessary for this type of learning to take place. For observational learning it is not necessary for the learner to experience the presence of a reinforcing stimulus to acquire the behavior of the model.

A model of observational learning. Bandura believes the following process takes place during the acquisition of a behavior through observation of a model. First, the visual experience of the behavior of the model involves a process of sensory conditioning in the absence of reinforcement. The vari-

Fig. 3. Children mimic adult roles. (H. Armstrong Roberts.)

ous behaviors engaged in by the model become associated with each other simply by the fact that they occur contigously, that is, following one another in time. These contiguous events are coded and stored as a memory function. Second, these contiguous stimuli undergo a process of verbal coding. Symbolic verbal labels are attached to the events observed by the learner. After the stimulus events associated with the behavior of the model have been verbally coded and stored, they function as mediators. They are stimuli governing the behavior of the learner when he experiences stimuli similar to those associated with the behavior of the model. Through the process of sensory association of visual experience and verbal coding of this experience, the subject learns the behavior that was performed by the model.

Learning becomes evident when the subject is placed in a situation similar to or identical with that in which the model was observed. In this situation the environmental stimuli lead to the retrieval of the encoded images and verbal symbols that resulted from observation of the model in that situation. The retrieval of this information leads to the performance of a behavior by the subject similar to that of the model.

Example of observational learning. Numerous theories have been formulated to explain the acquisition and development of aggressive behavior in children and adults. These theoretical positions are logical and at first glance seem to provide a useful method of understanding behavior. However, as is the case with many theories postulating the presence of inner causes as explanations of behavior, theories of aggression have lacked utility. Specifically, most theories of aggression postulate some internal mechanism, which is not available for observation or direct manipulation, as the governing factor in the development of aggressive or hostile behavior. In recent years researchers in learning and behavioral sciences have demonstrated more clearly some of the antecedents of aggressive behavior.

Bandura and Walters (1963) have demonstrated through experimentation that one need not rely on internal mechanisms as explanations for the acquisition of aggressive behavior. One famous experiment involved the acquisition of aggressive behavior in children through observational learning. Male and female children observed the behavior of adult male and female models. The models engaged in a variety of specific aggressive behaviors against a large inflated plastic doll. The model could be seen to push the doll to the floor and pound on its face, pick the doll up in the air and throw it, strike it with a wooden mallet, and kick it with great force. After observing the behavior of the model, the children were placed one at a time in the environment in which the model had engaged in the aggressive behavior. The children proceeded, without further contact with the model or anyone else, to engage in aggressive behavior highly similar to that of the observed model. If the child had observed the model pounding the doll with a mallet, a mallet was used by the child in a manner very similar to that of the model. Parents who allow their children to watch violence on television are likely allowing them to learn violent behavior.

Other experiments in related areas of behavior have led to the conclusion that observational learning alone is sufficient to account for many of the forms of behavior often attributed to some inner psychic process. The importance of this discovery lies in the fact that the behavior of a model can be manipulated to produce very specific effects on the behavior of the observer. Explanation of behaviors such as aggression in terms of inner mental processes leads to efforts at modification that must be indirect. They are much less efficient in comparison to those based on observational learning theory.

Controlling conditions. Several conditions are necessary if observational learning is to take place and be demonstrated by the subject. First, various components of the response to be learned must occur contiguously. If an individual is to learn a particular sequence of modeled behaviors through observation, the behaviors in that sequence must follow one another in their natural temporal order. Second, the individual must pay attention to the relevant stimuli associated with the behavior of the model. Simply allowing an individual to view another person engaging in some behavior is not sufficient for observational learning to take place. If the learner is not watching the behavior of the model but is attending to some irrelevant stimulus in the environment, observational learning will not take place. Third, the individual must be capable of retention of the coded symbols that represent the behavior of the model. If the individual is to be able to reproduce the behavior in the absence of the model, he must be capable of retaining the information gained from that observation. Fourth, the subject must be capable of motor reproduction of the observed behavior. Motor reproduction occurs most efficiently when the observed responses require the reorganization of existing behaviors into the new patterns exhibited by the model. Reproduction is not efficient when the responses of the model include behaviors with which the observer has had no experience or that he is incapable of performing.

Finally, if an observed pattern of behavior is to be reproduced by the observer, there must be sufficient motivational support in the environment. The observer should be in a situation similar to that in which he observed the model, and the reproduction of the modeled responses should be associated with positively reinforcing stimulus events. If such a situation occurs, it is likely that the observed behavior will be quickly reproduced. However, if the environment in which the observer is placed is very dissimilar from that in which the model was observed, and if a variety of punishing consequences are associated with the reproduction of the observed behavior, it is unlikely that such reproduction will take place. Movie censorship boards that require criminals to be punished at the end of the movie operate in consonance with this principle.

LEARNING AND SOCIAL BEHAVIOR

Numerous utopian social systems have been proposed to optimize conditions of human life and interpersonal relationships. Skinner (1971) has postulated the existence of behavioral laws affecting all human interactions. He makes the significant point that principles of learning exist and influence, but they seem to be denied by practically everyone. Instead, people rely on principles derived from theology and common sense, which are often at great variance with the actual existing principles. The false principles inform people what they should do, without noting that behaviors are contingent upon reinforcing consequences. A person should do something, but there is no provision for reinforcing whatever he does.

Fig. 4. Father's fantasies, son's dreams. (H. Armstrong Roberts.)

It is further postulated with such inaccurate thinking that what a person should do should not be reinforced, since this detracts from his freedom and dignity. Skinner believes the traditional concepts of freedom and dignity are illusions that have detracted significantly from the development of more appropriate human behavior and social institutions. Only by ridding ourselves of the illusion that positive behavior will be maintained without reinforcing consequences can we achieve a more adequate existence. If dignity and freedom are defined in terms of desired behavior and contingencies of reinforcement are instituted, utopia in the truest sense may be achieved.

Illogical evaluative thinking and its imposition are governed by very complex schedules of reinforcement. The major problem with the existence of these forms of moralistic behavior is that they do not provide the individual within society an efficient means of developing socially approved behavior. The contingencies of reinforcement governing the emission of moralistic behavior can be redesigned to emphasize positive rather than negative reinforcing contingencies, thereby recognizing man's nature as a behaving organism and increasing the probability that man will be able to live productively, peacefully, and happily.

MOTIVATION, FEELING, EMOTION, AND LEARNING
Differentiation

Motivation as a behavioral concept is often confused with feelings and emotion. Some people typically describe their emotional state as unmotivated. Motivation properly refers to a set of conditions quite different from those that define feelings and emotion. Motivation can be most simply defined as a discriminative stimulus for a particular behavior. For example, hunger is a motivating condition. It can be referred to as such because the presence of hunger indicates conditions under which food-seeking behavior has previously taken place and been reinforced.

Feelings and emotion, on the other hand, can be considered as both discriminative stimuli and operants. The presence of a particular feeling or emotion may indicate the presence of conditions under which some associated behavior, such as crying or striking out physically at a person or object, has been previously reinforced. Feelings and emotion, as operants, are components of emotional states that can be observed.

Defining characteristics of feeling and emotion as operants

Feeling and emotion as operant behavior can be understood in terms of two components that may or may not occur simultaneously (Reynolds, 1968). First, feeling and emotion include components of expressive behavior. Expressive behavior refers to observable physical movements—for example, smiling is generally indicative of happiness. Frowning is an expressive behavior generally denoting sadness or anger. Second, feeling and emotion include a verbal component, the verbal statement of the individual in naming or describing his emotional state. Words such as afraid, angry, happy, ecstatic, joyful, depressed, and anxious are all verbally reported components of emotion.

The existence of emotion and feeling does not occur within the "mind" of the individual. In almost every case a person's emotional state is reflected in his behavior, whether it is expressive, a simple verbal report, or both. It is actually more useful in understanding human behavior to define emotion and feeling solely in terms of expressive behavior and verbal report. In attempting to deal with feeling and emotion, we are always limited to dealing with one or both of the components. It is impossible to work with emotion that is not expressed by some form of behavior. Speculation about the presence, absence, and/or quality of feeling and emotion in the absence of behavioral components will often obscure significant individual behaviors that could be used productively to understand the person.

Controlling conditions in feeling and emotion

Feeling and emotion may be either innate or acquired. Innate emotional behavior is usually thought to be reflexive in nature, that is, a particular unconditioned stimulus (such as pain) will always elicit a specific emotional unconditioned response (in this case, fear). Through the process of respondent learning, innate emotional responses come to be associated with conditioned stimuli. The subsequent conditioned responses may be considered either normal or abnormal, depending on the conditioned stimulus that elicits them.

It has also been demonstrated that emotional behavior can be acquired and understood through the principles of operant and observational learning. When the emission of an emotional response such as smiling is regularly reinforced, it may become a very high-probability expressive behavior. If an individual regularly observes those in his environment emitting particular expressive behaviors in certain circumstances, it is likely that he will learn to behave in a similar manner under similar conditions.

For understanding human behavior it is of the utmost importance, if efforts at modification of emotion and feeling are to be attempted, that feelings and emotion be understood as behaviors governed by the same principles of learning that control other aspects of behavior. If feeling and emotion are placed in a metaphysical status and assigned spiritual or moral qualities, it becomes impossible for the individual to either modify or productively understand behavior. Spiritual and metaphysical qualities are neither observable nor open to change through human intervention.

INTERACTION OF HEREDITY AND ENVIRONMENT

One of the most pervasive problems in the behavioral sciences and the mental health field in general is the tendency of individual scientists and technicians to divide the human organism into hereditary-biological and environmental components. For many years there has been a raging controversy in the behavioral sciences to determine whether heredity or environment is the determining factor in human behavior. Logic and research suggest that relying on either biological or environmental events as explanations of behavior in the absence of each other can lead only to confusion and wasted effort. Human behavior is a function of both biological and environmental influences. If we are to effectively understand and deal with behavior of any sort, it is necessary that the entire man, both biological and behavioral, be considered in our analysis. Man does not function behaviorally independent of his physical body. Similarly, man as a biological organism does not function independent of environmental influence. To understand human behavior we must weigh the contribution of each carefully. If we are to understand behavior in terms of principles of learning, we must also be aware that the integrity of the biological organism is essential to learning. Likewise, understanding the effects of physical illness and dealing with it effectively require a knowledge of human behavior and emotion.

It is hoped that our division of man as a biological and a behaving organism in Chapters 2 and 3 will not lead to a division in the student's understanding of human behavior. We anticipate that the student will integrate the ideas and facts presented here to form a rational and effective approach for understanding human behavior.

REFERENCES AND SUGGESTED READINGS

Bandura, A. 1969. Principles of behavior modification. New York, Holt, Rinehart and Winston, Inc.

Bandura, A., and Walters, R. H. 1963. Social learning and personality development. New York, Holt, Rinehart, and Winston, Inc.

Hilgard, E. R., and Bower, G. H. 1966. Theories of learning. New York, Appleton-Century-Crofts.

Hill, W. F. 1963. Learning: a survey of psychological interpretations. San Francisco, Chandler Publishing Company.

Morgan, C. T., and King, R. A. 1966. Introduction to psychology. New York, McGraw-Hill Book Company.

Reynolds, G. S. 1968. A primer of operant conditioning. Chicago, Scott, Foresman and Company.

Skinner, B. F. 1953. Science and human behavior. New York, The Macmillan Company.

Skinner, B. F. 1960. Pigeons in a pelican. American Psychologist 15:28-37.

Skinner, B. F. 1969. Contingencies of reinforcement: a theoretical analysis. New York, Appleton-Century-Crofts.

Skinner, B. F. 1971. Beyond freedom and dignity. New York, Alfred A. Knopf, Inc.

4

THE PERSON AND GROUP MEMBERSHIP

In the beginning there was absolute nothingness. Masses of chemical elements were randomly assorted and coagulated throughout the universe with forces operating without meaning or design. Grand and spectacular cause and effect sequences, which we have come to know as physical and behavioral principles and laws, began to be formed. The world as we understand it had its beginning. The earth and all the other planets and celestial bodies became realities. The masses of elements were infused with a spark in some long-forgotten sea or swamp and life began. Creatures of beautiful simplicity were born, developed, and mutated to infinitely complex forms. Early versions of man gave way to more advanced ones. By natural laws of selection and development man came to be what he is today. Most importantly, man became the most highly developed and complex organism functioning in physical proximity and in relation to other men.

Humans are first and foremost distinctly social organisms. Man is like many other organisms in numerous ways, but most of us believe that there are unique qualities that make man different from social groups of gorillas, chimpanzees, and any other form of life. Everywhere and at all times men have lived with other men. Even to be a hermit requires the existence of other human beings, for by definition a hermit needs other people, whom he avoids, merely in order to be a hermit.

BASIC DEFINITIONS AND EXAMPLES

Much of the group influence on an individual's behavior is taken for granted to such an extent that we are usually unaware of the large degree to which our behavior is determined by group processes. We tend to believe that whatever we do is natural and results from our own decisions, rather than being caused by other people. When we decide that certain behaviors or events are good and proper, we are often amazed to find that people from other parts of the world, for example, believe the particular behavior or event is improper and bad. Individuals in some societies kill or allow to be killed their parents of advanced age, whereas Americans view such events with extreme disfavor. Such opposite beliefs and behaviors are formed by the guidance and teachings of the particular culture.

Culture

The term "culture" refers to the customs and traditions of a group of people and to the beliefs and emotional reactions they have about the significant aspects and events of their lives. They are transmitted via the social learning process to each newborn infant of the group. The infant begins a lifelong training process in the attitudes, beliefs, and behaviors appropriate to his particular culture. This cultural learning process is termed "socialization." The parents are the original group charged with the responsibility of transmitting the cultural heritage, and, of course, it was previously transmitted to them. Since all individuals are different, the degree to which one learns his cultural behavioral standards varies among individuals, which accounts and allows for social change within the framework of massive cultural stability.

Much research has been done on cultural differences. Comparing cultures with others is known as the cross-cultural method of ascertaining patterns of culture. The natural conditions under which people live have considerable influence on the formation of the cultural pattern. These include the kind and amount of food available to them, availability of natural resources, climatic conditions, characteristics of the land surface, proximity to oceans, and many others. Technology, religion, and the ultimate ideals of life existence are generally related to these factors.

Status and roles

Every culture has its own social structure, even though democratic and communistic nations in particular tend to avoid a focus on social structure and the existence of classes. Every society assigns a status, or actually several statuses, to every individual in the culture. Obvious statuses include those related to age, group, sex, occupation, and social prestige. Each status has an assigned role, which is a behavior pattern expected of a person holding such a status. For example, an 11-year-old white girl from a wealthy family exhibits and is expected to exhibit behaviors different from a 29-year-old black male from the ghetto. Their beliefs, attitudes, and interpersonal skills differ, and if either assumed behavioral patterns associated primarily with the other status, there would likely be a high level of emotional arousal from other members of the two groups.

It should be noted that people may have a particular status at one time and a different status at other times or under different environmental circumstances. An adult male in our culture has role behaviors expected in his place of business, but these are not exactly the same roles expected from him when he returns to his family at the end of the workday, nor expected when he goes to church on Sunday. He may have several statuses in the social structure and roles for the various aspects of his life.

It is not uncommon for a person to have a conflict of roles that can cause turmoil in his life and group functioning. The physician with the highest level of medical knowledge and skill is taught and is expected to assume a behavioral pattern characterized by confidence, ability, leadership, and authority. However, in situations of a social, political, and/or interpersonal type, these role behaviors may well be inappropriate and punished by others if he exhibits them. The new mental health worker who is accustomed to a role pattern of behaviors involving submissiveness and continually being told what tasks to perform and how to do it may suffer conflict when promoted to a supervisory position requiring the ability to work as a responsible, knowledgeable leader of other people. The roles learned in one status may not be appropriate in a new status.

The expectancy that groups have in regard to some behaviors may also exist among all other cultural groups. These are termed "universals," in contrast to particular rules or norms of behavior specific to a given cultural group. Norms of behavior associated with one group, such as the rules and regulations regarding food among Jewish people, are termed "particulars." Every culture has behavioral norms that can be categorized as prescribed, prohibited, or permissive. Prescribed behaviors are those that are demanded and for which negative reactions will occur when such behaviors are not exhibited. In early America people who did not attend church on Sunday or otherwise did not behave in the manner prescribed by their group could be placed in the stocks or receive some other form of punishment. Prohibited behaviors are those that cannot be exhibited; if they are, the person may be severely punished. Taboos, which may be either universals or particulars, fall into this category. One prohibited universal appears to be incest, for no cultural group on record has ever generally allowed such behavior. Permissive regulations pertain to behaviors that are open for the individual to express with little sanction or condemnation, other than appropriateness in terms of time, place, or other circumstances.

Social class

Social classes appear in all societies, with the status of individuals arranged on a scale of prestige. In our culture the social classes are primarily categorized on the basis of occupation, wealth, years of education, socioeconomic status of parents, area of residence, social and service club memberships, and others with a decreasing degree of importance. Associated with each class is a set of behavioral standards, which indicates which behaviors are appropriate for each class group. The highest socioeconomic class has the highest prestige and is usually and generally not supposed to relate closely to the lowest socioeconomic group. The highest class individuals raise their eyebrows when one of their group relates closely in any manner to a member of the lowest class, and vice versa. It is a surprising, unexpected, and at the least an uncondoned event.

Members of the highest class tend to have been taught that they are more important people, have the right to talk more in social groups, are more accepted as leaders, are more attractive to others, and feel more freedom to deviate from group standards. The reverse appears to hold true for the lower class. There are numerous and complex patterns that exist between these two extremes.

THE FAMILY

The arrival of a newborn infant is noted with the words: "It's a boy" or "It's a girl." These words reflect the importance of the newborn's sexual biology for the manner in which his parents and all of society will influence and react to him. The social role of men and women is acquired via the socialization process beginning with birth, and it has a highly pervasive influence on all of an individual's behavior. The parents have been taught their role behaviors and function to teach their new child.

There are numerous circumstances of learning, one of the most significant being modeling or imitation. Children are taught to perform many behaviors by imitating their parents. They are taught to imitate movements, including playing patty-cake, and language behavior, such as imitating the sounds "mama," "dada," or "kitty." Their motor and language behavior has many milestones and developmental sequences. The child usually takes his first steps between 12 and 16 months and says his first comprehensible words between 11 and 15 months. With the ability to move about in the environment and use language as a learning facilitator, the child is open to the majority of cultural influences.

Major behavior patterns that the parents influence involve those subsumed under the categories of dependency, aggression, achievement, and sexuality. In regard to all these areas there is a significant difference in the development of boys and girls. It is generally understood that little boys are taught to be independent, aggressive, sexual, and achievement-oriented outside the family, whereas in comparison little girls are taught to be more dependent, less aggressive, less obviously sexual, and more achievement-oriented within the family. Many writers have attempted to note the sequences in the development of these behaviors and the methods by which parents teach them or do not teach them behaviors considered appropriate for their sexual role by the larger culture. Clearly it is desired to find some optimal and effective behaviors in regard to these four categories, rather than an extreme of any. The person who is extreme in aggression at either a very low or a very high level is generally considered to have inappropriate behavior. Individuals high on aggression may be unable to relate to other people and may be very much avoided. Those who are extremely low on aggression may be unable to reasonably assert their rights as human beings. Such extremes for aggression and the other behavior categories undoubtedly exist, but usually it is the interaction and levels of all the role behaviors that are of primary importance.

Parental influence on behavior development

Children have two parents, and their mother and father, presuming both remain present, may be supplementary in their effect upon the child, or they may be very opposite and contradictory in their child development practices. On the basis of considerable research from numerous investigators, Becker (1964) has developed a model for parental behavior. He postulates three bipolar dimensions, these being warmth-hostility, restrictiveness-permissiveness, and calm detachment-anxious emotional involvement. The behavior of parents can be observed and rated and their behavior pattern plotted on a graph in terms of the interaction of these opposing dimensions. Regardless of their warmth-hostility and their restrictiveness-permissiveness, the degree to which they are effective is primarily related to calm detachment-anxious emotional involvement. This means that parents can exhibit many behaviors thought ineffective by others and still be very effective parents.

Parents who are warm and restrictive are often termed overprotective, but they may also be organized and effective if they are calm and mature. Parents who are warm and permissive may be quite democratic, but they may also be quite indulgent and negligent in their duties as primary teachers for their culture. This is particularly true if they are anxiously and emotionally involved, refusing to teach their children the values and standards of their cultural group. Older people view themselves as quite responsible and reasonable and perceive young people as irresponsible and juvenile. On the other hand, young people see themselves as open-minded and lacking in the conservative adults' hang-ups.

Parents who are very permissive and hostile toward their children may be seen as anxious neurotics. If they are calm and detached from intense interactions with their children, they are perceived as neglecting. Parents who are highly restrictive and hostile toward their children can be either rigidly controlling or quite authoritarian.

Children who develop in these various family atmospheres exhibit behaviors related to their family experiences. The children of warm and permissive parents who are not neurotically involved with them tend to be more creative, active, and socially outgoing. The aggressive behaviors of the children are more successful, and they exhibit less self-aggression. They are seen as being more independent, friendly, and capable of assuming adult roles. Children who grow up in families that are warm and restrictive, on the other hand, are more submissive, dependent, and overtly polite. They show much neatness, obedience, and orderliness. They tend to be much less aggressive and more oriented toward following the rules and regulations of society. Their peers do not perceive them as being very friendly, and creativity is minimal. They are viewed as quite compliant and not likely to be leaders.

Hostile parents, who can be either restrictive or permissive, are the ones who have problem children. Problem children are the result of problem parents, just as child abuse is performed by parents who have themselves been abused as children. Hostile and restrictive parents have children who are neurotic and socially withdrawn and who tend to be shy and have many quarrels with their peer group. They are low in adult role-taking ability and show neurotic behaviors, such as self-aggression or self-defeating patterns of behavior. Hostile and permissive parents have children who are not neurotic but delinquent. Their children get into many more difficulties with authority figures, including legal authorities. They tend to exhibit a high degree of aggression and little compliance with the rules and regulations of society.

The preceding model and research summary is consistent with numerous research studies, although it is clear that more intensive investigation of these dimensions and their interactions is necessary. A clear, definitive, and feasible method of changing currently unfortunate conditions of parent-child relationships, for which we have sufficient evidence, needs to be instituted.

Ceremonies

All cultural groups have specified important changes in the lives of their young members with various ceremonies denoting significant milestones of development. In primitive cultures there are rites of passage and initiations of several types. These may range from a minor degree of mutilation of the body of adolescent boys to a temporary but severe restriction on activities of any kind. To some degree these exist in our contemporary society with such events as the Bar Mitzvah, in which the young Jewish boy during a religious ceremony becomes an adult in accordance with Jewish standards. The American child's first day of school is also considered a very significant event, although many 5 year olds return home in tears complaining that they have not learned anything in school on the first day. A person's death is attended by ritual events that may be quite elaborate. Funerals are held to note the hereafter permanent absence of the person, and his friends and relatives, during the process of grief, break their emotional ties to the person to a sufficient degree that they may continue their own lives. Marriage is another significant event in the lives of people in almost all cultures, for no culture has been found that does not have some rules and regulations in regard to marriage and divorce. However, these are very different among cultures.

Loss of parents

When children grow up in families with only one parent, or when death or divorce claims one of the parents at an early age, children exhibit behavior patterns different from those who had two parents (Douvan and Adelson, 1966).

This is largely a matter of modeling, for little boys need fathers after whom they can model their own behavior in order to adequately understand the adult role behaviors of men. Little boys are much more susceptible to behavior problems if they do not have a father than if they do not have a mother. Nevertheless, it is certainly a truism that both little boys and little girls need both their parents if they are to be relatively assured of behavioral effectiveness as adults.

Boys who have lost their fathers at an early age from divorce tend to become very defiant and overassertive, being a caricature of masculinity. More than other boys, they show problems in self-control and coming to terms with authority figures, and they often bristle with aggression. What is lost in their development is apparently not simply the presence of the father, as occurs in death, but the loss of the father as an ideal of masculinity. In effect, they learn to reject any ideal and are always seeking out and simultaneously testing authority figures. Often the mother has anger toward the divorced father, which does not help the little boy in his search for an adequate male after whom he may model. Basically, their masculinity is superficially obvious, but it is often only a shell covering many problems. Since black boys often do not have an adequate father figure in the home, they tend to exhibit many of the aforementioned problems. It is also highly noteworthy that the assassinations of John Kennedy, Martin Luther King, and Robert Kennedy, all whom are generally accepted as adequate adult males, were performed by men who either did not have a father in the home when they were growing up or had a very inadequate one. The assassins' homes were dominated by a strong and rigid mother, and the father was at least psychologically not available as a model.

Formerly, both girls and boys from divorced homes remained with their mothers. Girls who have lost their fathers from divorce tend to be quite compliant but highly feminine on the surface. Unlike boys they do not rebel, but they psychologically withdraw. However, they also have developmental problems and, like boys, are always searching for a father figure, even when they are chronologically adults. Although they do not understand men very well, since they have not had a father in the home with whom to interact and learn, they test men differently from the testing shown by fatherless boys. Primarily this is exhibited in their compliance rather than hostility toward men in authority positions in school or business. Clearly, girls do not suffer as much from divorce and living with their mothers as do boys.

The death of the father leads to very different behavior patterns. For both boys and girls the effects are more situational. Problems resulting from the death of the father involve a lack of money in the family, more responsibility, premature seriousness, and less leisure time. In many respects these children are much more like those from intact families than those who have lost a parent through divorce.

Effects of siblings

There are numerous differences in the socialization process related to the number of siblings in the family and the particular sequence in which they are born. Only children are different from children from large families, firstborn sons are different from lastborn daughters, and middle siblings are different from any of their brothers or sisters. To a large extent these differences are related to envy of the other children's status and privileges and the effects that several children can have on each other in terms of their modeling of parent behaviors and the degree to which they serve as models for each other. In large families, of course, competition for attention and affection from the parents runs very high, whereas in small families the parents have attention and recognition for a smaller number of children.

Firstborn males tend to grow up to be very responsible and achievement-oriented. They are overrepresented proportionately in college classrooms, as numerous college professors, who sometimes have their students indicate whether they were firstborn, and in particular, firstborn sons in their family, will attest. Firstborn sons show numerous characteristics associated with the mature leader. Lastborn children are the babies of the family, and there is some evidence to suggest they they remain so in the eyes of their family and in their own self-concept. Even as adults they are often not informed of important family events until all decisions are reached. They tend to show a much more stable security and confidence in themselves, as if somehow people will always take care of them, and they sometimes seem to believe they are quite acceptable no matter what they do. Middle siblings have observed the oldest child dethroned from the highest status in the affectionate eyes of the parents, the same as happened to him, but the baby of the family has never been thus dethroned. Hence, the middle child tends to have ambivalent feelings toward the younger siblings. Basically, he finds it hard to believe that the youngest sibling has never been dethroned from the status of protected and highly rewarded baby.

These sibling competition effects are often noted in the psychological literature, and they were researched, significantly, by Alfred Adler, a latterborn son who worked with Sigmund Freud, a firstborn son. The competion between the mature and responsible Freud and the more social justice–oriented Adler was intense.

Modern living

Numerous changes have occurred in the last 100 years in society, including industrialization, urbanization, the changing status and roles of women, and the values in regard to the milestones of one's life. These changes have occurred in some parts of America to a greater extent than in others, but in view of the mobility of the population they appear to be quite pervasive and significant.

One hundred years ago the majority of the population lived on farms and were close to a very limited number of people. They tended to be born, mature, and die within a very limited geographical area. Only the most adventurous (and perhaps unstable and dissatisfied) journeyed from their homes to settle in the West. On the average today people move every 5 years, and it is by no means uncommon for a family to pack their belongings and move from New York to California. If the trend of the last 20 years of migration to the West continues, it may not be so many years before the trend reverses itself. City life has certain advantages in terms of sophistication, a larger group of people from which to select one's friends, better and higher paying jobs, general excitement, and many others. The disadvantages are becoming more apparent, these being overcrowding, pollution, highly expensive living, poor schools, crime, and many others. All these influence family conditions and the development of the child.

Industrialization is highly correlated with urbanization. People no longer work 10 hours a day in the fields tending crops and performing numerous duties

Fig. 5. Depersonalization and alienation in modern life. (H. Armstrong Roberts.)

associated with farming. Instead, they may work the equivalent of 7 hours for only 5 days per week in a factory performing the same task repetitively. Many workers in industry find their jobs lacking in gratification and boring. Writers have noted the change in man's behavior patterns associated with the effects of industrialization, and it is often stated that industry and cities are detrimental to the welfare of man. Groups of people have banded together to form communes in out-of-the-way places in order to return to what they consider a more natural mode of living and to escape from the negative effects of industrialized metropolises.

Women

The status and roles of women are much in the news. Changing views vary from the rational consideration of their lives by mature women to very strange expressions of disturbance by quite unrealistic women. Women have noted they are second-class citizens in comparison to men and are viewed by many as inferior. This is comparable to other minorities who have experienced intense discrimination. In the economic area there is a clear and poorly rationalized discrepancy between the salaries of men and women. Although there is no evidence in regard to genetic or biological inferiority in intelligence and most areas of production and performance, women are more often informed both subtly and directly that they should be nurses, teachers, or secretaries and perform other kinds of work in which they are definitely low paid and inferior to a man such as a principal, physician, or executive. In the family area they have been informed both subtly and directly that they should mop floors, carry out garbage, chauffeur, and perform other duties around the home regardless of their training and knowledge. In social role behavior they have had their inferiority shown by men who open doors for them, light their cigarettes, and otherwise place them in a submissive, lower, and weaker status.

Although some men have expressed the belief that this is in reality a masterful feminine plot against men, the facts indicate the reasonable anger of women in regard to their role and function in twentieth-century America. They are demanding and obtaining respect for themselves as human beings first, with their female biological status being a secondary and minor consideration. In other words, women are like men in terms of their membership in the human race. In the job market, family life, and social relationships they have made much progress, as exemplified by the saying: "You've come a long way, baby." Some men have noted that they will become truly free only when women become free.

By no means does this contradict the biological differences between men and women. It is recognized by behavioral scientists that biological differences do indeed exist, although they may be very subtle and highly susceptible influence via environmental learning. Furthermore, for the continuation of family life and our culture in general, women will undoubtedly retain some of their current role behaviors, regardless of the women's liberation movement. It is

noteworthy that many women very much dislike and disagree with the statements made by women's liberation advocates and prefer their traditional role
and status in society.

Perceived personality characteristics of adequate males, adequate females,
and disturbed patients have been studied. Professionals were asked to choose
adjectives that described each of these, and there was a high degree of correlation between descriptions of adequate females and disturbed persons. Both
adequate females and disturbed people were described as quite passive, submissive, dependent, and not achievement-oriented in terms of a career. If one were

Fig. 6. Women's rights are everybody's business. (Peggy Bliss, Editorial Photocolor Archives.)

to proceed strictly on the basis of this, one would have to conclude that the adequate female should be similar to the disturbed person, according to many professionals in mental health.

THE PEER GROUP

Infants immediately begin exploring their environment with their senses and begin the serious business of play. Playing is usually believed to be a matter of fun, which occurs on a random and occasional basis. This is a very incorrect viewpoint, for very young children visually explore their perceptual field, attempt to orient toward noises, manipulate objects, and otherwise behave in such a manner as to understand and control their environment. The seriousness with which this proceeds is well evidenced by the frustration and anger they exhibit when their parents interfere with their playing activities. Infants seem to have an inborn tendency to imitate, for they repeat sounds made by the family cat or dog and babble when their parents babble to them.

Play

At the youngest ages the child plays in a solitary fashion, which means he primarily does little in the way of interpersonal activities. As he grows older and if other children are available, he begins to play in a parallel manner with them, with two or more children performing activities in the same vicinity and perhaps with the same toys. Their play lacks a meaningful degree of interaction. However, children soon begin to play together, and their activities take the form of their own version of adult activities. They play husband and wife, doctor and nurse, and storekeeper and consumer. More complex activities involving groups of children and team competition require considerably more maturity and development, which is not very well acquired until the child reaches school age. The function of play is to learn within social contexts how to perform the role behaviors required of adults.

As children play together they form positive and negative feelings toward their playmates, which are the early basis for the development of friendships. Through interaction with other children they acquire an understanding of themselves that carries both intellectual and feeling components. This is the self-concept, which has had its earlier origins from the behavioral reactions of the parents. Their self-concept and understanding of their parents, siblings, and friends will be related to their behavior throughout development and highly influential into their adult years.

Most children become more intensely involved with the peer group when they begin school. The school provides many other children and adults with whom the child can interact and acquire higher levels of socialization. Most importantly, the school broadens his understanding of the culture far beyond that which could be provided by two parents and his siblings. Indeed, the school is second only to the family as a socialization agency. Teachers become the adults

significant in the child's life second only to the parents, and it is not at all uncommon for conflicts to develop in the child because of differences existing
between the parents' characteristics and objectives for the child and those held
by the teachers.

Although activities occurring within the school building are rather structured and highly influential in teaching the child about his society, it becomes
less significant as the person enters the adolescent years. In particular, activities
termed extracurricular occur, including parties, dances, athletic events, and
other social and intellectual group functions. It is from such peer development
that people obtain an understanding of themselves and formulate their goals
of future marriage and family life. Most important for boys, but increasingly
important for girls, is the development of vocational preferences during their
experiences both within and outside their school.

Vocational preference

There are no clear and definite indications of how individuals decide to
prepare for and enter specific occupations. There is considerable evidence to
suggest that the individual's development is of minor importance in obtaining
a particular kind of job. Factors such as the availability of particular jobs at a
given time and place and economic events usually seem to be predominant.
On the other hand, some individuals decide early to enter a specific occupation and actually follow their career plans. Holland (1966) has noted that career
choices represent an extension of personality and are an attempt to bring the
individual's behavioral style into the context of his life work. Second, an individual's perception of himself is projected into the world of work and into
occupational titles. Most people perceive the world of work in terms of the
occupational stereotypes, and they are at least partly based on reality and possess
some degree of accuracy. The stereotype a person holds about the various occupations reveals much information about the individual and expresses his preferred life style. Holland has categorized the life styles into the six following
areas.

Realistic. The realistic style is characterized by aggressive behavior, physical
strength, and masculinity. People oriented toward this role prefer concrete
rather than abstract problem situations and avoid interpersonal and verbal
areas. Such individuals tend to make vocational choices on the basis of this
personality style and enter such fields as farming, engineering, and truck driving.

Intellectual. The intellectual person tends to think rather than act and prefers to organize and understand rather than dominate or persuade. As a reflection of their style, they become chemists, biologists, and college professors.

Social. Social people are oriented toward close interpersonal relationships
and prefer to show supportive behavior toward others. As a reflection of their
personalities they become social workers and teachers.

Conventional. The conventional style is characterized by great self-control,
identification with power and status, and concern for rules, regulations, struc-

ture, and order. Interpersonal relationship are secondary. As a reflection of their styles such individuals become accountants, bank tellers, army officers, physicians, and nurses.

Enterprising. Enterprising people are highly skilled verbally, and they use such skills for influencing, persuading, and dominating other people. They are also concerned with power and status, but they aspire to power while the conventional person merely honors others who have already obtained it. Such individuals reflect their personalities by becoming salesmen, politicians, and businessmen.

Artistic. Artistic individuals show a high level of self-expression and relate with other people through their artistic expressions. They dislike structure and order and prefer tasks emphasizing freedom of self-expression. They tend to be highly concerned with the thoughts and feelings of people, although they are not highly sociable. Such individuals, of course, become musicians, painters, and writers.

Although Holland's viewpoint seems to have some utility, it is clear that all people show some degree of each of the six categorizations. There is no pure type in this or in any other complex psychological area. On the other hand, it appears that some people have high levels in one or two of the categories and quite low levels on several others. It is significant for the individual to understand what areas he would find most and least gratifying. It is obvious that there are countless thousands of people deeply dissatisfied with their occupations. Had they received vocational guidance or otherwise been helped to understand better their own characteristics and objectives, they might well have found more appropriate vocations. To accent the significance of vocational gratification, it is only necessary to point out that no heavens or paradises ever conceived have required the inhabitants to work.

ATTITUDES

Attitudes have been an interesting subject of scientific study by psychologists and sociologists for many years. An attitude is a tendency to respond in a favorable or an unfavorable manner to other persons, objects, or events. An attitude always involves a belief in regard to the person or event that is of an intellectual type and a feeling or emotional reaction. One cannot feel anger toward a minority group without having some beliefs about the group's existence, cultural heritage, or current behavior. The beliefs may or may not be true, but the person believes they are and is simultaneously emotionally aroused.

All individuals attempt to understand and exercise some control over their environment. Since the universe is currently complex beyond the understanding of mankind, although scientists are daily making numerous achievements, there is a necessity to simplify the universe to fit our intellectual ability. There is a tendency in the first instance to feel good or bad about anything. We either like or dislike something dichotomously, and there are few if any shades of gray between the positive and negative. We form conceptions that omit complex details and discrepancies, which is reflected in the stereotypes held by all people.

Stereotypes

A stereotype refers to simplistic understandings people have about an aspect of their environment, although they most often pertain to other people, in particular, minority groups. Since many black people are unemployed, they are seen by some white people as lazy and ignorant. This is done in spite of the evidence that indicates a person is not genetically caused to be lazy or ignorant, and in spite of the social and economic evidence indicating that adequate jobs and training programs are not often available. Nevertheless, by no means should stereotypes be considered totally false, for there is often a kernel of truth in many of them. If one were to gather evidence concerning the musical inclinations of black people, he might find they are proportionately overrepresented in professional musician groups. Jewish people are often stereotyped as industrious, shrewd, and intelligent. Since they are proportionately overrepresented in the college-educated group, there is indeed some degree of validity to the stereotype.

Prejudice

Contrary to scientific findings and usually in a quite inhumane way, stereotypes tend to be closely related to prejudice. Prejudice refers to the tendency to prejudge an individual on the basis of beliefs, which may be false, about a group and to think less of him as an individual regardless of his individuality. We have people who have many false beliefs and negative emotional reactions to others from numerous minority groups. Sometimes the prejudice is quite directly expressed, and sometimes it is expressed only in a very subtle manner. The prejudiced individual is often rather unaware that he has such attitudes. Prejudice should be clearly differentiated from discrimination, for discrimination refers to overtly negative behavior toward another person or group, whereas prejudice refers to the more pervasive feelings one has. Since there is no scientific substantiation that an individual's prejudice is genetically transmitted, it must be behavior learned in the same manner that any other behavior is learned.

In the United States prejudice is not only held by many white Anglo-Saxon Protestants (WASP) toward people with other characteristics but is probably just as strongly held by minority group members. Black people often refer to white people with the same hostility and lack of respect for individual differences as whites show them. They may also have very hostile reactions to Mexican-Americans, Jews, Indians, or any other group.

Authoritarianism and authority

Partly because of the events surrounding World War II, studies were done that culminated in the book *The Authoritarian Personality* (1950). The research showed there was a set of characteristics, often held in common, these being anti-Semitism (a dislike of Jews), ethnocentrism (dislike of any group different from his own), political and economic conservatism, and authoritarianism (anti-democratic ideas).

To the authoritarian personality, Jewish people are negatively perceived, people different from himself are inferior, the United States has never made a mistake in its relationship to other countries, the world is a threatening place against which one must defend and occasionally attack, and there is a clear, universal, and correct manner of sexual behavior.

The authoritarian personality tends to agree with the following kinds of statements:

1. In general Jews are pretty much alike.
2. It is best to prevent much contact between whites and blacks.
3. The American way is the only way.
4. Most men wouldn't work if they were not required to.
5. The most important virtues are obedience and respect for authority.
6. Every person should obey without question the decisions of supernatural power.
7. Our lives are controlled by secretly made plots.
8. Astrology can explain many things that are not understood today.
9. There are two distinct classes: the weak and the strong.
10. Homosexuals are really criminals and should be severely punished.

These attitudes have been studied in relation to the parental and peer backgrounds of the authoritarian personalities. The authoritarian was usually given harsh parental discipline in his childhood. His parents' love was given only when he showed behavior strictly in accordance with their desires. During development he tended to show little criticism of his parents and probably displaced much of his anger toward individuals and events outside his immediate family and peer group. The authoritarian has been taught to be highly moralistic and condemning, rather than permissive and open to new ideas and methods of behavior.

There has been some interesting research in regard to authoritarian personalities in mental health and educational organizations. Many staff members clearly show their beliefs of their clients' and patients' inferiority, although the majority express it in a more subtle manner. Statements in regard to the responsibility of the staff members to care for and control the lives of their clients and patients often have a subtle tinge of authoritarianism, for their statements imply that they are superior and must take care of the inferior mentally ill persons, for example. Some professional groups may show more authoritarianism than others, which is only partly related to their profession and most likely more related to their personalities, which guided them into their profession in the first place. Therefore, statements to the effect than certain professionals are taught to be authoritarians during their training should be viewed with some skepticism, because the individual presumably would never have entered the profession had he not been amenable to accepting such an orientation.

The difference between authoritarianism and authority is very important but seldom defined. Authoritarianism is a style that operates without a logical and scientific basis. In contrast, an authority functions on the basis of logical, generally substantiated, and delegated ability to perform some function. The physician in the operating room directly tells people what to do and fully expects they will do it immediately and well. He is functioning in his area of authority and must do so. He is the individual with the knowledge and skills to direct the surgery and prevent the loss of life. However, if he makes commands and becomes highly perturbed when people do not do what he wants them to do in other situations, such as at the junior league baseball game, simply because he is a physician, he is functioning in an authoritarian manner. Although this example concerns physicians, mental health workers can undoubtedly provide numerous examples drawn from education, mental hospitals, child guidance clinics, and other places that exemplify both authoritarian and authority behaviors and the degree to which they are appropriately and inappropriately expressed.

Attitude change

Because of the impact attitudes have on behavior and the damage that may occur, behavioral scientists have attempted to study and develop methods by which attitudes could be changed. Direct attempts to change attitudes by requiring contact, for example, between the black and white groups has been done. Blacks and whites living in one single housing project were assigned apartments without regard to color in one experiment. Interviews were conducted to study the attitudes of the white housewives toward blacks after residing in such proximity, and the researchers found a positive attitude change was considerably more frequent in integrated than in segregated housing projects.

Attempts to break down racial prejudice and improve attitudes between groups of people have been tried in other settings. There is no clear evidence that enforced contact, which is an authoritarian approach, is always or even often effective in achieving attitude change. In fact, there are some settings in which it has increased the degree of prejudice shown between the groups, with each group even more intensely disliking the other (Secord and Backman, 1964).

Verbal persuasion has been attempted to change attitudes. A very complex formulation has been derived that shows that *who* says *what* to *whom* through which *media* with what *effect* must be studied in great detail. The general findings suggest that attitudes are more likely to be changed when the communicator is regarded by the audience as honest and trustworthy and more similar to the audience than other communicators. The message is more likely to be accepted if it is designed to not allow much counterargument from the audience, if a desirable message is presented before undesirable information, or when the communication includes minor opposing arguments as well as arguments supporting the position of issue. In any case, it is clear that people with strongly ingrained attitudes and prejudices are very, very hard to change.

Cognitive dissonance

Since people have considerable resistance to attitude change, it is of interest to behavioral scientists to study what happens when inconsistencies or discrepancies between two beliefs do occur. Festinger (1957) has developed a theory of cognitive dissonance. It holds that tension resulting between the existence of privately held attitudes and overt behavior, which are discrepant with each other, is psychologically uncomfortable and will motivate the person to try to reduce the dissonance. He will then achieve more consistency between the two diverse elements. The person can either change his attitude to be closer to his actual behavior or decide that the dissonant factors are not important.

People who smoke heavily tend to devalue the medical evidence connecting smoking and lung cancer more than nonsmokers do. Heavy smokers may reject the scientific evidence and avoid additional information that increases dissonance. On the other hand, or in addition to this, the smoker may reassure himself that smoking is relaxing and therefore not sufficiently harmful. A person who believes mental hospitals are actually more harmful than helpful to the residents, and who continues to work in the hospital, may reduce dissonance by changing his attitude to be more consistent with his behavior. Or he may decide that it is the best organization currently available for severely disturbed people and has much opportunity for improving life conditions for the residents.

SMALL GROUP FUNCTIONING

There has been extensive research in regard to the functioning of small groups and the influence the group has on the behavior of its individual members. History is replete with accounts of the madness of crowds, both humorous and violent. Lynchings, riots, and other acts of group violence seem to derive from the pervasive group force, rather than the evil characteristics of one individual. The Nazis of Germany murdered millions of people in and outside of concentration camps. The common phrase during that period was: "I was only following orders." It is important to realize that conformity to group pressures, including participation in acts of violence, is not restricted to Nazi Germany. There is clear evidence that practically all people are subject to group social pressures and may conform to the most outrageous demands.

Conformity

Studies by Asch (1956), which were followed by others, exemplify this conformity. Asch formed groups consisting of one person as the actual subject of study and a number of other individuals who were confederates of the experimenter. In other words, they were not really the subjects of the experiment. There was one true subject, and he was unaware of this deception in the experiment. The confederates had been told beforehand to give incorrect judgments at certain points during a series of visual judgment tasks. The task involved three lines being projected on a screen with the group required to decide which of the three was equal in length to a standard line. Asch wanted to know how the genuine subject would respond, that is, whether he would yield to the group pressure. The genuine subject gave his judgment after the confederates had done so.

Group social pressure was shown to be extremely influential. Approximately one third of all the genuine subjects reported their judgments in the direction of the obviously false group judgment. They did this even though the difference between the correct line and the line chosen by the confederates was extremely large, and one would have to be quite visually impaired to give such a judgment if there were no group pressure. The variations of this study were also quite interesting. When there was only one confederate and one genuine subject, the subject tended to give accurate judgments without distortions caused by the confederate. When there were two confederates, conformity increased considerably. When there were three confederates, the conformity reached an extremely high level. Asch also inserted a "partner" into the groups who consistently gave the correct answer. Under this condition conformity was virtually abolished. Apparently, when one has the social support of only one other group member he is able to resist an otherwise overwhelming group pressure.

These early studies in regard to the degree to which people conform to the group were disturbing enough, but even more disturbing ones were done by Milgram (1964). The behavior of the subjects of his study is reminiscent of that shown by the Nazis and others who have committed atrocities under the influence of group pressure. He informed his genuine subjects that they were participating in studies on the effects of punishment upon learning. This was a collective teaching situation in which there was a team of three teachers. Two of these were actually confederates of the experimenter and they were supposedly involved in teaching a fourth person, the learner. However, the learner was also a confederate of the experimenter. The actual subject did not know that he was being deceived and that he himself was the object of study.

The teachers were informed that the learner must be shocked each time he made an error, and the teachers were to determine the amount of shock to be administered. The experimenter emphasized that they could stay at one intensity of shock, or they could raise or lower the level as they desired. The shock administered during any learning trial would be the lowest suggested by any of the three teachers. The experimental design called for the two confederate teachers of the experimenter to decide for a 15-volt increase each time the learner made a mistake on the learning task. The actual subject was always the last person asked to indicate the shock intensity to be administered to the learner. He was also the one to administer the shock by depressing a handle on a shock generator. Although the shock generator was made to appear quite authentic, it was actually incapable of delivering shock.

The learner was strapped in an apparatus resembling an electric chair in an adjoining room in full view of the teachers who could see him through a window. The experiment was arranged so that the learner would make many errors and the teachers could administer numerous shocks. The entire study was set up to ascertain the degree to which the actual subject as teacher would conform to the increasingly higher shock levels desired by the two confederates. The actual subject believed he was truly administering shock to the learner.

Grunts and groans and other verbal complaints had been prerecorded on tape and coordinated to certain shock levels. As the experiment progressed, the learner began responding with mild discomfort at the 75-volt shock level. When the shock level reached 120 volts, the learner began shouting that the shocks were becoming very painful. When the shock level reached 135 volts, the learner yelled that he wanted to be released from the experiment. He complained of a heart disturbance, which he had rather incidentally mentioned prior to the experiment. At 285 volts, which of course were not actually being administered, he responded with an agonizing scream. At 300 volts he shouted desperately that he would no longer give answers to the learning tests, and he remained mute on subsequent learning trials. As far as the genuine subject knew, the learner was dead.

The genuine subjects were highly influenced by the two confederate teachers. Twenty-seven out of forty experimental subjects administered shocks under the influence of the confederates, even after the learner had shouted that he wanted to end the experiment because of his heart condition. Seven out of the forty agreed to the maximum shock level of 450 volts when the subject appeared to be dead. This group of subjects was quite representative of the general population and included college professors as well as janitors. It should be clear to the reader that most of us are highly subject to the influence of group pressure, even when it causes serious damage or death to someone else.

Further studies of Milgram and others show that group influence can lead to humane behavior. When confederates defied the experimenter by refusing to administer any shock to the learner, thirty-six of forty subjects joined in defying the experimenter, although they thus also showed conforming behavior. While this indicates that man may also treat others with kindness and consideration, the impact of Milgram's original study provides evidence of brutality that can be rather easily prompted by social pressures to conform.

The degree to which these studies have meaning for human service workers should also be evident. In mental health settings there occasionally are decisions made by those in authority and their colleagues that inadvertently brutalize patients and clients. There probably have been many incidents in which inhumane treatment was being given while group members stood by quietly or even participated. For them to say or do anything against the group decision would be difficult indeed.

Creativity

In contrast to conformity is creativity. Creativity does not mean simply disagreeing with or doing something different from the group but involves better and different ideas and solutions to problems. Creativity is often confused with obstinance and strange behavior, and such behavior leads to unfortunate consequences. The adolescent who disagrees with his father or other authoritary figures may be expressing juvenile attitudes and behavior and no creativity whatsoever.

Individuals who are able to withstand group pressure and evidence creativity have been studied and found to have characteristics different from most people. Specifically, they tend to be more intelligent, original, and self-confident. They are able to cope effectively despite stressful circumstances, think highly or adequately of themselves, and are not highly anxious. They are also more tolerant, responsible, and dominant and lack disturbed, dependent, and neurotic relationships with other people. They also tend to be somewhat assertive and have a good sense of humor.

Leaders

Although creative individuals often become leaders in groups, there are other characteristics involved in leadership. Historians who have studied great leaders have two different viewpoints. Either natural leaders arise and by their actions change the course of events, or the tide of history causes leaders to arise who merely express the popular needs, rather than influencing them. The difference is whether Napoleon caused the events in Europe or whether events in Europe caused Napoleon to come to the forefront as a leader. Along with many of the characteristics previously noted, leaders are more likely to be quite active participants in their groups and socially popular. Leaders may be formal or informal. Formal leaders are authorized and carry titles or a recognized status, such as President, Director, or Chairman. Informal leaders are those without authorization who nevertheless function as leaders of the group. Sometimes this occurs with the informal leader giving opinions and suggestions that are quite different from those of the formal leader. The most advantageous situations occur when the formal leader also carries the influence that would otherwise be attributed to some informal leaders of the group.

Leaders tend to adopt three major styles for their leadership role, which are authoritarian, democratic, and laissez-faire. Under authoritarian leadership all policies are made by the leader. Techniques and steps in activities are dictated with only the leader having total information in regard to the final goal. Division of labor is done in fine detail and the authoritarian leader gives praise and criticism personally.

Democratic leaders make policy a matter of group discussion and decision. Democratic leaders assist, encourage, and consult. Entire projects and goals are discussed with the group members. The division of labor for tasks is decided by the group, and the leader is objective in his praise or criticism. He tries to be a group member and partially a worker.

Under laissez-faire leadership the leader allows complete freedom for discussions and participates at a very minimum level. The leader presents materials and information only when asked and does not participate in work discussions. There is no attempt to regulate the course of group events.

Under these three conditions there is very different behavior exhibited by the group members. Authoritarian leaders tend to create much hostility and aggression, which may alternate with extremely submissive behavior. Discontent becomes high, although it does not necessarily appear on the surface. Drop-out rates and pent-up frustrations increase. Dependency and a reduction of individuality occur.

Democratic leaders tend to create more friendliness and group-mindedness. Mutual praise, verbalizations, playfulness, and sociability are high. Work motivation continues in democratic groups even when the leader leaves the room, and there is more originality. However, the amount of work under democratic leaderships is somewhat less than the work quantity obtained in authoritarian groups.

Laissez-faire is definitely not the same as democracy, for democractic leaders perform leadership functions. In laissez-faire circumstances very little work is done, and the quality of work tends to be poor. There is considerable play and socialization, but the group members do not enjoy it. They tend to prefer democratic leaders.

These leadership situations are expressed in numerous settings, and the new mental health worker will have ample opportunity to know each. He will also have much opportunity as he progresses in his career to participate in groups as a leader of particular activities, and he should understand the negative characteristics associated with the authoritarian and laissez-faire styles, as well as the positive ones primarily shown under conditions of democratic leadership.

Group communication

The manner in which leaders and group members communicate is also important. When communication occurs only between the individual group member and the leader and is very limited or nonexistent among members, the leader functions partly as a dictator or boss. Feelings in regard to independence, restriction, and praising the boss tend to interfere with group functioning. In contrast, in communication structures involving openness, in which each person may communicate with any other person, the group members feel more independent and less restricted by the leader. Individuals in these open-ended communication systems believe their job is more satisfying.

Group members assume different roles in their group, which involve positive or negative reactions in the social-emotional area. Positive reactions include giving help, praise, agreement, and appropriate humor. Negative reactions include disagreeing, withholding help or praise, and expressing antagonism. In the task area the group members can either raise questions or give attempted answers. Questions involve asking for information, expressing feelings, and determining possible ways of action. Attempted answers involve giving suggestions, direction, evaluation, or opinion. In group activities discussion tends to begin with problems of orientation. Obtaining and clarifying information occurs near the middle part of group sessions. The final portion usually deals with further evaluation and the seeking of resolution of the group problem task. Positive and negative social-emotional reactions increase from the beginning to the end of most group discussions, with humor usually expressed at the highest level near the end of the meetings.

Halo and Hawthorne effects

The leader and group members operate in the maze of the group behavioral system. While attempting to achieve solutions to problems, two important kinds of events may occur, which are termed "halo effects" and "Hawthorne effects." Halo effects occur when group members are perceived as very positive in regard to one important characteristic and are thus considered positive in all. The reverse may also be true. When this occurs a group may function at a lower level than if they had objectively considered each suggestion or opinion from the person on its own merits, rather than being influenced by their general evaluation because of a specific positive or negative characteristic.

The Hawthorne effect refers to the injection of anything into the group functioning that subsequently increases group effectiveness and performance. Whenever the environment is changed to increase the probability of high performance, performance indeed tends to increase. On the other hand, making working conditions somewhat negative and uncomfortable also tends to increase performance. Children in average schools have been placed in very plush, carpeted, and well-lighted rooms. Their achievement significantly increased. Children from well-appointed schools have been placed in rather bare, dirty, and poorly lighted classrooms. Paradoxically, their achievement also increased. The increase presumably resulted from the attention and change, rather than the actual characteristics of their environment. Both Hawthorne and halo effects should be considered by the mental health worker in his specific work location in order to understand and improve the functioning of his group (Secord and Backman, 1964).

ORGANIZATIONAL BEHAVIOR

Most mental health workers function within an organization or institution with other mental health workers and professionals. Studies regarding organizational depelopment and functioning are quite illuminating. McGregor (1960) has contrasted two managerial viewpoints that influence the performance of the organization's members. These are termed Theory X and Theory Y.

Theory X and Theory Y

Managers of organizations with Theory X perspectives believe that people entirely dislike work and will do anything they can to avoid working any harder than possible. Therefore, the employees must be directed, totally controlled, and threatened with punishment in order to obtain their efforts to achieve the objectives of the organization. Most people prefer to be directed and will avoid their individual responsibility. More than anything the employee wants security. People simply have very little ambition, and wages and coercion should be emphasized.

Organizational managers with the Theory Y viewpoint believe that work is as natural as play or rest. People will show self-direction and motivation if they are committed to the goals of the organization. External control and the threat of punishment are not considered primary means of obtaining employees' work efforts. The employees are committed to the work objectives because their achievements obtain gratification for them. People not only do not avoid responsibility, they seek it. The Theory Y manager is not a "softy," but he is democratic, open, and aware of the importance of job gratifications.

The managerial grid

A more complex and somewhat different viewpoint of organizational functioning is taken by Blake and Mouton (1964). They view all organizations as necessarily involved in both performance (or products) and people. They have placed both concern for people and concern for performance onto a grid. Concern for people is rated numerically from one through nine, as is concern for performance. One is the lowest and nine is the highest for each. When concern for people and performance are both very low in an organization, there is little effort to get the work done and membership in the organization is only tentatively sustained. When concern for people is very high and concern for performance is very low in an organization, there is considerable and considerate attention made in regard to meeting the needs of people for satisfying relationships. There is a comfortable and friendly atmosphere, although high levels of achievement are neither required nor reached. When the reverse situation occurs, with concern for performance very high and concern for people very low, there is an efficiency in operations and a high performance level. However, the work is so arranged that human relationships interfere with performance at a minimum degree. There is a middle ground of concern for people and concern for performance, with both being at a medium level. There occurs a balancing of attempts to get people to perform at a high level with a maintenance of the workers' morale at a satisfactory level. All of these styles of organizational management have disadvantages, but they also have numerous advantages. There can be low performance, a social club atmosphere, or a middle level of both concern for performance and concern for people.

The highest results are obtained from a very high concern for people (rated nine) matched with a very high concern for performance (also rated nine). Under such conditions, performance is accomplished with highly dedicated employees. The employees have a high interest in the organization reaching its objectives. People who obtain job gratification tend to work well together, and personal relationships of trust and respect are engendered. In other words, people work very hard for and with other people who work very hard. They accomplish much and like each other.

Mental health and behavioral effectiveness organizations probably vary managerially as much as business organizations. Mental health organizations that have a social relationship atmosphere, with little concern for achieving their objectives, undoubtedly exist. They may function for many years with government support, but if they were a private business they would probably rapidly become bankrupt. There are probably fewer human service agencies with an exceptionally high concern for performance and a very low concern for people.

REFERENCES AND SUGGESTED READINGS

Adorno, T. W., Frenkel-Brunswik, E., Levinson, D. J., and Sanford, R. N. 1950. The authoritarian personality. New York, Harper & Row, Publishers.

Asch, S. E. 1956. Studies of independence and submission to group presence: I. A minority of one against a unanimous majority. Psychological Monographs, Vol. 7, Series No. 416.

Becker, W. C., and Krug, R. S.. 1964. A circumflex model for social behavior in children. Child Development 35:371-396.

Blake, R. R., and Mouton, J. 1964. The managerial grid. Houston, Gulf Publishing Company, Book Division.

Douvan, E., and Adelson, J. B. 1966. The adolescent experience. New York, John Wiley & Sons, Inc.

Festinger, L. 1957. A theory of cognitive dissonance. New York, Harper & Row, Publishers.

Holland, J. L. 1966. Psychology of vocational choice. Boston, Ginn and Company.

Kretch, D., Crutchfield, R. S., and Ballackey, E. L. 1962. Individual in society. New York, McGraw-Hill Book Company.

McGregor, D. 1960. The human side of enterprise. New York, McGraw-Hill Book Company.

Milgram, S. 1964. Group pressure and action against a person. Journal of Abnormal and Social Psychology 69:137-143.

Secord, P. F., and Backman, C. W. 1964. Social psychology. New York, McGraw-Hill Book Company.

Way, L. 1962. Adler's place in psychology: an exposition of individual psychology. New York, Crowell Collier and Macmillan, Inc.

5
METHODS OF BEHAVIOR ASSESSMENT

❧

Behavior assessment principles and methods were pioneered by psychology. The term "assessment" denotes the gaining of information that will lead to an understanding of behavior. It is important to differentiate between assessment procedures in terms of their goals. Some procedures are aimed at description, others designed for prediction, and some undertaken to ascertain specific causal relationships.

HISTORICAL BASIS OF BEHAVIOR ASSESSMENT
Early development in Europe

The first efforts toward the assessment of human behavior were made by Sir Frances Galton of England in the mid–nineteenth century with the concept of deviation from the average. This statistical concept had first been applied in the study of relationships between various physical characteristics of the natural environment. M. Quetelet, the Astronomer Royale of Belgium in the early nineteenth century, developed this concept in detail in reference to characteristics of planets and their movement. Galton applied this concept specifically in descriptive studies of the distribution of grades obtained by students taking the mathematical honors examination at Cambridge University (Galton, 1869) and such physical characteristics as the length and breadth of the head of individuals who lived near his South Kensington anthropometric laboratory. The results of his investigations were remarkably consistent with those that could be predicted on the basis of the formulas discussed by Quetelet (Galton, 1869). The results could be described with two important statements. The number of people who displayed extremes of any characteristic was very small, and the characteristics of the majority of people clustered around the average.

This led Galton to hypothesize that Quetelet's equations could be used productively for classifying men according to their natural gifts.

Around the turn of the century the French physician Alfred Binet also became concerned with the assessment of behavior. He and his associate, Theophile Simon, first began a study of individual differences to establish a scientific method for the diagnosis of mental retardation for use in the public schools (Binet and Simon, 1905-1908). Binet and Simon were faced with an almost complete lack of uniformity in the diagnosis of mental deficiency. Although at that time there was some agreement as to the existence of three levels of mental deficiency (morons, imbeciles, and idiots), it was impossible to find any large number of educators or physicians who could agree as to what sign or signs were appropriate in distinguishing among the various degrees of "inferior mentality." In order to overcome this problem Binet elaborated the concept of standardization. He initially developed a number of questions and problems that were presented in an identical manner to each individual for whom a diagnosis was to be made. In that way he hoped to overcome the various biases and prejudice that then accompanied the diagnostic process. After much revision Binet and Simon arrived at an instrument they felt was suitable for the assessment of deviations from normal intelligence. This instrument was revised by Terman of Stanford University for use in the United States. The Stanford-Binet and its further revisions became the standard against which the adequacy of all other methods of assessing intellectual function are measured.

The two concepts of deviation from the average as applied to human behavior by Galton and the idea of standardization as elaborated by Binet and Simon provided the foundations for behavior assessment.

Early development in the United States

Although some work in assessment was undertaken at various places throughout the United States and Europe during the years 1900 to 1920, the first large-scale application of the principles of standardization and deviation from the average occurred with the development of the Army Alpha Test (Cronbach, 1960). This instrument was constructed to facilitate screening of the large masses of men inducted for service during World War I. It was used not only to screen out those individuals who functioned at such a low level intellectually as to make them poor risks in military service but also to aid in the assignment of men to various occupations within the military service. There were many problems and difficulties associated with the use of this test for assessing the intellectual abilities of large numbers of men. One of the most controversial of these was the administration of the test to illiterate individuals.

The Army Alpha was meant to be a test of intelligence. However, in order to be used in the screening of hundreds of thousands of individuals, it could not be administered on an individual basis to each person, as was Binet's test.

For this reason the test was of the paper and pencil type, in which the individual had to respond to various problems presented to him on paper in a group situation. Since a large number of individuals were illiterate, it was necessary to make various modifications of the test to assess the individual's intellectual functioning in the absence of reading and writing skills. It was believed that a soldier needed very little education to function on the battlefield, although some intelligence in the form of good judgment and logical reasoning was essential for the safety of the individual soldier and his comrades. Although no clearly satisfactory solution to this problem was ever achieved, the military was able to formulate an instrument that, to their satisfaction, provided a legitimate assessment of abilities in the absence of literacy. Basically, it made extensive use of perceptual and motor test items rather than vocabulary and other language items so highly related to scholastic background.

Problem of culture

The problem of culture in behavior assessment first became apparent in attempts to translate the Binet-Simon test for use in schools in the United States. It was found that many of the questions, problems, and situations posed in the test were unique to the French culture and not applicable to or understood by American children. It thus became necessary to revise Binet's test for use in the United States. This revision by Terman involved not only a retranslation of Binet's original work but also a substitution of questions and problems that could be understood by and were appropriate for American children. A similar problem has arisen in the application of conventional assessment procedures to the measurement of intelligence of blacks, Indians, Mexican-Americans, and other ethnic groups within the United States. Each of these groups to a varying degree possesses its own cultural concepts, some of which are as broad as attitudes toward competition and others as specific as differing definitions for common words. In attempting to administer a test standardized on the total culture to members of a minority group, we may be asking them questions and imposing criteria for correct answers that are inappropriate for their cultural background.

One method of avoiding the problem of cultural differences has been to exclude nonwhites in the initial standardization of a test. Prior to 1954 and the Supreme Court decision concerning segregation in schools and the passage of the Civil Rights Acts barring discrimination in employment, this procedure could have been said to have some scientific legitimacy. Few nonwhites were ever in situations in the schools or in employment offices where an assessment of intellectual functioning was necessary. However, because of the effect of legislation, judicial decisions, and governmental attempts to end discrimination, more and more individuals of minority background are coming into contact with behavioral assessment procedures. This has resulted in increasing questioning as to the legal and proper use of assessment procedures standardized on white populations in making decisions concerning the intellectual capacities of non-white individuals. It has forced a reassessment of the use of tests in education and industry, in particular.

There is no easy or readily apparent solution to this problem. It has been proposed, for example, that new efforts at standardization be undertaken on individuals from minority backgrounds, and it has also been proposed that new instruments be developed specifically for use with individuals of different racial heritage. Both of these proposals leave much to be desired.

Tests are used to compare individuals, and the people who are to be compared must be tested with the same instrument. In the first instance, restandardization of existing tests with minority populations would not be legitimate because the tests in their present form contain many concepts, words, situations, and questions that are unique to Caucasian cultures. The minority individual would still be at a disadvantage. In the second case, developing different instruments for use with individuals of differing ethnic and socioeconomic backgrounds, legitimate comparisons would again be impossible since the same test would not have been administered to all the individuals to be compared. It is clear that great care must be taken in the evaluation of the result of any assessment procedure when administered to an individual from a culture different from that upon which the test was originally standardized.

Status of behavior assessment today

A basic fact of behavior assessment often overlooked by the layman is that tests are designed and constructed in an empirical and scientific fashion to facilitate the decision-making process in any given situation. Tests provide information to help make decisions about many important choices in a person's life, which often must be made rapidly and economically. Tests do not, as is so often thought by the layman, provide any direct information about the inherited intelligence or personality characteristics with which a persons enters life. The behavior of any person is a function of the interaction of the biological organism with his environment. Behavioral assessment procedures are instruments for measuring the result of this interaction with the environment in a standard and uniform way.

Although behavior assessment refers to a number of procedures, including interviewing, that do not involve the use of printed materials, most formal assessment techniques are of the paper and pencil type. There are a number of characteristics common to all modern procedures that define them as tests or instruments of assessment (Cronbach, 1960). These characteristics include the following:

1. There is a standard set of test items. In every case in which the procedure is used each subject is presented with the same questions, problems, or tasks.
2. The behavior of the individual doing the assessment activity is also

standard. His behavior in gaining the information necessary for the completion of the procedure is the same as that exhibited by any other person using the instrument.

3. The information gained from the use of the instrument is used to compare the behavior of the client with that of some other person or group.

In spite of many problems inherent in the use of assessment instruments, especially the problem of cultural variations, these procedures have proved themselves to be of great value in describing and predicting behavior and in determining causal relationships. However, the value of an assessment procedure is determined in large part by the knowledge and expertise of the person engaging in the activity. Unless the instrument is used in the manner in which it was intended—that is, in a standard and uniform way—the results will be of little value. Even when standard procedures are followed, if the person evaluating the assessment information gained is not familiar with the empirical background of the test and the limits of its predictive or descriptive power, his interpretation of the results may be not only misleading but potentially damaging to the client.

PSYCHOLOGICAL TESTS

Pioneering work during the late nineteenth and early twentieth centuries led to our current psychological testing or behavior assessment field. The purpose of psychological tests is to acquire as much useful and accurate information as quickly as possible in order to make predictions and decisions concerning the events of an individual's life, or to help him do so.

Standardization

Modern psychological tests are standardized tests. The word "standardized" refers to a systematic method of administration and scoring and the availability of norms. When a test is constructed and before it is published, the author administers the test to a large sample of the group about which the test later will be used to make predictions, decisions, or descriptions. The results of this initial administration of the test are generally published with the test and constitute the norms for the test (Cronbach, 1960). When a particular assessment procedure is administered to an individual, his score can be compared with the scores of others. This enables one to determine both how he is similar to and different from the people in the group upon which the test was standardized and is the basis for predictions. If one had administered the test to an individual and found that his score was very similar to people who are successful in college, one would be able to predict that he is likely to succeed in college.

It is important to note that an adequate knowledge of basic measurement concepts in behavioral science is absolutely essential to understand and use psychological tests. These are presented in Appendix A, rather than at this point, for purposes of simplification and continuity of language material.

Commonly used tests

Thousands of tests have been standardized and published in the last several decades, and some stand out as exceptionally useful for making predictions and decisions in mental health work. They may be classified into the areas of intelligence, projective, and objective tests.

Intelligence tests

Intelligence is probably one of the most commonly used terms in the assessment field. Literally hundreds of tests have been constructed that are supposed to measure it. But what is intelligence? What do we mean when we say someone is intelligent? What does an intelligence test measure?

The concept of intelligence is commonly thought by the layman to denote a person's inherited potential for success and achievement. Philosophers, especially in the nineteenth century, spent a good deal of time speculating about the nature of this concept. The question that they tried to answer was whether a man is born with a specific potential that he cannot exceed or whether everyone enters life with essentially the same potential for either failure or genius. In modern terms this question is termed the heredity versus environment problem. Is a person genetically predisposed to genius, or is his genius the result of an enriched, challenging, and rewarding environment? At this point in time there has been no satisfactory resolution of this problem.

Researchers in the biological and behavioral sciences have found that both genetic and environmental influences are important in determining one's level of intellectual functioning. These results have led behavioral scientists to look at intelligence solely in terms of behavior. In contrast, the nineteenth-century philosophers conceived of intelligence as an abstract cause of behavior and defined it in metaphysical terms, which made it unavailable for scientific observation and study. Since behavior is the only observable and measurable manifestation of intelligence, behavior is what intelligence tests measure. That is, an intelligence test does not give us any direct information about a person's inherited genetic potential or the richness or deprivation present in his environment. Rather, an intelligence test is a sample of a person's behavior, the results of which are used to compare the person with other people to facilitate prediction or description.

Stanford-Binet test. The Stanford-Binet test was the first standardized intelligence test to be widely used in the United States, and it was designed for the assessment of intellectual functioning in children. The questions or items are arranged in terms of year levels. That is, an average child is expected to answer correctly items appropriate for his age group. Thus, a child of 6 years would be expected, if he were of average intelligence, to answer questions as well as the average 6 year old. A child of 10 years of average intelligence should be able to answer questions as well as the average 10 year old.

The test is administered individually, only one child being tested at a time. The examiner first determines the basal age, which is the point at which the subject can pass all of the items of a subtest at a particular age level before he begins failing any. He continues presenting subtests at progressively higher age levels until he reaches a year level at which the child can correctly answer none of the items. This is termed the ceiling age level.

Items dealing with vocabulary, correct word usage, and memory are the most common. For example, an individual may be asked to define dog or logic, remember and report a spoken series of numbers, such as 9, 4, 7, 3, 8, or solve verbal reasoning problems. These items are included most frequently because successful performance is correlated with school success, vocational level, and socioeconomic status, thus suggesting they are the best indicators of general intellectual ability.

At the lower age levels questions and problems concerning information, the identification of various objects, and accurate perception of various forms are stressed. For example, a child might be asked to name the President, identify a picture of some common animal such as a cat, or place different shaped blocks of wood, such as a circle or triangle, into the appropriate shaped hole in a board of wood. At the higher age levels more emphasis is placed on the use of mathematical, verbal, and logical reasoning. The subject might be asked to solve an arithmetic problem or perform verbal abstract reasoning, perhaps explaining the similarity between love and joy.

The intellectual functioning of the subject is evaluated in terms of the following formula: intelligence quotient (I.Q.) equals mental age (M.A.) divided by chronological age (C.A.) multiplied by 100. The chronological age is the actual age of the subject at the time he was tested. The mental age is the level of ability obtained on the test in relation to children of other ages. If a child 10 years old were successful on all the items at year 10, one half the items at year 11, and none at year 12, his mental age would be 10 years and 6 months. The formula would be $\text{I.Q.} = \dfrac{\text{M.A.}}{\text{C.A.}} \times 100 = \dfrac{10.5}{10} \times 100$, or an I.Q. of 105. If this 10 year old had a mental age of 12, his I.Q. would be 120. If his M.A. were 7, his I.Q. would be 70.

The Stanford-Binet has become the standard against which most other tests of intelligence are compared. It is undoubtedly the best instrument of its kind for obtaining an estimate of general intellectual functioning in children. Essentially, it tells us how the child's intellectual growth compares with his chronological age. It further indicates the degree to which his mental abilities are consistent with his chronological maturation in comparison to children his age. However, the concept of mental age has proved inadequate for the measurement of adult intelligence. This is primarily because the kinds of abilities that are measured by the Stanford-Binet reach a plateau in adolescence. Following the early adolescent period there is relatively little change in Stanford-Binet mental ages, and the use of this test for assessing adult intellectual functioning is limited. Following age 14, there are no more true age level subtests. Intellectual functioning after this point is measured by only four more subtests, all with titles pertaining to adults.

The Stanford-Binet also lacks a clear differential method of assessing visual-motor performance, although some subtests require the subject to perform tasks requiring manual dexterity. It is difficult to assess visual perception and visual-motor coordination, which may be very important for a particular patient or client. An effective plan of treatment may require such information (Morgan and King, 1966).

Wechsler Intelligence Scale. Wechsler was one of the first to develop a test of intellectual functioning that provided a specific method for the comparison of verbal and performance abilities in adults. His original test, the Wechsler-Bellevue, has undergone extensive revision and modification. It is now known as the Wechsler Adult Intelligence Scale (WAIS).

The WAIS consists of a series of eleven subtests, six of which fall in the verbal category and five of which are in the performance category. It is administered on an individual basis and may require from 1 to 3 hours to complete. Each of the subtests consists of a progressively more difficult series of items of a given type, which the individual is asked to solve (Rapaport, Gill, and Shaefer, 1968).

Verbal subtests

INFORMATION. The information subtest is a series of questions, such as: "Where is China?" and "Who was Sophocles?" These questions assess the general information that a person has gained and reflect his level of education.

GENERAL COMPREHENSION. Questions such as: "Why should a person not steal?" or "If you were lost in the desert how would you find your way to a town?" are presented to the subject for solution. They measure the extent to which the individual possesses the social judgment necessary to function in society.

DIGIT SPAN. A person's score on this subtest is the result of combining his score on a "Digits Forward Task," in which he is required to repeat to the examiner increasingly large sequences of numbers, such as 4, 9, 2, 3, with his score on a "Digits Backward Task," in which the subject must repeat the numbers presented by the examiner in reverse order. For example, on the "Digits Backward Task," if the examiner said 2, 9, 7, the subject must repeat the sequence in the order 7, 9, 2. The score on the Digit Span Test is indicative of the adequacy with which he can store and retrieve information in memory.

ARITHMETIC. The person is presented with a series of problems to solve without the aid of paper or pencil. One of the simpler problems would be similar to: "How much is 10¢ and 20¢?" On one of the more difficult problems the examiner might ask the subject to solve a ratio problem, such as: "If four men can do a job in 10 days, how many days will it take ten men to do the same job?" This subtest measures not only the extent to which an individual has profited from his basic education but also how well he can reason with abstract symbols.

SIMILARITIES. These tasks require the individual to discover and report to the examiner the relationship between two seemingly different things. For example, the subject might be asked to answer the question: "How are a tree and a house alike?" This subtest provides an assessment of how well a person can reason with verbal symbols and his conceptualization level.

VOCABULARY. The subject is presented with a list of words to define. This is one of the most reliable subtests on the WAIS and correlates most highly with total I.Q. Thus, it is a good indicator of a person's educational level, verbal abilities, and general level of intellectual functioning.

Performance subtests

DIGIT SYMBOL. This subtest requires tht subject to match a series of symbols, such as X, O, and +, with a series of numbers, such as 7, 2, and 3, in a pre-determined fashion. The subject is allowed some practice matching these symbols. The actual test is begun by instructing him to work as quickly as possible, since he is only allowed 90 seconds in which to complete as much of the test as he can. This test measures the person's ability to learn and rapidly perform a simple but novel clerical task.

PICTURE COMPLETION. The subject is presented with a series of pictures in which some important part is missing. For example, he might be shown a picture of a house with no windows or a car with no tires. This subtest gives us information about the adequacy of the individual's visual perception and the degree to which he is sensitive to and aware of important aspects of the environment.

BLOCK DESIGN. This is probably one of the better known subtests of the WAIS. It requires the subject to put together colored blocks so that they match a pattern that is on a card in front of the subject. This subtest gives us information about the degree to which the subject can integrate logical reasoning with motor performance. It requires the ability to analyze and synthesize without heavy reliance on verbal skills.

PICTURE ARRANGEMENT. The subject is required to arrange a series of pictures, which are presented to him in a random order, to make a logical story. For example, the examiner may place before the subject three pictures, the first showing a man standing next to a falling tree. The second shows a man chopping on an upright tree with an ax, and the third shows the man looking at a upright tree while holding an ax in his hand. To obtain a maximum number of points for a correct answer the subject must rearrange the pictures in correct order in a specific amount of time. This subtest tells us how well the subject is able to think logically by examining a temporal relationship among events.

OBJECT ASSEMBLY. The subject is presented with a series of pieces of objects, such as a car, a face, or a hand, and he is required to assemble the pieces in their proper order as quickly as he can. The speed and accuracy with which he is able to perform these tasks tells us how well he is able to organize his visual perception meaningfully.

I.Q. scores. Once the entire test has been administered the examiner computes three separate scores. These are reported in the following terms.

VERBAL I.Q. This score tells us how well the subject is able to manipulate, organize, understand, and use verbal symbols in comparison to others in his age group.

PERFORMANCE I.Q. This score gives us information about the visual-perceptual and visual-motor coordination ability of the person in comparison to others in his age group.

FULL-SCALE I.Q. This score is a combination of the verbal and performance I.Q. and gives us a general evaluation of the overall intellectual functioning of the subject in relation to other people.

The norms available with the Wechsler Adult Intelligence Scales are excellent. Wechsler has also developed a children's scale, known as the Wechsler Intelligence Scale for Children (WISC). Like the WAIS, the WISC also provides us with full-scale, verbal, and performance I.Q.'s. The organization of the WISC in terms of subtests, construction, content, and method of administration is quite similar to that of the WAIS. The major difference between the WAIS and the WISC is that the content and norms of the WISC are appropriate for persons less than 16 years of age.

Other tests of intelligence. The Stanford-Binet and the Wechsler scales are probably the best instruments available for obtaining an evaluation of the intellectual functioning of an individual. However, these instruments also require highly trained personnel for their administration, are only administered to one individual at a time, and may require an excess of 90 minutes to complete. Hence, a number of other tests have been constructed for the purpose of assessing intelligence.

The Peabody Picture Vocabulary Test (PPVT) is a very commonly used instrument that requires neither a highly trained person for its administration nor a great deal of time to complete (Anastasi, 1968). To administer the PPVT, the examiner says a word to the subject, such as "cat." The subject is then required to pick one of four objects or events from a picture that best represents that word. If the examiner said the word "hurt," the subject might be presented with four pictures, one showing a little boy smiling and carrying a balloon, one of a dog, one of a man holding an umbrella, and one depicting a person pointing to a Band-Aid on his arm.

Another test of intelligence commonly used is the Otis-Lenon Mental Ability Test (Anastasi, 1968). It can be scored very rapidly, administered to large groups by a relatively untrained person, and completed in less than an hour. It is most often used in the screening of new or prospective employees in business and industry. The test requires the individual to solve a number of varied tasks, such as choosing the best definition of a word from several alternatives, solving arithmetic problems, and determining the next number that should appear in a series of sequential numbers.

Both the PPVT and the Otis-Lenon Mental Ability Test have been shown to correlate well with the Stanford-Binet and the Wechsler scales. Thus, to some extent we can be confident that they are measuring the same thing, but neither of these two tests gives us as reliable or as great an amount of information as the Stanford-Binet or the Wechsler scales.

Use of intelligence tests in mental health work. It has been demonstrated repeatedly that I.Q. scores are useful for predicting scholastic and vocational achievement and satisfaction. However, one of the most important uses of intelligence measures in mental health work is for isolating specific problem areas. A low score on an intelligence test can result from a number of factors. It is known, for example, that intelligence tests are related to educational achievement, socioeconomic status, and ethnic background. A number of other factors such as deprivation, emotional disturbances, and central nervous system dysfunctions can also affect an I.Q. score. When we evaluate the results of an intelligence test, it is important to ascertain whether any of these factors may be affecting the person's score and should be considered in treatment planning.

Projective tests

Projective tests are different from other types of assessment procedures in regard to objectives and the stimuli presented to the individual. The purpose of projective tests is to obtain information about the internal state of the individual, his thinking processes, fantasy life, relationship with other people, and view of himself. Many behavioral assessment experts question the use of the word "test" in describing these procedures and prefer the term "projective techniques" or "projective methods." Projective tests are based on the hypothesis that an individual, when asked to describe some ambiguous and unstructured stimulus, such as an inkblot, will reveal much information about the way he perceives and organizes his perceptions of the world that could not be obtained through the use of other assessment instruments. He projects his unique individuality onto the ambiguous stimuli.

Rorschach's test. The most well known of the projective tests is a set of ten inkblots named after its developer, Hermann Rorschach. Each inkblot in the set is presented on an individual card, half of them containing color. The examiner presents the inkblots to the individual twice, one card at a time. The first time the series is presented the examiner asks the individual to describe what he sees in the blot and notes the length of time it takes the person to respond and the nature of whatever he perceives. The second time the blots are shown to the subject the examiner repeats what the subject said the first time and asks the subject to state the specific details of the blot that determined his response. For example, if the subject said "a bat" initially, the examiner would inquire about what features of the blot suggested the figure of the bat to the subject. The scoring of the Rorschach is detailed and complex and requires considerable training and experience (Rapaport, Gill, and Schaefer, 1968). The results of this procedure often lead to valuable predictions and description, but the amount of training needed to make valid and useful inferences places it outside the usual realm of use by the human service worker.

Thematic Apperception Test. The Thematic Apperception Test (TAT) was developed by Murray (Cronbach, 1960) to assess one's various needs. This technique consists of twenty relatively ambiguous pictures about which the subject is required to tell a story. The story should contain certain elements, which include what is going on now, what led up to the situation, how it turns out, and what the people in the story are thinking and feeling. The examiner interprets the story in terms of the individual's personality needs and beliefs regarding environmental demands upon him. The TAT is rarely used by the new human service worker, although it is conceivable that he could at least administer it (Rapaport, Gill, and Schaefer, 1968).

Other projective tests. Projective testing is widely accepted by traditional mental health professionals, although the training required to adequately interpret results of the Rorschach or the TAT greatly limits their use by mental health workers. There are, however, other projective techniques that can be administered and to some extent interpreted by mental health workers.

The Rotter Incomplete Sentences Blank (Anastasi, 1968) consists of sentences in which only the first word or several words are given the subject, who is asked to complete the sentence. For example, the first words in one incomplete sentence might be: "My dog. . ." In responding to this stem the subject is expected to make a complete sentence. The Rotter can be scored for an indication of the person's degree of maladjustment, although the examiner usually attempts to understand the person from his responses without the scoring system.

Another very well-known projective technique which is easily administered is the Draw A Person Test (DAP). It requires only two sheets of paper and a pencil. The examiner asks the subject to draw a complete person on one sheet. The examiner asks, if necessary, whether the drawing represents a man or a woman. He gives the subject a second piece of paper and asks him to draw a person of the sex opposite that which he drew in the first picture. The quality of the drawing, sequence in which the sexes are drawn, relative proportion of various body parts, and presence or absence of body parts and clothing are used to assess the individual. If a man first drew a woman depicted without arms, the examiner might hypothesize that females are of greater than average significance in this man's life and that he generally perceives them as being powerless or helpless.

Another projective test of the drawing type is the House-Tree-Person test, which is more commonly used with young children. The child is asked to draw a house, a tree, and a person. It is believed that his drawing will contain elements of importance to him in his own environment and lead to a better understanding of how the child sees himself, his relationship with his parents, and his general environment.

Objective tests

Frequently the word "objective" is used to describe a test that has more standardized scoring procedures. For our purposes the objective test is distinguished both from the projective and the intelligence test by the fact that it requires less interaction between the examiner and the subject. They are used for the measurement of a number of dimensions, including achievement in school subjects or content areas and specific personality characteristics. They are highly standardized and rigorously researched.

In their most highly developed form objective personality assessment procedures are often used in conjunction with a computer or set of probability statements (actuarial table) to describe personality and formulate hypotheses and predictions about behavior. The actuarial use of personality assessment procedures is quite distinct from the clinical method. The term "actuarial" refers to the statistical study of the relationship between various dimensions measured by the test and behavior. In developing an actuarial method of utilizing an objective personality inventory, the researcher desires to obtain the highest degree of predictability. He may gather an enormous amount of data on a large group of people who have taken his test and systematically determine the correlation between all of the various dimensions measured by the test and all of the various classifications of data that he has collected. He may examine the relationship between the pattern of scores on a personality test and such dimensions as the age of the subject, type of disorder or emotional disturbance, number of siblings in his family, childhood health history, social adjustment, dating preferences, criminal record, marital status, length of courtship, age at time of marriage, extramarital relationships, characteristics of his mother and father, and numerous other factors relating to his total functioning. This research is undertaken from a purely statistical standpoint.

In contrast, the clinical method focuses on the individual and relies upon the examiner's expertise and experience. It should be clear that the human service worker could make good use of actuarial methods with objective tests.

Minnesota Multiphasic Personality Inventory. The Minnesota Multiphasic Personality Inventory (MMPI) is the most well-known and rigorously researched objective personality assessment instrument available for clinical use in mental health work. Several books have been written and computer programs instituted that were designed for use with this instrument in actuarial prediction. Considerable information is also available on the characteristics of this test, which enable it to be used effectively by the trained specialist in the absence of computer systems or actuarial textbooks.

The MMPI was originally constructed to provide an objective method of psychiatric diagnosis. Although this initial goal was not clearly realized, the usefulness of this instrument as a predictor of behavior and for generating descriptive statements is unparalleled in mental health work (Hathaway, 1966). The MMPI consists of four validity scales and ten clinical scales, all of which measure deviant aspects of personality. Scores on the various scales are plotted on separate profile sheets for men and women. The responses to each scale are converted to standard or t scores, which form a distribution with a mean of 50 and a standard deviation of 10. On an MMPI profile we would expect a relatively normal person to have no scores higher than 70 on any of the scales.

Validity scales. The four validity scales give some information about a person's personality, but their major importance is in determining whether or not the information the test gives is accurate. The first is represented by a question mark (?). This scale tells us whether or not an individual has left an unusually large number of questions on the test unanswered. If this is the case then we can have little confidence that the individual will be accurately described by the test. The second validity scale is known as the L (lie) scale. Questions on this scale give an indication of the degree to which a subject may be lying to the test questions. The third validity scale is the F scale. A high score on this scale indicates that the subject has endorsed a number of very unusual, deviant statements as being accurate descriptions of himself. If the F scale score is exceedingly high, it may mean that either the individual is purposely attempting to look very disturbed or that he does not adequately understand the content of the questions and is therefore responding in a random fashion. The fourth validity scale is the K scale. This scale is used as a correction factor on some of the clinical scales but also can give some information about the individual's personality. A very high K score indicates not only that the subject may not have been honest while answering the questions but that he tends to minimize and ignore his problems and generally views the world in a very naive and simplistic fashion. Hence, K is partly understood as an assessment of defensiveness.

A marked elevation on any one of the validity scales raises the question of the accuracy of the rest of the test as a description of the individual. If the t score on any of these scales is above 70, we can have less confidence that the rest of the test will give us a useful assessment of the individual. If the L, F, or K score is above 70, we might hypothesize that the person who took the test probably was lying on many of the items, may have been trying to appear much more disturbed than he actually is, or tends to deny the existence of any emotional difficulty for himself. We would not be able to interpret the rest of the scales on the test clearly; nevertheless, we would have gained some useful information about the person strictly from the validity scales, and perhaps some from the clinical scales (Marks and Seeman, 1963).

Clinical scales. The other ten scales of MMPI are known as the clinical scales. To describe an MMPI profile with the clinical scales, the highest three scores are reported in order of their elevation. For example, if a person obtained a t score of 100 on scale 8, 90 on scale 5, and 80 on scale 2, the profile would be described as an 852. Coding of MMPI profiles in terms of the three most elevated scales is the key to using an actuarial textbook. Examining an MMPI profile actuarially or describing the profile to another person is done by reporting the three most elevated scores in order.

Each of the clinical scales on the MMPI measures features of personality that are associated with behavioral abnormality and give a different type of information from that obtained on any other scale. However, the various scales are not completely independent of one another. An elevation of one scale is often accompanied by elevation of certain others, and it is the pattern that is important. The clinical scales include the following.

HS OR HYPOCHONDRIASIS SCALE. Elevation of this scale indicates that the subject is much more concerned than the average person with bodily function, illness, and somatic complaints. It is likely a person who receives a high score on this scale is experiencing much anxiety about his bodily functioning. It should be noted that elevation cannot be interpreted as proof that a person is a hypochondriac. Rather, it simply indicates that an individual probably spends considerable time worrying about his body. Whether or not this bodily preoccupation is justified must be evaluated medically.

D OR DEPRESSION SCALE. The D scale assesses the degree to which an individual is able to face everyday life with a normal degree of optimism. Elevations of this scale may be indicative of an inability to make reasonable decisions concerning the relative importance of events in one's life. High scorers are likely to spend a great deal of time worrying and tend to view the world with very gloomy and pessimistic attitudes.

HY OR HYSTERIA SCALE. Elevation on this scale indicates that the individual may be a very self-centered, immature person who is easily influenced and very likely to develop physical symptoms, such as headaches, that cannot be substantiated medically. An elevation on the Hy scale is often accompanied by an elevation of the Hs scale. In the absence of demonstrable physical illness, elevations on both of these scales suggests a person who is likely to behave in ways that will lead him to be labeled a hypochondriac or hysteric. That is, it is likely that the person is immature and self-centered, preoccupied with his own bodily functioning, and that he utilizes physical illness as a means of avoiding or escaping threatening or uncomfortable situations.

PD OR PSYCHOPATHIC DEVIATE SCALE. This scale is designed to measure the degree to which an individual can be described as a psychopath. Behaviorally, moderate and extreme elevations on this scale indicate that the subject is probably a confirmed nonconformist, very rebellious, has few if any lasting and deep personal relationships with other people, and is probably lacking in feelings for and loyalties to other people. His relationships with other people and society are generally marked by a lack of compassion and the absence of guilt or anxiety in relation to his own misconduct.

MF OR MASCULINITY-FEMININITY SCALE. An elevation of this scale in males indicates that the person is highly concerned with intellectual and esthetic pursuits. This orientation is often found in more highly educated males and should not be considered firm evidence of homosexuality or sexual deviance. However, an extreme elevation of the Mf in males (t score 80 or above) may indicate the presence of effeminate behavior and/or very strong interest in art and similar creative occupations. Similarly, an elevation of this scale for a female does not necessarily prove homosexuality but rather may show she is more interested in sports and other activities that are culturally defined as primarily masculine areas.

PA OR PARANOIA SCALE. Elevation of this scale is likely to be accompanied by suspiciousness, distrust of other people, and possibly feelings of persecution or exaggerated importance.

PT OR PSYCHOSTHENIA SCALE. This scale measures the extent to which an individual is able to function in his daily life without an excessive amount of anxiety and with a sufficient degree of behavioral flexibility to deal with the problems of everyday life with normal speed and efficiency. An extreme elevation of the Pt scale indicates that the subject is probably very rigid in his personal beliefs and work habits, worries excessively about his problems, has many disturbing thoughts, exhibits compulsive behaviors, and has significant guilt feelings. When accompanied by a higher elevation on scale 2 (the D scale), it can be hypothesized that the individual is probably depressed, generally feels that the situation is hopeless, has difficulty expressing his own feelings in relation to other people, and blames himself for his frustrations.

SC OR SCHIZOPHRENIA SCALE. The individual who obtains a moderately high score on this scale is likely to be perceived by others as being somewhat strange or eccentric. Extreme elevations on this scale are indicative of feelings of unreality, bizarre or disordered thinking, and the probability of delusions or hallucinations. The Sc scale is one of the most important indicators of severe emotional disturbance. Many of the items on this scale are also included on the F scale. Extreme elevation on the F scale will almost automatically be accompanied by an elevation on the Sc scale. If both of these scales are markedly elevated, it is likely that the profile is not valid and that the person is attempting to malinger—that is, he is attempting to look "crazy." However, a high Sc accompanied by an F score that is within normal limits (t score 60 or less) is a very good indicator of the presence of a severe disturbance.

MA OR MANIA SCALE. This scale measures the energy level of the individual, the degree to which he undertakes his daily activities with a normal amount of interest and enthusiasm. Very high elevations are indicative of restlessness and impulsiveness, which are probably accompanied by superficial happiness and gaiety. An individual with a very high Ma score is very likely to be unpredictable. When accompanied by a higher elevation on the Pd scale, an elevation on the Ma scale suggests the individual is prone to guiltless manipulation of others for his own purposes and is likely to operate in the criminal or delinquent fringes of society. This is a person who is often constantly involved in legal difficulties and who undertakes the pursuit of his own gratification at the expense of others. Elevation of Ma, when accompanied by an elevation of D scales, may be indicative of potential self-destructiveness. A person with an elevation on these scales is likely to be severely depressed and prone to impulsive behavior, which may take the form of self-destructive attempts, such as leaping in front of cars in the absence of warning signs or premeditation.

SI OR SOCIAL-INTERVERSION SCALE. The scale assesses the degree to which an individual is able to maintain satisfying and adequate social relationships. A person who produces an elevated Si score is likely to be shy, withdrawn, and generally inept and ineffective in social situations. Thus, we would expect that he has few friends, avoids gatherings such as parties or meetings, and prefers to spend his time alone.

Summary. A number of books known as atlases or cookbooks have been published to give much more detailed descriptions of various combinations of scales and their meaning in relation to a person's behavior than we have presented. Some of these works are listed by Marks and Seeman (1963).

It is of the utmost importance to remember, when examining the results of an MMPI, that it is primarily a method for clinical assessment. Its greatest use is for predicting or diagnosing abnormal or deviant thought or behavior patterns. It does not sample the universe of behavior patterns. It is probably one of the best assessment instruments available for use in mental health work. However, elevations on the various scales of the MMPI are not definitive indicators of emotional disturbance. Rather, they provide the mental health worker with hypotheses to be examined empirically. The results of the MMPI give us an idea of where to look for manifestations of deviant behavior; it does not definitely confirm the existence of such behavior. Maladaptive, inappropriate, or deviant behavior that is suggested by the MMPI must be confirmed through observation. Therefore, it is unwise to rely solely on an instrument such as this for evaluating an individual.

In human service work it sometimes occurs that the worker is called upon to help an essentially normal person find an appropriate job, discover an area of potential vocational success, or aid in the selection of a new career following a period of institutionalization. In cases such as this we are concerned with describing or predicting the behavior of an essentially normal person. The MMPI is, hence, an inappropriate method of assessment, for it was designed and constructed for use with highly deviant behavior and is of limited usefulness for describing and predicting normal behavior.

Other objective personality tests. Fortunately, a number of researchers have constructed rigorously researched instruments designed for use with average or normal people. They are used to compare an individual with other people on a number of personality characteristics not specific to psychiatric populations. One of the most widely used of these measures is the 16 Personality Factor

Questionnaire (16PF). From the results of the 16PF information can be obtained to help determine whether an individual is more or less intelligent, reserved or outgoing, self-sufficient, and suspicious or trusting than the average person. Information such as this can be of great value to help an individual make decisions about his life, as well as aid in the selection of individuals for employment. Another instrument with some similarity to the 16PF is the California Psychological Inventory (CPI) (Anastasi, 1968). It also gives information about how a person compares with the average individual on a number of personality traits important in understanding total behavioral functioning.

The Edwards Personal Preference Schedule (EPPS) is an instrument useful in guidance and counseling work. It provides information on interpersonal, occupational, and leisure-time preferences and shows how they compare with that of other people. The EPPS is valuable to help an individual understand himself and decide what type of career he would like to pursue.

Rating scales. Another class of objective assessment instruments is known as rating scales. These techniques differ from the preceding tests for they are usually completed by the examiner himself, not by the subject. Rating scales usually consist of a number of statements about the behavior of the subject, and the rater is asked to decide to what degree they are descriptive of the person's behavior. For example, a mental health worker might be required to rate the degree to which the statement: "He spent a lot of time talking with other people" describes the behavior of the subject. The examiner indicates the accuracy of the statement by assigning it a number. The number 1 might indicate that the statement is very accurate, the number 5 that it is very inaccurate, and the number 3 that it is of average applicability. If the worker observed that the subject very seldom talked with other individuals he would assign a number 5 to the statement.

Many rating scales are available for use in mental health work. The scores on these scales are helpful to classify patients or clients in terms of their level of behavioral functioning on numerous behavioral dimensions. The level of behavioral functioning may denote not only the presence or absence of maladaptive or inappropriate behavior but also the degree to which the person is able to adequately care for his own physical needs. Behavior rating scales are useful in examining the effectiveness of therapeutic programs and describing various characteristics of an individual or a group.

Other methods of behavior assessment

Up to this point we have discussed techniques of behavior assessment that provide a way of comparing one individual with another. There are other methods of behavior assessment, such as interviewing and obtaining social and developmental histories, mental status examinations, and case history information, that can supply very valuable information about a person and how he is functioning. They provide excellent opportunities for testing hypotheses developed about the person from the results of standardized psychological tests and further provide an opportunity to build a therapeutic relationship.

Interviewing. Interviews can take several forms, involve more than one interviewer and interviewee, and have many different purposes. Personnel officers typically interview applicants for positions, trying to assess the degree to which the individual meets the position specifications. The personnel officer makes some differentiation among all the individuals he interviews and, in conjunction with other information about them, makes his selection of employees. In human service work, interviews can be categorized first as those oriented toward obtaining information, with the interviewer primarily interested in a final recommendation or prediction on the basis of all the knowledge obtained from the person and from other materials. The second categorization in human service work pertains to psychotherapeutic interviewing, in which the interviewer is primarily a therapist attempting to help the individual better understand himself. From verbal statements and his understanding of the behavior exhibited by the client or patient, the therapist provides his perception to the client. In other words, he provides feedback to the client.

Our current focus will be on interviewing as a data collection method. The interviewer is clearly in a position of some authority, and he desires the client to express himself in an open and honest manner, encouraging the client to feel some trust in him. The interviewer observes the physical appearance, groom-

Fig. 7. Interviewing—a common assessment procedure. (Eugene Luttenberg, Editorial Photo-color Archives.)

ing, and behavior of the client. The client usually attempts to meet the desires of the interviewer, telling him what he wants to know and generally expressing his behavior in a manner that will favorably impress the interviewer. Sometimes the client may distort the actual facts about himself and others. He may or may not be aware of such distortions and inaccuracies, and it is the job of the interviewer to resolve discrepancies in the information given and to probe into unclear areas that are necessary for making adequate decisions and recommendations.

Interviews are typically categorized as structured and unstructured. A structured interview involves a form on which bits of information are noted, with blank spaces provided to allow room for the interviewer to write information. A structured interview schedule may resemble an application blank on which there are spaces for the client's name, date of birth, employment history, personality characteristics he would attribute to himself, future occupational goals, and anything else that might seem related to the purpose at hand. The interviewer may follow the form in a very orderly fashion, asking the questions quite directly and writing the information on the form. Structured interviews are often helpful for the person who is just learning how to become an interviewer.

However, with experience and increased levels of training, interviewers may feel much more comfortable and be more effective in their work with the use of an unstructured interview. Unstructured interviews are oriented toward collection of information in the same way as a structured interview, but the interviewer moves back and forth among the bits of information he is collecting. This occurs on the basis of the conversation between interviewer and interviewee, and the interview may well appear to be a relatively open verbal exchange between two people. That is, it appears to be a very natural and spontaneous situation, although to the individual not trained or experienced in unstructured techniques the interview may appear to be very vague and inadequate. Those who are lacking in experience are unable to perceive the manner in which the interviewer is operating to gather his information. The highly skilled unstructured interviewer may obtain information from a relatively brief interview that astounds the observer without such highly developed skills.

Social and developmental histories. The acquisition of a social and developmental history is another purpose of obtaining information by the interview method. It leads to an understanding of the total background of the individual and provides a basis on which to make predictions and recommendations in regard to the person. The history may be obtained either with the person whose behavior is the subject of interest or from some other individual, usually a family or peer group member, who knows the individual well. Initial interviews in mental health settings are commonly termed "psychiatric intake interviews." They have several purposes and may be done by any member of the mental health team, although traditionally they are done by social workers. The interviewee (or informant, such as a parent who will provide information about one of his children) arrives at the clinic or hospital for the first appointment. Presumably, the person believes he has a significant emotional problem, or someone else has told him he has, and he may enter the session feeling quite self-conscious, ill at ease, and defensive. Hence, the person may be very uncomfortable and somewhat afraid of what the session will be like. The interviewer must carefully note the entire behavior pattern of the person immediately and carry the responsibility for this initial session. The interviewer must establish a relationship with the client, attend to the client's characteristics, modify his behavior to increase rapport, give information about the services of the clinic, and help the client decide whether the clinic or some other agency will best meet his needs.

During some part of the interview the interviewer asks or otherwise obtains information about the client of a straightforward identification type. This includes the client's name, age, education, family status, and occupation. The interviewer will also help the client verbalize the nature of the problems that brought him to the clinic and attempt to determine the accuracy of the client's statements. The client may make statements that will have a bearing on the clinic's understanding of him, including his intellectual level, degree of self-understanding, ability to control impulses, and degree of disturbance. The initial intake interview may seem quite superficial, but it is an extremely important session that will have an effect on the client's feeling about the clinic and all his future visits.

Mental status examination. Partly during the initial interview, but most likely during later sessions, an attempt will be made to more definitively ascertain the client's condition or mental status. There are numerous areas of interest explored during the mental status interview, and they may be categorized as the following.

Attitude, appearance, and behavior. Is the client friendly and cooperative? How does his appearance compare with others of some reference group?

Mental content. Does the client have unusual fears, strange ideas, or preoccupations at a significant level?

Emotional tone. Are the person's facial expressions and manner of verbalizing his emotions consistent with the content of his statements? Does he say in a very flat, depressed manner that he loves his children?

Intellect. What is the person's level of intellectual functioning? (Results of brief tests of intelligence and orientation to time, place, and person will give a rough indication of this.)

Stream of speech. Is the person's speech coherent and organized? Does he speak either too rapidly or too slowly?

Insight. Does the person have adequate self-understanding? Is he clearly disturbed? Does he have any awareness of his condition?

Case history interview. After the initial psychiatric intake interview and the mental status interview, a case history interview is done to gather as much detailed life history information as possible. Prior to the interview the interviewer may also have available the person's formal records and reports from other agencies. These interviews cover the genetic and family background of the individual, conditions surrounding his birth, his early childhood development (such as age of walking and talking), difficulties in feeding and toilet training, relationships with other children within and outside the family, relationships with both parents, medical history, school experiences, occupational and work training and employment, dating pattern, and the marriage and family life.

Usually the person's history shows much information related to his current complaints and psychological condition. The astute interviewer's knowledge about the developmental acquisition of behavior problems will enable him to form many questions during the interview. He may or may not verbalize all his questions, depending on whether or not the client is able to respond effectively and adequately. If the interviewer had a question about the person's homosexual tendencies during adolescence, and if he were directly questioned, the interviewer might never see the client again. Therefore, if such questions are raised at all in these early sessions, it will probably be done in a very general and tentative manner. It is possible the interviewer will simply make a note concerning this possibility, of which the client may be very lacking in self-understanding, and the therapist to whom the client is later assigned may be helpful in exploring that situation with the client.

Behavior and emotional problems seldom or never appear with no history of learning; they are usually found to have a long developmental history with many complex and interacting determinants. Hence, there should be extensive exploration of significant turning points in the person's life that may have served as precipitants for his condition. It is very likely that a disturbed person will show a gross misperception of his own development and the actual freedom of alternative actions that he has. He may feel his life has been highly structured by others, that he is lacking in the ability to effectively consider alternatives, and that he may not be at all responsible for his behavior. The degree to which a person feels responsible and open to explore alternatives is a most meaningful question to answer during the case history interview. This information is of primary importance to the therapist.

People often forget the details of their development and present a picture of events that may be far different from the perception other people have of it. This is also a problem when parents are interviewed in regard to their children. They may have forgotten when the child began certain developmental tasks of importance, even to the extent of reporting a child began talking at the age of 11 months when in actuality he said his first word at the age of 2 years. To handle such problems interviewers have attempted to use interviewing statements of a more general nature. One form often used is the Vineland Social

Maturity Scale. The parent or teacher may be asked to describe the child's early behavior, and as the person relates the information the interviewer notes on a standardized scale, set up by age levels, at what point children performed specific behaviors of developmental significance. The parent is not asked directly at what age the child began doing certain things himself. Rather, he is simply asked to describe the child's early behavior. When information that is desired is not obtained, the interviewer becomes more and more specific in the questioning, probing from the general to the specific only as much as necessary. This appears to decrease the number of errors in information obtained from such sources.

Some general techniques by successful interviewers relate to the interviewer's individual human qualities. Interviewers who show empathy (the ability to understand the feelings and problems of the client), congruence (the ability to be a genuine, spontaneous, and caring person), and positive regard (a true rather than a stilted professional or phony caring and liking for the client) appear to be significantly more successful as interviewers. They develop feelings in the client that lead him to believe the therapist really wants to be helpful, likes him, and has some initial understanding of him. Such clients tend to return for more interviews, which take on more of a therapeutic rather than information-gathering flavor.

REFERENCES AND SUGGESTED READINGS

Anastasi, A. 1968. Psychological testing. New York, The Macmillan Company.

Binet, A., and Simon, T. 1905-1908. The development of intelligence in children. In Jenkins, J., and Patterson, D., editors. 1961. Studies in individual differences. New York, Appleton-Century-Crofts.

Cronbach, L. 1960. Essentials of psychological testing. New York, Harper & Row, Publishers.

Freund, J. 1960. Modern elementary statistics. Englewood Cliffs, N. J., Prentice-Hall, Inc.

Galton, F. 1869. Classification of men according to their natural gifts. In Jenkins, J., and Patterson, D., editors. 1961. Studies in individual differences. New York, Appleton-Century-Crofts.

Hathaway, S. 1966. MMPI: professional use by professional people. In Braun, J., editor. 1966. Clinical psychology in transition. New York, World Publishing Company.

Lyman, H. 1963. Test scores and what they mean. Englewood Cliffs, N. J., Prentice-Hall, Inc.

Marks, P., and Seeman, W. 1963. Actuarial description of abnormal personality: an atlas for use with the MMPI. Baltimore, The Williams & Wilkins Co.

Morgan, C. T., and King, R. A. 1966. Introduction to psychology. New York, McGraw-Hill Book Company.

Rapaport, D., Gill, M., and Schaefer, R. 1968. Diagnostic psychological testing. New York, International Universities Press.

6

THEORIES OF PERSONALITY

Personality is a word with which almost everyone is familiar, but behavioral scientists have experienced great difficulty in adequately defining it. It is sometimes said that a certain person has a great deal of personality, but this is usually meant as a value judgment of the person rather than an actuality. Each person has exactly the same "amount" of personality as any other person. To the behavioral scientist "personality" refers to process and product of the individual's behavior. A person who behaves in one way in a situation tends to behave in that way in comparable situations. This behavior is taken as a personality characteristic and illustrates the concept of process. A person who drives an expensive automobile is perceived differently from a person who drives an imported economy car. The automobile exemplifies products of the person's behavior—that is, he has purchased and drives it.

Personality is often discussed in such a way that the process and product of behaviors are rather far removed from the words used to describe the person. Behavior is extremely difficult to understand when taken out of context and separated from the behaving person. To reduce the complexity, observers note numerous behaviors in terms of both process and product and compare the individual with other persons of his age, social status, culture, and other factors. The observer tries to understand the person's behavior in terms of both heredity and environment and describes the person with words. For example, to say one person is very warm and friendly, the observer must have some basis on which to make such a comparative statement, and there must be some degree of agreement among people in regard to what the words mean. Complete agreement among behavioral scientists is rare to say the least, and the behavioral indications of personality characteristics are commonly argued. Furthermore, since all people have their own system of values, they tend to project these onto the individual. One who dislikes loud and aggressive people may perceive people he otherwise doesn't like as loud and aggressive. He will also indicate by his statements and reactions that loud and aggressive people should be viewed by others with disfavor.

In the behavioral sciences the personality theorist is one who studies behavior and attempts to categorize and better understand people. The data base is observable process and products of behavior, from which he make inferences to a more conceptual and meaningful level.

TRAITS, FACULTIES, AND PREDISPOSITIONS

People have tried to understand themselves and others since the beginning of time. History is replete with the work of personality theorists, including that of the great physician, Hippocrates. He proposed four personality types corresponding to body fluids, and there are some interesting contemporary parallels of his work. Hippocrates postulated the existence of the sanguine temperament, based on blood. This person particularly enjoys wine, women, and song. The melancholic temperament was based on black bile, and the melancholic person has a rather gloomy and depressed behavior pattern. The choleric temperament is based on yellow bile; an individual with such a personality is prone to violence and emotional acting out. The phlegmatic temperament is based on phlegm, and the phlegmatic person tends to be rather lazy and in need of body comforts.

Another milestone in the development of personality theory is termed "physiognomy," which is the art of inferring personality traits from facial features. For example, small eyes are supposedly indicative of stupidity and wickedness. A viewpoint related to physiognomy is phrenology, which is the art of inferring personality traits from the shape and bumps of the skull. Charts have been made on which sections of a person's head have been given numbers, which are supposed to show where certain personality characteristics are located on the person's head. A number 13 of the skull may pertain to will power and number 14 to affection. Physiognomy and phrenology are viewed by modern-day behavioral scientists as prescientific and worthless.

However, the central idea of a person having personality traits that influence all of his behavior remains. Faculties and predispositions, at least in the sense that they deal with the degree to which an individual possesses a stable, internalized, and characteristic way of behaving, have largely been retermed traits. Very sophisticated statistical and computer techniques have been used to help clarify the evidence regarding the existence and function of traits, which in one theory have been named "factors."

The statistical technique of factor analysis has been developed to a very high level by the psychologist Cattell (1957), who has made psychological tests measuring the primary characteristics of people. They are reported in terms of unusually high and unusually low scores on each trait. The following is a brief, slightly paraphrased description of Cattell's factor analytic results.

FACTOR A   Easy-going, warm-hearted, blunt, and generous versus obstructive, indifferent, and secretive

FACTOR B   Intelligence, alert, and wise versus stupid and silly

FACTOR C   Mature and patient versus childish and anxious

FACTOR D   Impulsive and overactive versus deliberate, leisurely, and self-controlled

FACTOR E   Confident, aggressive, and forceful versus modest, timid, and insecure

FACTOR F   Talkative, cheerful, and responsive versus brooding, seclusive, and quiet

FACTOR G   Conscientious, responsible, and loyal versus frivolous and undependable

FACTOR H   Brave, carefree, and overtly interested in sex versus overtly disinterested in sex, careful, and cowardly

FACTOR I   Introspective and intuitive versus hard, practical, logical, and self-sufficient

FACTOR J   Uncooperative and independent versus supportive, dependent, and collaborative

FACTOR K   Polished, polite, and reserved versus crude, awkward, and uncouth

FACTOR L   Jealous and skeptical versus trustful and unsuspecting

FACTOR M   Eccentric and complacent versus conventional, poised, and earnest

FACTOR N   Expedient and calculating versus indifferent, apathetic, and unskilled in analyzing the motives of others

FACTOR O   Depressed, compulsive, and moody versus cheerful, spirited, and self-sufficient

FACTOR Q1   Liberal and open-minded versus conservative

FACTOR Q2   Self-sufficient versus reliant on the group

FACTOR Q3   Controlled and careful versus careless and lacking in caution

FACTOR Q4   Conflicted and frustrated versus relaxed and composed

Other attempts have been made to categorize and understand individuals on the basis of their bodily structures. A physician named Sheldon (1954) argued for the existence of three basic body types, called somatotypes, each of which has characteristically associated personality traits. Sheldon believed that all people had some of the three extremes but that many could be understood as being primarily only one of the three.

The endomorph has dominant body structures associated with digestion. The endomorphic individual is soft, chubby, and lacking hard muscles. He tends to enjoy the good things of life and avoids problems. The mesomorph has a dominant body structure associated with strength and motor activity, which involves heavy, well-developed bones and muscles. He tends to prefer competition and the direct expression of his energy and feelings. The ectomorph has a dominant body structure associated with sensory and intellectual processes. He tends to be rather forgetful, delicate, and thin. He prefers to think, rather than to feel or do. Sheldon and other somatotype personality theorists have certainly contributed some to our understanding of people, but their work seems to have had little lasting impact on the field.

PSYCHOANALYTIC THEORY

The psychoanalytic viewpoint of personality development and functioning originated with Sigmund Freud (1953) in the late nineteenth century. All of Freud's concepts must be understood in the context of his personal background, culture, and numerous historical influences. He was originally trained as a physician in Vienna and did not begin publishing the psychoanalytic viewpoint until he was in his middle age. His medical background had significant influence through all of his writings. He was a biologically educated person interested in the behavior of individuals and behavioral science in general. He was Jewish and was subject to slights and prejudices throughout his life, which culminated in exile from Nazi Germany in his final years. He was also much influenced by the prudish Victorian tradition and, contrary to popular opinion, he was never able to personally escape from such values and attitudes. The Industrial Revolution had occurred, and Freud's writings are interspersed with analogies drawn from the world of production, including basic concepts of hydraulic forces, energy, and transformations of energy.

Freud has probably had more influence on our conceptions of human behavior than has anyone for at least 2,000 years. Although his ideas are somewhat out of favor with many professionals working with human behavior, the degree to which some criticize Freud stands as a ready testament to his influence. Psychoanalytic thought was perceived as very dangerous and threatening at its inception, and many continue to find it repulsive and anxiety arousing. However, it is impossible to understand the theory well without considerable expenditure of time and effort. It is very complex, with numerous interacting concepts. In regard to psychoanalytic theory, it is often stated that a little knowledge is a very dangerous thing, but most people who say they have studied psychoanalysis have not yet reached the danger point.

The following brief summary will not do justice to psychoanalytic personality theory, but it is hoped some degree of initial understanding may develop. The psychoanalytic formulation should also be understood as primarily developing before the behavioral sciences became dominant, and it has continued to develop somewhat out of the mainstream of behavioral sciences.

Structure and function of personality

Freud's theory begins with the birth of the individual. A person comes into the world strictly as a biological organism under the direct control of his physiological drives. Because of the individual's behavior being determined by biological predispositions, he is termed an "It." The word "It" was later translated from the German language into the English language as "Id." The Id is the original structure of human personality and drives the person to satisfy directly and without environmental influence his basic needs of thirst, hunger, warmth, and sexuality. The Id operates on the pleasure principle.

Nevertheless, the newborn infant learns that other people and circumstances beyond his control frustrate his needs for biological satisfaction, and the pleasure principle does not work sufficiently well. That is, although he may be hungry and crying desperately for the bottle, some time may elapse before the parents can satisfy this physiological need. Infants also are often placed on feeding schedules to which they must adapt. Newborn infants feel discomfort from wet and cold diapers and learn that a reduction of such discomfort sometimes occurs when the parents are ready, rather than when the discomfort begins.

As the child learns to tolerate such frustrations and accommodate to his parents and the world, he develops a concept of time, space, and a differentiation of himself from the universe. He develops an Ego, or self, which is the second structure of personality in the psychoanalytic system. The Ego operates on the reality principle. It serves as the executive for the Id, attempting to meet the demands of the Id while operating within the realm of realistic life circumstances. The pleasure principle of the Id remains in operation, but the Ego must meet the demands of the Id while simultaneously operating in the world of reality and other people.

The child learns from his experiences that some objects or events are pleasurable and that others are not. This is the beginning of a value orientation to all of life, which will later serve as a model for the highest level morality and compassion, as well as the most negative of human behavior and feelings. He learns that things are good or bad in a very dichotomous, black and white manner. Things are either all good or they are all bad, and only through considerable experience and intellectual development is he able to make some degree of differentiation in terms of varying shades of gray. Many adults, however, find it very difficult to think of events in shades of gray, and under extreme stress, they resort to dichotomous thinking.

Not only does the individual attach good and bad orientations to external objects and events, he begins to attach them to himself. He develops a positive or negative perception of himself, which is not necessarily based strictly on his behavior. The value orientations are conceived of as the conscience, which Freud termed a Superego. It serves as the value judgment device for both the Id and the Ego. The Ego must be aware of the drives of the Id, the reality aspects of the world, and the values imposed by the Superego. Thus, the stage is set for considerable frustration, conflict, and many behavioral difficulties. The structure of the personality, including the Id, Ego, and Superego, is completed in the first few years of life, and changes in the relationship of this basic structure are possible but not very probable.

Motivations and memories of life experiences may be conscious, or at an awareness level that can be verbalized. They may also be unconscious, or not at a verbalizable awareness level. Unconscious motivations and memories have much influence on a person's behavior, although by definition he does not know or understand it.

Driving forces behind behavior

Freud termed the driving forces behind behavior the Libido. He also believed that all pleasure, which is the object of the Id, is sexual. Importantly, he defines sexuality as pleasure, which is such a broad definition that many critics find it unacceptable. A person's Libido is an energy force that can be altered in many ways, but as long as the individual is alive it exists in some manner. In effect, it is the life force, which in his early writings Freud termed Eros. This includes all the very positive feelings and behaviors such as love, affection, warmth, sexuality, and creativity. In the later period of his life Freud seemed to become more depressed and pessimistic about human beings and developed a polar opposite of Eros, which is termed Thanatos. This includes all the negative emotions and behaviors, including hate, hostility, aggression, destruction, and death. Eros and Thanatos operate in mutual antagonism throughout one's life.

Psychosexual stages of development

Oral stage. When an individual is born he obtains primary satisfaction from reducing the drives of hunger and thirst. The newborn infant is driven to use the areas around the mouth, having an instinct to suck. Oral behavior may later be influenced by experience, but in the first instance it is a drive. If it were not an instinctual pleasure area, the newborn infant would die from a lack of sustenance. This set of oral behaviors is sexual in the sense that it is pleasurable. Throughout life the person will to some degree continue finding oral behaviors to be pleasurable and sexual, as evidenced by kissing. The newborn infant is very dependent, and any significant events occurring during this stage will influence later behavior in the area of dependency. Affection also becomes related to the oral stage, since the parents show positive emotions when meeting the child's oral needs. The oral stage is dominant for the first year and a half or so of a person's life, although it never actually disappears as an area of drive satisfaction.

Anal stage. Near the age of 1½ or 2 years the anal areas become more significantly pleasurable to the child. This corresponds rather closely to the toilet training period. The child has learned to walk and talk and is generally becoming more difficult for his parents to control. He is able to move about the room quickly, perhaps breaking things. He learns words, some of which are not necessarily accepted in polite society, and he is clearly in need of behavioral guidance from his parents. Pressures to find the appropriate time, place, and method of expulsion of feces and urination become strong. Unlike the oral stage, the child in the anal stage is the recipient of expectancies for his behaviors, and there often results a quite observable pattern of hostile behavior from both the child and his parents. In almost all cases, of course, the parents will win this battle and the child will become toilet trained. Because the parents win, it is said the child must will the inevitable.

Oedipal stage. At approximately age 3 or shortly thereafter the child has become completely toilet trained, is learning numerous words daily, and in general has acquired a fantastic amount of information. His thought processes are becoming very complex, and his energy appears without limit. The child expends his energy until he practically collapses in sleep. He becomes very aware of the fact that he has two parents, one of whom is similar to himself and the other less similar, but more desirable.

The child learns that he will grow up to probably be with a member of the opposite sex, but he will himself be more like the same sexed parent. However, before these concepts become firm and realistic, the child has a very major hurdle to overcome.

The oedipal child has primary pleasure in the genital area. This happens between the ages of 3 and 5, not at adolescence as is commonly believed. Obviously, the child is poorly equipped to be effectively adult in the genital sexual area. The little boy or girl will openly state that when they grow up they will marry their mother or father. This is met with some amusement on the part of the parents and others, and they slowly begin to teach the child that this is an incorrect assumption. Interestingly, if the adolescent reports he is going to marry his mother, this is met with considerably less amusement by the parents.

Freud took as his model for this stage the play *Oedipus Rex*, in which a king of a Greek city was told by a soothsayer that his newborn son would grow up, kill him, and marry his mother. The king had a subject take his son outside the city to be killed, but instead the child was given to a passing caravan. The child grew up in another city and later, in his wanderings, met an older man with whom he began arguing. He killed him and went into the city, fell in love with an older woman, and married her. The city was beset by disastrous events, and the citizens were powerless to combat them. Finally, a wise old man of the city reported why the city was beset by so many calamities. He reported the current king, Oedipus, according to his prediction of years earlier, had indeed killed his father and married his mother, although he was unaware he had done so. Oedipus felt great guilt and put out his own eyes, saying: "None are so blind as those who will not see."

Since this play has continued throughout the centuries to draw a good audience, elicits an intense emotional reaction, and has a theme expressed in uncountable plays, books, and movies, Freud believed it was an experience had by everyone, including himself.

The child is attached to the opposite sex parent, not just in terms of affection but in terms of being motivated toward sexual intercourse. Little boys and girls, however, have a very different experience. Little boys become aware that their fathers are angry, even though the anger may be expressed very subtly, and they develop the notion that the father will damage them. The damage takes the form of castration. Freud termed this feeling "castration anxiety." The fear becomes so intense that a resolution must be made, which occurs in the form of trying to become the father. The little boy identifies with the father and attempts to imitate his every behavior. He then gives up his orientation toward his mother and begins looking outside the family for his ultimate mate. This transpires at the time the child begins formal education, and the school and everything with it become his primary areas of energy disposal. The little boys become very industrious, interested in all areas of knowledge, and obvious sexual interests are no longer observed.

The little girl becomes sexually attracted to her father and competes with her mother. Her mother is viewed with disfavor partly because she is lacking obvious sexuality. She believes that she and her mother once had a penis, but that they have been castrated. They are now inferior to men, and her mother is not a worthy model for her own behavior. Freud termed this condition "penis envy," which, of course, very much angers women's liberation groups. The psychoanalysts view the groups' denial and anger in regard to penis envy as an obvious substantiation of its very existence. The women's groups lose either way they go. The little girl never really identifies with a mother to the extent that the little boy identifies with the father, and although the little girl ultimately looks outside the family for her marriage parner, she remains oriented toward finding a more mature and capable male. That is, the young woman is much more apt to marry an older man than is the young man to marry an older woman. The popular song "My Heart Belongs to Daddy" is taken as minor evidence for this belief.

Fairy tales and myths are loaded with symbolic accounts of the oedipal situation. For example, Hansel and Gretel had a very high sexual interest, in this instance toward each other, and were frustrated by their mother. The witch in the gingerbread house, whom they pushed into the hot oven, was actually a symbolic representation of their mother, who would not allow them free sexual expression. Rumpelstiltskin is the story of a young girl who was sexually interested in an older man (her symbolic father), which is transposed into a denial of him and a desire for a younger man. Snow White was not content with one older man but had seven.

The concept of the oedipal stage probably arouses the most heat and anger of any psychoanalytic ideas. It is substantiated by the psychoanalytic theorists, according to them, with considerable indirect evidence, which their critics consider extremely far-fetched and indicative of the unusual qualities of the psychoanalyst. One point that should be made, however, is that the first opposite sexed person of significance in practically everyone's life is one of their parents. Little girls learn what adult men are like, in the first instance, from experiences with their father, and little boys learn what adult women are like, in the first instance, through their interactions with their mother. The degree to which these learning experiences later influences their behavior is hardly disputable, regardless of the emphasis Freud placed on sexuality. Freud noted that whatever is feared or denied with extreme hate and anger must be very much desired, which is also taken as a counterpoint to the critics of the oedipal stage.

Latency stage. The elementary school years are times of learning. Freud had little to say about sexuality during this period other than pleasure is derived from becoming more effective and competent in the world. It is further stated by many that Freud probably underemphasized the importance of sex during these years, for it is clear that elementary school children are not disinterested in sexuality.

Genital stage. The genital stage, which is the second upsurge of genital sexuality, begins at adolescence. Memories of the original upsurge during the oedipal period are reactivated, but it is quite clear to the adolescent that he must move outside the family. Adolescence is an extremely trying time for both parents and adolescent. There is now another sexually mature person in the family who is further beset by many problems involving his peer group and by striving for maturity in the educational and vocational areas. If life experiences up to the time of adolescence have given the individual some degree of security and the ability to cope with daily problems, adolescence will be less stormy and the person will soon become a mature adult with a family of his own.

Defense mechanisms

Throughout life, but in particular during the formative years, people have life stresses that require them to protect themselves. They develop techniques the psychoanalysts term "defense mechanisms," which are coping methods to reduce feelings of discomfort and anxiety and to handle conflict and frustration. Conflict can occur between the Id and the Ego, the Ego and Superego, or the Id and the Superego. The desires of the Id may conflict severely with the values and conscience of the Superego. That is, one may want sexual satisfaction but believe that in terms of the time, place, or partner it is very wrong. Humans are the organisms that are subject to such a strong and pervasive conflict, which further indicates that the particular conflicts and frustrations of the sexual drive are learned from experiences, to a large degree at a very early age. The animals of the barnyard exhibit few or no such conflicts or frustrations. A conflict between the Ego and Superego exists when a person quite objectively comes to a rational decision but becomes frustrated when his religious teachings, for example, make him feel his decision is wrong or cynical.

Every person must learn methods to handle conflicts and frustrations, and there is no person who does not protect himself with defense mechanisms. Furthermore, the defense mechanisms are largely exemplified by verbal statements and are considered detrimental to the person only when they are used very extensively, when there is a focus by the person on a very limited number of mechanisms, or when they become ineffective by not working well. The categories of defense mechanisms are somewhat arbitrary and should be understood as guidelines for understanding behavior, rather than mutually exclusive categories. They are primarily unconscious and automatic.

Regression and fixation. Fight and flight reactions are evidenced by organisms as basic methods of escaping anxiety-arousing situations, these being related to aggression and withdrawal. There are also protective mechanisms termed regression and fixation. Regression occurs when an individual reverts to a manner of behaving that was considered appropriate during earlier years but is no longer. For example, an 8-year-old child who has no brothers or sisters may be suddenly confronted with the arrival of a new sibling. Although he previously had sucked his thumb, as all youngsters do, he has outgrown the need for such self-satisfaction. However, with the arrival of the new child, he begins sucking his thumb as he once did, which suggests a reactivated need for affection and bodily self-satisfaction.

Fixation is somewhat different, for it pertains to a manner of behaving that is appropriate at a given developmental stage but that the individual retains rather than developing more appropriate behaviors. This is seen in the child who is preoccupied with matters relating to going to the toilet, as many 2 year olds are, and who retains such an interest at a very high level when he is considerably older.

Fixation and regression are two of the most primitive and significant of all the defense mechanisms, and they are observed in a rather clear form in people who are placed in mental hospitals. Severely disturbed individuals such as schizophrenics and autistic children exhibit many behaviors suggestive of fixation and regression. It is not unusual for oral and anal behaviors to be expressed in an early developmental manner by institutionalized people.

Denial. Reality events sometimes become so painful and anxiety arousing that the person cannot accept them at all. They may handle the problem by denying the reality of the event. Children do this, for example, when after being severely beaten by the parents they insist that their parents dearly love them. They may also deny the existence of their brothers and sisters when they do not receive sufficient affection and attention from their parents. This pattern is also observable in severely disturbed people, such as occurs when people in mental hospitals deny that they are in an institution and insist the institution is, perhaps, a shoe factory of which they are the president. Often disturbed people will deny significant aspects of themselves, such as a hospitalized person insisting that he is a genius and holds numerous college degrees and patents on inventions.

Projection. Projection is often associated with denial. It refers to significant aspects of the self that are denied and projected onto another person or group. In psychoanalytic theory these projections have sexuality and aggression conflicts at their base, although on the surface they may seem to have only to do with everyday matters not associated with sex and aggression.

A person may be extremely angry toward himself because he has received information that he is not perceived as a highly worthy individual. He denies his lack of self-esteem and projects inferiority onto others. That is, he may express statements about the inferiority of blacks, Jews, Chicanos, or particular other groups with some characteristics different from his own. Another common example comes from the area of developing sexuality. The teenage girl may have intense sexual desire for her teacher, uncle, or other adult male. Since she has learned that these are unacceptable desires, to protect herself she denies their existence for her. She then projects the sexual desire onto the male and may even inform her parents that her teacher has made sexual advances toward her. The newspapers regularly report such events. They sometimes result in a court case, during which the truth becomes known.

Hospitalized patients categorized as paranoid schizophrenics exhibit the mechanisms of denial and projection to an extreme degree. They may report they are Napoleon, Jesus Christ, or any other famous person. Sexuality and aggression motivations exist but are denied, and the person projects these onto other people whom he believes are unjustly doing bad things to him. The false ideas of delusions of persecution they develop require substantiation, and the person ultimately decides he is being persecuted because he is a great person. The delusion of grandeur that he is a great person comes after he has denied his personal difficulties and decided that external events and other people are to blame for his problems.

Identification. Identification is usually thought of as a developmental process, but it should also be understood as a protective technique. Children develop behavioral patterns associated primarily with the parent of the same sex, the little boy imitating his father and the little girl imitating her mother. Although there have been obvious adaptions of parental behaviors in the first few years of life, the most meaningful peak of identification occurs during the oedipal stage, which has been discussed previously. To decrease his castration anxiety the little boy attempts to become like the father as much as possible. The little girl is in more difficult and complex circumstances. Although she is aware of the similarity between herself and her mother and attempts somewhat to become like her, the little girl never really gives up the idea that the father is the clearly superior and more worthy person. In adult life this difference in identification is observed in some career women, for example, who are continually compelled to compete with men and who show their deep inferiority feelings by constantly saying how adequate they are and how inadequate many men are. In the extreme form such women are termed castrators, probably most commonly by men who have castration anxiety.

The little boy, of course, retains some deep fears of physical castration, which he transforms into a fear of psychological punishment. Hence, as an adult he may be unusually afraid of failure in his business or profession. Sometimes such individuals with a high state of anxiety do the reverse of what is expected and may become dare-devils, automobile racers, and participants in other clearly dangerous activities; the person is compelled to perform in order to continually test his ability to master his fears. This is known as counterphobic behavior.

Repression. Repression is an unconscious practice of forgetting and not becoming aware of internal basic impulses or highly anxiety-arousing external events. In effect, it is a lapse of memory. According to the psychoanalysts, the most significant repression occurs during the oedipal period, although many aspects of the oral and anal stages have repressed elements affecting adult behavior. Penis envy and castration anxiety, in the basic sense of each concept, are repressed. Indeed, they must be repressed if a person is to become an effective adult. Whenever a person reports he has no memory of the oedipal situation, it is taken by the analyst as a matter of course that he has repressed his memory. If the person as an adult clearly remembers the oedipal situation and/

or other meaningful events during the oral or anal stages, it is believed the person has suffered a breakdown of repression that will probably severely interfere with his functioning, if it has not already done so. An adult male who daily thinks about having intercourse with his mother is probably quite disturbed. The degree to which this is a taboo area with extreme fear-arousing components is evidenced by the great anger shown when a person is called certain profane names linking mother and intercourse.

Repression may have an extremely useful function for most people. It is only when it is used to an extreme degree and the person behaves in ways he does not understand because of inappropriate repression of some events or an overuse of the mechanisms, or when repression does not work well, that it has negative consequences for the individual. Everyone represses much, but severely disturbed persons repress either more than others or repress events of which they need to be aware to function adequately. Repression may break down, and they are flooded with memories that greatly upset them.

Suppression. Suppression is considerably more conscious than is repression. It is basically a half-way conscious forgetting of events that are too anxiety arousing and that have negative effects on the person if he continually thinks about them. Human beings are aware of their ultimate death, but if they are preoccupied with these thoughts daily they are less able to function. Hence, we place such thoughts out of our minds and proceed to live each day without compulsive preoccupation with our ultimate decline and death. Animals apparently have extremely poor memories, and it is a good thing they do. A rabbit highly aware of its numerous daily brushes with death would probably be immobilized by fear, knowing how quick and probable his death may be at any given time. People who hear an otherwise amusing story on the way to a funeral will probably not find it mirth provoking, which indicates they are suppressing normal reactions under this particular circumstance.

Displacement. Displacement occurs when a person has a feeling state that he is unable to express directly for any number of reasons. It may be that if he were to express his feelings toward a particular individual who has raised his anger level he would find himself in very unfortunate circumstances. When a person is receiving angry statements from his employer, he may well feel motivated to retaliate in kind. If he expresses his anger to his supervisor he may be fired and in need of a new job. Therefore, the employee goes home at the end of the day and displaces the anger he felt toward the supervisor onto his wife, irritably telling her the dinner was not very good and/or she did not do well in disciplining the children today. The wife, of course, finds such behavior difficult to understand until her husband relates the negative events of the day, presuming he can.

Displacement may also occur on the part of the wife who cannot express her anger directly toward her husband, since she might be struck or otherwise receive some kind of punishment. She may displace her anger onto one of the children by spanking him for a very slight misbehavior. The child does not understand why he received such treatment, and since he cannot act out his anger directly toward his mother, he may kick the family dog. Displacement can also occur with any kind of feeling state, although psychoanalysts usually think sexuality and aggression are of primary importance.

Reaction formation. Reaction formation is the denial of unacceptable thoughts or impulses by the person and the returning of the thought or behavior into its exact opposite. This is a protective mechanism believed to be expressed in groups trying to increase the severity of pornography laws. People sometimes band together, deciding the citizens are being sinfully stimulated by erotic films and magazines. They attempt to close down theaters and otherwise decrease the amount of pornography available. Their reaction formation is evidenced by the unusually long periods of time and the efforts to which they go to observe sexual behavior. They sometimes spend more time viewing pornographic movies than anyone else. One group recently made their own antipornography movie, which was to be shown to citizen groups in order to motivate them to join an antismut campaign. The U. S. Post Office did not allow the movie to be sent through the mail because they considered it too pornographic.

A legislator in one state has introduced bills to make the sale of erotic materials a felony, which is such an extreme punishment for a natural behavior that one can only question the degree to which this person has adequate personal integration. Mothers sometimes smother their children with such saccharin sweetness and superficial love that one questions the motivations for their behavior. Are such mothers really harboring resentment toward the children who keep her from participating in many activities outside the home and obtaining personal and occupational fulfillment?

Intellectualization. Intellectualization is overusing thought processes to protect against unacceptable anxiety-arousing feelings. The person focuses on the intellectual content to such an extent it is apparent he has little emotionality invested. He isolates his feelings because it would be much too painful to include them, and he talks in a highly intellectual manner. College students may spend hours discussing anything from free love in communal living, to complete pacificism, to anything else. They talk about such topics without really being involved with their feelings. Beating around the bush is by no means only done by college students. People also talk about their families and jobs as if they had no feelings at all about them.

SOCIAL LEARNING: A PERSONALITY THEORY PERSPECTIVE

People have always been aware that behavior can be altered by doing something to the person after he has behaved in a certain way. It is clear that animals alter the behavior of their offspring during their development. The lion mother fetches and slaps her cub whenever he wanders too far from her, provides the cub with many rewards such as food and a good washing, and teaches the cub how to hunt successfully. Mankind's awareness of and experience in modifying behavior has been acquired slowly, partly because of moralistic and magical thinking. In the late nineteenth century the Russian physiologist Pavlov and the American psychologist Thorndike (Woodworth and Sheehan, 1964) almost simultaneously made significant discoveries that would alter our thinking about the learning process.

Pavlov noted that a meat powder presented to a dog caused the dog to salivate. He paired a bell with the meat powder, with the sound of the bell coming immediately before the presentation of the meat. He deleted the meat powder after a number of trials, simply presenting the sound of the bell. The dog then salivated whenever the bell sound was presented, even though there was no meat. This has become known as classical conditioning and is taken as a model by some for the manner in which much human behavior is acquired or changed.

Thorndike's discovery resulted from his work with cats, which he placed in a cage with a food reward immediately outside. The animal had to use trial and error methods to escape from the cage and obtain the food. After a number of trials the animal became very adept at getting out of the cage. For example, the first time the animal was placed in the cage he might require an hour to free himself, the tenth time 5 minutes, and the hundredth time 4 seconds. This is termed instrumental or operant conditioning, since the organism must perform some behavior and operate on the environment in order to obtain the reward or reinforcement. Many believe this is the more accurate model for understanding the acquisition and modification of most human behavior.

Merging with the research findings in the area of learning was thinking in regard to the psychoanalytic and sociologic areas. An early and significant version of the merging trends occurred in a book co-authored by Dollard and Miller (1950), which they dedicated to Pavlov and Freud. They attempted to bring these two major and sometimes conflicting viewpoints of human behavior into a meaningful single perspective. An emphasis was made that behavior has been learned in social situations and can be unlearned or more appropriate behaviors learned in comparable situations. This is not exceptionally different from the newer psychoanalytic thinkers becoming more attuned to social factors in behavioral development and change, although psychoanalysts often omit or rarely use the word "learning" in their writings, preferring the word "experience." The laboratory psychologists who studied learning have generally not been receptive to the work of Dollard and Miller, although there are points of agreement. Certain of the learning theorists attempt only to substantiate laboratory principles of behavior and entirely avoid any psychoanalytic concepts and terminology.

Dollard and Miller focus on four major concepts:

1. *Drive.* Drive is a desire or physiological need and is somewhat comparable to the freudian Libido and motivation in general. All people have

a number of drives. In terms of problems in everyday living and satisfaction of needs, sexuality and aggression have important positions.

2. *Response.* A response is any behavior of the person and can be of a very large or very small type. In the event of a high state of drive the organism tends to respond to reduce the desire by obtaining satisfaction.

3. *Reinforcement.* A positive reinforcement is a reward that meets the individual's needs and reduces his drive state. By definition, any object or event that tends to increase the probability of a response is a reinforcer.

4. *Cue.* A cue is any environmental object or event that provides information to the person and functions as a stimulus to direct the person to a reinforcer or drive reducer.

Fig. 8. Strong families develop mature and effective behavior. (H. Armstrong Roberts.)

An example of the entire sequence occurs with a child and cookies. The child has a hunger or drive for food, since it has been several hours since he had lunch. The mother moves near the cookie jar with which the child is familiar, and the child begins receiving cues. The drive state is moved to a higher level and the child begins responding in ways designed to get the mother to give him a cookie. As soon as the mother reinforces him by giving him the cookie, he stops responding to the cues and focuses on eating the cookie. The next time the child is hungry for cookies he will probably behave in much the same way as he did immediately prior to his mother giving him the cookie. Thus, the effect of a positive reinforcer is to increase the probability of behaviors that occurred immediately prior to reinforcement in previous situations. This is also taken as a model in which behavior is acquired that other people term abnormal or deviant.

More recent theorists in this framework are Bandura and Walters (1963), who move into a more direct use of learning principles with humans that is derived from experimental research. Although they are somewhat critical of psychoanalytical principles, they retain a focus on problems of behavioral acquisition during development and those associated primarily with human beings rather than animals. Their chapter titles relate to dependency, aggression, and sexuality. Their terminology is much more from the field of learning than from psychoanalysis. Our earlier discussions have noted that more recent learning theorists have emphasized rigorous laboratory study. They sometimes receive criticisms of being stilted, rigid, and lacking in a broad vision.

SELF-ACTUALIZATION THEORY

There are numerous viewpoints of human behaviors oriented around the concept of motivation. One of the more influential personality theorists is Maslow, who has outlined a theory known as self-actualization. Maslow (1954) postulates five levels of needs arranged in an order from the most basic to the highest level. The needs are listed in the order in which they appear in the development of all people. The more basic needs must be satisfied before people can move to satisfying needs at a higher level.

Physiological needs. Newborn infants are primarily oriented to satisfying their drives for hunger, thirst, and other body conditions.

Safety needs. Safety needs include personal security and stability. Safety needs do not become highly observable until the person has satisfied his physiological needs, and he will act to satisfy hunger needs even at the loss of personal security. It is said that man does not live by bread alone, but this seems to be true only if there is sufficient bread.

Belonging and love needs. With development of the individual and general satisfaction of physiological and safety needs, the person becomes motivated toward affection, affiliation, warmth, and support from other people.

Esteem needs. People who have achieved adequate satisfaction of physiological, safety, and love needs become motivated for obtaining prestige, success, and self-respect. They want to think highly of themselves and for others to think highly of them.

Need for self-actualization. After all the preceding needs are adequately met, people have a natural tendency to develop all their potentiality to the highest level. Self-actualizing persons are more often creative, exhibit less hostility in their humor, are oriented to humanity and its welfare, enjoy their occasional privacy, are somewhat selective in their friends, are self-accepting, and are able to feel comfortable within the rules and regulations of society. They are not neurotically driven to achieve, although they may be exceptional achievers in any given occupational or professional field.

Maslow's self-actualization theory is acceptable to many theorists who have made additions or different emphases. Although it appears to be appropriate for understanding any person, it is believed that the emphasis on self-actualization has more relevance to the most effective and highly functioning members of society. The severely disturbed, including those in mental hospitals, are more involved with satisfying needs lower in the hierarchy.

Carl Rogers (1961) basically agrees that self-actualization is the ultimate goal of the person. The major reason people develop psychological difficulties is because others have interfered with the person achieving an adequate degree of need satisfaction. Hence, the person cannot proceed to the self-actualization level. Rogerian therapy is formulated to allow the person to satisfy some of the lower needs in order to become more aware and capable of satisfying self-actualization needs.

EXISTENTIAL THEORY

The existential personality theorists (May, 1961) seem somewhat closer to the fields of philosophy and religion than to the behavioral sciences. They are primarily concerned with the problems and questions posed for the individual by his very existence and the effect that the resolution of these conflicts has on the person. The existentialists note that we should try to be "that self which one truly is." A person is considered a being who is acutely aware of his being and subject to anxiety at the threat of nonbeing. Unlike animals, all people are aware of their ultimate physical death and suffer existential anxiety and despair.

Three key words of existential theory are freedom, responsibility, and courage. Man has the freedom to make choices. He has the responsibility of fulfilling a purpose and giving some meaning to his short life. Hence, the significant question is whether man has the courage to be. Existential theory focuses on the freedom people have in regard to alternative courses of action in their lives. They are not robots at the whim of some master agency. People must be responsible for their own behavior and cannot continue to blame others for the negative things that happen to them. Once a person acknowledges his freedom and responsibility, and if he has the courage to be, the person is no longer

Fig. 9. Sensitivity groups—a new way of developing personal awareness. (Arthur Sirdofsky, Editorial Photocolor Archives.)

overwhelmed by anxiety and despair in regard to his human condition. He is able to encounter life and all his experiences in an open, honest, and effective manner.

Encounter groups have recently sprung up throughout the country. They focus on increasing the awareness, sensitivity, and experiences in the world for all participants. They use techniques involving touching, feeling, seeing, hearing, and other sensory aspects influenced during development, which people tend to forget or misuse. Many participants in encounter groups report a very positive experience, although some increase their anxiety and despair.

RATIONAL-EMOTIVE THEORY

Since there is a general agreement that human beings are able to think and feel about their experiences and that experiences have much to do with the development of human personality, Ellis (1962) has formed a set of concepts that he has termed rational-emotive theory. People distort and misperceive their lives and at the extreme develop ideas bound to make them less effective and perhaps disturbed.

The following paraphrases central principles of rational-emotive theory:

1. Irrational thinking and behaving is a natural human state, and all of us sometimes behave in a neurotic manner.

2. Many people are born with biological problems that life experiences will not significantly alter.

3. The person who behaves abnormally is repeating childhood conflicts to himself and perpetuating his emotional disturbances, rather than automatically following his parents' unfortunate demands.

4. Emotions are closely allied to and are the products of thinking; they rarely have an independent existence in themselves. Emotional disturbances consist of mistaken and incorrect meanings that the individual has acquired, and because of this he feels and behaves in a self-defeating manner.

5. Disturbed behavior can be acquired at any time in a person's life, regardless of the adequacy of the first 5 years with his parents.

6. The idea that some person must be blamed for everything that goes wrong is the core of all human disturbances. To become more effective one must stop blaming himself and others.

7. An individual has the ability to change and conquer his basic hostility.

8. Adults do not need to be accepted and loved by everybody, even though it would be good if such were the case.

9. Unfortunate events in and of themselves do not cause psychological harm to people. It is their interpretation or perception of the events that is of concern.

10. Irrational ideas commonly held by disturbed people include the following:
   a. It is necessary to be loved or approved by virtually every person.
   b. One must be absolutely competent and achieve success in everything if he is to be worth anything.
   c. Some people are evil and wicked and should be severely punished.
   d. When things are not the way one would like them, the entire world is in an extremely terrible state.
   e. Since unhappiness is caused by external events, people have practically no ability to control their own happiness.
   f. It is easier to escape or avoid everyday problems than to face them.
   g. The person's past history determines his current behavioral condition. The person can do nothing to improve his circumstances, for the past will continue to have an effect forever and ever.

COMMENT

Personality theorists may seem to be like the blind men in the fable who attempt to understand an entire elephant by touching and feeling a small and limited part of the animal. Although what they say about the total on the basis of the part may be partially true, none has a completely acceptable and comprehensive viewpoint. Furthermore, when one attempts to combine viewpoints into an eclectic one, there appear numerous discrepancies that are not easily resolvable. Parts of the puzzle are missing and others simply do not fit together well.

REFERENCES AND SUGGESTED READINGS

Bandura, A., and Walters, R. H. 1963. Social learning and personality development. New York, Holt, Rinehart and Winston, Inc.

Cattell, R. B. 1957. Personality and motivation structure and measurement. New York, Harcourt, Brace and World.

Dollard, J., and Miller, N. E. 1950. Personality and psychotherapy: an analysis in terms of learning, thinking, and culture. New York, McGraw-Hill Book Company.

Ellis, A. 1962. Reason and emotion in psychotherapy. New York, Lyle Stuart, Inc.

Freud, S. 1953. Complete psychological works of Sigmund Freud (translated and edited by James Strackey). London, Hogarth Press and Institute of Psychoanalysis.

Maslow, A. H. 1954. Motivation and personality. New York, Harper & Row, Publishers.

May, R., editor. 1961. Existential psychology. New York, Random House, Inc.

Rogers, C. R. 1961. On becoming a person: a therapist's view of psychotherapy. Boston, Houghton Mifflin Company.

Sheldon, W. H. 1954. Atlas of men. New York, Harper & Row, Publishers.

Woodworth, R. S., and Sheehan, M. R. 1964. Contemporary schools of psychology, ed. 3. New York, The Ronald Press Company.

7
BEHAVIOR DISORDERS

✤

We use the term "behavior disorders" for this chapter, and it is in many ways similar to chapters or entire books entitled "abnormal psychology." Behavior disorders, as a descriptive phrase in the mental health field, is relatively new, but we prefer it because it more precisely describes our true area of study. Behaviors may be considered socially inappropriate, ineffective, or self-defeating, which indicates the behavior is at least somewhat lacking in reasonableness and control and suggestive of disorder.

We do not believe science has substantiated disease as a medical concept to be adequate for understanding behavior disorders. There is no doubt of the reality or existence of the behaviors under consideration, but we do not agree that people who behave in an unusual or difficult to understand manner should be termed sick or mentally ill in a highly definitive physical and medical fashion. It so happens that the behaviors usually considered disordered fall into patterns that can be somewhat separated and categorized in the traditional manner. They provide a meaningful starting point for understanding behavior disorders. Nevertheless, by no means should these be considered clear-cut and accurately agreed upon diagnostic labels.

The mental health worker will be working with traditional professional people. Since psychologists, psychiatrists, and others often use the words and concepts of traditional abnormal psychology for diagnosis, the worker needs to be sufficiently conversant with such terms to work with these other professionals. Applying a diagnostic label should inform others of a person's behavior problems, but labeling a person a schizophrenic is often simply that. To describe his behavior problems specifically in terms of what they are and how they developed leads to an understanding of and implications for altering the person's behavior problems.

NORMAL AND ABNORMAL BEHAVIOR

Abnormal behavior has been defined by Ullmann and Krasner (1969) as behavior that so violates a group or culture's interpersonal rules or norms of behavior that it is acceptable for mental health professionals to intervene in the person's life. Therefore, terming a person abnormal is a social act under prescribed conditions. When a person's social behavior creates embarrassment, inconvenience, or damage to others or himself, he may be committed to a mental hospital or other institution, either full- or part-time. Since there are numerous ifs, ands, or buts involved in such social actions, it should be clear that there is no obvious and definite distinction possible between normal and abnormal behavior. Basically, the act of labeling behaviors as normal and abnormal depends on the characteristics of the individual being labeled, the characteristics of the labeler, and numerous cultural characteristics.

People simply do not have mental illness in the sense they have physical illness. A person either has a kidney disease or does not, but one cannot say that a person has or does not have schizophrenia. On the other hand, there occasionally is some utility for conceptualizing a person's behavior as schizophrenic, but he does not *have* schizophrenia. There is a significant difference between having a disease and conceptualizing a set of behaviors with a verbal label for communicating meaning about a person's behavioral condition to another person.

For purposes of understanding disordered behavior, it may be helpful to give an explanation of ordered and appropriate behavior. Marie Jahoda (1958) has suggested six criteria of behavioral effectiveness.

1. *Attitudes toward oneself.* A person is objectively conscious of his functioning and accurately understands and accepts his abilities and limitations. The person knows who he is, where he has been, and where he is going. He does not feel deep and basic doubts about his identity.

2. *Growth, development, and self-actualization.* The person strives to realize his potentialities and does not stagnate in his development.

3. *Integration.* The person has coherence in his functioning and a unifying philosophy of life. He is not overwhelmed by the frustrations and tensions of coping with everyday kinds of problems.

4. *Autonomy, independence, or self-determination.* The person clearly understands himself and obtains gratifications from his dependence upon himself, rather than relying too heavily upon others for support and direction.

5. *Perception of reality.* The person is free from distortion and misinterpretation of events to suit his own needs. He views the world realistically, tests reality, and proceeds on the basis of his best mature judgment. Because the person is free from distortion in regard to himself, he has empathy, social sensitivity, and concern for others.

6. *Environmental mastery.* The person adapts successfully. He has the ability to care and manifest adequacy in love, work, or play. He is able to relax after

work and enjoy freedom of expression in leisure-time activities. His interpersonal relationships are good, and he has a feeling of belonging to a group. His problem-solving behavior is effective, and he feels positive about himself when success is achieved.

It should be clear that legal, religious, and other social concepts have always influenced any set of statistics in regard to disordered behavior. Statements in textbooks involving percentages of the population that can be categorized under mutually exclusive labels simply do not attend to the fact that everyone has problems of living, that these are more severe at certain times, and that everyone probably exhibits all of the behaviors described within this chapter to some degree during a lifetime. Statistical accounts do not sufficiently account for fluctuations in the ability of people to solve their own problems over given periods of time.

For the statistically minded reader who desires numbers in which to place some of his faith, the following may be of some use. In the United States there are at least 1 million people with transient disorders, 10 million with psychoneuroses, 20 million with psychophysiological disorders, 1 million with psychotic disorders, 2 million psychopaths and criminals, 5 million alcoholics, 6 million mental retardates, and 1 million persons with disorders associated with organic brain impairment. The number of drug abusers may be any where from 50,000 or 10 million or more, depending upon whether the usage of marijuana is considered drug abuse, as it is by some writers. The number of children and adolescents with significant behavioral problems is listed in the many millions. All of these statistics should be taken with a heavy dose of salt, for a highly accurate accounting not only has not been done but, in terms of our orientation to the field, is quite impossible to do.

CHILDREN

It has been said that childhood is a nightmare, but we remember primarily the good things occurring during our development. Traumatic and painful events have been forgotten, although they may have influenced our behavior and continue to do so outside our usual realm of awareness. Children develop deviant behavior primarily within the context of unfortunate and damaging family conditions and relationships. These behaviors are usually elaborated in the school, and it is not uncommon for them to first arise in the school situations. Children are also born with physical problems, or they may acquire physical problems during development, that significantly become associated with their behavior disorders. This sometimes functions as a cause of a behavior problem and sometimes as an effect. Children's behavior problems are considerably more flexible in their occurrence, that is, they have not yet acquired a firm and habitual manner of deviant behavior, as is the case with adults. Furthermore, children are less able to verbally relate their problems, and much of their behavior must be understood from the point of view of the observers. We will discuss categories of childhood behavioral disorders accepted by the majority of traditional mental health professionals.

Although children are of the same species as adults, they are much different from adults and have been much less adequately categorized in terms of patterns of disordered behavior. The standard definitions, descriptions, and explanations of childhood behavior disorders are considered useless or at least misleading by some professional mental health workers. Many simply do not use them at all but operate with consideration only of specifically defined problem behaviors.

Fig. 10. Is childhood a nightmare? (Harold M. Lambert.)

Adjustment reaction of childhood

One categorization uses the phrase "adjustment reaction" of childhood to describe the negative reactions of children to immediate situational conflicts. These are considered relatively minor and transitory, being subdivided into habit disturbances, conduct disturbances, and neurotic traits.

Habit disturbances. Habit disturbances include nail biting, thumb sucking, enuresis (bed wetting), inappropriate masturbation, temper tantrums, and other annoying behavior problems. These behaviors are habits that may have been acquired in association with traumatic events. They have been learned and continue to be maintained like any other learned behavior. Many professionals view these behaviors as symptoms or symbolic representatives of deeper and more pervasive conflicts. That is, thumb sucking is interpreted as evidence of unsatisfied dependency needs, nail biting as hostility and anxiety turned against the self, and enuresis as the child's method of expressing his impotent rage against his parents.

While some believe that these actions are symptoms of underlying problems, others believe that they are specific behaviors that have been learned and are, hence, subject to unlearning. The difference is a most important one, applicable not only to these examples but to the majority of the field of behavior disorders. Undoubtedly, all children periodically exhibit problem behaviors during development. They are considered habit disturbances only when they do not drop out from the child's repertoire of responses. A 2-year-old child who sucks his thumb is seen quite differently from a 10-year-old thumb sucker.

Conduct disturbances. Conduct disturbance is a second subcategory of childhood adjustment reactions. The behavior problems are exhibited in social misconduct. A child who steals, hits other children, destroys personal property, is cruel to animals, or otherwise behaves in an acting out, aggressive manner is said to have a conduct disturbance.

Neurotic traits. Neurotic traits are reactions involving repetitive body movements, sleep walking, stammering, irrational fears, or similar behaviors. It should be obvious that the professional often has great difficulty differentiating between neurotic traits, habit disturbances, and the more severe and chronic behavior disorders.

Psychoneurotic and psychotic behavioral conditions to be discussed in regard to adult disorders are also exhibited by children. All or most of the behavior disorders exhibited by adults can be learned and expressed during the developmental period. Parents who evidence inappropriate behavior, unfortunately make excellent teachers for their children. The father who swears and physically strikes out at members of his family often has sons who behave in a remarkably similar manner. The phrase "like father, like son" does not always have a positive evaluation. Professional workers who are having difficulties with a child in school may call the parents in for a conference and be amazed at the behavioral similarity between the parent and the child.

Childhood psychoses

The childhood psychoses are usually categorized as childhood autism and childhood schizophrenia. Much research has been done to differentiate the two, but there has eventuated little agreement or practical utility. Primarily, both psychotic behavior patterns involve the expression of little interest in other people, unusual emotional responses, strange and repetitive mannerisms, self-stimulated thought and speech, and in some cases behavior that appears similar to that of severely retarded children. Behaviors range from considerable apathy and withdrawal to highly uncontrollable and destructive behavior. Psychotic children are very difficult to teach or socialize, and the majority are restricted to institutions or their own homes, usually never attending public schools.

The recent research and thinking in regard to childhood psychosis indicate genetic, metabolic, and physical injury causes for the condition. Although there is some evidence concerning cold and aloof behavior patterns on the part of the parents, this does not appear to be severe enough to cause the children to become psychotic. Indeed, the parent's behavior may be effects of the child's behavior, rather than the cause.

Factor analysis of children's behavior problems

Because of the apparent transitory and flexible nature of most childhood behavior disorders, attempts have been made to identify more stable patterns with the use of the statistical technique of factor analysis. Quay and Quay (1965) and Peterson (1961) have obtained frequencies of occurrence of rather specific behavior problems and the number and severity exhibited by individual children. They have identified four major factors or categories: subcultural delinquency, immaturity, personality problems, and conduct problems.

Subcultural delinquency. Subcultural delinquency refers to behavior patterns that are reinforced by the neighborhood or small group but condemned by the larger society. For example, children may be taught by their parents and sub-cultural group that stealing and fighting are not only allowed but desired under certain conditions, even though the larger society view these behaviors with disfavor. Children in ghetto schools are often reinforced for behaving in ways that would be severely punished in suburban, middle-class schools. It is not uncommon for professionals who have worked in schools located in wealthier sections of a city to be shocked at behaviors permitted by children when they visit or become employed in poverty areas or minority group schools.

Immature personality. The immature personality factor includes the relatively mild behavior problems indicative of retardation in social development. Children who exhibit such behaviors have not been taught to behave in a manner consistent with their current age status. Children are less often referred for mental health services when this pattern is dominant. The children are much more often referred for these services for behaviors termed personality or conduct problems.

Personality problems. Personality problems are characterized by adjectives such as nervous, spoiled, sensitive, depressed, and irritable. The child often expresses feelings of inferiority and may withdraw from interaction with others.

Conduct problems. Conduct problems, on the other hand, are described by words such as temper tantrums, sexual delinquency, hostility, destructiveness, lying, truancy, and stealing. In contrast to the personality problem children, conduct problem children turn their feelings and conflicts outward and onto others, instead of inward and largely against themselves.

These four main factors are not mutually exclusive, and a child usually shows some of the behaviors categorized under each factor on a rating scale. For example, one child may have fourteen behaviors listed under conduct problems, ten under personality problems, and one under immaturity. Another child may be described with twenty-two behaviors under personality problems, four under conduct problems, and two under subcultural delinquency. It is the pattern of behavior that remains most important, rather than a clear-cut diagnosis.

ADOLESCENCE

Adolescence is a bridge between childhood and adult status. As the adolescent stands on the bridge, he strives, wavers, and occasionally regresses. He is simultaneously pushed by his past and pulled by his learned conceptions of his future. The adolescent has three major conceptions—what he is, what he has been, and what he will become. These define his identity, and his integration of them is central to his behavioral effectiveness. The adolescent is quite painfully aware of himself, for he is both too young to be a productive and fully accepted citizen and too old to be a child with the numerous advantages of childhood. Freud has stated that the purpose of living is to love and work, and the adolescent is seriously and often conflictively immeshed in both areas. Behavior disorders that existed in childhood may continue, those for which the stage was set during childhood may emerge, and problems rather strictly related to adolescence and of a transient type may occur.

There are common problems of evolving peer group relationships, dating and preparation for family life, training and skill development for acquiring a means of livelihood, and rebellion and testing of authority figures in regard to societal conventions and norms. However, there are many adolescents who exhibit various kinds and degrees of more significant behavior disorders. These include school phobias, suicide, and a psychotic lack of contact with reality. The adolescent period is often considered stormy and stressful, not only for social reasons but for biological ones as well. The adolescent is becoming physically and socially mature. The period of adolescence may roughly be considered as lasting from age 12 to about age 18, in terms of both social and biological criteria. A person who does not adequately resolve his problems of living during adolescence may have numerous problems throughout the adult

Fig. 11. Peer groups influence adolescent behavior. (Harold M. Lambert.)

years, just as the child with numerous unresolved conflicts upon reaching adolescence will likely have problems during this period. Development is cumulative, never ceases, and each period of learning influences subsequent periods.

School phobia

Within the family and school there is a sometimes painful awareness that the adolescent is becoming biologically mature. Numerous rules and regulations are specified for the adolescent. Obviously, in our society he must attend school and obtain knowledge and skills increasingly appropriate for his adult status. Some adolescents, as well as some children, give highly irrational but adamant refusals to attend school. They give extremely vague or unreasonable excuses. An adolescent girl may unexplainably burst into tears during class, bolt from the room, and return home. Later she may explain that she was afraid her house was burning down, her father killed in a car wreck, or her mother seriously injured. She may further explain that she had to find out if her fears were justified and if there was anything she could do to be helpful in this situation. Her teachers and parents find both the fear and the behavior quite difficult to comprehend. If her behavior is repeated and becomes a chronic school phobia, in the sense that she cannot remain in class but must leave for the some supposed reason, a mental health person may be asked to consult with school personnel in regard to this situation.

Research on school phobias, according to some, substantiates the existence of fears that are actually unconscious and unacceptable wishes. That is, our particular adolescent girl may be extremely angry at either or both of her parents, wishing them ill or injured, but she may be unable to understand or accept her rage. Therefore, she does not admit such anger into her awareness, but it breaks through during inopportune times and she is driven to do something about it.

It is also not uncommon for such school phobias to involve unacceptable feelings and desires in the sexual area. The mental health person may discover that the girl has a crush on her teacher or classmate and, at some level of awareness, may be having sexual fantasies. When she becomes more aware of these fantasies, she becomes very fearful and attempts to escape from the physical vicinity of the object of her feelings. Hence, she dashes from the room but is unable to adequately explain her behavior. School phobias are often quite astounding to those closely and subjectively involved with the person, but they are quite understandable in terms of unacceptable responses that have been stimulated.

Adolescent suicide

Although few children commit suicide, it is by no means a rare occurrence among adolescents. The numerous problems associated with this developmental period causes many adolescents to believe they are incompetent, inadequate, evil, or worthless. They may then turn their anger against themselves and commit suicide either by degrees or in one fell swoop. They may become drug addicts and kill themselves over a period of years, or they may commit suicide directly. Although girls talk about suicide and make more gestures than do boys, they commit suicide less often. Apparently, they are asking for help from others, and their gestures are often of a passive type with prior warning. They often somehow inform others that they are going to damage themselves and choose a means of suicide in which it is possible to intervene. They take poison or cut their wrists, and because of the time span prior to death, another person may discover and abort their actions.

On the other hand, boys give little prior warning and choose methods that are more active and final. They jump from buildings, shoot themselves, and otherwise make actual attempts rather than suicidal gestures. Although they make fewer suicidal gestures, boys are more successful in committing suicide than girls.

Suicide seems to reach a peak during adolescent years at the end of high school and the beginning of college. Suicide is believed to often be the expression of anger toward someone else, which is denied but turned against the self. It has been said that no one commits suicide without first wishing someone else dead. This someone else may be a parent or an important person in the individual's life, such as a girlfriend, boyfriend, spouse, or employer.

Adolescents may also exhibit any of the behavior disorders that will be discussed for adults. They are more similar to adults in terms of their behavior disorders than they are to children. This becomes increasingly true as the adolescent grows older, for he becomes more socially and biologically mature.

ADULTS

The definition of adult maturity and effectiveness in American society is highly complex and varies in regard to social groups and geographical areas. To be fully acceptable to most members of our culture the individual must leave his original family, get married, have a family of his own, obtain a job and continue working in an economically gratifying manner, and exhibit behavior that is within the general norms of our culture. It is a rare or nonexistent person who does not at least occasionally exhibit behavior considered inappropriate, disordered, or disturbing to others.

Adjustment reactions

At some period in our lives, all of us experience very stressful events, such as the death of a loved one, a debilitating illness, loss of a job, or exposure to an extremely dangerous situation. Any of these may necessitate a rapid and effective readjustment of our early patterns of behavior. Many people are able to face these difficulties and modify their behavior effectively with a minimum of distress. However, there are others who do not possess the responses or flexibility in their repertoire of behavior and as a result display inappropriate, ineffective, or disordered behavior, but this is often transistory. The following are several examples of reactions to severe life stresses.

A young soldier was sent to Vietnam. He was a married, college graduate who had never shown disordered behavior of any consequence. To all observers he was as stable as the average person. After being on the front lines for several weeks participating in and observing much combat and the deaths of several members of his platoon, changes began to occur in his behavior. He began to be increasingly irritable, complaining about the slightest inconvenience, sleeping poorly if at all during many nights, and having very bad headaches. He became increasingly withdrawn from social interactions with the other soldiers and began spending much of his time simply sitting and staring into space. He began losing weight and his speech became more and more difficult to understand. When he did talk in a relative sociable manner, the content was primarily related to events in his childhood rather than the stresses and strains involved in being in a battle zone. As his behavior became more disordered, his superiors became aware of his condition and finally had him transferred to a rest area. He did not regain effective control over his behavior rapidly and was ultimately transferred to the United States for the rest of his service commitment. A 1-year follow-up of this individual found his behavior back to normal, and he had apparently reconstituted his functioning quite well.

A young woman was preparing for her wedding day and had sent invitations, selected her trousseau, and otherwise prepared for the ceremony. She had known her fiancé for many years, and the marriage was encouraged by both sets of parents. As the wedding date approached she began having nightmares in which her husband-to-be was killed, and she became very tense and forgetful. Invitations to the grandparents were somehow forgotten, and her anger was easily aroused by the slightest difficulties. She caught a cold and was unable to completely lose it, and she coughed and sneezed for several weeks. Finally, several hours before the wedding she disappeared, and her frantic relatives were unable to locate her. Two weeks later she called from a large metropolitan area and informed her parents that she never really loved her fiancé and finally realized that she could not marry him.

While a young married couple was expecting their first child, the husband became increasingly difficult to get along with. Although he was at first happy about the impending event, he soon stopped talking about it and no longer participated in buying new clothes and furniture for the baby. The couple's marriage relationship deteriorated badly, he began going out with his old friends, and he generally showed little interest in either his wife or unborn child. As soon as the baby was born he filed papers for divorce. After the divorce was granted and he resumed his premarital style of living, he became more interested in his former wife and child. The couple finally entered counseling, in which it was discovered the husband had deep but largely unconscious fears of being supplanted in his wife's affection and attention by the child. After coming to an understanding and some resolution of his conflicts and fears, the couple was reunited in marriage.

A business executive had worked very hard in hopes of obtaining a promotion, which was finally granted. He began complaining of stomach pains and headaches. It became evident that he had been worrying intensively about his abilities to perform in his new position, although his overt behavior gave little indication of his severe anxiety. After receiving support and encouragement from his supervisor, his physical complaints were reduced and ultimately disappeared.

These examples of reactions to stress occur by the thousands daily. The great majority of them are short-term, being resolved during the usual course of living without intervention by professionals in mental health. If they do not resolve themselves or if therapeutic intervention is not made or is not effective, the person may develop more severe and chronic behavior disorders.

Psychoneurosis

Whereas adjustment reactions tend to be acute, indicative of panic, and found in situations of high stress in which the person has no effective responses in his behavioral repertoire, psychoneurotic conditions are more chronic and severe but occur in situations in which most people feel less stress. In other words, there has not been a catastrophic event but only a long-term tension-arousing set of circumstances, and the person is upset. He has learned his behavioral reactions just as other behaviors have been learned.

It is said that the psychoneurotic builds castles in the sand, the psychotic lives in the castles, and the mental health professional collects the rent. That is, the neurotic certainly has his long-term problems but, unlike the psychotic, he has not lost touch with reality. Rather, he copes strenuously with reality events, but he behaves ineffectively.

Psychoneurotics exhibit behavior that can be understood largely in terms of roles. All individuals learn behavior patterns appropriate for given circumstances. The teacher behaves in one manner when he is lecturing but in different ways at professional conferences. The auto mechanic has a set of behaviors he exhibits at home with his family, but a somewhat different role is exhibited at his place of business. The major problem with neurotics is not their behavior per se but the circumstances under which it is exhibited and the difficulty of identifying and understanding contingencies that govern their responses.

Until quite recently the behaviors that we today term psychoneurotic were attributed to the workings of demons or the effects visited upon one for "sinful" misdeeds. Much of our understanding of the psychoneuroses derives, at least originally, from the clinical study and theoretical formulations of Sigmund Freud. Freud noted in his work as a neurologist that numerous patients had no physical causes for their strange behavior. Since the behavior problems were strictly psychological, Freud resorted to psychological means for changing his patients' behaviors. He believed the behavior disorders resulted from unacceptable wishes and impulses. The person used defenses for self-protection, but these defenses were ineffective or highly subject to breakthroughs into conscious awareness. When this happened the person exhibited strange behavior. Importantly, Freud used little terminology from the area of learning.

The psychoneuroses are characterized by repetitive maladaptive patterns of behavior that the individual finds extremely distressing. He is highly motivated to obtain psychotherapeutic intervention, although paradoxically he goes to great lengths to avoid learning about himself and changing his behavior. Behavior disorders termed psychoneuroses are usually not severe enough to cause the person to be institutionalized, although institutionalized patients, who are usually classified as psychotic, exhibit many neurotic behaviors. In our discussion the neurotic conditions will be broadly categorized into the (1) hysterical and dissociated behaviors, (2) the phobic and obsessive-compulsive disorders, and (3) depressive reactions.

Hysterical and dissociated behaviors

Conversion hysteria. A young man enters a drugstore and begins looking over the magazines. He picks up a copy of *Playboy* and while thumbing through it comes upon the centerfold picture of a seminude pretty young girl. He drops the magazine, stares upward toward the ceiling with a fixed gaze, and shouts with terror that he is blind. Most of us recognize that a rapid degeneration of the retina has not occurred, nor has any other physical disability suddenly happened.

Instead, the young man is showing behaviors we term conversion hysteria. He has converted a psychological problem into a physical one. It is important to note that 100 years ago the majority of people might think of this as being strictly a physical problem, not a psychological one. The writings of psychologists and psychiatrists have increased public understanding to such an extent that the majority of people today probably know more about behavioral problems than professionally knowledgeable people 100 years ago.

What function has the young man's behavior served for him? First of all, he has avoided the stress-provoking centerfold, and his escape behavior is understood as a response stimulated by the picture. Importantly, he will also obtain from some people what is termed secondary gain. Since he exhibited this inappropriate behavior, it is likely that his parents have taught him this was an appropriate response, or at least he somehow came to that conclusion as a result of his development within their home. The secondary gain is the sympathy, care, and concern that the parents, in particular, will probably exhibit to him. They will reinforce and maintain escape behavior, which has occurred under circumstances that most of us would find pleasurable rather than frightening.

Hysterical personalities. Hysterical personalities are usually more subtle, do not evidence definite conversions, and rarely show disordered behavior as dramatic as the preceding example. Today such behavior as this and other conversion reactions are evidenced primarily by people with low levels of general education, below-average intelligence, low socioeconomic status, and lifetimes of problems with their parents and families. There is often an element of sexuality and hostility that the person does not find acceptable, or in other words a denial of a significant part of being a biological organism. According to the psychoanalyst, the hysteric also has a strong element of sexual interest toward the opposite sex parent. Learning theory formulations either do not focus on this clinical impression or take a slightly different perspective by conceptualizing the person's problem in a learning history manner. In any case, practically all viewpoints of the hysterical personality emphasize the fear and avoidance reactions that are exhibited in complex and sometimes very subtle ways.

The hysterical personality is also very susceptible to suggestion and under the influence of authority figures can be rather easily persuaded. The notions of placebo and hypnosis are particularly applicable in regard to hysterical personalities. Hysterics are rather easy to hypnotize, and some of the earliest work during the eighteenth and nineteenth centuries was done with people whom we would term hysterics today. If one attends a demonstration of hypnosis in night clubs, he will observe some people quite actively volunteering to be subjects of the demonstration. They are often chosen by the showman-hypnotist to be subjects, for they will be the first and easiest to hypnotize. Since they are highly suggestible, they can be told to perform some of the most outrageous behaviors. The audience finds this highly amusing and marvels at the skill of the hypnotist. His skill, however, largely rests in selecting in the first instance individuals who are the most susceptible to persuasion and suggestion. An authoritative figure can sometimes simply inform them in a matter of fact tone of voice that they are hypnotized, and this is sufficient to make them play the role of the hypnotized person.

Hypochondriasis. Hysterics may become irrationally concerned about their physical functioning, become preoccupied with their bodily processes, and believe that something is physically wrong with them. This pattern is known as hypochondriasis. They may believe they have kidney disease or cancer and find it very difficult to sleep at night because of their concern. While these may be partially realistic fears, their visits to physicians who inform them they are not ill fails to convince them. They simply go to another physician who performs further laboratory studies, and he too may tell them there is no physical illness. Finally, they may either undergo an unnecessary operation because they have found a physician who is taken in by their statements of pain or, if they are lucky, they obtain psychotherapeutic help.

Placebo. The physician himself often gives such help in the form of a placebo. He may be quite vague about the physical condition but prescribe "medication." The patient later informs the physician the "medication" relieved the pain and profusely thanks him. Actually, the physician prescribed capsules with sugar or some other noneffective substance, which is a placebo. He did nothing of definitive significance, but the patient thinks he did.

Hysteria and sexuality. Hysterical personalities not only have problems with the parents during development, but their marriages are often disastrous. Hysterical personalities tend to be female more often than male, which indicates the learned role-playing aspects of the disorder. Women are taught that certain impulses and behaviors are inappropriate, and to avoid and escape such responses on their own part, which they obviously cannot do as long as they are alive, they behave inappropriately. Men are more often given freedom to express these behaviors more directly, since they are taught from an early age that it is admissible for boys and men to be aggressive and sexual. Many are taught that if they do not directly exhibit such role behaviors, they are less than adequate as an adult male in our society.

The following are examples of behavioral conditions categorized as hysterias.

A soldier in Vietnam engaged in hand-to-hand combat with the enemy and ultimately killed him with a knife held in his right hand. The next day the soldier reported he could not move his right arm at all, but a physical examination revealed no physical causes for the paralysis. The examination clearly pointed to a paralysis with no muscular, neural, or skeletal associations. Therefore, the paralysis had to be a result of a thought and feeling process that eventuated in a paralysis as an operant behavior. It served the functions of removing him from the combat area as the primary gain and of obtaining support and concern from others as the secondary gain. It may also have relieved guilt feelings engendered by the killing, since in our culture we are taught to not participate in such activity.

Many people question whether this is malingering or a hysterical disorder. Malingering is the conscious intent to avoid an unpleasant situation, such as when a child reports to his parents he is sick on the day he is scheduled to have an arithmetic test at school. Hysteria is a condition marked by the calm, detached insistence by the individual that indeed he is paralyzed or otherwise incapacitated. Even under intense questioning he does not alter his account, although he still remains highly susceptible to suggestion that his physical disorder will disappear under certain conditions.

A college girl from a rather rigid and fundamentally religious family was on a date with the somewhat notorious lover boy of the campus. He began an attempted seduction by touching her legs, after which she slapped him and pushed him away. The next day she informed her roommate that her legs were paralyzed and she couldn't get up from bed. She was taken to the emergency room of a hospital, but after a physical examination she was informed there was no physical causes that could be ascertained for her paralysis. Her behavior disorder was strictly psychological with no actual physical components. The primary gain, secondary gain, and self-punishment were learned role behaviors similar to that of the combat soldier in many respects. She was effectively removed from further sexually exciting situations, obtained sympathy from others, and made herself feel better for her probable sexual interests by assuming paralysis. She exhibited little overt concern about her paralyzed legs but went to great lengths to inform her roommate and the physician about her problem. Although her verbalizations were replete with details, she showed an unusual lack of feeling and fear, a condition which has been described as "la belle indifference."

Another example of conversion reaction occurred with a famous violinist who had given numerous performances ending with standing ovations. However, he read a very insulting and critical review of one of his performances prior to a scheduled solo concert. Immediately before going on stage he noticed his fingers were numb and rigid. Try as he might, he could not increase the sensation and movements of his fingers to the degree to which he had been accustomed. The concert was cancelled and he was given a physical examination. The results were similar to those noted previously and were understood as an avoidance reaction at a level of awareness that he could not verbalize. There was no stigma attached to the cancellation, for who would find fault with a famous violinist who suffered an immediate loss of ability to perform?

Amnesia and fugue. Sometimes the hysterical personality does not exhibit general and pervasive patterns of inappropriate behavior, nor does he evidence a conversion reaction. At the more severe levels dissociation may occur, which is borderline between the psychoneuroses and psychoses. The person may suffer a loss of memory with no known physiological correlates, which is an amnesia. A highly stress-provoking event may be blotted from the memory, which is one way of avoiding and escaping from the situation. If the person also flees from unpleasant situations, he is in a state of fugue. Amnesias and fugue are sometimes described in the newspaper, as was the following.

A relatively successful middle-aged businessman vanished from his home and business. All attempts to locate him were to no avail and he was presumed dead after a number of years. Twelve years later in a town over 1,000 miles away a man from the missing person's original home town met a service station operator who looked and behaved amazingly like his former friend. Questioning elicited no connections between the service station operator and the other person, but the traveler was not satisfied. An investigation of all records and acquaintances of the missing man and the service station operator pointed out numerous consistencies. The service station operator had arrived in town only 1 week after the other was reported missing. The missing man's former wife and children ultimately visited the town and it was finally verified that they were indeed one and the same. During psychotherapy the service station operator came to an awareness of his amnesia and fugue and began understanding his operant behavior. His relationship with his former wife was not very gratifying, he had seven children with whom he did not get along very well, and his business was beginning to fail badly. Amnesia and fugue resulted, and he had now married a second woman and had begun another family.

When the public reads of such accounts, they suspect a high degree of fraud, and in a sense they may be correct. However, from the professional viewpoint, and in view of the entire behavior pattern, this is understood to be a case of dissociation. Escape from a highly punishing or nonreinforcing situation has occurred. Such events commonly happen in battle zones, as occurred with the young soldier in Stephen Crane's *The Red Badge of Courage.*

Somnambulism. Sleep walking or somnambulism is another kind of dissociated reaction. When the person is asleep and his usual levels of coping are decreased, he may arise from bed and in a trance-like state perform unusual behaviors. Accounts are reported in which unhappy individuals telephone their supervisors at their homes in the middle of the night and give them a good lesson in profanity. The next day the person has no knowledge of his behavior, but often his supervisor has recognized his voice and informs him. This is strongly denied by the employee, but sometimes to no avail. More violent and highly sexual events can occur, but they are very rare. If the sleep walker is awakened, which is usually not too difficult to do, he can easily be put back to bed by a simple statement that he should do so. Sleep walkers sometimes hurt themselves by walking into doors or falling out windows, so this condition should not be considered an amusing one.

Multiple personality. The most dramatic dissociated personalities involve what has become known as the multiple personality. The book and movie *Three Faces of Eve* clearly exemplified a case of multiple personality. A young Southern girl was quite dissatisfied with her marriage to her backwoods husband. She received little gratification from her marriage and in effect was not allowed to respond in ways consistent with her biological impulses. She was a very depressed, constricted, and unhappy person who verbalized little understanding in regard to her predicament. However, she developed an entirely different set of behaviors, in the sense of occasionally behaving with great energy, abandon, and exuberance. She was found by her husband in motel rooms with other men, but his reactions were met by great hostility from her. These two alternating personalities were termed Eve White for the constricted role and Eve Black for the acting out, sexual role. In psychotherapy a new behavior pattern developed, which was termed Jane. This person was neither constricted nor promiscuous but was more stable, realistic, and rationally effective. This person with multiple personality ultimately divorced her husband and was remarried, although there were numerous conflicts and behavior problems yet to be resolved.

Multiple personalities are very rare, but they are highly interesting to both professionals and members of the public. They also show how behavior patterns or roles are learned and how more appropriate behaviors can be learned in place of them. Reinforcement is shown to be as useful a concept with hysterical and multiple personalities as with any other behavior.

Phobic and obsessive-compulsive disorders

Phobias. Phobias are fears an individual has in regard to an object or event that most people see as quite irrational. The phobic person may also believe his fear is irrational, but he is compelled to behave in accordance with his fear. The object or event functions as a stimulus for the person's response, which is an avoidance or escape behavior. Much has been written about the rather strange and sometimes amusing phobias people have, and they are given names with Greek prefixes such as claustrophobia (the fear of being closed in), acrophobia (the fear of height), zoophobia (the fear of animals), and many others. The student should disregard these terms, for they primarily obscure rather than clarify. It is much better to simply state what the person fears.

Children exhibit many phobias, for they are lacking in experience and to a large degree are simply behaving with avoidance and escape in a manner that will change as they gain more experience and knowledge. Many children are afraid of dogs but fewer adults exhibit obvious avoidance and escape reactions to dogs. They may have some realistic fear because, after all, dogs have been known to bite people, even adults. In other words, phobias often have a realistic basis but they persist and may become quite an interference in a person's life.

Phobias are highly susceptible to study in the laboratory. A famous experiment by Watson and Rayner (1920) with a child named Albert is a case in point. Little Albert was a happy child who was placed in the vicinity of a rodent, and he often reached for and otherwise exhibited approach behaviors. They paired a very loud noise with the animal, the loud noise frightening Albert. When the animal was presented, so was a very loud noise. After a number of trials be became tense, cried, and otherwise showed emotional behavior when the animal was presented. The loud noise was dropped out of the experimental situation and only the animal was presented. His phobic reaction to the rodent was clearly shown, for now the previously neutral animal elicited crying and escape behavior. Such direct conditioning of a classical or respondent type probably accounts for many phobias.

Nevertheless, the concept of generalization is often required to understand how individuals have acquired their phobias. Stimulus generalization occurs when objects or events have a meaningful degree of similarity, such that the person does not discriminate well or at all between the stimuli. The person who has a phobia about rats, which is an avoidance response, may also avoid rabbits and cats. All of these animals have four feet and fur and are small. They are in many ways quite similar, and the avoidance response is elicited by all of them. As people develop they acquire verbal labels to attach to objects and events. The label may become a discriminative stimulus for avoidance. A person who has one or a few negative experiences with arithmetic, for example, may attach the word "difficult" to arithmetic, thereafter be convinced that arithmetic is too difficult for him, and avoid situations in which arithmetic skills are needed. Hence, he learns a phobia about arithmetic.

By avoiding stressful and negatively reinforcing events prior to their occurrence, or by escaping from them if he has not been able to avoid them, the person removes himself from the situation. His response rate is maintained by escape from aversive stimulation. Nevertheless, he has also effectively removed himself from the situation and is, therefore, unable to learn that his fears are irrational and that avoidance and escape are not necessary. That is, had he remained in the situation he would at least have had the opportunity to learn more appropriate behavior. This thinking forms the basis for methods of removing phobias to be discussed in Chapter 8. There is no reliance on strange-sounding words and conflicting ideas, and there need not be. Our formulation of phobias is quite understandable not only to professionals but to the public, and there is little doubt that research substantiates the superiority of learning principles for the modification of phobic behavior.

Phobias often lead to self-fulfilling prophecies, which involves believing something will happen and then planning and behaving so that it will occur. Furthermore, events that do not occur because the phobic person was avoiding them can serve as a rationale. An individual who refuses to fly on an airplane may say he is extremely fearful he will be killed. He substantiates his good reasoning by telling others that since he is alive and has avoided flying, he is alive because he has not flown.

Obsessive-compulsive disorders. Obsessive-compulsive disorders may result from phobias, and in a sense they are more severe and pervasive phobias with one highly distinctive characteristic. Whereas phobics, in the simplified sense, merely avoid stressful objects and events, the obsessive-compulsive also attempts to do something about his irrational fears. In effect, there is a kind of spontaneous attempt at getting rid of the phobia by thinking or doing something about it. In many ways this is similar to what behaviorally oriented professionals have them do, but the obsessive-compulsive person is unsuccessful. On the other hand, many obsessive-compulsive personalities achieve some measure of success in attempting to alter their behavior, but these are not well documented and usually do not come to the attention of the mental health professional.

Textbooks of the past usually separated obsessions and compulsions, often into two distinct chapters. An obsession pertains to thought processes, the person being obsessed with an idea or thought sequence. Compulsions pertain to overt behaviors that the person feels compelled to perform. In actuality, obsessions and compulsions are practically impossible to differentiate. One who is obsessed almost always has some compulsion to act.

Obsessive-compulsive behaviors are operants. They are behaviors emitted by the person that are followed by some reinforcement. By definition, if these behaviors did not lead to reinforcement, they would soon extinguish. Therefore, they function to help the person avoid or escape from more stressful stimuli, such as his own thoughts or external situations. They take the place of something else in the person's behavioral repertoire.

Obsessive-compulsive behaviors often occur when the individual is thinking or doing something that he finds unacceptable and that arouses his guilt or negative self-evaluation. He may have been taught that there are strict and clear-cut standards for appropriate behavior and that he must not do or think otherwise. Since no perfect person has yet been found, everyone probably resorts occasionally to obsessive-compulsive behaviors. When one behaves toward a colleague in a way that probably offends or insults him, he may attempt to resolve the guilt by ruminating about what caused him to behave in that manner. He attempts to find good reasons for his behavior, and he goes over and over his rationale until he achieves some degree of satisfaction that he behaved appropriately. Since sexuality and hostility are two behavior patterns with many social rules and regulations taught in regard to their expression, they are often the stimulus events leading to the obsessive-compulsive responses. It may be that hostility is the more common stimulus and that obsessive-compulsive responses are more often exhibited by men than by women.

The following are examples of obsessive-compulsive behavior disorders.

A young wife was preparing to go on a picnic with her family. She was making the house ready for her departure and found she was continually wondering whether she had turned off the gas on her kitchen range. She went to the kitchen several times and checked the knob on the range to be certain it was off, but within 5 minutes she had to return to check it again. She kept wondering what would happen if the range was left on, fantasizing that the house would become filled with gas and ignited by a spark. It so happened that she had much anger toward her husband and children and was not able to express her dissatisfaction with her life style of dishwasher, floor sweeper, and diaper changer. Her obsessive-compulsive behavior is understood as an operant manner of expressing her anger, which she found unacceptable because direct expression would lead to punishment.

Hand-washing compulsions are rather common, with a famous one occurring in Shakespeare's *Macbeth*. Lady Macbeth had been instrumental in the murders of her husband's friends and colleagues, thereby helping him achieve the throne. Thereafter, she was obsessed with the thought of blood on her hands and compulsively washed them to be certain no blood remained. She was unsuccessful in convincing herself that her hands could ever be truly clean again, and as the play continued she became even more severely disturbed.

The rituals and ceremonies that obsessive-compulsive persons perform have their normal counterparts. There are rules and regulations in courts of law, the military, and educational organizations. Students and teachers, defendants and judges, and privates and generals have elaborate rules of behavior. When one deviates from the accepted and mandated behavior pattern, superiors are filled with great consternation and demand that the deviant behave in the conventional manner.

Superstition may be largely understood as obsessive-compulsive behavior. The baseball manager whose team won when he wore the same uniform two games in a row may believe his wearing the dirty uniform has something to do with winning. He associates the two and decides the dirty uniform has functioned as a stimulus for the response and reinforcement for winning the baseball game. He may persist in wearing the dirty uniform until his team loses, which extinguishes this response. Superstitions are begun by quite random reinforcement, but they may be continued far beyond the individual by storytelling and news reporting. These function as methods by which modeling and vicarious reinforcement may occur.

Depressive reactions

Depressive reactions involve verbal statements and general behavior indicative of a lessening of the energy level and slowed activity. The person states he feels bored, without love, worthless, or generally without a desire to live an active and fulfilling life. Depressive reactions may occur when a person loses his spouse through death, is fired from a job, or otherwise loses something of great significance to him. Many individuals place the blame of these unfortunate events upon themselves, deprive themselves of fun, and verbally ruminate about their loss.

This verbal and general behavior indicates the person has lost the positive reinforcers and maintainers of his enthusiasm. To a large degree he is informing others that he needs new operant behaviors and reinforcers, which he attempts to acquire through trial and error. As he begins to obtain positive reinforcement, his energy level increases and he begins operating again in the mainstream of life. It is important to note that the depressive neurotic person may emit much verbal behavior about his unfortunate condition. A danger is that he may obtain the interest and concern of others to such a degree that they reinforce his depressive neurotic behaviors. The listener who is not knowledgeable about reinforcement may serve to maintain the depressive neurotic condition, rather than helping him obtain new operants and reinforcers.

The depressive reaction is to some degree normal role playing. It is believed quite natural and normal for a person to go through a period of mourning when a loved one dies. He is performing the socially appropriate role behaviors in such circumstances. When one is terminated from a job, it is likewise considered normal and natural for him to feel negative toward himself and express his feelings of worthlessness and inferiority to his friends. However, within socially defined periods of time the person is expected to find new operant behaviors and acquire substitute reinforcers. Indeed, this is the usual course of events that keeps the number of depressive neurotics at a reasonable level.

Character disorders, sociopathy, sexual deviations, and addictions

We are including a number of behavior disorders under this section that are different from neurosis in many ways, yet they are not severe enough to generally be understood as psychotic disorders. Furthermore, these behavior disorders are often quite difficult to clearly identify in the sense that the observer has a very adequate perception that the disordered person fits into any specific category.

Character disorders

Character disorders involve behavior deviations that are not marked by a high degree of chronic discomfort, as is the case with the psychoneurosis. They are usually separated into categories of personality trait and personality pattern disturbances. The disorders may take many forms, since it is possible for human beings to behave in uncountable ways that are not effective and self-actualizing. These behaviors are exaggerations of quite normal patterns of behavior and often are simply understood as eccentricities. They develop as distortions during the early childhood years, acquire reinforcing properties, and continue into adulthood. The analogy usually given is in regard to the bent twig of childhood becoming distorted into a leaning tree. As an adult the person may seem somewhat inhibited or impulsive or show any exaggeration of behavior. The following describes common types of character disorders.

The compulsive character is usually neat, stubborn, inflexible, and orderly to a pronounced degree. Interestingly, in certain occupations these may be quite positive qualities, such as in accounting, engineering, and science. Their behavior patterns may be disturbing to others, but they are quite acceptable to the individual.

The hysterical character is often a dramatic, narcissistic, and enthusiastic person who is similar to the child who is "showing off." His self-expression and shallow emotional attachments may be a nuisance to others, but his needs to be attractive and loved are quite acceptable to him. In accordance with the reinforced social roles, more women than men tend to be hysterical characters. They may become famous actors or great artists of many types.

The paranoid character has a lack of basic trust, and he tends to be unusually sensitive to the hostility or criticism of other people. He appears to be quite alert that others may find him imperfect, and he sometimes is more offensive than defensive. That is, he attacks and condemns others as a defense.

The manic and depressive character disorders involve behaviors ranging from depressed feelings to exaggerated energy and motivation. Occasionally these may oscillate. The depressive character seems to always have a cloud of gloom over him, although he is neither highly anxious nor out of contact with reality. The manic character is so wound up that people find him quite unreasonable and overbearing in terms of his activity level.

The schizoid character is a somewhat withdrawn person who shyly avoids interaction. He is usually quite compliant, lonely, and overly sensitive. Although he is a social "lone wolf," he has many fantasies about his abilities to perform, including interpersonally. He is often aloof and secretive.

Other behavioral distortions are here classified with character disorders, since there is little good reason to separate them. They include inadequate, emotionally unstable, and passive-aggressive personalities. These are probably as common as character disorders.

The inadequate personality is one who is generally ineffective in meeting the ordinary demands of life. He continuously shows poor judgment and little responsibility. He may get into few legal or interpersonal difficulties, but somehow he manages to respond to immediate gratifications and thereby not obtain reinforcements occurring only after long periods of responding. For example, such a person seldom, if ever, obtains a college degree, although he may have attended a few classes. Sitting in class for 4 years is simply too strenuous for the later reinforcement, and he would rather be having fun.

The emotionally unstable personality lacks a reasonable degree of self-control and often expresses anger and fear when it will most harm him. His interpersonal relationships are brief and unstable. He tends to be seen as impulsive, unpredictable, and quite childlike.

Passive-aggressive personalities are common, maddening, and rather easy to understand. In our society there is much emphasis on learning to control angry behavior. Many individuals do not acquire sufficient skills in this area and behave aggressively or passively to extremes. The passive-dependent type strikes one as being quite helpless and clinging. He seems to demand continuous support and guidance from others, but there is an underlying hostile attitude toward those who give him such reinforcement. It is as if he has tremendous hostility that he has learned to repress, and instead he behaves in a quite opposite manner.

The passive-aggressive type evidences behavior that seems quite passive but is obviously obstructive and hostile. He has learned that he cannot aggress directly and finds ways in which he can defeat or interfere with activities by becoming quite passive. Students often become this way toward their teachers, somehow managing to interfere with classroom learning situations while simultaneously being so subtle and indirect that the teacher cannot reasonably confront them directly about their passive-aggressiveness. Employees do the same to the supervisor by exhibiting inefficiency, procrastination, and sullenness. Nothing seems to please them. They complain in particular about authoritarian figures, perceiving even the kindest supervisor as a domineering tyrant. The secretary who files all letters under L, to her supervisor's consternation, is another example.

The aggressive type, like other passive-aggressive personalities, is just as fearful and dependent as they are, but the aggression is directly expressed and has a clear defensive quality. He may be quite sarcastic, dependent, and demanding. Also, like the other passive-aggressive personalities, in educational and work groups aggressive persons can be extremely demoralizing to their colleagues and sabotage the most reasonable job functions. Typically, they are dismissed from such organizations, but they are prone to institute lawsuits against their employers for supposed discrimination and unfair treatment.

Sociopathy

Sociopathy refers to behaviors that are usually illegal and highly discrepant from social norms. We categorize them as antisocial reaction, dyssocial reaction, juvenile delinquency, sexual deviation, and addiction. The latter two are included under sociopathy as a matter of commonly being associated with the others. The term formerly and generally acceptable for these behaviors was "psychopathic," but the newer term "sociopathic" emphasizes the social causes and effects of such behaviors. Some theorists believe that sociopaths are just as disordered as psychotic persons but do not clearly show their loss of contact with reality. Their disorder has been characterized as the mask of sanity.

Antisocial reactions. The behaviors expressed by sociopaths categorized as antisocial reactions are quite diverse and heavily influenced by social value judgments. They usually show only a few of the behaviors noted here. The antisocial sociopath does not respond to usual kinds of reinforcement and seems to play his own game of life, which involves rules different from those of society. He often presents himself as charming and effective, for he has a highly developed set of verbal behaviors. However, verbalizations are different from other behaviors, and it often occurs that only after a period of time are people aware that they have been conned by a sociopath. He is very impulsive and has little ability to delay gratifications or reinforcements, often being a chronic liar, but others are able to identify his deceit only with great difficulty. He has little anxiety, guilt, or self-understanding, and he does not profit from experience, tending to repeat his self-defeating behaviors. Many sociopaths would probably be wealthier and generally more successful because of their charm and good presentation of self if they were not sociopathic.

The antisocial sociopath dislikes educational situations because they require a degree of discipline and submission to authority, neither of which he can accept. He treats others as objects rather than as people and uses them to his advantage, instead of developing meaningful interpersonal relationships. He lives for today with little foresight about tomorrow.

Although there is much research in regard to inherited sociopathy, the inheritance is most likely cultural transmitted as learned patterns of behavior. The antisocial sociopath, like practically all other behavior disorders, has learned his role, although there is some evidence that he is less susceptible to conditioning than other people. That is, experimental work indicates the sociopath does not condition as rapidly as others, which is parallel to the clinical findings that the sociopath does not learn from experience. He is unusually oriented toward seeking stimulation and has a minimal tolerance for sameness.

Dyssocial reactions. An antisocial sociopathic behavior pattern is unlike dyssocial behavior, although there is some commonality in terms of the degree to which their behavior is legal or illegal. The dyssocial person may be a quite good father and husband and otherwise show deep emotional attachments to people and organizations. He does not live strictly for himself in a pleasure sense and may often show quite good judgment in terms of achieving his goals. On the other hand, the dyssocial person may be a quite dangerous criminal. Members of organized gangs or groups, such as the Mafia, exhibit illegal and dyssocial behavior. The Godfather, as portrayed in the book and movie of the same name, may request a member of his "family" to kill someone, and the action is carried out quite efficiently. The person exhibits little guilt, for he has learned to accept and follow orders from his superiors. Within his subgroup his behavior is not only acceptable but demanded.

Juvenile delinquency. Juvenile delinquency, which is the committing of illegal acts by children and adolescents, is a concept heavily influenced by varying state laws and local customs. Statistics in regard to delinquency generally refer only to those who have been caught, thereby coming to the attention of legal authorities. Obviously, juveniles from wealthier homes will more often be released to their parents, whereas juvenile delinquents from lower socioeconomic or broken homes will be detained and perhaps institutionalized.

Juvenile delinquents in the past were usually males; females were so termed primarily because of sexual behavior deviating from accepted norms. More recently, young females have been involved in drug usage, burglaries, and other illegal activities, and it is believed they may soon equal males in frequency of delinquent behaviors. Girls are more often released to their parents instead of being institutionalized, for they are considered less dangerous. Many state hospitals, in fact, have maximum security wards for men but not for women. If women's liberation has its way, there may soon be more maximum security wards for women.

Many juvenile delinquents fall into the categories of antisocial or dyssocial reactions, but a significant number are merely expressing their neurotic conflicts. The individual who commits a burglary and leaves a note signed with his name is clearly asking to be apprehended. This is a neurotic disorder and not totally antisocial or dyssocial, assuming the person is not mentally retarded.

Sexual deviations. Sexual deviations are defined by the norms of a particular culture and even cultural subgroup. Every culture has sexual rules and regulations, the United States being no exception. Interestingly, rules and regulations in regard to sexual behavior vary throughout the country and sometimes within regions. Sexual behavior considered quite within normal limits of liberal, suburban Chicago may be viewed with great disfavor by rural, fundamentalist persons in Southern Illinois.

The most common sexual deviations occur among married couples; the wife may be frigid (unable to achieve orgasm) or the husband impotent (unable to attain sexual gratification). These problems are usually strictly psychological. They are learned behavior patterns based on fear and are highly susceptible to modification.

Voyeurism refers to obtaining sexual gratification by looking at others who are sexually stimulating. Men who attend strip shows are considered voyeurs, although they are obviously not as extreme as the legendary Peeping Tom. Exhibitionists are those who obtain gratification by showing themselves to others. It has been said that every good exhibitionist needs a good voyeur.

Fetishism refers to obtaining sexual pleasure from an unusual stimulus. It is exemplified by the male who finds womens garments or other feminine objects stimulating. When women find their underwear missing from their clothesline, it is often a fetishist who has done the stealing. Transvestism refers to obtaining sexual gratification by dressing as a member of the opposite sex. Men who wear panties and bras are transvestites, although it is more socially acceptable for women to wear slacks or men's shirts. In other words, men are more subject to the rules and regulations of society than are women in this respect.

Sadism refers to obtaining sexual excitement by inflicting pain on another person. Men who torture women may obtain a high degree of sexual excitement. Masochism refers to becoming highly sexually excited while being subjected to pain and torture by another person. It may also be said that every good sadist needs a good masochist.

Rape is a forceful sexual attack in which a person fails to attend to probable punishing events after the act or to attend to negative verbal stimuli prior to the event. That is, the person either does not adequately judge the situation or note the probability that he will be severely punished after it. Almost all legally defined rapists are men, most of whom are married and in their early adulthood.

Homosexuality refers to obtaining sexual gratification from a member of one's own sex. Kinsey (1953) has found that as many as 40% of adult males and 20% of adult females have had some homosexual experience. The rules and regulations of society in regard to homosexuality are clearly more punishing toward males than females. Men who go out of their way to attack and physically punish known homosexual men are usually considered latent homosexuals, which means they are protecting themselves from their own sexual impulses by punishing the known homosexual. Female homosexuals are usually considered amusing rather than frightening or dangerous to society.

Clinical work has indicated that much homosexual behavior is a result of phobias learned in regard to the opposite sex. The young man who has been taught that heterosexuality is wrong may begin responding sexually to members of his own sex. Men in prisons sometimes exhibit homosexual behavior simply because the appropriate sexual partner is not available. Apparently, the same occurs with women in prisons and other institutions.

Many homosexuals are quite satisfied with their behavior and not desirous of changing. However, many others are not satisfied and seek counseling for better understanding of themselves in changing their behavior.

Addiction. Addictive behavior is usually divided into alcoholism and drug addiction. The personality characteristics and developmental learning histories of drug addicts and alcoholics are rather comparable, the main difference largely being the chemical substance they find most reinforcing.

Addiction refers to a physiological need that has been acquired as a result of using drugs or alcohol. Over a period of time metabolic changes occur that create a continuing demand for the substance. Psychological dependency refers to the learned reinforcement value the substance has for the person, and it is often quite separate from physiological addiction. The person may crave the substance, but he is not physiologically addicted to it. Abuse refers to an observer's belief that the person is overusing the substance and damaging himself. It is a social evaluation with no clearly defined limits. The obese housewife who takes amphetamines more often than her physician prescribes in order to lose weight may in her husband's viewpoint be abusing the drug.

Drug addiction and abuse are by no means new, although usage of LSD, marijuana, and speed, in particular, are much more common than a few years ago. Marijuana, of course, is a controversial drug. Many would like to have it legalized on the basis that it is neither addictive nor dangerous and is less damaging than alcohol. It is probable that frequency of positive feelings caused by using illegal drugs is matched by the frequency of positive feelings caused by legally prescribed medication. Many anxious and depressed persons with sufficient money can obtain medication from their physician to make them feel better, whereas young and poor people resort to buying drugs from a "pusher" in order to obtain their positive feelings.

Alcoholism, which is a learned operant behavior with reinforcing consequences, and certainly not a disease, also has a long history. Alcohol in quantity is a depressant, but it also reduces anxiety feelings and makes the person feel more adequate and powerful. This reinforcement is sufficiently more gratifying for some individuals than the punishing consequences, which accounts for some people becoming alcoholics. Physiological addiction and psychological dependency often result. Over a period of time an alcoholic may suffer irreversible brain damage and exhibit memory loss and confusion usually found in senile people. A small percentage of alcoholics will exhibit delirium tremens, or D.T.'s, which involve hallucinations and tremors. The hallucinations may be auditory or visual, with the alcoholic both seeing and hearing things that do not actually exist.

The successful treatment of alcoholism tends to occur with two methods, although others continue to be used. Alcoholics Anonymous is often quite successful, and it includes a somewhat rigid set of attitudes and behaviors. Interpersonal support and guidance is a central aspect of the program, and the alcoholic must totally abstain from drinking. The second method is direct behavioral modification. There is a pairing of aversive stimuli with drinking alcohol. This technique may include giving the person Antabuse, which makes him violently ill when he consumes alcohol. More recent techniques based on learning principles include retraining the alcoholic to drink in a socially appropriate manner rather than attempting to teach total avoidance of alcohol.

Psychoses

The psychoses are the most deviant and disturbing behavior disorders. Individuals diagnosed as psychotic by professionals are usually institutionalized. Their behavior is so different and disorganized that they are said to have lost contact with reality, which in our viewpoint means they are not responding to stimuli in a manner other people would. They often evidence delusions (false beliefs) and hallucinations (sensory experiences other people do not have). There are many researchers and theorists who have written about psychotics in terms of the genetic, metabolic, and brain damage determinants of their disordered behavior. Since the great majority of psychotic patients cannot be shown to have such physical causes for their behavior, we will proceed with a learning orientation to the development and expression of their behavior disorders. This is not meant to suggest that some highly disordered people do not have physical causes for their behavior problems, nor that physical treatments are not effective, but our focus is on the functional psychotics rather than brain-injured or physically defective persons. The two major categories of functional psychosis are schizophrenia and the manic-depression. Our discussion will omit certain subcategories found in other textbooks because of the unreliability of the labels and the fact that they are derived from theories with little scientific substantiation.

Schizophrenia

Traditionally, the schizophrenias are categorized into four classic types, although there are several additional categories. One should understand that a disturbed person usually will not readily fit into any of these categories, and if he does, his behavior may change in a short period of time to warrant reclassification. However, on the basis of observed behavior and history, it sometimes happens that an individual does seem to be more like a given type than the others.

The *simple* type of schizophrenia is characterized by behavior indicative of indifference, apathy, and marginal social and occupational adjustment. The person is a loner or drifter, existing outside the mainstream of life. He usually has no friends and does not keep a job for any length of time. Only under psychological testing or intense questioning do his illogical thinking and very different ideas and attitudes become apparent. Otherwise, he simply exists rather than lives, at least in the conception of most people. He may be institutionalized if his behavior comes to the attention of professionals in mental health or the legal authorities.

The *hebephrenic* schizophrenic, in contrast, is highly noticeable. He may find the most everyday occurrences highly amusing, giggle profusely, and behave with ritualistic mannerisms. Since such behavior is so highly observable, he readily comes to the attention of authorities who are concerned about the apparently internally stimulated aspects of his behavior. He uses words illogically and may combine portions of words to form new ones, which are called neologisms. He may be extremely incoherent, irritable, and changing in his mood. In mental hospitals he may find a quiet and rather secluded spot and sit for hours, apparently hallucinating, which the observer understands as talking to himself. Since the hallucinations are solely the individual's private stimulation, the person is indeed talking to himself. It should be pointed out that all people do this occasionally, as if they were attempting to resolve conflicts and rehearse role behaviors appropriate for an impending situation, which may be of a crisis type. Therefore, the real difference between the so-called normal person and the hebephrenic schizophrenic is in terms of degree rather than kind. Even under external stimulation, it is most difficult to get the hebephrenic to attend to external rather than internal cues, whereas if we are privately engrossed in our rehearsals most of us can readily shift our attention from internal to external events.

The *paranoid* schizophrenic behavior pattern is characterized by illogical thinking, delusions, and occasional hallucinations. Hostility and aggression are usually involved, with the person believing others are out to do him harm (delusions of persecution) and/or that he is an exceptionally great and powerful person (delusions of grandeur). It may be that delusions of persecution precede delusions of grandeur, with the person believing that he is being persecuted because he is so grand and great. He arrives at this insight, but it is false.

Paranoid schizophrenics in mental hospitals are often deluded to an exceptional degree, with their false beliefs being held in the most obviously discrepant ways. Not only are their delusions inconsistent with each other, but they are clearly different from reality as perceived by others. For example, a patient may insist that he is the director of the hospital, the purpose of the hospital is to make shoes, he could leave from the hospital whenever he wishes, and the young man now speaking with him will be sent to Mars if he doesn't stop asking such absurd questions. These verbal behaviors may transpire with great rapidity and anger, with the patient failing to attend to actual stimuli in the environment.

There are numerous paranoid characters who are not institutionalized. Many of them are probably as lacking in attention to actual stimuli as institutionalized patients, but their behavior simply has not come to the attention of authorities, or they have somehow managed to avoid the authorities. People who join extreme political groups and spend their days and nights looking for Communists plotting to overthrow the country, or Fascists who are doing likewise, are often termed paranoid by members of the press and public. Their suspicions, distrust, and frantic searching for plotters behind conspiracies are perceived as unusual and deluded by others. Occasionally, such individuals are stimulated sufficiently to respond with action. They may decide some political leader is indeed the evil one who is causing their problems and protect themselves by assassinating the political figure.

Paranoid schizophrenics may arrive at religious delusions, proclaiming that they are the risen Christ or the new Satan. There is an interesting account of three such individuals being placed together, each of whom insisted he was Jesus, which is reported in *The Three Christs of Ypsilanti* (Rokeach, 1964). Their far-fetched verbal rationalizations in regard to why each was the Christ and the other two were imposters make fascinating reading, although each of the individuals continued to hold his own delusion through to the end.

There has recently been a rash of sightings of flying saucers that have not been scientifically substantiated. Nevertheless, some people have banded into groups and are on the lookout for invaders from distant planets, who, of course, are perceived as dangerous and destructive. Slightly paranoid characters, again oblivious to science, decide that the movement of stars has influenced their development and controls the future. They have become "astrology nuts" and have little understanding of the reality stimuli.

Paranoids also become deeply involved in scientific matters, and some of them have the grandest schemes for irrigating the Sahara Desert with water from the polar ice caps or of communicating with men from Mars by twitching their left earlobes. Often their delusions and schemes have a flavor of authenticity upon first hearing them, but upon closer analysis they are obviously delusions.

The *catatonic* type of schizophrenia is most marked by unusual motor behavior, which can be great agitation and movement or severe rigidity of the body. The person may sometimes have parts of his body moved around as if he were a plastic doll, staying in whatever position he has been placed. The catatonic person behaves somewhat like the injured possum, but he can be violent. The catatonic state tends to be of short duration, with the person moving into one of the other types.

The other categories of schizophrenia are less adequately defined and tend to be used as a kind of wastebasket for those who do not fit in those previously defined. The words of the categories exemplify this state of affairs, these being *acute undifferentiated, chronic undifferentiated, schizoaffective,* and *residual* schizophrenia. If the professional labeler does not know into which category the person should be placed, he can pick and choose from these with some degree of confidence.

Since schizophrenic conditions are the most common diagnosis given for admissions to hospitals, and since there is a tendency for such severe disturbances to accumulate, the visitor or employee of state hospitals often gets the impression that schizophrenia is simply a synonym for institutionalized patient. There is probably a degree of validity to such a perception. Furthermore, the very nature of mental hospitals, as discussed in various portions of this book, tends to reinforce the schizophrenic patient for remaining a schizophrenic patient. In effect, there is reinforcement for schizophrenic types of behaviors.

Schizophrenic behaviors can be understood as being like any other emitted behaviors. They are learned on the basis of experience, which may range from reading about what schizophrenic patients' behavior is supposed to be like or from hearing what a deviant relative did to get committed to modeling the behavior of so-called patients in movies. Within state hospitals the patients have an infinite number of behaviors to imitate. They soon become amazingly adept at showing crazy behavior when reinforced for doing so, just as they become very capable of defeating the most well-laid plans of the staff members for altering their behavior.

It is probable that anyone who attempts to cure schizophrenia has set himself an impossible task. On the other hand, if he understands the behaviors as operants with reinforcing consequences, he has a method with which to change the behaviors by changing the consequences of the behaviors. Institutions are bureaucratic organizations, unfortunately, which in numerous ways maintain or exaggerate the deviant behavior of the inmates. Our basic viewpoint is that schizophrenic behaviors are subject to modification, just as any behavior is.

Schizophrenics tend to come to the attention of authorities in early adulthood, although intensive and adequate social histories will usually show a lifetime of unfortunate events with which the individual was unable to cope. He was not taught coping behaviors, or if he was, he may have had constitutional defects that prevented him from learning coping behaviors at an adequate level. It is rare that a single traumatic incident in a person's life is sufficient to create the bizarre responses we conceptualize as schizophrenia. The books and movies that stress a single traumatic event making a person schizophrenic are simply incorrect. Most schizophrenics have a lifetime of failures, few or no people who cared for them at all, no adequate adult model who functioned as a guiding hand, and few general life gratifications. Those diagnosed as schizophrenic are usually of the lower socioeconomic class with few vocational skills and a somewhat lower educational level. State hospitals, in particular, have patients who come from the inner city, the ghetto, and very poor rural areas. All of these characteristics are indicative of a nonreinforcing environment for behaviors considered appropriate in the larger culture and to the middle class mental health professional.

Schizophrenic behaviors are under the stimulation-demand characteristics of the environment, just as so-called normal individuals are, but the atmosphere of institutions often obscures this fact. Many human service workers have had an experience similar to the one reported by Ullmann and Krasner (1969). In one of his early group therapy sessions with patients in a mental hospital, one psychologist attempted to use a rather nondirective approach. He entered the room with a number of patients who sat generally in a circle. The therapist waited expectantly for a patient to verbalize his feelings and reactions, but none did so. The patients remained mute, periodically staring, occasionally glancing at each other, but for the most part all looked down at the floor or gazed absentmindedly out the window. The patients not only did not attend to each other, but they gave little attention to the therapist. Apparently, they were rather strictly attending to self-generated stimuli and were fantasizing away. It suddenly dawned upon the therapist that he was behaving much like the patients, and if an observer entered the room he would have found it very difficult to ascertain any difference among any of the participants. It was, therefore, necessary to begin priming the behavioral pump, with the therapist making verbal statements to and about the group members and otherwise attempting to elicit responses on the basis of stimuli external from each patient. This was far more effective and clearly indicated that the patients had the capacity to attend to reality.

Ullmann and Krasner (1969) point out that the major deficit in schizophrenia is attention. The schizophrenic does not emit the operant of paying attention to the stimuli to which others attend. He emits operants that are not appropriate in terms of time or place, and when direct questions are made he responds in a way that indicates he has not been paying attention. His responses seem illogical, concrete, and indicative of poor social judgment. He is not intellectually impaired, but he simply does not know what is going on and responds with self-stimulated responses. In the schizophrenic this aspect is different from the normal person only in terms of its severity and degree.

Furthermore, observers find it extremely difficult to not reinforce schizophrenic behavior with attention, concern, and statements of advice. The schizophrenic is being reinforced for these operant behaviors, but it is difficult to identify either the stimuli or reinforcers. The observer notes the responses and must unravel the sequence of operants and reinforcers before intervention can be effective. Everything a schizophrenic says and does has meaning in the sense that he is obtaining some gratification or reinforcement. Those who brush aside his statements as being simply crazy and without meaning are actually only indicating their lack of understanding of the individual patient's behavior. Much work has been done in regard to changing schizophrenic behaviors of disorganized thinking, apathy, social withdrawal, and bizarre verbalization. Experimental work has shown clearly the effectiveness of the operant method for modifying schizophrenic behavior.

Manic and depressive disorders

Manic and depressive disorders are characterized by extreme affective or mood states. The person may be either depressed or manic, and he may occasionally alternate between these two extremes. The numerous subclassifications in this disorder will not be reviewed here, since it is often difficult even to identify differences between neurotic depression and psychotic depression. The psychotically depressed not only have an extremely low energy level and feelings of worthlessness, but they sometimes have clear delusions and hallucinations in regard to why they are so depressed. They may run the gamut from beliefs that they have participated in the crucifixion of Jesus to any other possible reason of which the human mind is capable. There is a meaningful probability of suicide in depressed states.

The psychotically depressed generally have a long history of little positive reinforcement, but their psychotic condition is often precipitated by the loss of a highly reinforcing person or event. For example, a person may lose a spouse through death and decide he is responsible for the loss. He becomes quite delusional and believes there is nothing else worth living for. These behaviors are understood as reactions to the loss of major sources of reinforcement that have not been replaced. Therefore, the method of treatment clearly involves finding new reinforcers for appropriate behavior.

Among other individuals there may exist a manic condition. The person has a high degree of elation and activity, perhaps talking loudly and becoming extremely boisterous. He may also be quite angry and engage in violent behavior. He cannot sit still and must respond so rapidly that he comes close to being the kind of raging maniac sometimes portrayed by Jerry Lewis. If this alternates with depression, which is somewhat rare, it can be understood as spontaneous attempts to obtain new reinforcing stimuli. Delusions and hallucinations may also occur in manic states.

Physical treatments of depression, including psychotropic drugs and electroconvulsive therapy, are sometimes quite effective. Hence, it is suggested by some that there is a physical cause of these manic and depressive disorders, which is not necessarily the case at all. This kind of thinking is analogous to believing that since aspirin reduces the pain of headaches, the cause of people's headaches is a lack of aspirin in the bloodstream. Until evidence contrary to the learning viewpoint is provided, we will continue to believe that manic and depressive disorders involve behaviors that are learned like any other behaviors. They are operants maintained by reinforcement, and an important method of treatment involves behavior modification techniques. By no means, however, do we suggest that physical techniques are not relevant or appropriate.

Psychophysiological disorders

There are many disorders that have components from both the physical and the psychological areas. The term "psychophysiological disorders" conveys information that the person is actually physically ill, although there may be significant indications of behavioral disorders that have caused the physical illness.

Whereas hysterical conversion disorders are understood as operant responses, psychophysiological disorders are understood as largely respondent disorders. The psychophysiological reactions are partially a result of chronic and exaggerated conditions of normal physiological expressions of emotion. The person with a psychophysiological disorder is increasingly understood by laymen as expressing psychological problems, and there is an element of humor and degradation in many such perceptions. This is most unfortunate, obscuring the fact that the person is not only truly physically ill, but it is also inaccurate, because by no means can all psychophysiological disturbances be shown as directly and only caused by emotional problems. Cause and effect usually are confounded. Furthermore, such an orientation sometimes prevents adequate physical treatment and can lead to more body damage and even death. Psychophysiological disorders always require the knowledge and skills of the physician, although experts in the mental health field also may be centrally involved in providing services for the person.

There have been many theories and research studies done in regard to the causes of physiological disorders, and, as might be expected, they range from the strictly physical to the strictly psychological, with many combinations between. Hereditary factors may be involved, but they have not been shown to account for any meaningful number of disorders.

Other biological viewpoints stress the concept of body organ specificity. Some psychoanalysts believe that the affected organ system is symbolically related to the specific emotional condition. The body part affected adequately expresses the problems of the person. Others believe that some individuals are born with certain weak organs that then become highly susceptible to disorder because of environmental stress and strain. The person has a kind of physiological Achilles heel.

Physiological disorders include in some diagnostic systems practically all physical problems our flesh is heir to.

1. Skin disorders include dermatitis, which may originate as a physical disorder but becomes quite severe as a result of scratching, which is, of course, a behavior. It may be that in such conditions an operant response has occurred and is reinforced by the care and concern by other people.

2. Musculoskeletal disorders involve the musculoskeletal system and include backaches, muscle cramps, and rheumatism.

3. Respiratory disorders include bronchial asthma and other breathing problems, such as hiccoughs. The psychoanalytic viewpoint emphasizes the asthmatic attack as a cry for help, stressing that the asthmatic has suppressed great needs for dependency and care of frustrations occurring during childhood. During periods of stress, when the asthmatic has a higher need of good mothering, the asthmatic attack occurs. Biological viewpoints stress the frequency with which asthmatic conditions occur in families, believing there is a constitutional respiratory weakness that becomes more severe and that is expressed during situations most people are able to handle.

4. Cardiovascular disorders include migraine headaches, essential hypertension (chronic high blood pressure), and other vascular problems.

5. Gastrointestinal disorders include peptic ulcers, constipation, heartburn, anorexia nervosa (the refusal and inability to eat and keep adequate life-sustaining food), and obesity. It is rare for obese persons to have strictly physical disorders as a cause of their problem. Rather, they simply overeat, according to some, as an expression of their need for love and affection. They have somehow associated the eating of food with the acceptance of affection, and they eat instead of loving.

6. Genitourinary disorders include menstrual dysfunction, possibly constipation, and sometimes frigidity and impotence.

7. Nervous system disorders include vague body complaints and chronic general fatigue.

Physiophysiological disorders clearly involve both body and behavior. In contrast to formulations that stress only the biological or only the psychological causes of behavior, there is an emphasis on the effects of physiological processes and behavior in consort with body functions. Psychophysiological disorders have certain adaptive functions in the same sense that neuroses and psychoses do. The person, if physically sick instead of being neurotic or psychotic, is allowed to have the physically sick role with all the attending reinforcers.

These disorders also may serve the function of protecting a patient from a psychosis, which sometimes occurs when the patient is stripped of his defenses and verbal rationalizations. For example, a young man's asthmatic attacks were clearly precipitated by anger from other people. A friend informed him that his asthma was an indication that he was still tied to his mother's apron strings, could not cope with other people's hostility, and copped out by having an asthmatic attack. The attack functioned to elicit care and concern from others instead of hostility. The interpretation, although having some validity, had a very negative effect on the young man, creating nightmares and a morbid preoccupation about his stability. With such friends one does not need enemies.

Treatment of the physical disorder without psychotherapy will probably lead to a maintenance situation for the physical illness. Psychotherapy is needed in the great majority of psychophysiological conditions to help the person understand himself and his behavior. It sometimes happens that psychotherapy in conjunction with medical treatment leads to a disappearance of the physical disorder.

Central nervous system disorders

Central nervous system disorders can result from genetic factors, injury, diseases, or metabolic malfunction. Any of these can create damage to the central nervous system, and since it integrates and coordinates all behavior, the individual's behaviors can become quite disordered. Severely mentally retarded and geriatric patients usually have a significant degree of damage to the central nervous system, although such damage can only be clearly substantiated by an autopsy, if then.

Mental retardation

The three factors defining retardation are intelligence quotient, social adjustment, and duration of the defect. "Mentally retarded" is a term reserved for those who have had the deficit since birth or shortly therafter, are socially incompetent, and score low on intelligence tests. It does not apply to adults who receive a brain injury and thereafter function at low levels.

Mental retardation is classified by degree of impairment, which include the descriptive terms of profound (I.Q. below 20), severe (I.Q. 20 to 35), moderate (I.Q. 36 to 52), and mild (I.Q. 53 to 69). Most profoundly and severely retarded individuals require considerable care, life maintenance, and supervision from others, for they are generally unable to take care of themselves or function as adults. Some classifications simply term them custodial, although it is clear that behavior modification techniques can be used to help them take care of their physical needs.

With intensive training the moderately retarded can learn academic skills to approximately the fourth grade level. Although they need some guidance and supervision, they can often be equipped to function in unskilled or semiskilled occupations. In educational classifications they are termed trainable.

The mildly retarded are termed educable in educational classifications and can learn academic skills to approximately the sixth grade level. Their social and economic adjustment is often quite adequate, although under periods of serious stress they may become more maladjusted. Otherwise, as adults they are often undistinguishable from the general population. It is said that they are labeled as mentally retarded primarily during their school years.

Physical causes are more prevalent at the lower I.Q. levels, although most retarded children are not severely or profoundly retarded. There are genetic causes for mongolism, Turner's syndrome, phenylketonuria (PKU), gargoylism, cretinism, and microcephaly, among others.

Cases of mental retardation that do not have an identified genetic or biological base are termed cultural-familial. They tend to be less severe and are largely understood as simply being the lower end of the distribution of general intelligence. Cultural factors and learning opportunities are also believed to be highly involved, for children from poverty-stricken and deprived families are overrepresented in this category. Retarded children from wealthy families with high levels of educational attainment tend to have more clearly defined biological causes for the retardation.

Brain disorders

Brain disorders may be acute or chronic, the classification depending upon the reversibility of the damage. Individuals diagnosed as having brain disorders usually show behavior indicative of mental impairment rather than mental retardation. Acute brain disorders result from temporary impairment of brain function, such as occurs from alcoholic intoxication, poison, head injury, and meningitis. It is of relatively brief duration and the person recovers from the disorder. In contrast, chronic brain disorders occur when there is irreversible damage to the brain with consequent behavioral impairment. It can result from syphilis, arsenic or other poisons, severe brain injury, cerebral arteriosclerosis, and the numerous physical dysfunctions from growing old.

The degree of behavioral impairment is not necessarily highly associated with the degree of brain damage. There are many social and personal factors involved. A person may have a very slight degree of brain damage but show marked confusion, disorientation, and instability. Another may have a rather severe degree of brain damage with little noteworthy behavioral impairment. Presumably, differences between such individuals are related to the past histories and current environmental and social conditions.

There has been a significant increase in the number of older people; senior citizens now constitute an increasing proportion of our population. Many become senile as a result of the aging process and exhibit behavior disorders ranging from pervasive childishness to almost complete incapability. They may exhibit much behavior similar to that of both depressives and schizophrenics, and the treatment of their behavior disorders is often secondary to maintaining biological life.

PROBLEMS OF DIAGNOSIS AND LABELING

We have discussed most of the major diagnostic categories used to conceptualize deviant behavior. Many writers discuss other categories and often separate them differently. Most research evidence indicates that the assumptions underlying the process of diagnosing deviant behavior are lacking exceptional validity and reliability. It is important to be aware that the labeling process may have serious detrimental effects upon the individual, with the labeled person learning to behave in accordance with the assigned label. Furthermore, anyone who has ever assessed the behavior of a disordered or disabled person is well aware of the tremendous difficulties involved in trying to accurately obtain information that will enable him to neatly categorize others. A patient or client may show some or all the behavior problems noted in this chapter and be simply impossible to meaningfully categorize. Undoubtedly, the majority of patients show some behaviors associated with several of the classifications, rarely if ever only one of them.

REFERENCES AND SUGGESTED READINGS

American Psychiatric Association. 1968. Diagnostic and statistical manual of mental disorders, ed. 2 (DSM-II). Washington, D. C., American Psychiatric Association.

Cameron, N. 1963. Personality development and psychopathology: a dynamic approach. Boston, Houghton Mifflin Company.

Coleman, J. C. 1964. Abnormal psychology and modern life, ed. 3. Chicago, Scott, Foresman and Company.

Crane, S. 1962. The red badge of courage. New York, P. F. Collier, Inc.

Eysenck, H. J., editor. 1961. Handbook of abnormal psychology. New York, Basic Books, Inc., Publishers.

Jahoda, M. 1958. Current concepts of mental health. New York, Basic Books, Inc., Publishers.

Kessler, J. W. 1966. Psychopathology of childhood. Englewood Cliffs, N. J., Prentice-Hall, Inc.

Kinsey, A. C., Pomeroy, W. B., Martin, C. E., and Gebhard, P. H. 1953. Sexual behavior in the human female. Philadelphia, W. B. Saunders Co.

Peterson, D. R. 1961. Behavior problems of middle childhood. Journal of Consulting Psychology 25:205-209.

Quay, H. C., and Quay, L. 1965. Behavior problems in early adolescence. Child Development 36:215-220.

Rokeach, M. 1964. The three Christs of Ypsilanti. New York, Alfred A. Knopf, Inc.

Telford, C. W., and Sawrey, T. M. 1967. The exceptional individual: psychological and education aspects. Englewood Cliffs, N. J., Prentice-Hall, Inc.

Thigpen, C. H., and Cleckley, H. M. 1957. The three faces of Eve. New York, McGraw-Hill Book Company.

Ullmann, L. P., and Krasner, L. 1969. A psychological approach to abnormal behavior. Englewood Cliffs, N. J., Prentice-Hall, Inc.

Watson, J. B., and Rayner, R. 1920. Conditioned emotional reactions. Journal of Experimental Psychology 3:1-14.

8
TECHNIQUES OF BEHAVIOR CHANGE

❧

We use the term "techniques of behavior change" to designate numerous methods for altering behavior. Some of these techniques are designed specifically for use with disordered behavior, although many others can be applied to the modification of behavior whether it is labeled deviant or not. After presenting key ideas in this area, we will give examples of each technique.

Psychotherapy is not a branch of life

Psychotherapy, which is the traditional term for attempts to change the behavior of an individual or group, is a very recent development in its systematic form. People have managed to survive the horrors of war, pestilence, famine, and man's inhumanity to man for centuries without the aid of psychotherapy, relying solely on themselves, their peers, or an occasional magician, sorcerer, or priest for altering their deviant behavior. It should be clear that formal psychotherapy as a technique is not a necessary condition for behavioral change or the continued existence of an individual, despite the quality of the distress in which he finds himself.

Deviant behavior often decreases in the absence of any formal attempt at therapy. Human service workers have sometimes found it necessary to limit the number of disturbed individuals whom they treat. In later following up some of these untreated cases in order to institute a therapeutic program, it is often found that the client for whom services were initially unavailable is no longer in need of those services. He has somehow managed without the aid of formal treatment to come to some workable resolution of his problems. Although efforts at behavior change can be helpful in speeding the return of an individual to a normal life pattern and easing the stress he experiences, it is a tribute to the adaptive capabilities of the human organism that an individual may, without intervention of a systematic therapeutic sort, continue to lead a satisfactory life.

165

Physical and behavioral science

An understanding of both the physical and behavioral sciences is essential if one is to adequately understand the behavior of an individual. Nevertheless, the importance of the role of the physical in this understanding process has been grossly overemphasized. The medical model of mental illness as a vehicle for understanding deviant behavior has until this decade been the major force governing the design of therapeutic programs. In terms of improvement in the humanitarian aspects of treating deviant behavior, this orientation has been immensely helpful. However, time and again it has been noted that this orientation has not led to innovative and effective treatment methods.

Conflicts and compatibility. With the refinement of principles of learning and nonmedical perspectives on psychotherapy, the dominating influence of the medical model has lessened. The reduction of this influence is primarily a result of the documented improvement in therapeutic effectiveness that has accompanied the emergence of nonmedical treatment methods. Conflict has arisen, nevertheless, between those whose primary area of expertise is the physical functioning of the organism and those who are concerned primarily with the individual as a behaving organism.

The medical orientation toward deviant behavior, which is herein termed mental illness, commonly assumes that deviant behavior is simply symptomatic of some underlying pathology that can be ultimately understood in biological terms. Sociological and behavioral orientations to deviant behavior, on the other hand, have refuted the notion that such behavior can be adequately understood in terms of biological dysfunction. It is pointed out that the idea of an underlying cause of deviant behavior, whether hypothesized to exist in the biological structure of the individual or his underlying personality, has limited usefulness for treating deviant behavior. We have noted previously that deviant behavior can be understood as a function of the principles governing the individual, both as a biological and as a behaving organism.

Much of the conflict in mental health work results from the tendency of various professions to view their orientation to deviant behavior as the only correct system upon which an effective means of treatment can be based. It can be shown that some forms of behavioral disturbance result directly from biological dysfunction. However, it has also been demonstrated that the great majority of behavioral disturbances are not understood or effectively treated from a biological viewpoint. Mental health people may be united in their orientation toward helping others in distress, but they sometimes divide themselves into hostile factions to prove by vote or dogma that their one particular orientation is correct. Compatibility is yet to be achieved.

Practicing psychotherapy without a license. As a result of the long-standing tradition of medical treatment for deviant behavior, training programs have tended to follow traditional models of medical education. It has been assumed that many years of extensive education and supervised experience are necessary to produce an individual who can engage in the treatment of disordered behavior. In several states there has been controversy in regard to legislation that allows individuals without medical training, such as psychologists and social workers, to engage in the practice of psychotherapy. Typically, it has been argued they should not be allowed to practice psychotherapy, because deviant behavior is mental illness and clearly a medical problem. Fortunately, enough research has been completed to show that medical training is not necessary and is largely irrelevant for the treatment of deviant behavior. In most areas of the United States professionals without a medical degree but with sufficient training can provide psychotherapeutic services, after being duly examined and licensed through state boards.

Psychotherapy is defined as an attempt to change the social behavior of another individual or group, and it encompasses a very broad range of activities and perspectives. Everyone studies the behavior of others, hoping to discover behavioral antecedents and alter the behavior by changing its consequences. The mental health technician is one who is likely to experience some hostility from other professionals in the field of mental health, partly because his training generally does not follow traditional lines. He is not licensed by state boards in mental health technology, although in a few states the nursing profession provides him licensure. Thus, the technician may sometimes be made to feel that he is practicing psychotherapy without a license. The technician should recognize that psychotherapy is not the sole domain of any one professional group. Traditional methods learned from long-term professional programs are not the only way in which one can become an effective agent of behavior change.

TRADITIONAL DIRECT METHODS

Traditional direct methods of behavior change unfortunately are often overlooked because they are so obvious. They are discordant with the viewpoint that psychotherapy is an esoteric form of magic. Typically, they are not defined as psychotherapy by traditional mental health professionals. Since direct methods have as their goal some form of behavior change, they can legitimately be considered psychotherapeutic activities if they focus on social behavior. Even if the direct method emphasizes academic or vocational behavior, improved social behavior often results.

Education

One of the most established and comprehensive social institutions designed to facilitate changes in behavior is the educational system. Educational systems are formulated to provide training for skills in academic, vocational, and social areas. The job of the public schools is to alter behavior, and beyond the family they generally have the most significant effect of any social institution.

When a child first enters school he is both physically and socially incapable of functioning independent of parental support. He can neither read nor write and has no marketable job skills. He has little idea of the structure of the various institutions of the society or of how he must relate to others. As he matures, the educational system provides him with these skills. In dealing with individuals who display deviant patterns of behavior, it is not at all unusual to find that they have experienced many educational problems. For a variety of reasons the person may not have acquired adequate education or may have learned inappropriate ways of behaving within the educational system.

Some human service agencies employ the services of professional educators in order to bring the level of the client's educational skills to a satisfactory level, and sometimes to compensate for negative experiences within the educational system. The activities of educators in human services include comprehensive evaluations to determine the present level of individual educational functioning, individual instruction in areas of particular difficulty, and preparation of the patient for completion of high school or other equivalency examinations. An educator in a mental health agency might evaluate a client and discover that he has few academic skills beyond the second or third grade level and that special areas of difficulty include arithmetic and reading. The educator would operate on the basis of his evaluation of the individual's level of intellectual capacity and design a program to compensate for areas of difficulty and specific learning disabilities. Depending upon the educator's assessment of the educational potential of the client, this program may have a variety of goals. If the individual is thought to have a relatively low intellectual capacity, the program may be designed to simply provide the basic skills in reading, writing, and arithmetic necessary for the individual to function in our society. If the individual is thought to have exceptional educational potential, the objectives may include the attainment of a high school equivalency certificate and specific preparation for college work.

Rehabilitation

Rehabilitation has some similarity to education, for it directly instructs the individual in skills for living. However, the rehabilitation therapist more often deals with people who have concrete physical problems, such as central nervous system damage as a result of an automobile accident, or who have experienced a decrement in social functioning associated with institutionalization. One emphasis the rehabilitative therapist has is concern with returning the individual to his former level of competency.

Rehabilitative therapies programs usually include professionals of varying educational backgrounds whose training enables them to deal with specific problem areas of the client. There may be staff members whose specialty is the evaluation of current job skills and potential for employment. This part of rehabilitative therapy may include job assignments such as industrial or occupational therapy. This is done to give the client an opportunity to learn and maintain good work habits, such as promptness and efficiency, give him experience in a specific job, or evaluate his capability for performing similar types of tasks.

Rehabilitative therapists also include specialists in the areas of speech and hearing and visual, perceptual, and motor skills. These specialists are generally concerned with identifying specific problems and developing a course of treatment for overcoming these deficits. For example, a speech and hearing therapist would assess the vocal and auditory abilities of the client and design a program of therapy to help compensate for any defects that are discovered. The physical therapist, dance therapist, and music therapist often undertake similar assessment activities to determine the overall level of perceptual-motor functioning of the client. To treat problems discovered through their assessment, these specialists use techniques such as dancing, playing music, physical manipulation of body parts, and a variety of other methods to help the client, both physically and behaviorally.

One focus of the rehabilitation therapist is neurophysiological. The rehabilitative therapist works to correct or compensate for a defect in the physical structure of the individual and he plays an important role in the treatment of individuals recovering from nervous system damage. He also is involved in the treatment of individuals who may have less specific neurophysiological problems.

It is assumed by some mental health professionals that a diagnosis indicating the presence of some central or peripheral nervous system damage means that nothing of substance in the way of psychotherapy can be done for the client. This is a false assumption and often reflects nothing more than the narrow scope of training that many traditional mental health professionals have experienced. Although some nervous system problems can never be repaired, in many cases rehabilitative therapists are able to effectively return an individual to a more normal level of behavioral functioning.

Remotivation

Remotivation is a technique primarily used in mental hospitals to help the individual return to the outside world after a period of institutionalization. It is designed to make the individual aware of the environment outside of the institution and arouse a spark of curiosity and interest in the world, which may have been lost.

Remotivation is largely a group activity conducted along lines quite different from other forms of therapeutic groups. Such a group attempts to remotivate and renew the individual's interest in the world by working with the unwounded areas of the patient's personality. Through group discussion of topics brought up by the leader and examination of various interesting objects from the outside environment, such as seashells, unusual foods, or interesting artifacts, it is expected that the clients will begin to experience a renewed interest in the outside world. The thrust of the remotivation group is stimulation of the client by giving him something to think and talk about besides his troubles. It primes the behavioral pump by making the client more aware of his environment.

Remotivation has been found to be a very successful technique in the treatment of chronic, severely disturbed behavior. It takes some of the dullness and drabness out of institutional life, enables the client to again come in contact with external reality, and facilitates the development of a good relationship with the leader and the group members.

Environmental modification

Sometimes in working with an individual it becomes obvious that the most reasonable solution to his problems will involve modification of the environment in which he lives. Such modification may take several forms. The most direct forms of environmental modification include those that can be undertaken by the individual himself, such as escape or avoidance of troublesome situations. Direct attempts at environmental modification include efforts by the human service worker, the client, or both in changing the behavior of others to have a favorable influence on the client. One may have found through many years experience that he is incapable of dealing effectively with his relatives with whom he lives. Depending on the circumstances, he might well be advised to simply remove himself from the situation. Another individual, rather than leaving, might utilize the services of a human service worker in helping to confront his relatives with the way he feels and work toward an acceptable solution without leaving. In both these cases the effort at modification is very direct. Either the individual removes himself from the situation or something concrete and specific is done to change the behavior of others so the client can function normally.

INDIRECT METHODS

Indirect methods of behavior changes are distinguished from the traditional direct methods and the methods discussed in the following section by the fact that they are concerned with bringing about a change in overt behavior through the subtle manipulation of verbal symbols. Verbal interaction between the client and the therapist is used to bring about a resolution of the problems or conflicts involved in the behavioral disturbance. This method of therapy in its more systematic form began in late nineteenth century Europe as the talking cure, primarily resulting from the work of those who first discovered and described hypnosis and the profound effect that this procedure could have on behavior. Hypnosis has had a central role in the history of psychotherapy, although it is often conceptualized as a placebo.

The term "placebo effect" has been used to describe the results of hypnosis and some attempts at psychotherapy. The placebo effect refers to the fact that in many cases, no matter what procedure is followed, the result is some positive effect. Researchers in industrial settings have provided working conditions that will optimize production and found that many kinds of changes stimulate production. One may attempt to change behavior through forceful persuasion or more passive means, such as simply listening to what the other person has to say without offering suggestions. In both these cases a positive effect may follow, with the client reporting he feels better.

The placebo effect is often seen when dealing with a client whose primary need is for some attention from a person of status, power, or prestige. He probably has few friends and no one in whom he feels he can place trust and confidence. The mental health worker may function as a sort of professional friend to this individual. "Placebo effect" describes the fact that no matter what specific form the friendship takes, the effect likely will be positive. The individual will begin to feel better in spite of goals and techniques being vaguely stated.

The placebo effect is the result of specific characteristics of the client and his problem. Although many different forms of psychotherapy may have positive effects, this does not mean that psychotherapy is simply a placebo. Traditional indirect methods are sometimes criticized on these grounds. The placebo effect is not limited to traditional methods and should not by any means be considered an indictment of the effectiveness of psychotherapy. Indeed, it is suggested we should make maximum use of the placebo effect. Numerous research studies also have demonstrated that certain types of psychotherapy are effective as behavior change methods, rather than simply as a placebo effect (Eysenck, 1966).

Psychoanalysis

Psychoanalysis originated from the work of Freud and Breuer on the treatment of hysteria. Freud discovered that the effects of hypnotic treatment of this disorder were transitory and, while working with this problem, developed the methods of psychoanalysis. These methods are oriented toward resolving subconscious conflicts, which he believed were responsible for the disorder (Freud, 1943). Classical psychoanalysis has some unique components and others that are held in common with several systems of therapy.

The functioning of the therapist is one of the most important aspects of psychoanalytic treatment. In the course of training the psychoanalyst, it is traditionally required that the student-therapist undergo analysis himself. This didactic analysis is necessitated by the existence of transference and countertransference. Transference refers to the interpersonal process between analyst and client during psychoanalytic treatment, which is similar to stimulus generalization. The client identifies the therapist as a part of his on-going life problems and transfers onto him much of the feelings associated with these problems. These are primarily of the parent-child type, usually the client relating to the analyst as if he were his father. Psychoanalysts generally agree that it is the presence of the transference relationship that makes possible the resolution of subconscious conflict. The client's problems developed during his early years and were repressed. The father-figure analyst reactivates the conflicts originally acquired in association with the parents and thereby enables the client to begin to understand himself. However, if the therapist has not himself undergone analysis, it is highly probable that he will develop interfering feelings toward the client, with the therapist investing and projecting much of his own personal ideas, beliefs, and feelings as if the client were his child.

This latter phenomenon is known as countertransference, and it is thought to be an inhibiting factor in the therapeutic relationship. In order to minimize the effect of counter transference, the analyst-in-training is required to undergo personal analysis. This minimizing or at least awareness of countertransference results in a particular pattern of behavior in the psychoanalytic therapist.

During an analytic session the psychoanalyst attempts to objectively understand his own feelings about the client and experience and analyze the client's statements and relationship to the therapist. The psychoanalyst often will say very little during therapy. The client may recline on a couch or be seated in a very comfortable chair with the analyst sitting behind him. A principal way in which the therapist openly communicates with the client is through interpretation. Interpretation is the therapist's expressed integration of the symbolic content or meaning of the client's statement. Interpretation in analytic therapy is largely based upon the technique of free association, the client stating whatever comes to mind with limited conscious control over the stream of thought. Dream interpretation is also often employed.

Psychoanalytic therapy in the traditional sense is a long process, sometimes spanning several years before conclusion. Although recently the techniques and success of the analyst have received much criticism from psychotherapists committed to the application of learning principles in therapy, this technique may be very beneficial to some. It holds greatest potential for those who can afford it, for quite intelligent and rather young adult patients, and for neurotic patterns of behavior. It appears much less effective with individuals of average or lower intelligence, for those from lower socioeconomic background, or for those who display psychotic patterns of behavior.

Although analysis may be very helpful with specific individuals, expertise in this technique requires years of training. Treatment is a long and expensive process, and traditional psychoanalytic treatment is rarely provided by government funded agencies. The payoff does not seem to justify the investment in many instances.

Client-centered counseling

Client-centered counseling, as originated by Carl Rogers (1951), concentrates on providing the individual with a situation in which he can discuss his innermost feelings openly and without fear of retribution. Rogers believes that deviant behavior largely results from an individual placing conditions of worth on himself based on his behavior. There are certain behaviors that lead the individual to positively evaluate his worth as a human being. However, there are other behaviors that lead to negative self-evaluation. The presence of conditions of worth leads to neurotic behavior. A condition of worth results from the individual having received only conditional positive regard during his development. Conditional positive regard refers to others making their positive evaluation of a person's worth dependent upon certain behavior. For example, a parent who only expresses affection toward his child when he is doing what the parent feels is appropriate and who withdraws affection and berates the child as a bad person when he behaves inappropriately is imposing conditional positive regard. The conditions of worth that an individual learns to apply to himself as the result of experiencing only conditional positive regard are the targets of the client-centered therapist. The therapist attempts to communicate a feeling of unconditional positive regard to the client. Unconditional positive regard refers to the perception by the individual that he has positive values as a human being independent of his behavior. The therapist may not value the person's behavior, but he values the person.

Carkhuff (1972) has further studied the methods of client-centered counseling and identified several factors important in the course of therapy. The term "client-centered" pertains to the behavior of the therapist, who imposes minimal structure on the conversation of the client and attempts to respond by reflecting the feelings of the client in respect to his current predicaments. Carkhuff has found that the qualities of accurate empathy, warmth, and genuiness in the therapist are positive assets. The degree to which the therapist communicates to the client that he is respected as a person (warmth), that his feelings are correctly understood and to some extent experienced by the therapist (empathy), and that the therapist is genuinely interested in the client and is honest in his conversation (genuineness) increases the probability that therapy will be successful. Carkhuff has developed specific procedures for training individuals in what he calls "the art of helping." The behavior of a helper-therapist who has received Carkhuff type training is very similar to that of the client-centered therapist and by no means highly different from that of therapists of many other theoretical persuasions.

Many psychotherapists have hypothesized that the communication of attitudes such as warmth, genuineness, and empathy is a necessary condition for successful therapy, regardless of the theoretical school of psychotherapy that the individual practitioner endorses. Whether or not an individual is receiving client-centered counseling or rational-emotive psychotherapy, successful therapists are communicating similar feelings to the client. Basically, this feeling that is communicated can be described as unconditional positive regard (Rogers, 1951), referring to the client's feeling that the therapist respects him as a human being and is interested in him as a person. Once this feeling is established in a client it becomes easier for him to talk freely with the therapist about his personal feelings without fear of retribution or rejection. Often the idea of unconditional positive regard becomes confused with the idea of condoning inappropriate, antisocial, or criminal behavior. This should not be the case. While discussing with an individual some antisocial act, such as a robbery or vandalism, the therapist should carefully avoid communicating to the client the approval of such action. The therapist should let the client know that he understands the feelings associated with the act and that these feelings are not morally reprehensible and are, in actuality, perfectly acceptable.

The communication of feelings of positive regard to the client is especially important in the initial interview or contact. It is at this time that the client learns either that the therapist understands him, accepts him, and wants to help him or that the therapist is no different than the many other representatives of the agency or institution who have only been interested in him as a patient, in this sense as only an object to be questioned and analyzed. This is the time when both the client and therapist are sizing each other up. The client and the therapist will both come away from this initial meeting with very definite feelings about each other in terms of how well they can work together or whether or not they want to work together at all. It is of utmost importance that the therapist make it as easy as possible for the client to express his feelings, both about himself and about the therapist. The lines of communication must be kept open if each is to get an accurate picture of the other. The easiest and probably the most effective way to accomplish this goal is for the therapist to attend to the feelings expressed by the client during his conversation, rather than strictly to the actual content of what he is saying. Attending to the feeling

Fig. 12. Open exchange in counseling. (EPA Newsphotos, Editorial Photocolor Archives.)

means interpreting to the client the therapist's perception of how the client is feeling at the moment about what he is saying, the significant others in his environment, his present condition, and, most important, the therapist himself. These interpretations must be given in an open, relaxed, and nonjudgmental manner if the client is to really feel positive regard and begin to trust in the therapist.

However, this task is often made very difficult for the therapist by the intrusion of his own feelings into the conversation. These obstructive feelings in the therapist may be described as pressure or anxiety and may result from a number of attitudes that the therapist holds concerning his role in the therapy situation. These ideas and attitudes include, but are not limited to, the following ones.

The therapist may feel that he has an obligation to "keep the conversation going." In many cases the therapist feels obligated to keep the client talking, especially when there has been a silence of some duration. The therapist may feel that he is somehow a failure if the client is silent, and this fear of failure may cause the therapist to impose questions or topics of conversation that are unrelated to the true concerns of the client.

The therapist may feel an obligation to "cheer the client up" when the client is discussing negative events or feelings. This may take the form of trying to point out something positive in the client's present situation with the hope of making him feel better. These attempts may be motivated by fear or failure on the part of the therapist. Many individuals seem to feel that if they do not make the client feel better right away, they have failed as therapists. These attempts may also be motivated by personal problems the therapist has experienced that are similar to those of the client, thus leading the therapist to avoid discussion of these topics by offering the client a brighter picture of the events, even though it is not congruent with the feelings of the client.

The therapist may avoid answering any of the questions the client asks him. Questions may be avoided through the use of some reflective maneuver, such as a statement like: "It is really important for you to find out the answer to this." After making a statement such as this the therapist may continue to refuse to answer the client's question. Sometimes the client is asking for more than a simple answer and may be telling the therapist something quite important. In these cases it may be important to focus only on the feelings associated with the question. However, there are many instances in which the client will ask a question, such as: "How are you going to be able to help me?" or "What are your qualifications?" These deserve and demand an immediate and honest reply from the therapist. The client has a right to know just what the qualifications of the therapist are and how it is possible for him to be of help. In avoiding questions such as this the therapist may be reacting to his own feelings of inadequacy and the fear that the client will reject him as a therapist. This avoidance of legitimate questions through the use of reflective interpretation will often leave the client feeling that there is something very wrong with him and that the therapist really does not understand him.

The therapist may feel that he must at all costs find out "what the problem is." This effort is most apparent in an interview that is conducted along the lines of an interrogation rather than a conversation. The therapist may continually bombard the client with questions and leave him feeling somewhat like a bug on a pin under a microscope. These attempts are also often motivated by fear of failure in the therapist. This usually takes the form of feelings of inadequacy in the therapist when he is not able to report the specific conflict that has led to the client's emotional disturbance.

The therapist may feel that he must offer the patient a concrete solution of his problem. This attempt will usually be sabotaged by the client or answered by the statement: "Yes, but I have already tried that," thereby leading the therapist to continue posing further solutions rather than to concentrate on the feelings of the client. These efforts to propose solutions are often the result of the therapist feeling that he has to "help" the individual and that the only way to do this is to tell him what to do. Telling a client what to do is probably of little benefit, and it tends to create dependency or gives the client the feeling that the therapist really does not understand.

Finally, the therapist may force the client to remain in the interview for a specific length of time. This time period is usually predetermined by the therapist in the absence of the client. During the interview this may lead the therapist to ignore messages from the client that represent requests to leave the situation and give the client the feeling that the therapist really does not care about him. This also may be motivated by fear of failure on the part of the therapist. The therapist may feel that if the client wants to leave the interview it will mean that the client does not like him and that he therefore is not a good therapist.

It is important to be aware of these problems and styles of communication and to avoid them during initial contact with a client if he is to feel understood and valued by the therapist. One of the most effective methods of improving communication with a client is to utilize the talents of one's fellow workers in analyzing the content of conversation in therapy. Probably the easiest way to do this is to tape record individual therapy sessions and play them back, using another individual as a critic. Another method is to have someone sit in or observe therapy while it is actually in progress and discuss the session following its close. The single most important question that should be asked in reviewing the therapy is: "Why did I say that?" To answer this question the therapist should be able to report specific behavior of the client that led the therapist to make the statement. The answer to this question should be based solely on the behavior of the client and not reflect a reaction to the therapist's own internal state. In other words, in answering the question: "Why did I say that?" the only satisfactory reply is one based upon the behavior of the client. Any reply that includes or is based upon the feelings of the therapist about himself as a consequence of the behavior of the patient is indicative of poor communication between the therapist and client.

This does not mean that at other points in therapy any of the styles of communication discussed in the preceding six points are inappropriate. For example, it may be determined that it will be of benefit to the client to focus directly on the conflict that has led to his seeking treatment and that the best way to do this is the use of an interrogative style by the therapist. It could also be the case that specific suggestions as to solutions to the conflict should be given by the therapist. However, at later points in therapy the decision to use any one of these styles should be a rational one based on observation and consideration of the responses of the client. It is important to differentiate this rational decision from the use of these techniques by the therapist when they are motivated by such feelings as fear of failure or the need to be liked by the patient. In these cases the decision is not based on rational consideration of the client's need but rather on the feelings and attitudes of the therapist toward himself. This will most likely lead to mistrust on the part of the client and a general slowing down of therapeutic process. If it is possible for the therapist to avoid these styles of communication during the initial therapeutic interview and focus on letting the client know that he and his feelings are important and accepted by the therapist, the result will be the development of basic trust in the relationship and a sound basis upon which to build a treatment program acceptable to both the client and the therapist.

Specialized techniques

There are a variety of other techniques currently employed as indirect methods of psychotherapy. Many of these techniques are designed for the treatment of specific problems such as phobias. More generally used specialized techniques include gestalt therapy, psychodrama, and numerous variants of psychoanalytical treatment.

Gestalt therapy was developed primarily by Perls (1951) and is based on the belief that the neurotic has been unable to integrate his behavior, feelings, and thoughts into a whole, or gestalt. The techniques of gestalt therapy are designed to help the person achieve wholeness. The therapist is usually very active and may sometimes appear rather belligerent. A primary method is confronting the client with discrepancies that appear between the feelings he is expressing and the behavior accompanying this expression. An individual may be discussing some very disturbing incident in his life but smile and laugh while doing so. The gestalt therapist might simply say to the client: "Why are you smiling?" and then point out that the subject matter that the client is discussing is not really very pleasant material. Gestalt therapy sessions are usually quite animated and lively. It has most frequently been applied in private practice and out-patient settings, and there are few data to support its use with psychotic individuals.

Psychodrama (Moreno, 1959), although based on a different theoretical system than that of a gestalt therapy, involves a similar process. Through the use of psychodrama the client is made aware of how others perceive him and of discrepancies that exist in relation to his behavior, his perception of himself, and others' perception of him. The technique involves groups of clients working together as a kind of therapeutic group of actors, with each of the clients under the supervision of the therapist portraying different roles of significance to the group members. Sometimes the client-actors play out their roles on a stage. One of the key components of psychodrama is role reversal. After a pair or group of clients have played their roles, they are required to switch with each other, thus enabling each client to see himself in the actions of another person and move toward greater self-understanding.

The many variants of psychoanalytic treatment include those of Reich, Horney, Sullivan, Jung, Rank, and Adler. All of these systems share with traditional analytic therapy an emphasis on the understanding of the relationship between client and therapist, and they rely heavily upon interpretation as a method of learning. The primary differences among these systems involve theoretical disputes about the nature of man's psychic apparatus and about what behavioral, interpersonal, and conversational components of therapy are most important. All of these analytical methods generally are governed by similar requirements in terms of therapist training, client intelligence and socioeconomic status, and duration of treatment. Therefore, these variants of traditional psycho-analysis are also not often encountered in the treatment programs of government supported agencies.

THERAPY AS A LEARNING PROCESS

The principles of learning can be applied to the prediction and control of human behavior outside the laboratory and make more explicit and useful the statements of several personality theories. Our discussion of learning principles has thus far been related to acquisition of behavior generally considered normal or appropriate. In this section we are dealing more specifically with methods of altering behavior considered socially abnormal or inappropriate.

The medical model of mental illness has as one of its cornerstones the idea that abnormal behavior is caused by some underlying pathological entity, whether physical or psychic in nature. This model has led many individuals to falsely believe that abnormal behavior is acquired in a manner quite different from normal behavior. If this position were true, then the use of principles of learning derived from the observation of normal individuals would be inappropriate in dealing with abnormal behavior. The assumption that an underlying physical or psychic cause is responsible for all abnormal behavior leads them to assume that changes in behavior, which are the result of treatment based on learning principles, will be transitory. A similar form of abnormal behavior supposedly will occur because the underlying cause has not been removed.

The vast majority of research available on the effects of treatment based on learning principles indicates that this assumption is erroneous. It has been established that the acquisition of abnormal patterns of behavior can be understood clearly with learning principles, without reference to underlying physical or psychic entities as explanations. The exceptions, of course, are the identified instances of brain damage or physical dysfunction. It has also been shown that when a program of treatment based on learning principles is well formulated and carried out with consistency, new patterns of abnormal behavior will not appear unless the individual is placed in an environment in which the contingencies of reinforcement promote the reappearance of such behavior.

It is both logical and efficient to employ learning principles as a basis for therapy. The application of learning principles to therapy can greatly increase the efficiency of the therapist, reducing the amount of time needed to return a client to normal patterns of behavior and increasing the resistance of the individual to the development of new behavior problems. In a sense, all psychotherapy is education, but not all education is psychotherapy. Both rely on the principles of learning.

Positive reinforcement, behavior shaping, and the Premack principle

One technique for behavior change based on the principles of learning is positive reinforcement. Application of this method has the most general use of any learning procedure, primarily because of its flexibility, compatibility with other treatment approaches, and the presence of fewer technical, environmental, and ethical problems, such as those associated with the use of extinction and punishment.

The use of positive reinforcement has the distinct advantage of clearly specifying for the client the type of behavior that will be followed by reinforcement. It involves none of the bothersome respondent behaviors typically accompanying extinction and punishment. The use of operant learning for shaping a pattern of behavior involves the manipulation of various reinforcers commonly present in the individual's environment, such as food or social approval, and increases the rate of emission of adaptive responses (Coleman, 1964). Behavior shaping with the method of successive approximation has been used successfully in the treatment of severely disturbed behaviors (Isaacs, Thomas, and Goldiamond, 1960). Initially, the therapist reinforces any behavior approximating the desired behavior. As response rate begins to increase, he then reinforces only closer approximations to the desired behavior. Inappropriate behaviors are continuously extinguished through the lack of reinforcement, until the patient exhibits behaviors that were the therapeutic objective.

For some time the use of shaping as a method of behavior change appeared to be limited to individuals who were very severely disturbed. The use of learning principles was often criticized as being irrelevant to most behavior problems because the technique relied on simple social approval or tangible awards, including money or pieces of candy as reinforcing stimuli. It was found that in some cases no reinforcing stimulus of this type could be discovered. It became clear that the definition of positive reinforcing events was too narrow for wide applicability. However, Premack (1959) discovered that reinforcement could be more broadly defined.

This new definition of reinforcement is known as the differential probability hypothesis, or the Premack principle. It states that for any pair of responses the most highly probable one can be used effectively to positively reinforce the less probable one. The application of this principle involves the observation of the frequency with which various behaviors are emitted by the client. The frequency of emission is used as an estimate of the probability of occurrence of a particular behavior. In order to increase the response rate of a behavior that is observed to be of low probability in a situation, the therapist arranges a contingency, in which the opportunity to engage in a high probability behavior is made contingent upon the emission of the lower probability behavior.

If a patient were observed to constantly spend his time talking with other individuals and only rarely performing basic self-care functions, such as taking a bath, the frequency of bathing could be increased by making the opportunity to interact with other individuals contingent upon bathing. The therapist would tell the patient and the individuals with whom the patient most frequently interacted that the patient would not be allowed to speak to them and that they were not to talk to the patient until he had taken a bath. If this contingency were maintained, the rate of bathing would increase and the contingency would be removed after the response rate had reached an acceptable level. This method is often used effectively by parents in increasing the amount of time children spend studying or doing school work. The contingency may specify that the child will not be allowed to go outside and play, watch television, or engage in some other highly preferred behavior until he has studied for a specified amount of time. The Premack principle has been found to be extremely effective as a method of defining reinforcement for use in the modification of human behavior. This principle bridged the gap between the application of tangible reinforcers, such as food as applied to animals in the laboratory, and the productive application of the principles of operant learning to human beings in social situations.

Much of the initial work in the application of operant principles to the modification of human behavior was done with the mentally retarded. In these early studies the goals of the shaping procedure were usually very simple behaviors. Subsequently it has been shown that principles of positive reinforcement and behavior shaping can be used to quickly and efficiently modify disturbed behavior. One notable case involves the treatment of a 3-year-old autistic child (Wolf, Risley, and Mees, 1964). Five areas of behavior were chosen for modification. They were:

1. Temper tantrums—the child engaged in severe self-destructive behaviors, such as head banging.
2. Bedtime problems—the child would not go to sleep, forcing one or both parents to remain at his bedside.

3. Wearing of glasses—he would not wear the glasses, which had become essential to avoid adult visual impairment.
4. Verbal behavior—he had no socially appropriate verbal behavior, although he was far from mute.
5. Eating behavior—he would not use silverware, he stole food from the plates of other children, and he threw food around the room.

To modify tantrums, bedtime problems, and inappropriate eating behavior, a combination of mild punishment and extinction was used. To eliminate eating problems, the child's plate would be removed for a few minutes, such as when he ate with his fingers. The child himself was removed from the dining room, whether he had finished his meal or not, whenever he threw food or when he took food from other children. At no time was the child reinforced with attention while engaging in any of the undesired behaviors.

The method of successive approximation was used to imitate the wearing of glasses and expand verbalizations. Food was found to be an effective reinforcing stimulus in both cases, with the child being reinforced for successive approximation to the desired behavior. While shaping the wearing of glasses, he was first reinforced with food when he looked at them, then when he held them, and so on, until he had learned to place them on his head in a proper manner. A similar procedure was followed to institute appropriate verbal behavior. Each time the child emitted an approximation of an appropriate verbal response, he was reinforced, and subsequent reinforcement was made contingent upon closer approximation to normal speech.

Complete removal of all the major problem behaviors was accomplished in a 7-month period. Six months after the child had been returned home the mother reported that he continued to wear his glasses, did not have tantrums, slept normally without disturbing the family, ate in an appropriate manner, and was becoming increasingly more normal and appropriate in his verbal behavior.

In this instance, as in any other successful application of learning principles to the modification of behavior, success of the procedure hinged upon the skill of the staff in presenting the reinforcing stimuli and remaining consistent in their behavior. When therapists who apply learning principles to modify behavior are able to devise a comprehensive program based on a sophisticated analysis of the patient's behavior and ensure that the contingencies arranged will be carried out by all those who have contact with the patient, the success of the program is almost certain. Unfortunately, some individuals who apply learning techniques do so in the absence of an adequate analysis of the patient's behavior, design their program with only superficial knowledge of learning principles, and do not ensure that other individuals who come in contact with the patient will cooperate in maintaining the therapeutic contingencies of reinforcement. In cases such as this, a positive result is simply a matter of chance, and more often than not the procedure will not lead to behavior improvement but will promote the development of more inappropriate behavior.

Verbal learning

One of the first researchers to apply the principles of learning to verbal behavior was Greenspoon (1955). He was able to demonstrate an increase in the rate of verbal emission of nouns for subjects who were reinforced verbally (the experimenter said "hum-mmm") every time a plural noun was emitted. Subsequently, other researchers have demonstrated that the effect of reinforcement on verbal behavior is quite pervasive and not limited simply to discrete components of speech such as single nouns. Hildum and Brown (1956) showed that verbal reinforcement using the word "good" was sufficient to produce changes in verbally reported attitudes toward general education in college students.

Some believe that concepts of verbal learning can be applied to increase our understanding of traditional indirect methods of psychotherapy, as well as in developing more efficient treatment programs. Generally, it is hypothesized that psychotherapists using traditional indirect methods function as reinforcing agents to change the verbal and social behavior of the clients, often to be more consonant with the therapist. This is vigorously denied by many traditional therapists, but Rosenthal (1955) has confirmed that changes in attitudes and behavior following psychotherapy are rated by the therapist as improved when they indicate movement toward his own personal style. Thus, therapy in the traditional sense involves, at least to some extent, the communication by the therapist of his own personal beliefs and styles of behavior to the client.

It has been suggested that an improvement in the efficiency of psychotherapy as a learning process could be accomplished if the therapist would make an overt effort to manipulate the contingencies of reinforcement in therapy that control the verbal behavior of the client (Krasner, 1966). It is apparent that therapists are already doing this, but the activity is carried out covertly and often without the awareness of the therapist or scientific planning and is, therefore, not maximally efficient. The application of the principles of learning to the verbal behavior of the client in therapy involves a direct effort at behavioral analysis by the therapist. That is, the therapist analyzes the verbal behavior of the client, determining which aspects of this behavior need to be eliminated, which need to be increased, and what new patterns of verbal behavior need to be developed. After such an analysis, the therapist decides which components of his own behavior can be used as reinforcing stimuli and then proceeds to design contingencies of reinforcement that will lead to an increase in the desired verbal behavior of the client.

These methods are often used in managing and altering the speech of the severely disturbed. For example, in dealing with irrelevant patterns of speech, extinction and successive approximation are used. If a patient is observed to spend the vast majority of his time with the therapist speaking in incomprehensible phrases and only rarely making a statement that can be understood, the therapist might arrange a program of contingencies. Initially, he would not respond in any way to irrelevant speech (that is, begin an extinction procedure) while simultaneously reinforcing any relevant comment by the patient with an appropriate social response or some simple phrase such as: "I understand," "Uhmm-hmm," or "Good." As the effect of the extinction procedure on the irrelevant speech becomes more pronounced, the rate of emission of appropriate verbal responses would also be observed to increase, and after a relatively short period of time it is likely that the patient would spend almost all of his time in conversation with the therapist using appropriate speech. Once appropriate patterns of speech are relearned, the therapist can then proceed to arrange contingencies that will lead to the emission of verbal reports indicative of more general changes in the patient's attitude toward himself and his environment.

Although these procedures are very effective, they cannot be expected to work in the absence of environmental change or behavioral change by the patient. Simply reinforcing positive attitudes will not lead to lasting changes in behavior unless the individual can find some objective basis for attitude change. Therefore, it is important that efforts at verbal learning in therapy be backed up by consistent application of the principles of learning to help the individual modify other troublesome aspects of his behavior.

Extinction and punishment

Two of the most powerful techniques of behavior change derived from the principles of learning are extinction and punishment (or aversive conditioning). When these techniques are used properly almost any behavior can be eliminated, although the application of these methods is fraught with difficulties when dealing with humans. The greatest problems lie in the areas of technology, control of environmental contingencies, and ethics.

In Chapter 3 we discussed the concept of extinction in reference to both respondent and operant learning. The use of this method to modify abnormal behavior is designed specifically for the removal of a particular behavior pattern. In the case where an individual has acquired a deviant pattern of behavior (such as withdrawal from people) through respondent conditioning, the therapeutic procedure is respondent extinction. The conditioned stimulus is presented repeatedly in the absence of the unconditioned stimulus. If one had acquired an incapacitating fear of dogs as a result of being bitten by them several times, the fear might be extinguished by repeatedly exposing the person to a dog (the conditioned stimulus) in a situation in which the bite (the unconditioned stimulus) would not occur. After many such exposures to the dog in the absence of an aversive event, the individual would eventually be able to cope with the dogs in his environment.

The bothersome behavior of young children, such as temper tantrums and long periods of crying, can be removed through an extinction procedure based on the operant model of learning. Observation of the acquisition of these types of behavior indicates that they are maintained by the presence of attention or some other reinforcing stimulus. In order to eliminate this behavior it is simply required that the reinforcing stimulus event be removed. In the case of a young child who consistently cries for increasingly long periods of time after being put to bed at night, making it virtually impossible for the parents to get any rest because they comfort the child when he cries, a simple extinction procedure would be very effective.

The attention of the parents maintains the crying of the child. In order to eliminate the crying through extinction the parents simply have to begin ignoring consistently any crying at bedtime by the child. It should be remembered that the removal of the reinforcing stimulus will initially produce an increase in the rate of emission of the operant. This makes the use of extinction a difficult procedure for dealing with operant behavior. The parents might feel that they were making the child worse. Rather than continue the extinction procedure, they might periodically return to pay attention to him. In effect, this would place the child on a partial schedule of reinforcement and render the bothersome behavior much more resistant to extinction. However, if the parents were able to tolerate the initial increase in rate of responding following the onset of extinction, the rate of emission would soon begin to drop rapidly and within no more than 5 to 10 days the child should cease crying at bedtime, unless there is some physiological basis for his tears (for example stomach ache, headache, or other physical pain).

For these simple examples the extinction of respondent and operant behaviors is relatively speedily and easily accomplished. However, there are patterns of abnormal behavior in which the behavior itself is intrinsically reinforcing, such as sexual deviations, alcoholism, drug addiction, and patterns of behavior in which the reinforcing stimuli cannot be modified or even clearly specified. These are much more difficult to treat through extinction. In the case of intrinsically reinforcing behavior, extinction is either extremely difficult or almost impossible, for the process cannot occur unless the behavior is emitted. Since the behavior itself is a reinforcing event, it is a technical impossibility to remove the reinforcement in the presence of the behavior. Extinction is equally as difficult when the reinforcing stimulus event cannot be manipulated or specified. For example, if the parents in the case cited before would not cooperate with the extinction procedure, refusing to allow themselves to be manipulated as therapeutic agents, the procedure could not be instituted. Similarly, if a behavior is maintained by an event that is not observable, such as hallucinations, extinction cannot be used because the reinforcing event cannot be removed.

Punishment or aversive conditioning is an alternative method of eliminating undersirable behavior, often being employed in cases for which extinction is impractical. Punishment must be severe and consistently applied before well-practiced behaviors can be eliminated. Punishment is used in both respondent and operant approaches to the modification of deviant behavior.

One of the most widely known uses of punishment of a respondent type involves attempts to eliminate the consumption of alcohol by alcoholics. The act of drinking alcohol is the conditioned stimulus, and the feelings that accompany ingesting are the unconditioned responses. For respondent learning treatment of alcoholism, some chemical substance, such as emetine, is mixed with the alcoholic beverage. This causes unpleasant physical side effects, including nausea and vomiting, when alcohol is ingested. Through the use of such chemicals the unconditioned response to alcohol ingestion becomes unpleasant rather than pleasant, and drinking becomes a conditioned stimulus for these feelings of unpleasantness.

This procedure may be carried out either individually or in a group situation. A glass of alcoholic beverage containing emetine is placed in front of the client and he is invited to drink from it. Shortly after ingesting the alcohol he will become nauseous and vomit. This procedure has been relatively effective, although there are several problems associated with it. One of the most obvious is that the procedure is quite messy. It is also very hard on the client physically and in some cases cannot be used. The greatest technical problem with this method is that the individual himself is aware that the drink that he is ingesting is different from those outside the therapeutic situation, even though there is no difference in taste. Thus, one common effect of this procedure is that the individual simply becomes unable to consume alcohol in the environment in which he has undergone the aversive respondent learning procedure, but he is perfectly capable of consuming alcohol outside of the clinic or hospital in his normal environment. These problems are common to most attempts at removal of deviant behavior through punishment in a respondent learning model. In most cases the individual is very aware of the fact that the aversive unconditioned response that is being manipulated in the therapy session will not occur outside of therapy or will be under his control.

The operant use of punishment involves an aversive stimulus being made contingent upon some behavior, and it is applied on either a continuous or partial schedule of reinforcement. Although partial reinforcement of the behavior with an aversive stimulus reduces the probability that the behavior will reappear in relation to the use of a continuous schedule, if punishment is intense enough the punishing stimulus need only be presented a very few times in order to eliminate the behavior. It is important to remember that an aversive stimulus for use in operant punishment is defined in terms of response rate, rather than from the guesses of the therapist. Some events, such as spanking a young child, logically can be thought of as punishing, but it may in some individuals lead to an increase rather than a decrease in response rate. The attention that accompanies punishment may serve a reinforcing function, outweighing the physical discomfort and leading to an increased rate of responding.

An operant approach to punishment that has been used with some success for alcoholics involves the client ingesting a long-acting drug (Antabuse) that produces nausea when alcohol is ingested. In this case each time drinking behavior is emitted, if the individual has been taking the drug regularly, nausea will follow. As long as the drug is taken consistently, the punishing effect of nausea will reduce the response rate to near zero. However, once the individual is taken off the drug the response rate often returns to its previous high level.

Sexual deviations such as homosexuality or fetishism have also been dealt with through operant application of punishment. An individual who is obsessed with handling and wearing of ladies' undergarments might be placed in an environment in which behavior is followed by an intense electric shock. Homosexuals have received shock when they showed measurable responses of a positive type, such as an erection, when viewing pictures of nude male models.

Potential physical damage and the individual's knowledge that the punishing stimuli are found only in the therapeutic environment reduce the effectiveness of these procedures. However, if punishment can be administered ethically, without physical or emotional harm to the client, and on a consistent basis in the person's normal environment, its effect in eliminating undesirable behavior will be rapid and relatively permanent.

Satiation and deprivation

Two other techniques similar to extinction and habituation are deprivation and satiation. Deprivation is used to increase the value of some event, which may have lost its effectiveness as a positive reinforcer. The client is placed in a situation that includes a number of discriminative stimuli associated with the presence of reinforcement following a particular activity. He is not actively encouraged to emit the particular behavior, but he is surrounded by stimulus events that commonly precede that behavior. He may be encouraged to engage in certain behaviors that are an early part of the pattern and that ultimately would lead to reinforcement. After a sufficient length of time with the early behaviors, the individual will begin to emit the final desired behavior, and the reinforcing stimulus will once again come to control response rate.

For example, to reinstate eating in an individual who for some reason has decided that he should not eat, a deprivation procedure might be used with some hope of success. The patient would be placed in a situation where he is able to observe others eating enjoyable and highly preferable foods. The patient himself, however, would only be allowed to smell and watch and not engage in eating. After a relatively brief period, it is likely that the patient would begin to express some interest in eating. However, deprivation usually is continued for a period after the individual first expresses an interest in performing the desired behavior in order to further enhance the effectiveness of the reinforcing stimulus. Soon after this the patient will likely be observed to express a very active interest in eating, and at this point the therapist might allow him to sample one or two of the foods surrounding him. Soon the therapist will observe the patient becoming increasingly more interested in eating and demanding to be allowed to eat what the others are consuming. At this point the therapist may then allow the individual to eat an entire meal. It is probable that interest in food will be maintained after this point.

Deprivation is often a necessary method to counteract the effects of attention an individual receives when he refuses to perform an activity, such as eating or some other behavior of biological necessity. Often the simple act of refusal gains the individual a great deal of attention and interest from other people. These activities become more powerful reinforcing agents than the food itself. Therefore, the success of a deprivation procedure requires that the therapist ensure that no attention is paid to refusal to engage in the desired behavior and that social approval is withheld until the activity itself again assumes the role of a reinforcing stimulus. In the preceding example, praise and positive social interaction with the therapist would be withheld until the patient had begun to eat in a normal manner. Thus, deprivation involves the use of extinction through the removal of social reinforcement for inappropriate behavior and a return of the person's behavior to the control of appropriate reinforcing stimulus events.

Satiation is a technique based on the principle of habituation in respondent learning; conditioned stimuli lose their power to elicit behavior if they are continuously presented in the absence of the unconditioned stimulus. Habituation also can be applied to the removal of the controlling value of a reinforcing stimulus in operant learning. Habituation of a positive reinforcer will occur when it is presented in a noncontingent manner. That is, the reinforcing stimulus follows any behavior that the individual emits, rather than only one particular behavior. If one wished to eliminate money as a reinforcer for working, all that would be necessary is to disburse the money on a noncontingent basis. No matter what behavior the individual engaged in, he would receive money for it. Money would then soon lose its power to maintain work, and the person would probably begin to engage in other, more highly preferred activities. Satiation has been applied to those who tend to hoard things and others who engage in some potentially destructive behavior, such as smoking to excess.

To treat a patient who tends to hoard articles of clothing, a satiation procedure involves making the desired articles available to the person at all times. Initially he will accumulate a large supply of articles, but within a very short time he will begin to dispose of them and return to more normal behavior. To eliminate or decrease smoking, the therapist may place the individual in a small unventilated room with a group of other people who also smoke to excess and require that all of the people smoke continuously. After 1 or 2 hours the people will find smoking much less desirable and will either not smoke as much or cease smoking entirely.

The use of satiation and deprivation must always be undertaken with concern for the welfare of the patient. It is not necessary to carry deprivation or satiation to extremes for either to be effective. Although these techniques will generally work, they are not the only methods available for modifying deviant behavior. The therapist must be most careful that the client understands the procedure being used and that he has the right to refuse such treatment at any time.

Escape and avoidance

The best measure for a client to take in order to increase his behavioral competency may be to remove himself from the situation that serves as the stimulus for his deviant actions. Escape and avoidance are two methods of accomplishing this goal.

Escape procedures usually involve training the individual to be able to remove himself from a punishing or aversive situation. To help a person deal more effectively with his family and control his own behavior, it may be necessary that he leave the situation before it becomes so aversive as to serve as a stimulus for deviant behavior. In other cases it is sometimes necessary for the therapist himself to intervene in removing the person from this situation. While helping a child who consistently behaves inappropriately in the classroom, it may be discovered that the teacher or some other student in the class is the stimulus for such behavior. The behavior of these people may be so aversive to the child that he feels that he is forced to behave inappropriately as a means of getting himself removed from the room. Should it prove impractical to modify the behavior of those who are causing the child to act in this way, the child can be allowed to escape permanently from this situation by having him placed in another class.

In avoidance training the client is taught how to avoid the undesirable consequences of his behavior by changing the behavior itself. A widely known avoidance technique is the Mowrer (1938) apparatus for the treatment of nocturnal enuresis, or bed wetting. Such behavior can be extremely disruptive to the life of the client and his family. No organic causes can be found in a great majority of cases, and treatment through avoidance learning, which is at least 85% effective, should be employed. Unfortunately, this technique is not commonly used. Instead, the client is put through a long and involved process of traditional indirect psychotherapy or chemotherapy. Although indirect methods may be effective, they are much less efficient than the use of avoidance learning to rapidly return the individual to normal patterns of bladder control.

The Mowrer apparatus consists of a pad and a buzzer or bell, which is activated when the pad becomes wet. The pad is placed on the client's bed and should he urinate during sleep the sound of the buzzer or bell will awaken him. Being awakened during the night is generally an aversive event, and the child will quickly learn to control his bladder and avoid being awakened.

The apparatus can be purchased through the catalogues of major chain department stores and is a very inexpensive and humane method of helping the client eliminate enuresis. The effect is usually quick, and contrary to the opinions of some professionals, the use of this procedure does not lead to symptom substitution. Indeed, it generally results in a marked improvement in family, school, and peer relations.

Modeling

Modeling as a technique of behavior change generally takes one of two forms. First, the client may simply observe the therapist or some other individual engaging in appropriate behavior in a situation that has been a problem for the client (observational modeling). Second, the client may actually participate in the practicing of appropriate behavior with the therapist (participant modeling). Both participant and observation modeling have been used to help people gain control over their behavior in a number of situations. Participant modeling has been used as a means of helping people who have a profound fear of water learn to swim (Hunziker, 1971). Observational modeling has been used to increase the verbal behavior of autistic children, modify the amount of cooperative and domineering behavior of hyperaggressive children, and increase the amount of social interaction in groups of withdrawn children (Bandura, 1969).

Modeling techniques have generally been found to be most effective when the model shares some degree of similarity with the observers. Otherwise, the same controlling conditions discussed earlier in reference to the acquisition of behavior through modeling apply. Human service workers of any agency or title function as behavior models for their clients and patients. Workers in mental hospitals, for example, serve as teachers of social behavior, and if one condones and demonstrates acting out hostility, the probability increases that patients will behave in a similar manner. The principle applies to drinking, drugs usage, clothing styles, verbalized negative attitudes toward authorities, and any other aspect of behavior.

Homework/rehearsal

A technique associated with the use of a variety of other therapeutic programs is the assignment to the client of specific tasks to perform or practice outside of the therapy situation. Desensitization and assertive training, which are discussed later, both often employ these techniques. Homework may involve the client completing a particular task, such as construction of a hierarchy for desensitization, testing his ability to approach feared objects, or engaging in social behaviors of which he formerly was not capable. Rehearsal refers to the client practicing some behavior or behavior pattern. As a part of assertive training the client may be asked to rehearse appropriate behavior in front of a mirror at home.

Masters and Johnson (1970) make extensive use of homework and rehearsal as a part of their program for married couples with sexual problems. Clients are instructed to perform specific foreplay sexual behavior and indications of affection, which they are to practice at home until they feel comfortable and aroused. Practice and rehearsal occur for each separate part of the sexual act. Initially the clients might be instructed to hold hands and caress each other without kissing or having intercourse. This practice would be continued until both partners felt comfortable and aroused. Then they might be instructed to continue engaging in caressing but also to kiss and fondle each other more actively. Eventually the couple would, through practicing each separate part of the sexual act, be able to return to a normal pattern of sexual behavior.

Rational emotive therapy (Ellis, 1962) also makes extensive use of home-work assignments to achieve behavioral change. Ellis believes that many of the problems of everyday life are the result of irrational assumptions about the consequences of behavior. To modify behavior Ellis uses a very direct approach, confronting the client with his irrational assumptions and demanding the individual accomplish certain behavioral objectives as homework assignments. For a client who is afraid to ask a woman to accompany him to some activity, Ellis would confront the client with the irrational nature of his fear. It is usually found that the client fears he will be rejected by the woman and assumes that such rejection would be a complete and utter disaster with far-reaching consequences for the rest of his life. The therapist confronts him with the illogical nature of this assumption. He points out that his rejection actually has little objective relationship to his life at all and that his inability even to ask a woman for a date results from his irrational assumption. At the close of the sessions the therapist assigns the client some homework task, which must be completed before the next therapy session, such as talking to a woman to whom the client feels attracted.

The use of homework assignments and behavioral rehearsal outside actual therapeutic situations is increasingly common. This method greatly enhances the effectiveness of therapy by reducing the number of sessions required to bring about an improvement in behavior. It further increases the resistance of improved behavior to extinction after therapy is terminated. These techniques are compatible with almost any form of therapy and should be used at every reasonable opportunity.

Bibliotherapy

Bibliotherapy is similar to the homework rehearsal techniques noted previously but is distinguished by the fact that it involves the client reading some assigned material from a topic area suggested by the therapist. There have been a number of manuals published describing materials and techniques of bibliotherapy (Association of Hospital and Institutional Libraries, 1971).

The process of bibliotherapy has much in common with education. It has been shown that individuals are able to gain much insight into their problems, and as a result they effectively modify their own behavior through reading. To help a child adjust to the loss of his parents, the therapist might recommend the child read a biography about some well-known and respected parental figure. For a little boy he might recommend reading a biography on Babe Ruth, and a little girl might be asked to read about Clara Barton. Once the client has completed some of the reading, the content and feelings are discussed, either with the therapist alone or in a group. Sometimes members of the group may even act out the parts of different characters in the books. Through discussion and role playing, the similarity of content read by the client to his own life is emphasized, and he is invited to contemplate and understand how the material applies to him and how it can be of help. The use of bibliotherapy is sometimes overlooked in favor of indirect or other forms of therapy. It should be noted that this need not be the case, since bibliotherapy is compatible with any other form of therapeutic procedure and can result in considerable behavioral improvement, including that which occurs in the absence of interaction with a therapist.

Persuasion, suggestion, relaxation, and hypnosis

Persuasion, suggestion, relaxation, and hypnosis all share some similarity in terms of the behavior of the therapist, but they are distinguished by the degree, intensity, and depth of change desired. To some extent these procedures in practice are related to placebos.

Persuasion as a therapeutic technique is not very different from the concept as applied to salesmen. In some cases it may become clear to the therapist that a concrete solution to the problems of the client is available and that the only major problem preventing improvement is unwillingness on the part of the client to accept the advice of the therapist. In such a case the goal of the therapist may become very similar to that of a salesman selling vacuum cleaners. The salesman has a specific behavioral goal in talking to the customer and attempts to persuade the customer to emit that behavior, which is writing out a check for the vacuum cleaner. Similarly, the therapist who decides to use persuasion as a technique also will have a specific behavioral objective in mind for the client. Often this goal is simply that the client accomplish some task that he finds difficult to complete because of environmental or personal problems.

The individual may want to leave home and begin living independently. In cases such as this it is usually found that the emotional problems of the client are a direct result of a pathological pattern of interaction in the family, in which the client is encouraged to remain dependent in spite of his desire to leave and become an independently functioning adult. The client subtly may have been made to feel that it is wrong to want to leave his family. The therapist may elect to persuade the individual through a rational examination of all various aspects of the situation that there is nothing wrong with his desire to leave and that he and his family would be much happier if he did.

Persuasion commonly has three elements. First, the therapist must agree with the client that there is a need for change. Second, the therapist must prove that the change that he is suggesting is reasonable and will result in an improvement in the quality of the client's life. Third, the therapist must provide the individual with the knowledge, emotional support, and understanding necessary to accomplish and maintain the desired goal.

Persuasion is differentiated from suggestion by the fact that a persuasive approach is more direct. It involves the therapist giving specific suggestions and arguments for the desired behavioral goal. Suggestion, on the other hand, may be much more subtle and involve the therapist supplying ideas for the client to think about and act upon. Suggestion is used as a method of providing an individual with alternatives to his present situation, which he may not have yet discovered or which for some reason he may find so unacceptable that he is unable to talk about them with the therapist. Through suggestion the therapist may accomplish two functions. The most desirable is that the subject will immediately begin to feel better and believe that his problems are being solved. A more probable response is that suggestions will make it possible for the client to discuss with the therapist thoughts, feelings, and courses of action that he previously was unable to verbalize. For the example discussed before the use of suggestion might involve the therapist making a statement such as: "You were thinking of leaving home." Suggestions also may be made with statements such as: "You are feeling better today," "Everything is really all right now," or "You are really very angry."

The key feature of suggestion is that the therapist presents the idea in such a manner that the client begins to perceive it as reality. The statements of the therapist are made so as to elicit acceptance by the client, in spite of the fact that they may be to some degree incongruent with the way the individual is actually thinking and feeling. The therapist may make statements such as: "You are really feeling much better" in the absence of evidence indicative of improvement. Suggestions when presented in this way sometimes result in an actual change in the behavior of the client.

Relaxation is a method of treatment that has quite a long history in mental health work. The basic techniques involve the relaxation of muscles in various parts of his body. Relaxation is often used to help individuals who are chronically nervous, agitated, and fearful to learn to calm down and relax when discussing or experiencing uncomfortable topics or situations. The basic technique of relaxation involves the tensing and releasing of tension in various opposing muscle groups in the body. Relaxation sometimes may be accomplished simply through suggestion. However, it usually has been found that a combination of suggestion and muscle tension release is most effective. First, the therapist constructs a list of various muscle groups in which tension will be removed and explains the list to the client. The client practices tensing and releasing the tension in these various muscle groups. For example, in relaxing the arms the client would first practice tensing his hand by making a very hard fist for about 10 seconds and then opening his hand. Next he would practice stretching his fingers and hand back and as far apart as possible, then returning the hand to a normal position. Following this he might flex the arms to make the biceps extremely hard and then stretch out his arms to flex the triceps as hard as possible. Suggestions may be contributed by the therapist when the client is tensing a particular muscle group. The therapist suggests how uncomfortable and painful the tension in those muscles becomes. When the muscle group is relaxed and returned to a normal position, the therapist suggests how much better that part of the body feels, how relaxed it is becoming, and invites the client to contemplate the difference between the sensation of tension and the feeling of relaxation.

The muscle relaxation procedure often is carried out on opposing muscle groups from head to toe. This may involve, initially, about 30 to 45 minutes to complete, but after a little practice the individual will be able to perform the exercises much more rapidly and without the aid of suggestion from the therapist. The feeling that accompanies thorough muscle relaxation is very pleasant, and the vast majority of individuals who undergo this treatment enjoy it very much.

When undertaking a muscle relaxation procedure the therapist must be careful not to require or suggest to the individual that he perform exercises of which he is incapable or that will result in physical damage. Prior to beginning a relaxation procedure the therapist must ascertain whether or not the client has had any orthopedic problems that might be aggravated by tensing of muscles. Another difficulty commonly encountered is the wearing of contact lenses. When tensing the muscles around the eyes the individual may be required to squint. If contact lenses are worn when squinting takes place, physical damage is a possibility. The simplest solution to these problems is to avoid tensing muscle groups in areas where orthopedic problems have been present and to have the client remove contact lenses before relaxation is begun.

Techniques of persuasion, suggestion, and relaxation are sometimes employed simultaneously. This type of activity is referred to as hypnosis. It is distinguished by the fact that, at the suggestion of the therapist, the client enters into a state similar to sleep, which is known as a trance. When an individual is in a trance state, the effect of suggestion and persuasion is much more pronounced. Posthypnotic suggestions for behavior are often employed. The client is given a suggestion to behave, which is carried out after leaving the trance state. Hypnotists in the entertainment world often use posthypnotic suggestions in their acts. After having hypnotized and released a subject, the hypnotist-performer at some time gives a sign or signal that serves as a stimulus for the subject to engage in the previously suggested behavior.

Hypnosis has been used in mental health work for many years with positive effects. It has also been used to aid in the removal of bothersome, self-destructive behaviors or habits such as smoking, alcoholism, and drug dependence. However, because of the use of hypnosis as an entertainment medium by performers, its value as a method of altering behavior is sometimes grossly overestimated. It is assumed by some that hypnosis is a magical procedure that enables the client to behave in ways of which he is quite incapable when not in the trance state. It has been known for years that hypnosis does not enable the individual to do things he is not normally capable of doing, and it differs in effect very little from suggestion and persuasion applied vigorously to an individual who is not in a trance state (Hull, 1933).

Desensitization

The technique of systematic desensitization was developed by Wolpe and Lazarus (1966). It is based on the concept of reciprocal inhibition and has been thoroughly documented as an effective treatment technique, particularly in dealing with phobic disorders.

Reciprocal inhibition pertains to a method of removing anxiety responses associated with inappropriate conditioned stimuli. Anxiety is believed to be the basic motivating factor in many neurotic behavior patterns, but it can be inhibited by incompatible physical responses. For example, the anxiety associated with a fear of a particular person or object is incompatible with a state of pervasive muscular relaxation. Therefore, muscle relaxation can be used to inhibit anxiety. Sexual responsiveness and appropriate social assertiveness are also compatible with anxiety. Hence, they can be used in its inhibition.

In the course of treatment through systematic desensitization, there are two major elements. The first is training the client in muscular relaxation. The second is the construction of a hierarchy of anxiety-provoking situations. To treat someone with a disabling phobia of an animal, the therapist would ascertain those situations involving the animal that were anxiety arousing and arrange them in order of the magnitude of the anxiety response associated with each situation. Once the client has mastered muscle relaxation, the therapist proceeds to work through the hierarchy with the client in a relaxed state. While in the relaxed state the client is repeatedly asked to imagine the weakest stimulus situation in the hierarchy until it no longer arouses any anxiety. Progressively stronger stimuli are then introduced and similarly treated until all of the items on the hierarchy have lost their anxiety arousal properties. Finally, the client can imagine any scene from the hierarchy without experiencing any anxiety.

Several variants of the basic desensitization method are now widely used. One of these is in vivo desensitization, in which the patient is exposed to real rather than imagined stimuli. An in vivo procedure involves the construction of a hierarchy of progressive anxiety-provoking situations, but interpersonal circumstances rather than muscle relaxation are relied upon to provide the emotional reaction inhibiting anxiety. A famous example of in vivo desensitization (Jones, 1924) involved the removal of a child's fear of rabbits. The incompatible response was the consumption of food, and the hierarchy consisted of moving a live rabbit closer and closer to the child as he ate. After a relatively short period of time the rabbit was placed close to the child, who showed no fear response and was soon observed to touch the rabbit and pet it.

Group desensitization is another variant of the desensitization procedure. It is essentially identical with the individual desensitization procedure, except that several clients with similar phobias are treated simultaneously. A third variant of desensitization is the use of anxiety-inhibiting emotive images to eliminate phobic reactions in children. This technique consists of four steps. The first is the construction of the hierarchy of anxiety-arousing situations. This is accomplished in a manner similar to that of other variants of desensitization, which is by questioning the client or by having him develop the hierarchy as a homework assignment. Second, the therapist discovers through conversation with the child the content of his fantasy life regarding heros, how the child identifies himself with them, and the kinds of activities of the hero in which the child would like to engage. Third, the child is asked to shut his eyes and imagine a scene he might encounter in his environment. A story including elements of the content discovered in the second step is then introduced into the scene. Fourth, the therapist begins to include sequentially in the story the items in the hierarchy. He begins with the least anxiety-arousing scene and proceeds until the child can imagine a situation in which elements from the most highly anxiety-arousing situation in the hierarchy are included without becoming distressed.

Systematic desensitization is a very flexible procedure. Although muscular relaxation is often utilized as a major anxiety-inhibiting method, it should be remembered that this is not always necessary. The success of the technique depends primarily on the skillful construction of a hierarchy and the presence of responses by the client that are incompatible with anxiety. Although muscular relaxation is a very effective competing response, the effectiveness of desensitization is not reduced and may even be enhanced through the use of some other anxiety-inhibiting response. In some instances it is not necessary to clearly specify any competing response on the part of the client. It has been demonstrated that simply practicing approach toward some fear-eliciting stimulus will result in the elimination of anxiety, often as effectively as conventional desensitization in which a competing response is clearly specified and performed by the client (Bandura, 1969).

Assertive training

Assertive training is a method of treatment directed primarily toward those who have developed incapacitating anxiety responses to situations involving social interaction. The anxiety limits the expression of feelings and the performance of adaptive behaviors (Wolpe and Lazarus, 1966). Assertive behavior is the appropriate expression of feelings and beliefs by an individual and is incompatible with the expression of anxiety. In the presence of assertive responses the anxiety aroused by the situation is inhibited. Assertive training was initially developed as a method for inhibiting anxiety. When assertive training is used as a method for the reciprocal inhibition of anxiety, it is assumed that the client presently possesses adaptive behavioral social skills and that inhibition of anxiety will make it possible for him to display these skills.

However, it has been noted that it is not unreasonable to assume that the client may never have learned how to behave in an appropriately assertive manner. The observed inappropriate behavior of the client results from a behavioral deficit, rather than the presence of anxiety. In either case the procedure involved in assertive training effectively teaches the individual to behave appropriately. Assertive training is conducted in either individual or group situations. When done on an individual basis the therapist constructs a hierarchy of situations in which the client has difficulty asserting himself. They are discussed and the client and therapist mutually arrive at a decision regarding the appropriate behavior for each situation. The situations are acted out with the therapist and client each playing a specified role. The client plays himself and the therapist takes the role of the other person or persons. Sometimes this may be reversed and the therapist will attempt to model appropriate behavior for the client by taking his role.

The procedure in group assertive training is similar to that followed for individuals. There are many factors associated with group assertive training that make it preferable to individual assertive training, including efficiency in terms of the number of clients who can be treated by a single therapist. The most notable advantage of group assertive training is that the situation itself increases the probability that stimulus generalization will occur. When assertive training is conducted individually, the client learns behavior in the presence of only one stimulus (the therapist). The therapist stimulus is usually quite dissimilar from the kinds of people encountered by the client in everyday life. In the group situation the client learns to respond appropriately to a variety of stimuli (the other group members and the therapist), who are much more apt to be like the people encountered outside of therapy.

In the assertive training group each group member, as well as the therapist himself, takes part by planning roles and performing tasks. The tasks in an assertive training group are typically arranged in a sequence. After introducing himself to the group and explaining the treatment, the leader invites the group members to engage in a task of free association. The group members may be seated in a circle, and during free association every person in the circle states aloud the first word that comes to mind. This task is repeated until all the group members appear to be relatively relaxed and comfortable while stating their association. In the second task, the group members practice giving and accepting compliments. The third task involves each group member turning to the other and saying; "Hello, how are you?" This task, like the prior task, is practiced until all the members appear comfortable with it. At this point the therapist may elect to introduce variants such as introducing oneself to an acquaintance or a stranger. The fourth group task involves small talk. One group member is invited to pick a nonthreatening topic, such as the weather or flowers, and choose two other members of the group to discuss this topic for a period of time specified by the therapist. The length of time is initially short, perhaps 10 to 15 seconds. As the group members become more comfortable with this task, the time is increased gradually up to 1 to 3 minutes. The final task in group assertive training may be role-playing situations that pose particular problems for each of the group members. As a homework assignment the therapist invites the group members to think about what problems they would like to work on in the group. In the group the members and the therapist discuss specific problems and situations, devise strategies for dealing with them, and practice those strategies with each other through role playing, until each of the group members feels confident that he can carry out that strategy when faced with the problem in his natural environment.

Assertive training is an effective technique for modifying the behavior of people who are either chronically and ineffectively very passive or very aggressive, these behaviors resulting from overwhelming anxiety or behavioral deficit. These individuals usually avoid making direct eye contact with other individuals, tend to speak in a monotone, very rarely show much facial expression, avoid contradicting others, and seldom use the first person pronoun when speaking. Therefore, in both group and individual assertive training the therapist requires that the client begin to emit all of these behaviors in their appropriate form. The individual is encouraged, for example, to make eye contact by the therapist, being criticized when eye contact is not present. Immediate reinforcement in the form of verbal praise is given when eye contact is established. The same procedure is used for other behavioral areas. The effect of this immediate feedback is enhanced in the group by the presence of others. After the members of the group have become accustomed to each other, and with a sufficient amount of encouragement from the therapist, each will begin to actively participate in praise and criticism. Within a very short time these common activities result in a very cohesive group that becomes animated and enjoyable for both the clients and the therapist.

Assertive training is ideal for use with persons described as inadequate personalities, producing very rapid improvement that is resistant to change in the environment. Assertive training especially should be cautiously used with psychotics and those who give some evidence of thought disorder. Assertive training with psychotics in group situations sometimes increases inappropriate behavior.

Implosive therapy

Implosive therapy is to some degree a productive combination of psychoanalytic theory and learning principles. This technique is based on the assumption that intense elicitation of the anxiety associated with repressed conflict, through the visualization of scenes depicting that conflict, will result in the extinction of the anxiety response (Stampfl and Levis, 1967). In direct contrast to desensitization, implosive therapy purposely overloads the person with intense discomfort.

The therapist must ascertain the important fears or repressed conflicts in the life of the patient from interviews. Once a determination of the specific problem area is made, the therapist may place the client in a state of muscular relaxation and proceeds to graphically describe scenes associated with the problem. For example, implosive therapy might be used to treat a client with a phobia for chickens, which interferes with attending picnics and sleeping on a pillow, because they involve fried chicken and feathers. The therapist suggests that the client imagine a chicken entering the room, and then more and more chickens entering, approaching the client, looking him over, touching him, and finally pecking and running all over him. The client visualizing the scene becomes extremely anxious.

The scenes which the client is asked to imagine during implosive therapy are very detailed. When the technique is working effectively it is expected that the client will experience a profound degree of emotional discomfort. However, after one or two descriptions of the scene by the therapist, habituation will take place and the client will be able to function without experiencing the degree of anxiety that existed prior to therapy.

GROUP METHODS

Many of the techniques discussed in the preceding section are adaptable for use in groups. However, there are several forms and methods of therapy specifically designed to be used in a group situation, the dynamics of the group being viewed as an integral part of the therapeutic process.

Traditional

In its traditional form group therapy consists of a small number of people, with no more than six to ten clients and one or two therapists. The techniques for traditional groups are generally derived from psychoanalytic and client-centered viewpoints.

Psychoanalytically oriented group therapy involves analysis of the relationships between the various group members and the therapist. The analysis is done along similar lines to classical analysis with one individual. The group members are allowed to associate freely, and the therapist provides occasional interpretation in an attempt to integrate the symbolic meaning of the members' associations into a form that will produce insight and behavioral change.

Client-centered groups involve the therapist providing a situation in which each of the members in the group can learn to experience and provide others with unconditional positive regard. In the client-centered group the role of the therapist takes the form of clarification of the feelings that the group members express toward one another, rather than the symbolic interpretation that characterizes the therapist in the analytic group.

A third form of group therapy, very similar in theory to both learning and psychoanalysis, is transactional analysis (Berne, 1964). The therapist's role is the discovery and clarification for the participants of the "games" which they play in an effort to help them begin communication with one another on an adult and productive level, rather than in a childlike or parental fashion.

Emerging

In recent years there has been an explosive growth in the field of group therapy, and a number of techniques differing markedly in both client and therapist roles has resulted. Sensitivity training, nude marathon groups, and others have been well publicized. Many of these emerging group methods have resulted from the work of client-centered and gestalt therapists, and a number of institutes and retreats have begun around the country where an individual may go for such group experiences. Some of these emerging techniques have been scientifically developed and may be of great benefit. However, in some cases they have been promoted by irresponsible individuals and have proved to be potentially harmful to their participants. Taking part in group therapy is not a recreational activity and should not be entered into for purposes of entertainment.

Training and experience are necessary if one is to conduct a safe and effective group. Much planning about one's goals is necessary before participating in such a group. In participating or leading groups it is important that the individual recognize that pressures toward conformity exist that may force an individual to stay in the group even though he is being harmed by it. Therefore, the leader has an unusual degree of responsibility and must remain in close contact with the participants of the group in order to prevent adverse reactions. In general, psychotherapy in any form is a very uncomfortable and sometimes even painful process for an individual to undergo. This is especially true in therapeutic groups. They should not be entered into with the thought that they are going to be fun, because often one person's enjoyment and recreation in this situation will occur at a very great expense to the other members of the group.

Token economy

The token economy is one of the most recent therapeutic techniques to evolve from the application of learning principles to the treatment of deviant behavior. Token economies are essentially miniature societies in which each individual receives reinforcement contingent upon appropriate behavior, as defined in a very complex and detailed treatment plan (Ayllon and Azrin, 1968). The entire system is similar to capitalism as an economic method for controlling behavior.

Sophisticated analyses of human behavior reveal that man is governed by complex contingencies of reinforcement. One way of looking at deviant behavior is to recognize that it results from the presence of unusual contingencies of reinforcement in the individual's environment. When a person is placed in a token economy for behavior change, the goal is to retrain the individual to behave appropriately by presenting him with contingencies of reinforcement that will lead to adaptive rather than maladaptive behavior.

There are two major parts to treatment in the token economy. During the first phase the behavior of patients in a mental institution or disturbed children in a classroom, for example, is assessed to determine what patterns of maladaptive behavior currently exist. The result is a behavioral baseline. Contingencies are identified that appear to be maintaining those patterns. Finally, there is an accounting of events functioning as positive reinforcing stimuli for the patients or children. Once the initial assessment phase is completed, the treatment phase begins on the basis of the information gained from the behavioral assessment. The therapist develops a treatment plan consisting of specific contingencies designed to increase the rate of emission of appropriate behavior and decrease the amount of inappropriate behavior.

Most often token economy procedures rely primarily on positive reinforcement. This reinforcement is dispensed in the form of tokens, which may be pieces of colored plastic with some marking identifying them as belonging to a particular individual. They can be obtained by behaving appropriately and exchanged for certain objects or for being allowed to engage in particular behaviors. It is like receiving a salary for working and being allowed to buy a car or take a vacation. Deprivation procedures, such as placing the patient in seclusion for a short time, are also sometimes used. However, punishment is rarely employed. An assessment of a particular patient might indicate that he consistently uses obscene language inappropriately, never takes a bath, wears ill-fitting and filthy clothing, and spends his time either lying in bed asleep or watching television. A treatment plan in a token economy for this individual could involve making preferred activities contingent upon the performance of less perferred activities. Whenever the patient engaged in appropriate behavior such as bathing, wearing clean clothes, using appropriate speech, or working, he would receive some specified number of tokens. They could later be exchanged for goods such as candy or for the opportunity to engage in a preferred behavior, such as watching television, lying in bed, or talking to his therapist. Inappropriate behavior would be eliminated through simple extinction or the use of mild deprivation.

The contingencies closely resemble those present in the normal environment. An individual must dress, speak appropriately, and work if he wishes to watch television or have a bed on which he can rest. He also must work to afford to talk with his psychotherapist. Thus, in the token economy the patient is placed in a situation in which he learns how to function normally within society. Although the example just discussed is relatively simple and uncomplicated, token economy procedures have been applied successfully to the treatment of chronic psychosis and character disorders, both of which have for many years appeared to be complex conditions for which there was little hope of change.

In a typical token economy in schools and institutions the contingencies of reinforcement that are a part of the treatment plan should be explained to the children or patients. Explaining conditions under which reinforcement will occur greatly increases the effectiveness of any procedure based on positive reinforcement. In order for contingencies to be effective, however, it is necessary that all of the treatment staff who have any contact with the children or patients be well trained in learning principles and be committed to the use of this procedure. It is also necessary that the administration of the organization in which a token economy is instituted fully and unconditionally support its methods. If either staff members or administrative personnel do not understand or support the token economy, the contingencies of reinforcement will be applied inconsistently and not function at maximal efficency. This inconsistency may lead to the appearance of new patterns of deviant behavior or render other existing abnormalities more resistant to treatment.

CHEMOTHERAPY

One of the most significant developments in the treatment of deviant behavior within the last 100 years has been the introduction of psychotropic medication. The use of psychotropic drugs for treating behavior disturbances is referred to as chemotherapy. Psychotropic drugs can be classified as belonging to one or more of the following groups: antipsychotic drugs, antidepressant drugs, antianxiety drugs, and sedatives and hypnotics (Wolberg, 1967). Although these drugs do not cure mental illness, they tend to have positive behavioral effects and are assumed to make the individual more accessible to other methods of therapy. They have also resulted in more humane conditions within institutions by reducing the incidence of violence and disruptive behavior, thereby lessening the need for such measures as physical restraint and seclusion.

It should be noted that each individual reacts in a unique manner to chemotherapy. This results from physiological differences among individuals, differences in personality, and attitudes toward and expectation of results of medication. The administration of a program of chemotherapy must always be under the direction of a physician, and the reaction of the patient to medication must be consistently monitored by the physician and other observers.

Antipsychotic drugs

Antipsychotic drugs are part of a group of chemical compounds known as phenothiazines. The two phenothiazine derivatives that have antipsychotic effects and that are most widely used are chlorpromazine (Thorazine) and thioridazine (Mellaril). They have been found to be most effective for helping very anxious patients, and they may eliminate hallucinations and reduce the pervasiveness of delusions. Generally, individuals who are diagnosed as schizophrenic, manic depressive, or involutional psychotic respond to these medications.

Antipsychotic drugs are generally not used with neurotics or with individuals who have liver disease. Common side effects of antipsychotic drugs include the following: drowsiness, dry mouth, constipation, skin sensitivity to light, and dizziness. There may also be impairment of sexual functioning, such as impotence or amenorrhea.

Antipsychotic drugs are relatively safe in terms of potential danger as a result of patient abuse. They are considered nonhabituating, they rarely cause withdrawal symptoms, and suicide as the result of overdose is rare.

Antidepressant drugs

Commonly used antidepressants include stimulants, which are generally amphetamine derivatives, and more specific antidepressant compounds such as monoamine oxidase (MAO) inhibitors. The effects of these various antidepressant medications are varied and beyond the scope of this discussion. In some cases antidepressants will be used in conjunction with antipsychotic agents. In many instances of depression these drugs will be useful in returning the patient to a normal level of activity. However, they also may increase the level of anxiety and tension experienced by the patient and produce side effects such as constipation and reduced sexual activity. The amphetamine derivatives, in particular, are potentially dangerous. They are addicting, and prolonged usage may result in organic brain damage and emotional instability. Occasionally, amphetamine addiction has been reported to lead to psychosis, and withdrawal after prolonged usage is very severe. It is of utmost importance, therefore, that the use of antidepressants, especially the amphetamines, be closely supervised by a physician.

Antianxiety drugs

Antianxiety medications are also known as minor tranquilizers. The most commonly used antianxiety drugs include chlordiazepoxide (Librium) and meprobamate (Miltown, Equanil). These drugs are generally used for the alleviation of tension, anxiety, and depression of short duration in nonpsychotic patients. They are helpful in giving rapid symptomatic relief to alcoholics who are agitated and hallucinating. The possibility of addiction is present in the use of some minor tranquilizers, and drowsiness often accompanies use of these medications. Therefore, care should be taken that individuals for whom such medications are prescribed do not engage in activities such as operation of a motor vehicle or other machinery for which alertness is necessary for safety.

Sedatives and hypnotics

Sedatives and hypnotics generally are barbiturates but also include other compounds. They are not as widely used today as prior to the advent of other tranquilizing medications. They occasionally are used as daytime sedatives, but they are more often employed as aids to sleep. They may be helpful for reducing tension and anxiety, and some are used to control convulsions. All of these medications are addictive when used over a long period of time and are dangerous when combined with the ingestion of alcohol. When taken in large doses they are fatal. They are rarely made available in large quantities to depressed patients or those who are prone to excessive consumption of alcohol.

Other somatic treatments

A number of other treatments for disturbed behavior are medical in nature, although not relying specifically on drugs for their effect, and they are in wide use. Probably the most well known and effective of such treatments is electroconvulsive therapy (ECT). When properly administered, ECT is a relatively simple and safe procedure that may be very helpful in alleviating depressive and schizophrenic patterns of behavior. ECT involves the induction of convulsions in the patient through the application of electric shock to the forebrain. The number of times this treatment is necessary, the voltage, and the use of other medical procedures, such as psychotropic medication; is determined by the physician. The most widely found side effect of ECT is a loss of memory for recent events. This effect generally disappears within a relatively short time after treatment.

Other somatic treatments, such as hydrotherapy, are not as well documented as having some positive effects, although they are still in use today. The human service worker in settings such as mental hospitals may be requested to assist in certain medical treatments. If he is properly trained and supervised by medical personnel, he may perform a valuable service for the patients. On the other hand, without legal sanction, training, or supervision, the mental health worker should not participate in either medical or certain behavioral change procedures. He should know his limits of authorization and competence for using behavior change techniques in both biological and behavioral areas and rely on the higher trained professionals for consultation and direction.

RESEARCH ON EFFECTS OF PSYCHOTHERAPY

Research in the area of psychotherapy has been plagued by a number of problems, especially a lack of control groups, placebo treatment groups, and groups treated with another form of therapy thought to be effective with the same behavior disorder. As a result of these problems and the statistical difficulties that arise from the poor reliability of a psychiatric diagnosis, the results of research on psychotherapy has been frequently confusing, conflicting, and sometimes misleading.

Eysenck (1966) has made an extensive study of the effectiveness of various forms of psychotherapy, and it is his belief that the traditional indirect methods of psychotherapy are no more effective than nontreatment for returning a neurotic individual to normal patterns of living. That is, people who have not received any form of traditional psychotherapy appear to improve just as quickly as those who receive traditional therapy. It is his belief that at the present time only those forms of therapy based on learning principles are capable of producing behavioral improvement more effectively than the person's regular interaction with his environment during the simple passage of time without treatment.

Two points should be remembered in thinking about research on psychotherapy. The first is that research such as that reviewed by Eysenck is based on large groups of mostly neurotic people. The results indicate that on the average improvement as a result of traditional psychotherapy is no bettter than would be expected in the absence of treatment. However, various individuals within these large groups may improve as a result of treatment and still others may feel much more positively toward themselves, even in the absence of a demonstrable therapeutic effect on behavior. Thus, although on the average traditional treatment may not appear effective, in many cases it can be helpful to the individual. Second, it should be remembered that therapy based on learning principles includes all of the techniques discussed in this chaper, with the exception of techniques derived from the physical sciences. It is not limited to a simple dispensing of tangible reinforcers but includes numerous techniques that rely upon verbal interaction between the patient and therapist for their effect.

The relationship between client and therapist is of great importance even when therapy is based on learning principles. A program of therapy based on these principles is minimally effective when carried out in a mechanistic and automatic manner. Although research indicates that traditional methods of therapy may not be exceptionally effective, this does not mean that verbal interaction is an inappropriate medium of therapy. Rather, the work of Eysenck points out that for therapy of any form to be effective, the interaction between client and therapist must be based upon scientific principles that have been demonstrated to be useful in the understanding of behavior, rather than on armchair theorizing about the metaphysical components of the mind.

We agree with Eysenck that traditional psychotherapy is not maximally efficient. In contrast to him, we believe that traditional psychotherapy should be continued and improved.

REFERENCES AND SUGGESTED READINGS

Association of Hospital and Institution Libraries. 1971. Bibliotherapy methods and materials. Chicago, American Library Association.

Ayllon, T., and Azrin, N. 1968. The token economy: a motivational system for therapy and rehabilitation. New York, Meredith Corporation.

Bandura, A. 1969. Principles of behavior modification. New York, Holt, Rinehart and Winston, Inc.

Berne, E. 1964. Games people play: the psychology of human relationships. New York, Grove Press, Inc.

Braun, J. 1966. Clinical psychology in transition. New York, World Publishing Company.

Carkhuff, R. 1972. The art of helping: a guide for developing helping skills for parents, teachers and counselors. Amherst, Mass., Human Resource Development Press.

Coleman, J. 1964. Abnormal psychology and modern life, ed. 3. Chicago, Scott, Foresman and Company.

Dollard, J., and Miller, N. 1950. Personality and psychotherapy: an analysis in terms of learning, thinking, and culture. New York, McGraw-Hill Book Company.

Ellis, A. 1962. Reason and emotion in psychotherapy. New York, Lyle Stuart, Inc.

Eysenck, H. 1966. The effects of psychotherapy. New York, International Science Press.

Freud, S. 1943. A general introduction to psychoanalysis, ed. 3. Garden City, N. Y. Garden City Publishing Co.

Greenspoon, J. 1955. The reinforcing effect of two spoken words on the frequency of two responses. American Journal of Psychology 68:409-416.

Hildum, D., and Brown, R. 1956. Verbal reinforcement and interviewer bias. Journal of Abnormal and Social Psychology 53:108-111.

Hull, C. 1933. Hypnosis and suggestability: an experimental approach. New York, Appleton-Century-Crofts.

Hunziker, J. 1971. A comparison of participant modeling and vicarious extinction in the treatment of fear of the water. Unpublished master's thesis, Arizona State University.

Isaacs, W., Thomas, J., and Goldiamond, I. 1960. Application of operant conditioning to reinstate verbal behavior in psychotics. Journal of Speech and Hearing Disorders 25:8-12.

Jones, M. C. 1924. A laboratory study of fear: the case of Peter. Pedagogical Seminary 31:308-315.

Krasner, L. 1966. Behavior control and social responsibility. In Braun, J., editor. Clinical psychology in transition. New York, World Publishing Company, pp. 140-145.

Masters, W., and Johnson, V. 1970. Human sexual inadequacy. Boston, Little, Brown and Company.

Moreno, J. 1959-1969. Psychodrama. Beacon, N. Y., Beacon House.

Mowrer, O., and Mowrer, W. 1938. Enuresis: a method for its study and treatment. American Journal of Orthopsychiatry 8:436-459.

Perls, F. 1951. Gestalt therapy: excitement and growth in the human personality. New York, Julian Press.

Premack, D. 1959. Toward empirical behavior laws: I. Positive reinforcement. Psychological review 66:219-233.

Rogers, C. 1951. Client-centered therapy: its current practice, implications and theory. Boston, Houghton Mifflin Company.

Rosenthal, D. 1955. Changes in some moral values following psychotherapy. Journal of Consulting Psychology 19:431-436.

Stampfl, T., and Levis, D. 1967. Essentials of implosive therapy: a learning theory based on psychodynamic behavioral therapy. Journal of Abnormal Psychology 71:496-503.

Ullmann, L., and Krasner, L. 1965. Case studies in behavior modification. New York, Holt, Rinehart and Winston, Inc.

Wolberg, L. 1967. The technique of psychotherapy, ed. 2. New York, Grune & Stratton, Inc.

Wolf, M., Risley, T., and Mees, H. 1964. Application of operant conditioning procedures to the behavior problems of an autistic child. Behavior Research and Therapy 1:305-312.

Wolpe, J., and Lazarus, A. 1966. Behavior therapy techniques: a guide to the treatment of neuroses. London, Pergamon Press Ltd.

9
PHYSICAL CARE AND FIRST AID

❧

The tasks of the mental health worker in providing human services sometimes include carrying out a variety of procedures pertaining to the person as a biological organism. In some institutions these duties may compose a major part of the job. This chapter is designed to introduce the mental health technician to a variety of physical care procedures. It is not intended to provide a sufficient background to enable him to perform the many complex physical care tasks that have often been a major part of his role in the past. The new mental health worker is a generalist, and his primary duties involve understanding and promoting behavior change. However, in his job he may be required to work with medical personnel such as physicians, nurses, and others, and sometimes he may be called upon to perform important physical care activity in unusual situations. Therefore, it is important that the mental health worker be familiar with certain procedures used by other professions and with emergency first aid.

Prevention should be the major concern of the mental health worker, rather than treatment of physical problems. He is in a position to observe behavior and environmental conditions that may lead to injury or illness. Concern for safety, cleanliness, and the personal hygiene of himself, his patients, and others with whom he works are significant for preventing injury and illness. In order to determine the presence of illness or injury and its severity, it is essential that the mental health worker know certain signs and symptoms.

SIGNS AND SYMPTOMS OF ILLNESS AND INJURY
Objective signs and symptoms

Objective signs and symptoms of illness or injury include those aspects that can be observed or measured by the mental health worker without a verbal report from the client.

Vital signs. Vital signs are measurable indications of the functioning of the physical organism. Changes in any or all of these signs may indicate the presence of illness or injury.

Temperature. Temperature is a measure of the heat generated by the body in conjunction with the life process. Normal temperature is approximately 98.6° Fahrenheit by the oral method. Elevations or depressions of temperature more than 1° above or below this are generally indicative of bodily malfunction. Body temperature may be determined by three methods.

It may be determined *orally* by inserting a thermometer under the tongue and closing the mouth for 3 minutes. Care should be taken that the patient does not bite with his teeth on the thermometer, since broken glass and the substance contained in the thermometer may cause serious physical damage.

Body temperature may be determined *anally* by insertion of a clinical thermometer lubricated with petroleum or liquid petroleum into the rectum for a period of 3 minutes. The patient should be lying on his side with his knees flexed when the thermometer is inserted. It should be noted that normal rectal temperature is usually 1° higher than temperature taken by mouth.

Body temperature may also be determined by placing the thermometer in the *armpit (axilla)* for a period of 10 minutes. The bulb end of the thermometer should be in the hollow of the armpit and the stem should point out from the patient. The patient should rest his hand on the opposite shoulder. Temperature determined by the axillary method is the least accurate method and usually yields a normal temperature 1° lower than that obtained when temperature is determined orally.

Pulse. Measuring a person's pulse is a way of determining at what rate his heart is beating. The pulse can be measured by putting pressure with the fingers on an artery resting on a bone, against which it can be compressed. A number of factors influence pulse rate, including sex, weight, age, posture, and the use of medication. Exercise, emotion, bleeding, and high body temperature are associated with an increase in pulse rate. Normal pulse rate for adults usually ranges between 70 and 80 beats per minute, although for some individuals the range of normal pulse varies between 50 and 90 beats per minute.

Respiration. Respiration or breathing is the process of exchanging oxygen and carbon dioxide in the lungs. After air is inhaled the oxygen is transferred from the lungs to the bloodstream and utilized by the body. The chemical reactions in the body requiring oxygen give off the waste gas carbon dioxide, which is released through the lungs when one exhales. In determining respiration rate, the rise and fall of the chest is counted as one respiration. Normal respiration rate ranges between 16 and 20 respirations per minute.

Blood pressure. Blood pressure refers to the force exerted by blood on the walls of the arteries. Blood pressure depends upon the energy or force of the heartbeat, varies from day to day, and is influenced by changes in physical or mental activity. Blood pressure is measured using a sphygmomanometer and a stethoscope. Two readings, the systolic and the diastolic blood pressure, are recorded.

Other objective signs and symptoms. Aside from vital signs, there are other aspects of a person's behavior and bodily function that can be observed by the mental health worker and that may be indicative of physical dysfunction. Significant indications of illness or injury should be reported to a medically trained professional.

Response to the environment. A person's general responses to his surroundings and other people may suggest physical problems. One who is experiencing some degree of physical distress is generally less capable of responding normally to his environment. He may seem preoccupied, lethargic, withdrawn, irritable, or depressed. A noticeable change from usual in the way an individual responds to his environment should alert the mental health worker to the possibility that the person is physically ill.

Skin condition. Illness may be evidenced by changes in skin color, the appearance of a rash, or other skin disturbances, such as pimples or boils. Often the appearance of rashes or pimples is indicative of the presence of serious infection. For example, syphilis usually first manifests itself through the development of a pimple or chancre in the genital area. Other conditions, such as diabetes and heart disease, may show themselves through changes in skin color, moisture, and texture.

Motor functioning. The degree of facility with which an individual is able to control the movement of his limbs can also alert the mental health worker to the presence of illness of injury. Physical dysfunction may manifest itself in a loss of normal control over patterns of movement. For example, when a person faints, appears very clumsy, moves extremely slowly, tends to avoid the use of a particular limb, or moves in a spastic or sudden manner, he should be referred for physical examination.

Bowel movements. The frequency and characteristics of bowel movements are good indicators of illness or injury. One who is constantly constipated, produces movements of an unusual color or texture, or is incontinent may have infection or injury to his body. Incontinence poses a particular problem for the mental health worker, for it is likely to arouse anger and may often be thought of as simply a device for manipulating staff and gaining attention. In some cases this may indeed be an operant behavior that can be modified with the use of learning principles. In many other cases incontinence results from genuine physical disability and may be indicative of serious illness.

Bleeding and other discharges. Bleeding is one of the most obvious signs of infection or illness, and immediate efforts should be made to stop or slow the flow of blood. Simply stopping blood may not solve the problem that caused it. Other discharges that can be observed by the mental health worker may also be important indicators of illness or injury. Drooling at the mouth, constant discharge from the nose, a discharge from the ears or eyes, and unusual bowel discharges may be indicative of illness.

Subjective signs and symptoms of illness or injury

Subjective signs and symptoms of illness or injury include those that cannot readily be observed by another individual but that are reported by the person who experiences them. These signs and symptoms are equally as important as objective ones and often are the earliest indicators of illness or injury. When an individual reports that he has muscle stiffness, aches, pains, tingling sensations in some part of his body, an upset stomach, dizziness, or a headache, the mental health worker should be aware that such verbal reports may be extremely important.

Summary

In order to provide the best possible service to those under his supervision, the mental health worker in many work locations must be alert to the significance of indicators of illness and injury. If he is to be an effective agent of behavior change and prevent needless suffering by his patients, signs and symptoms of physical illness should never be ignored or dismissed as simply manifestations of deviant behavior. Too many lives have been lost by routine dismissal of these important signs and symptoms. Whenever there is a meaningful possibility that an individual is physically ill, it is the responsibility of the mental health worker to obtain the expert help of the medically trained professional.

ASPECTS OF PHYSICAL CARE

There are a number of aspects of physical care performed by mental health workers to varying degrees in different job situations. Most often they are supervised by a registered nurse, physician, or other expert. This section will introduce certain terminology and procedures, but an extensive discussion is beyond our scope.

Nutrition. Nutrition is one of the most important aspects of somatic care that is sometimes overlooked by the mental health worker. The technician should be careful to see that the client is receiving adequate nutrition. This is most easily accomplished in institutional settings by accompanying the patient to meals. When dealing with individuals on an out-patient or community basis, it is sometimes necessary to question the individual to determine his eating habits and instruct him in the essentials of good nutrition.

Every individual needs to daily consume proteins, carbohydrates, fats, vitamins, minerals, cellulose, and water if he is to function normally on the biological level. The specific amount of each must be determined by the size, age, sex, and weight of the individual, as well as the nature of the environment in which he lives. In harsh environments a person often will need more of a particular substance than he would in others.

Guidelines for good nutrition should be determined in conjunction with a dietitian, nurse, or physician. In some instances one's physical condition or medication requires that he consume only certain foods. Special diets are often used in the treatment of physical disorders, such as ulcer, diabetes, and phenylketonuria, and some medications require that the intake of certain foods be restricted or eliminated. For example, individuals who are receiving a monamine oxidase inhibitor must restrict their intake of cheeses.

Personal hygiene. Personal hygiene is very important for the prevention and communication of disease. The mouth is the body orifice through which most disease germs enter. Infections of the mouth should not be thought to be limited in their effect to that area, since the disease may be transmitted to the respiratory and digestive tract from the mouth. Neglect of oral hygiene may cause bad breath (halitosis) or lead to serious dental problems. Brushing the teeth with an appropriate dentifrice after meals is the easiest and most effective way to maintain good oral hygiene. The mental health worker should be certain that his patients or clients maintain good oral hygiene.

Adequate care of the skin includes regular bathing. Baths allow the wastes of the body to be discharged through the skin more efficiently, stimulate circulation, provide muscular relaxation and mild exercise, and reduce objectional body odor. Good care of hair is also important, for dirty, greasy hair is unhealthy and unattractive. The hair should be washed frequently with a good shampoo.

Shaving is another activity that is an important part of personal hygiene. The mores of American culture indicate that men be generally clean shaven about the face and that women shave the axillary area and their legs. To a large extent, however, shaving is a matter of personal preference, and it should not be thought that a patient must always shave or that a patient will not improve if he does not. Body hair may become a part of the self-concept; a man may wear a beard because he feels more protected with it. This is usually appropriate and acceptable, and he should not be forced to shave simply on the basis of another's rigid personal beliefs. However, it is important for health reasons that facial and other body hair be kept clean, just as the hair on the head must be clean in order to avoid dangerous skin conditions, unsightly appearance, and odor.

Bowels. While working with disturbed and physically ill persons, the mental health worker may be required to aid in the care of bowels. The primary problems faced are cleanliness and incontinence.

A catheter, which is a special tube, may be inserted through the urinary tract to the bladder in order to help control incontinence, obtain a sterile urine specimen, or relieve bladder distension for the patient who is paralyzed or in a coma.

Enemas are used to produce a bowel movement, for the cleansing of the large intestine, and to provide medication or nutrition when these substances cannot be taken by mouth. An enema is given by inserting a lubricated rectal tube into the colon through the rectum.

Enemas and catheters are only given when ordered by a physician. They are unpleasant tasks, but their necessity and benefit to the patient have been well documented. Evacuation and cleansing of bowels are normal body functions. Helping an individual under his care to properly perform these functions need not be a source of dread for the mental health worker.

Hot and cold applications. The application of moist heat or dry cold is often used in the treatment of injury and infection. Heat may be used to lessen pain, relieve muscle cramps and swelling, promote circulation, and localize infection. Cold may be used to relieve headache, slow hemorrhaging and swelling, relieve pain, and reduce body temperature.

Heat and cold may be applied with hot water bags, ice bags, hot compresses, steam inhalations, or tepid sponges or by placing the patient on a hypothermia mattress. The application of heat and cold is usually used to aid the body in healing. The application of heat leads to dilation of blood vessels, thereby increasing the supply of oxygen and blood to injured tissues. Conversely, the application of cold results in a contraction of blood vessels, thus reducing the flow of blood and oxygen to a body part.

FIRST AID

While working with people who exhibit disordered behavior, it is not uncommon to encounter emergency situations in which a knowledge of basic first aid may save a life.

Common emergencies

Wounds. Wounds are commonly known as cuts in the skin and are of four types. Abrasions are wounds that occur as a result of friction of the skin against an object. Incised wounds are generally very regularly shaped openings in the skin that bleed freely. Lacerated wounds are irregular openings in the skin. They may not bleed freely but may involve a great deal of damage. Puncture wounds are those produced by the penetration of a sharp instrument through the skin.

The chief concern of the mental health worker in an emergency situation is a wound that is bleeding severely. The first step to take is to stop the bleeding at once. Where possible this should be done by placing a clean cloth directly over the wound and applying pressure. Bleeding can in almost every case be controlled by direct pressure over the wound. A tourniquet should never be used unless it is the only possible means of reducing blood flow to an acceptable level. Once a tourniquet has been applied, its improper release may lead the individual to go into shock and die. Loss of the limb through use of the tourniquet may also occur. A good general rule is that the mental health worker should never apply a tourniquet unless he is willing to risk the loss of the limb in order to save the patient's life. If a tourniquet must be applied it may only be removed by a physician in a facility where the effect of shock can be controlled.

In some cases injury or illness may lead to internal bleeding, which only becomes apparent when blood is discharged from mouth, nose, or ears. First aid in this case involves raising the head and shoulders if there is difficulty in

breathing and seeking medical care immediately. If the patient becomes unconscious, he should be placed on his side with the head and chest positioned
lower than the hips to prevent blood from being absorbed in the lungs.

Burns. First aid for burns is aimed at the relief of pain and the prevention
of infection. First-degree burns produce redness and soreness, second-degree
burns are those for which blisters develop, and third-degree burns involve
destruction of layers of tissue below the skin. It is often difficult to determine
the degree of burn when it first occurs. Danger to the individual from infection
is highest in second- and third-degree burns. First aid action involves keeping
air out of the burn. This is accomplished by the application of a thick layer of a
dry cloth dressing material. The dressing should be sterile to prevent contamina-
tion and infection.

Fractures and dislocations. A fracture is a break in a bone. These breaks
are classified as either simple fractures, in which the skin around the bone is
not broken, and compound, in which a bone fragment penetrates the skin and
is visible. A third type of fracture, the comminuted, involves several breaks in
the same bone. It may be enclosed by the skin or penetrate the skin as in a compound fracture.

A fracture should be suspected when swelling and tenderness are present
following an injury. Fractures can only be accurately evaluated through the
use of x-ray equipment, since an individual may be able to move the broken
bone and associated appendages may be mobile without pain. Therefore, first
aid should be administered when pain, swelling, and tenderness to the touch are
present on the assumption that a bone has been fractured. First aid for fractures
involves keeping the injured limb or body area quiet, limiting movement in
adjacent muscles and joints, and treating for shock. It the skin has been broken,
bleeding should be controlled first. A protruding bone should never be pushed
back through the skin. The manipulation of fractured bones, splinting, and
traction are best undertaken by a physician. These activities should never be
attempted by an individual unless medical treatment is completely unavailable
at the scene and the victim must be transported a great distance to receive
medical attention.

Dislocation involves the displacement of a bone from a joint. The symptoms
of dislocation are very similar to those of fracture, and first aid should follow
the same pattern as that used when a fracture is suspected. Under no circumstances should the individual giving first aid attempt to replace the bone in the
joint socket through manipulation. Sometimes this will occur spontaneously, but
medical attention is necessary if further injury and future physical handicap
are to be avoided.

Shock. While rendering first aid to individuals who have suffered severe
burns or wounds, one of the primary concerns of the mental health worker
is the control of shock. Traumatic shock is a term that refers to depressed
functioning of the body as a result of reduced blood flow through the circula-

tory system following serious injury. Traumatic shock may also follow fractures and should be expected to occur in any injury where a large quantity of blood is lost. The most important indicator of traumatic shock is weakness of the victim and skin that is pale, moist, and cool to the touch. Nausea, dilation of the pupils, a weak pulse, and shallow or irregular breathing often also indicate shock. However, symptoms of shock are not always present even when an individual is severely injured. The patient may appear wide awake, aware, and optimistic but then suddenly collapse from shock. The best course to follow is to treat any seriously injured person for shock. The patient should lie down, and a blanket should be placed beneath him. If the outside temperature is cool he should be covered lightly with a blanket. The blanket should not lead to sweating, and when the temperature is warm a blanket may not be needed. The objective in applying a blanket is to prevent the loss of body heat; it is not necessary if the environmental temperature is high enough to maintain body heat. It may be advisable to raise the feet 8 to 12 inches for the individual who has lost a considerable amount of blood. This elevation should be avoided for patients with suspected head injury, if it results in difficult breathing, or if pain results from such movement.

Poisoning. When an individual has taken some poison by mouth, appropriate action is to dilute the substance as fast as possible and then, in some cases, induce vomiting. The most readily available substance for dilution of poison is water, but milk is preferred, since it coats the digestive tract and slows absorption of poison. Vomiting may be induced by having the individual drink a large amount of fluid or by using a finger or spoon in the mouth to promote gagging. When an object is used to promote gagging through the mouth, care should be taken that vomitus is not released into the air passage. The universal antidote (activated charcoal) should be available and administered.

This procedure applies in most cases of poisoning. However, when an individual has ingested a strong acid or alkali, strychnine, or kerosene or when he is unconscious, convulsing, or exhausted, different procedures must be followed. When a strong acid has been ingested a solution of milk of magnesia or baking soda should be given to the patient, but vomiting should not be induced. Administration of this solution should be followed by ingestion of milk, egg white, or olive oil in order to protect the lining of the digestive tract. If a strong alkali has been taken, vinegar or lemon juice should be diluted with water and ingested by the patient in order to neutralize the poison. Vomiting should not be induced and olive oil, milk, or egg white should follow the taking of the neutralizing solution. For an individual who has taken strychnine, fluids may be given and vomiting induced only if these procedures are used immediately after the poison was taken. If 5 or more minutes have elapsed since the poison was taken, these procedures or any other attempt to treat or move the person may induce convulsions. Medical care should be sought as quickly as possible. When the patient is unconscious or in a coma, it is likely that the poison has already been absorbed by the body. In these cases the patient should be kept warm, but fluids should not be given and vomiting should not be induced.

In any case of poisoning, even though first aid measures may lead to optimism, the human service worker must always ensure that the individual receives medical attention as soon as possible.

Fainting. Fainting is a reaction of the central nervous system leading to a reduction of the blood supply to the brain and causing unconsciousness. Usually fainting occurs in conjunction with some stressful event; it is not the same as unconsciousness caused by illness or injury. For an individual who reports that he feels faint, the best immediate aid is to have him lie down on his back. When this is impossible or inconvenient, lowering the head to knee level will be helpful. A person may collapse, with loss of consciousness being the result of fainting. He will regain consciousness soon after collapse if he is able to lie level with the floor. When fainting occurs frequently, or if the individual remains unconscious for some period of time, simple fainting has not occurred. The person should receive prompt medical attention, since unconsciousness is an indicator of more serious injury or illness.

Convulsions. Convulsions are associated with a variety of conditions. The two most common causes of convulsions are high fever associated with infection of the central nervous system and epilepsy. Convulsions take many forms and are a manifestation of the uncoordinated and simultaneous action of large groups of nervous tissue in the brain. The convulsion that is of greatest concern to the individual giving first aid is that involving jerky, spasmodic contraction of the large muscle groups of the entire body and loss of consciousness. The greatest danger during such a convulsion is that the individual will fracture a bone by striking an object or bite his tongue severely. When such a convulsion occurs the bystander should not attempt to restrain the individual in any way, since restriction of movement may lead to a fracture. He should remove any objects that the victim might strike and place some firm object, such as the edge of a book cover or a wooden tongue depressor, between the teeth to prevent tongue injury. After the convulsion has ceased some attempt should be made to determine its cause. If it is the result of an epileptic attack and is recognized as such by the victim, all that remains to be done is ensure that he has regained equilibrium enough to manage movement. However, the victim may not be aware that he is epileptic. He may appear to have a high fever, and the convulsions may not cease within a relatively short period of time, which indicates that immediate medical attention is urgent. Serious infection and poisoning often result in convulsions, and this reaction of the body indicates that death may be imminent without treatment.

Head injury. Injuries to the head are one of the most common causes of death. Death most frequently occurs from head injury in traffic accidents. However, diving into shallow water or tumbling from bicycles and horses also accounts for many head injuries. The symptoms indicating head injury are varied and may be very subtle. The most noticeable and positive signs are unequal size of the pupils, paralysis of a body part, unconsciousness, or headache. In some cases the individual may manifest very few symptoms at the time. Thus, head injury should be treated in any accident where a good deal of force has been involved, such as an automobile crash or fall. The most important action to be taken is to keep the person quiet. If he is unconscious the head should be turned to the side so that secretions will be discharged from the mouth. It may also be advisable to raise the head 1 or 2 inches by placing a pillow or some other object beneath it. Clothing about the neck should be loosened, and if the patient is awake, he should be instructed to lie quietly on his back. Whenever head injury is suspected no stimulants such as coffee should be given. For apparent scalp wounds, care should be taken not to place pressure on the skull. A dressing should be laid lightly over the injury and a full head bandage applied.

Heart attack and stroke. Heart attack is most common in people who are of middle age or older. Heart disease usually develops over a long period of time and in most cases an individual will seek medical attention before he suffers an acute attack. However, when an acute attack occurs rapid action is essential if life is to be sustained. The most common symptoms of heart attack are pain, usually in the chest, and shortness of breath. First aid for a heart attack involves helping the individual take his medication if he is already under medical care for a heart condition. Persons reporting feeling faint should lie down and the legs should be raised slightly. When shortness of breath is reported the head and chest should be raised to a position the patient finds comfortable. The pain associated with heart attack may be extremely severe and extend to the neck, arms, or abdomen. Having the person lie down on his back is helpful for relieving pain, but such a position may be difficult for the patient to assume initially. This position puts less strain on the heart and the patient should be informed calmly that it will be to his benefit if he will lie down. Transportation of a heart attack victim may be dangerous since it adds more strain, and it should not be undertaken unless it is impossible for medical aid to be administered within a reasonably short period of time. The patient should be disturbed as little as possible and remain lying on his back while he is being transported.

Stroke, or apoplexy, involves a blood clot or hemorrhage in the blood vessels of the brain. Strokes vary in severity, but when extensive damage is done the patient will be unconscious, breathing heavily, and possibly paralyzed in parts of his body. Smaller strokes may not be accompanied by unconsciousness, although dizziness, headache, memory loss, speech defects, ringing in the ears, or difficulty in movement may be indicators of stroke when they occur suddenly. The proper procedure for suspected minor strokes is to advise the patient to seek medical care and protect him from overexertion or injury that might result from the symptoms. When a severe attack is suspected, the patient should be kept lying flat. If breathing is labored he should be turned on his side so that whatever secretions are present will drain from the mouth and not be discharged into the air passages and lungs. No fluids or food should be given and medical care should be sought with the utmost speed.

Foreign bodies. It is not uncommon to encounter situations in which some foreign body has become lodged in the eye, throat, or food passages. When a foreign body such as a piece of hair or dust becomes lodged in the area of the eye, it most commonly lies on the inside of the upper eyelid. First aid involves removing the object by placing slight pressure on the lid with some blunt object while turning the inner surface of the eyelid outward. The foreign body will often fall from the eyelid when this is done. A particle remaining on the inner surface of the lid sometimes may be removed by touching it with the corner of a clean piece of cloth. When the particle or object can be seen on the surface of the eye the patient should be instructed to blink his eye several times. This will often dislodge the particle. However, if it is imbedded in the eye or is not dislodged by blinking, under no circumstances should an attempt be made to remove it. Medical care must be obtained at once for cases of scraping or penetration of the eye. The patient should close his eye and a pad of cloth or cotton should be placed over the closed lid. When an object is imbedded in the eye, serious injury is likely even when damage appears slight. Transportation to medical attention should be rapid and stress on the eye should be minimal.

When a foreign body lodges in the throat or air passages choking will result. The first action of first aid is to let the patient attempt to cough out the object by himself. Probing with the fiingers may push the object farther down and is no more effective than coughing itself. The patient should not be distracted from his coughing by alarm or questions. The individual should be taken to a physician or the nearest hospital, and if breathing ceases artificial respiration is essential for the maintenance of life.

It may be apparent that a foreign body has been completely swallowed and has entered the digestive organs of the body. Even such objects as open safety pins can pass harmlessly through the digestive tract. However, there is a good deal of danger that the object may become lodged in the digestive tract or will enter an air passage. Unless the object has become struck in the throat, symptoms are usually absent. One who has swallowed a foreign body should be taken to a physician for examination as soon as possible.

External cardiac pulmonary resuscitation (ECPR)

It is unusual to find only one of the common emergencies discussed here occurring at a time. Generally injuries tend to occur in groups. For example, an individual who has been in an automobile accident may be unconscious, have suffered fractures of various bones, be bleeding profusely, and exhibit symptoms of shock. When groups of serious injuries occur or in the case of any serious injury, it is possible that the heart will stop beating and respiration will cease. Once this has occurred the first aid administered in the next several minutes is of utmost importance. When heartbeat and respiration have ceased ECPR should be instituted. The heel of the palm of the hand is placed on the sternum and used to compress this bone against the heart. Pressure should be applied and released rapidly, approximately once per second. After approximately twelve to fifteen such compressions, resuscitation by mouth should be given twice. It is accomplished by placing the mouth over that of the victim, tilting his head back, closing his nostrils with the fingers, and exhaling deeply. After this is done two times, the sequence of chest compression and respiration is repeated until skin color of the victim becomes normal and heartbeat and respiration are resumed.

It is extremely critical that ECPR be administered immediately. If 3 or 4 minutes pass without heartbeat and respiration, damage to the brain becomes severe because of lack of oxygen. Courses in ECPR are made available by local heart associations, and every person should take the time to learn the proper method of administration.

Transportation

Accidents that result in serious injury often do not occur in locations where medical attention is readily available. For this reason it may become necessary to transport the individual some distance for adequate medical treatment. Transportation of the injured should be undertaken carefully if further needless injury is to be avoided. For persons who must be carried, an adequate stretcher or litter is needed. If the victim will be transported by car, the driver should avoid bumps and other road hazards that may cause needless movement of the patient. Many injuries, such as those to the head or spinal cord, require that special precautions be taken in the transportation of the individual to avoid permanent disability or death. Instruction in proper modes of transportation and first aid in general is available through the American Red Cross. Every person should take the opportunity to enroll in one of these courses.

PSYCHOLOGICAL CONSIDERATIONS IN PHYSICAL CARE

When rendering first aid or carrying out various physical care procedures, one of the most important considerations is the manner in which these functions are accomplished by the worker. Physical illnesses sometimes place much of the burden for understanding and compassion on the shoulders of the therapist, and these factors have been shown to have major effects on the outcome of physical treatment. When rendering first aid a calm, understanding, but firm approach is best. No attempt should be made to diagnose injury or make suggestions as to prognosis. These areas are the concern of the physician, and inaccurate or incorrect information supplied by an untrained individual may cause needless worrying and sorrow for the patient. When helping an individual with personal hygiene or carrying out other physical care procedures, it is important that the worker show positive regard and respect for the patient, explain to him the procedures that will be undertaken, and proceed in a calm and efficient manner.

When it is needed, reassurance should be given. The individual should never be made to feel that he is a burden. The attitude and manner of a worker in carrying out physical care activities for chronically ill patients may enhance the patient's concept of himself and lead to more speedy recovery, or the behavior can contribute to despair and loss of the will to live. Therefore, it is most important that the mental health worker seek to maintain an understanding and therapeutic relationship with the patient for whom he is providing physical care.

REFERENCES AND SUGGESTED READINGS

American National Red Cross. 1957. First aid textbook. Garden City, N. Y., Doubleday & Company, Inc.

Mayes, M. E. 1970. Abdallah's nurse's aide study manual. Philadelphia, W. B. Saunders Co.

10

HUMAN SERVICE AND
MENTAL HEALTH TECHNOLOGY

❦

The concept of human service workers and mental health technicians as an independent or at least interdependent professional group effective in providing the general psychotherapeutic services required by persons who are in distress is quite recent and innovative in the field of helping services. Several indications of the need for the mental health worker concept have been noted (Albee, 1959; Arnoff, Rubinstein, and Speisman, 1969), and attempts have been made to supply the manpower on the basis of identified demands, including:

1. The personnel must be produced for work in a short period of time, both in order to fulfill manpower needs and to compensate for the rather large turnover rate.

2. Many more additional personnel need to be trained and made available for positions in the field.

3. The personnel must be produced and placed in positions relatively inexpensively. It is said that what this country needs is not a good 5¢ cigar but a good $5 an hour psychotherapist.

4. The new mental health personnel's skills need to be very broad and general, while at the same time in sufficient depth to be effective.

It is generally recognized that the first training program for preparing college-educated mental health workers in a full 2-year curriculum began at the Fort Wayne Campus of Purdue University under the direction of Drs. John Hadley and John True in 1966. There were historical events and faltering steps taken prior to this program, including the important research by Margaret Rioch and others (1963), who demonstrated the high level of ability college-educated housewives had when given a degree of specialized training in psychotherapy. Programs designed to train individuals to deal therapeutically with others have sprung up in community junior colleges all over the country. There currently are over 100 such training programs, which carry such titles as human service worker, mental health technician, child counselor, psychology assistant, counselor aide, and many others. They have in common the orientation toward helping people with problems and a curricular emphasis in the behavioral sciences. These programs are directed toward practice and skill development, rather than only academic knowledge.

The community junior colleges primarily operate the programs because they tend to have much more flexibility and openness to serving community needs, although some 4-year universities have shown interest in developing programs and are beginning a few. Attempts are being made by many of these community junior college programs to become adequately coordinated with 4-year universities to allow graduates with the associate of arts or science degree to enter the university and obtain a 4-year bachelor's degree in a helping services area. It is probable that this will become an actuality rather than simply a desire as the community junior college training programs become more adequate and well defined. Appendix B provides information about programs currently identified, most of which was supplied by Dr. True through the National Institutes of Mental Health.

Many of these programs, such as the one at Maricopa Technical College in Phoenix, Arizona, were initially developed to answer the need for trained personnel at local mental hospitals. At present, however, the movement is away from an emphasis on hospital-oriented training programs designed to meet the needs of the institutionalized individual and toward the training of new professional generalists and technicians in the helping services field. The community junior college–based programs are becoming more attuned to the numerous agencies providing services to people, not just to the mental hospitals. The curricula of these training programs have much in common, although there are many significant differences. The Mental Health Technology program description at Maricopa Technical College is included here to give the reader an indication of the purpose, content, sequence, and methods of such programs.*

MENTAL HEALTH TECHNOLOGY AT MARICOPA TECHNICAL COLLEGE

The professional groups providing services to our citizens under the broad rubric of mental health have become increasingly aware of the need to reach those who are presently not receiving services or are receiving them ineffectively and inadequately. Traditional concepts of training have emphasized ideal

---

*It was originally intended to place the program description in the Appendix. However, since the mental health worker is what he has learned to be, it was decided to make the curriculum description a part of this chapter, rather than placing a training description in a portion of the book that might be overlooked. Furthermore, the variations in purpose, orientation, and content of other programs should be studied by those interested in this rapidly enlarging field. It is recommended the interested reader write to the program directors listed in Appendix B to request their program descriptions. Those who wish a comparative analysis of programs should consult the references listed at the end of this chapter.

conditions and characteristics of both the professional and the client, which the present status of our society clearly indicates is unrealistic and unworkable.

The major reorientation to the problem is the development of educational programs to prepare personnel to perform numerous tasks formerly assigned to the relatively few members of the traditional mental health professions. The immediate and most important question is whether such an educational program at the associate of arts degree level can equip students with the knowledge, skills, and attitudes to meet the responsibilities of a capable mental health generalist. Research evidence leaves no doubt that such personnel can function quite well, sometimes surpassing the more highly educated professional with particular clients and groups.

The purpose of this program is to increase the manpower in the mental health field, with a training sufficiently broad to enable graduates to function well in diverse settings, rather than limited to a certain position in a specific location. Throughout the curriculum there is an emphasis on developing skills with which the students can increase the behavioral effectiveness of clients.

Mental health technology, Year I courses   **Total credit hours 64**
First semester
   mh 101—Orientation to Mental Health Technology   CREDIT HOURS 1

An introduction to contemporary mental health services. Particular emphasis is placed upon the generalist role of the mental health technician.

   py 101—General Psychology   CREDIT HOURS 3

An overview of the general areas and applications of psychology with consideration of history, scientific methodology, concepts of measurement, biological bases of behavior, learning, development, abnormal behavior, personality theory, and social processes.

   bi 110—Biology Concepts   CREDIT HOURS 3

An overview of the general concepts of biology designed to meet the general education requirement for a liberal arts program and for preprofessional students.

   en 101—English   CREDIT HOURS 3

A development of communication skills, including reading, listening, writing, and speaking. Some secondary orientation on both a group and an individual basis will be made to the mental health area.

   so 101—Introduction to Sociology   CREDIT HOURS 3

An introduction to the study of human societies, social forces, and collective behavior. Special emphasis is placed on the study of contemporary problems, such as those concerned with race, immigration, the family, child welfare, economic security, education, crime, and others.

mh 106—Practicum   CREDIT HOURS 3

An introduction to practice in community, educational, family service, and child treatment agencies, all under professional supervision.* (12 hours per week)

TOTAL HOURS 16

Second semester
en 106—Technical Writing   CREDIT HOURS 3

Presentation of the fundamentals of technical report writing. Organization, diction, clarity, and conciseness are stressed.

mh 103—Deviant Behavior   CREDIT HOURS 3

Theory and research regarding ways in which people become maladjusted, diagnostic categories of behavior disorders, methods of identifying commonalities and differences within and between diagnostic categories, sociological considerations, and therapeutic interventions.

mh 105—Group Process   CREDIT HOURS 3

Presentation of the history, research, and theory of group process, including the utilization of skills in social and work situations. An introduction to therapy with groups is made.

mh 105—Group Process (Laboratory only)   CREDIT HOURS 1

The laboratory is oriented toward acquiring understanding of intrapersonal and interpersonal processes, with a more particular emphasis on self-understanding in relationship to other students in the group.

mh 108—Behavior Assessment   CREDIT HOURS 3

Introduction to basic concepts of behavioral measurement and understanding of test scores. Behavior rating scales and other commonly used psychometric instruments will be emphasized. There will be some experience using assessment techniques relevant to the mental health technician's occupation.

mh 107—Practicum   CREDIT HOURS 3

An introduction to practice in the assessment and treatment of disturbed and impaired adults, the mentally retarded, geriatric patients, and abusers of drugs and alcohol, all under professional supervision. (12 hours per week)

TOTAL HOURS 16

Mental health technology, Year II courses
Third semester

*The practica are more specifically described later.

mh 209—Group Process (Laboratory only)　　　　　CREDIT HOURS 1

A continuation from the second semester.

mh 204—Behavior Modification　　　　　CREDIT HOURS 3

Advancement of principles of individual behavior modification and group methods, including token economy systems. Project reports regarding supervised experience in utilizing behavior modification techniques within the operant framework will be required.

py 215—Personal and Social Adjustment　　　　　CREDIT HOURS 3

Normal development and adjustment with consideration of physical, intellectual, personality, and social variables.

mh 205—Principles of Human Learning　　　　　CREDIT HOURS 3

Historical development of theories of learning placed in perspective. The emphasis will be on present concepts, research evidence, and application possibilities of generalizations regarding how behavioral changes occur. Operant treatment with individuals and groups will be introduced, primarily of an academic rather than a social type.

so 109—Introduction to Social Work　　　　　CREDIT HOURS 3

An introduction to the major viewpoints, skills, methods of operation, and organization of social work services. Some supervised experiences will be provided in selected agencies.

mh 206—Practicum　　　　　CREDIT HOURS 3

The students will be involved in the social service, rehabilitation, adult education, and professional psychology areas. Agencies include selected divisions at the state hospital and community agencies. There will be a comprehensive overview of social work techniques and advanced experience in assessing and altering behavior with both individuals and groups. (12 hours per week)

TOTAL HOURS 16

Fourth semester

mh 210—Group Process (Laboratory only)　　　　　CREDIT HOURS 1

A continuation from the third semester.

mh 208—Group Therapeutics　　　　　CREDIT HOURS 3

A presentation of theories and specific techniques designed to lead to self- and interpersonal understanding among group members, research regarding behavior changes resulting from these behavior techniques, and supervised experience in working with groups. The focus is on group behavior in therapy settings.

hl 203—Drugs and Behavior   CREDIT HOURS 3

A review of basic terminology regarding drugs, the various methods of administration, and physical and behavioral effects. This will include drugs presently illegal and those used to excess, as well as therapeutic drugs. Problems of alcoholism are presented.

co 151—Counselor Aide Practices I   CREDIT HOURS 3

Counselor training for a wide range of supportive service activities under the direct supervision of professional personnel in the development of leadership and skills for individual and multiple client discussion groups, planning and recording counseling activity, observational methods, establishing relationships, and giving information. The student is prepared to recognize his limits in counseling activities and to maximize his working effectiveness in social service, educational, and private agencies.

Humanities   CREDIT HOURS 3

Elective courses that meet this requirement are Philosophy, Art Appreciation, Drama III, Literature Courses, Music Appreciation, or Foreign Languages.

mh 207—Practicum   CREDIT HOURS 3

The final practicum is designed to meet the individual educational and experential needs of each student. They may continue to work in agencies to which they were assigned the preceding semester or in certain programs in which they have developed an interest for future employment and/or in which they need further development. (12 hours per week)

                                                                TOTAL HOURS 16

Mental health technology practica

The experiences to be obtained during the practica are recognized as necessarily being unusually important and broad in scope, with certain of the very specific skills relegated to the future actual work situation. That is, at times the emphasis will be on acquiring widely applicable skills rather than those of more depth but limited applicability, this being consistent with the desire to prepare personnel for diverse human service settings rather than to fill specific positions in a particular location.

Basically, the skills in working with clients and patients involve techniques to perform an assessment of the problem areas, design and implement an adequate and appropriate treatment program, and continuously evaluate the effectiveness of client services. Experiences will include numerous and various locations, kinds and degrees of disorders, and age groups.

Objectives

The students will improve their skills and clarify their roles in performing or assisting in performing in the listed areas. They also require ever-expanding knowledge and skills in ascertaining the behavioral difficulties of the client in order to understand who should be consulted, that it, to whom should the client be referred for more appropriate and adequate assessment and treatment.

Rehabilitative therapies. The student will obtain increasing skills and knowledge in assessment and modification of the clients' occupational abilities, speech and hearing, perceptual motor functioning, general physical needs, recreation and leisure needs, arts and crafts, and other rehabilitative therapies.

Psychological therapies. The student will obtain orientation and improvement in individual therapy, group therapy, behavior therapy, token economy systems, and other basic psychological therapies.

Nursing and first aid. The student will obtain the knowledge and skills to participate in the assessment and treatment involving personal hygiene, first aid, and physical care skills.

Community psychiatry and social services. The student will obtain education in regard to social services, his role and functioning within a therapeutic community, token economy systems, correctional programs, and other social therapies. Furthermore, the development of functional relationships with community agencies will occur.

Management and supervision. The student will obtain education in participating in administering programs and supervising other personnel. His role and function in human service systems undergo continuous revision and must be clarified and altered.

Adult education. The student will be educated to work in the adult education program, which involves skills in tutoring, functioning as discussion leaders, and other significant roles.

Practica sequence Year I   CREDIT HOURS 3
Practicum 106, first semester

Practicum 106 will be a set of educational experiences that will occur with families, with a focus on children and their parents in interactive process. It is believed that most disordered behavior is caused by, or at least developed within, the context of family relationships, the family being considered the smallest unit of the community within which maladaptive behavior coping techniques are expressed. Skills include obtaining information with recognized social and psychological methods, organizing and assessing the data, and implementing behavioral change methodologies to effect more successful and socially appropriate feelings, behaviors, and relationships. Locations for these experiences will include educational, social service, and mental health agencies organized to help families and children. Social welfare agencies, child guidance centers, several programs under various departments at a state university, and the child treatment unit and outpatient clinic of the state hospital are included. Locations that will be secondary, but only because their interest is more focused on the child, include the numerous kinds of educational institutions, public, private, and specialty.

While learning about man as a developing behavioral being, the student's need for a focus on and orientation to man as a biological being will be met through lecture and practice in supervised settings. Skill development will include remotivation, first aid, and basic physical care procedures.

Practicum 107, second semester   CREDIT HOURS 3

Practicum 107 will be located primarily on several adult treatment divisions at the state hospital that emphasize treatment and services. Included will be a token economy system, which is a model of the appropriate behavioral system existing outside the mental hospital. By this time the students will have obtained the basic knowledge, skills, and facilitative attitudes to perceive how disordered behavior develops. This knowledge will be employed with adults who are in the process of establishing a more effective psychological equilibrium. Part of the student's experiences during this period will involve rehabilitation therapies. Behavioral assessment, social work techniques of obtaining and organizing information, and orientations to individual and group therapies will occur as part of the assignments from the didactic courses of this semester.

In completing the cycle of human development, students will move to the geriatric areas, acquiring new knowledge concerning the geriatric person and, with modification, applying their skills to disordered persons of advanced age. Their proficiency in the physical, psychological, and rehabilitation areas will proceed on the basis of working with patients as functioning totalities. There will be coordinated experiences in boarding and extended care homes in the community.

The students will concentrate on special and significant problems of mental retardation. Locations will be the state hospital, public and private schools, and residential centers for the retarded. Professional groups functioning in these locations will provide orientation to their specialties.

The students will acquire knowledge about the problems of drug and alcohol abuse. Community centers and the state hospital serve as locations for these experiences.

Practica sequence Year II
Practicum 206, third semester   CREDIT HOURS 3

Practicum 206 will involve increasing the students' ability in the areas of social and psychological services. The social service area will include students working under the supervision of social workers in community agencies and on selected treatment divisions at the state hospital. The orientation will be toward a more intensive and comprehensive overview of techniques of social work. The professional psychology areas will provide advanced field work in assessing and modifying behavior with both individuals and groups. The students will work in a number of community agencies, including those whose population consists of armed service veterans, those dealing with hard-core unemployed, mental health outpatient clinics, agencies serving Indians having alcohol and drug abuse problems, agencies whose population is composed of emotionally disturbed and mentally retarded children, and high school counseling offices. Many students will obtain experiences teaching in adult education programs. In all of these placements the students obtain experience in interviewing clients and their families, assessing and modifying behavior, knowledge of other community agencies for referral purposes, teaching, and individual and group counseling.

Practicum 207, fourth semester   CREDIT HOURS 3

Practicum 207 is designed to meet the individual needs of each student. Students may continue to work in the agency to which they were assigned the preceding semester to further increase their ability and competence in the areas of social and psychological services. Students also will be assigned to certain programs in which they have developed an interest, in which they have made a commitment to be a future employee, and/or in which they need further training. In addition, some students may be viewed as potential leaders and supervisors in human service work and will receive training in techniques of supervision, research, and program development. Each student is informed of the broad goal that we expect him to achieve in each agency placement, but the specific learning experiences are unique to each agency in which they are placed.

Agencies and experiences

More specifically, for the Maricopa Technical College program practicum agency experiences include, but are not limited to, the following.

1. The Devereux Day School is for children of average intelligence having emotional problems that cannot be dealt with adequately in a public school setting. Four students are in the Devereux School to acquire skills in interacting with children, tutoring, observing behavior, effectively using behavioral rating scales, and group therapy. The first-year students work primarily with mental health professionals and one teacher for approximately 13 weeks. The second-year students spend approximately 20 weeks in this agency, performing more advanced activities with an expected higher degree of competency. In addition, second-year students assist with the supervision and instruction of beginning students.

2. The Head Start and Day Care Program on the Salt River Indian Reservation is for the children of the Pima and Maricopa Indian tribes. Nine students are in this agency. This is their initial contact with two of the Indian tribes located in Arizona and is partially an attempt to recruit students from the Indian groups. Students working in this agency develop an understanding of the Indian culture in dealing with families, with the primary focus being upon the child.

3. The Perry Rehabilitation Center is for mentally retarded children residing in school districts that have neither the funds nor trained teachers for special education classes. In addition to tutoring, testing, and observing behavior, the

four students who are in this agency develop an understanding of the specialized programs for the mentally retarded and their various behavior problems.

4. The Jane Wayland Child Guidance Center is located in the Phoenix inner city area and provides both professional consultation and special education services to emotionally disturbed children. Families utilizing the services of this agency generally are from minority and lower socioeconomic groups. Two students are in the Jane Wayland Center special education classes and are primarily involved with tutoring and assessment activities.

5. The Child Psychiatry Treatment Division of the Arizona State Hospital serves as a practicum base for four non–hospital employed students, primarily because it is the only recognized residential treatment center for emotionally disturbed children in the State of Arizona. The student act as co-supervisors of the children in a cottage living situation and assist in the classroom activities.

6. The Phoenix Union High School, located in the heart of the Phoenix inner city, provides experiences with students from Afro-American and Mexican-American groups. Two students work primarily with the School-Community Workers, who are representatives of the minority groups. These students tend to function more directly with the high school students in their home environments.

7. The Roosevelt School District provides practicum bases for four students in special education classes for retarded children. The students tutor, assist with social activities, and in general work as a teacher's assistant. They also obtain experiences with mental health workers in the district.

8. The Veterans Administration Hospital has four students under the supervision of psychologists. These students are working primarily in the day care center and community agencies to which clients have been referred.

9. The Concentrated Employment Program, located in the inner Phoenix area, has four students involved in group and individual counseling, bilingual basic adult education classes, evaluations of client progress, and community agency referrals.

10. The Alcohol and Drug Abuse Program at the Sacaton Indian Hospital on the Sacaton Reservation is a new federally funded program begun in 1971. They currently have three students involved in the development of in-service training programs, which will include various community agencies servicing the Indian community.

11. The Salvation Army has two students involved in home visits with clients, as well as referrals to appropriate community agencies.

12. The Social Service, Adult Education, and Rehabilitative Therapies Departments of the Arizona State Hospital are providing experience for four students. Skill acquisition includes interviewing, referral and placement in other agencies, family contacts, individual tutoring in basic education, perceptual-motor testing, and work evaluation.

13. The St. Luke's Mental Health Center has one student whose skill acquisi-

tion includes interviewing, individual and group therapy, behavior assessment, and treatment of alcoholic patients.

14. The Paradise Valley High School has one student functioning as a counselor under supervision. This student is involved in interviewing students and their families, behavior assessment, referrals, individual and group therapy, and classroom tutoring and supervision.

15. The Valle del Sol Narcotic Prevention Project, located in the Phoenix inner city, deals primarily with hard-core Mexican-American drug addicts. Experiences include individual therapy, interviewing, referral, and follow-up evaluations.

CAREER LADDERS

Along with the increased training provided by community junior colleges in the mental health and helping services areas, the opportunity for career employment and advancement has been developing in a number of agencies and states. The State of Arizona Personnel Commission has formulated job descriptions for mental health workers in the State of Arizona. It is a career ladder with clearly specified job functions and qualifications for advancement. Since it provides an example of the type of opportunities available to those who wish to pursue a career in mental health, the basic outline of the qualifications for the series of positions is given.

Classification	Minimum qualifications
1 (a) Mental Hospital Worker Trainee	Tenth grade education, merit examination
(b) Mental Hospital Worker	One year's in-service and on-the-job training
2 (a) Mental Health Worker Trainee	High school degree or GED
(b) Mental Health Worker I	High school degree or GED, 1 year's experience including on-the-job training
(c) Mental Health Worker II	High school degree or GED, 1 year's in-service and on-the-job training, plus 3 years' experience
3 (a) Mental Health Technician Trainee	Two years' college credits
(b) Mental Health Technician I	Two years' college credits, 1 year's experience with in-service and on-the-job training; or A. A. degree in mental health technology area
(c) Mental Health Technician II	Two years' college credits plus 3 years' technician experience including in-service and on-the-job training; or A. A. degree in mental health technology area plus 2 years' technician experience
4 (a) Mental Health Specialist I	Bachelor's degree, preferably in psychology, guidance and counseling, or a closely related area
(b) Mental Health Specialist II	Bachelor's degree, preferably in psychology, guidance and counseling, or a closely related area plus 2 years' experience comparable to Mental Health Specialist I. A master's degree in psychology, guidance and counseling, or a closely related area may substitute for the required experience.

These positions exist at the Arizona State Hospital, although other state agencies providing helping services use comparable job specifications more appropriate to their own specific area. The job descriptions for the mental health worker series of positions emphasize, but are not restricted to, duties involving physical care activities and maintenance functions at the lower levels. At the higher levels there is an increasing emphasis on psychosocial assessment and therapy techniques, community relationships, and duties involving teaching and supervising other mental health workers. There is the possibility of administering particular treatment programs, and there is less custodial, maintenance, and physical care duties with patients.

Personnel in most parts of the country who are working in the public schools, welfare organizations, and community mental health clinics generally do not have a highly structured career ladder, but as these organizations select, train, and make more efficient use of these personnel, it is expected that their job structure will become more organized and definitive. There appears to be a basic fault in mental health worker career ladders, for the most effective ones, upon reaching the top of the scale, tend to switch to an accessible traditional mental health profession, such as nursing or social work.

ROLES AND FUNCTIONS

The orientation and content of this book has been meant primarily for the education of workers who will function as human service or mental health technicians and generalists. The location of employment and the actual roles and functions of any mental health worker will depend on the organization and beliefs of the particular agency in which he works, the specific training he has obtained, political, legal, and budgetary matters, and other factors. In the past, many words have been used to describe what we now term the new human service worker. He has been characterized as the subprofessional, paraprofessional, preprofessional, and numerous others, which indicate beliefs that such personnel are less adequate or at a lower level of performance and professionalization than others.

Since no traditional professional group has evidenced they can rid our world of human problems, it is highly questionable that the new mental health generalist should be viewed as lacking in professional ability. Since mental health generalists will provide services in all areas associated with the traditional professionals and will have been given specific techniques and skills in mental health work, we may find that the new mental health generalists will become recognized as the most numerous and effective workers in the field. It is conceivable, in fact, that mental health generalists have always been the group that carried the major weight for providing services in some agencies, such as mental hospitals. The traditional mental health professions may become more strictly the teachers, researchers, administrators, and consultants in behavioral effectiveness agencies.

The roles and functions of mental health generalists have long been considered highly significant in Head Start programs, special education classes, and counseling offices. Educators have been aware of the value of such personnel, particularly since they often come from the community in which the school is located. School administrators and teachers often live outside the school communities in which their services are most badly needed. In ghetto and inner city areas most of the educational personnel live outside the immediate vicinity of the school, which may seriously detract from their educational efforts. By bringing members of the community into the school as helpers in the educational process, many direct and indirect benefits have occurred.

Authorities have developed lists of roles and functions that are or could be performed by the new mental health generalists. Such lists are often quite general, vague, and overlapping, or they are quite specific and compulsively detailed, in either case being open to serious question when selection and training are not specified in conjunction with the roles and functions. We take the position that anyone who is adequately selected and trained for particular tasks will be able to provide services in the mental health and behavioral effectiveness areas.

For example, Margaret Rioch and others (1963) selected eight, middle-aged, college graduate women, several of whom had been in personal psychotherapy. She gave them intensive training in counseling skills. Their subsequent performance in working with disturbed people was excellent, marking a turning point for the conceptualization of the capable new mental health worker. Other studies have substantiated this finding, although the trainees of other researchers usually have not been so well qualified prior to specific skill development.

AN EMERGING PROFESSION

There is much evidence that the new mental health workers are receiving a more adequate education and are assuming new duties, responsibilities, and indications of status. They also are receiving more monetary compensation than did the aides of former years. It is believed the new mental health workers are beginning to emerge as a distinct profession, and it is important to consider the aspects of groups that define their degree of professionalization. The following five points are generally accepted criteria for professional status, and we have followed each with a statement in regard to the new mental health workers.

There is an organized and accepted body of knowledge. Obviously, the worker has a body of knowledge, but it is not very well organized and is drawn from several professional areas. On the other hand, it is important to note that few professions, if any, have mutually exclusive bodies of knowledge. In regard to the assessment and treatment of most behavior problem areas, it is apparent that the psychiatrist and the psychologist, for example, have a large amount of overlapping skills and knowledge. The physician and the registered nurse also have many such common areas.

The entrance standards are determined by the members of the group. This is one area in which mental health workers are generally not operating. Personnel departments and highly specialized traditional professionals generally ascertain who will or will not be admitted to these positions. However, at the Arizona State Hospital a beginning has been made by assigning one mental health technician to the Department of Education, Mental Health Technology. He participates in the selection procedures as a completely equal staff member.

Educational standards are set by the group. This is another criterion that in practice is not completely true for most professional groups. For example, there are psychologists in departments of psychiatry in medical schools, there are sociologists involved in the training of psychologists, and physicians often serve as instructors for nurses. It is true, however, that the ultimate power of authority is held by the particular professionals. Several mental health workers have participated as instructors and practicum supervisors in education programs at Maricopa Technical College.

The group has a code of ethics. The National Association of Human Services Technologies has developed a statement concerning its ethical positions.

An elaboration and extension of this statement of ethical behavior would be appropriate. The traditional professions have rather consistent codes of ethics and could serve as models.

The professional group is self-policing and self-supervising. In most hospitals mental health workers are directly supervised by nursing departments and in public schools by teachers, although in some community agencies they may be supervised by other professional groups. An attempt to provide some of the self-supervising functions for mental health workers has been made at the Arizona State Hospital and others.

A meaningful organization of mental health workers began approximately 10 years ago when the California Society of Psychiatric Technicians helped form the National Association of Psychiatric Technicians. They planned to help the state associations standardize training and levels of performances to develop effective mental level workers in mental health and related fields. Work in corrections, social welfare, schools, and others were included, and ultimately it was decided that the organization's name was not appropriate. Hence, the National Association of Psychiatric Technicians changed its name to the National Association of Human Services Technologies at its 1970 convention. Its new title was more clearly indicative of the variety of personnel with many different kinds of occupational titles working in mental health and behavioral effectiveness areas.

Dr. John True, the former director of the Purdue program, has become director of the Center for Human Services Research, a component of the Johns Hopkins University Department of Psychiatry and Behavioral Sciences. The Center is doing research on the effectiveness of education programs designed to train 2-year mental health workers. It is also investigating the impact on roles and functions of these workers on the mental health field. They publish a newsletter entitled "Karuna," which provides much useful information about program

Code of Ethics
NATIONAL ASSOCIATION OF HUMAN SERVICES TECHNOLOGIES

The Psychiatric Technician's work is based on democratic humanitarian ideals, dedication to service for the welfare of mankind, disciplined use of recognized body of knowledge about human beings and their interactions and promotion of the well being of all without discrimination.

As a member of the National Association of Human Services Technologies, we commit ourselves to conduct our professional relationships in accord with this Code of Ethics and subscribe to the following statements:

1. Precedence to our professional responsibility and personal interest.
2. Responsibility for the quality and extent of the service we perform.
3. Respect for the need of dignity, privacy, individuality of the people we serve.
4. Responsible use of information gained in professional relationship.
5. Respect for the findings, views and actions of colleagues and use of appropriate channels to express judgment on these matters.
6. Practice of our profession within the recognized knowledge and competence of the profession.
7. Acceptance of the responsibility to help protect the community against unethical practice by any individual or organization engaged in the Psychiatric Technician profession.
8. Readiness to give appropriate professional service in public emergencies.
9. Statements and actions in public as an individual must be clearly distinguished from those representing the organization.
10. Support of the principle that professional practice requires professional education.
11. Contribution of knowledge, skills, and support to programs of human welfare.
12. Relations with others based on their qualities as individual human beings, without distinction as to race, creed or color, economic or social status.
13. No invasion into the personal affairs of another individual without his consent, except when in an emergency we must act to prevent injury to him or others.

developments obtained from training directors and other interested professionals throughout the country. Another indication of development is the publication by the Arizona Society of Mental Health Technology of the *Journal of Mental Health Technology*, with the first issue appearing in 1972.

PROFESSIONAL CONFLICTS

In their natural environment animals exhibit a territorial imperative. They often define the boundaries of their territory by urinating around the perimeter and daily checking to see that the smell of their urine is adequate for other animals to sense and, therefore, keep off their territory. They will defend their territory from the presence of intruding animals and generally evidence by their behavior that an area is theirs to the exclusion of other animals.

There may be a parallel situation in the mental health field, for the traditional mental health professional groups spend much time and effort defining their territory and jealously attempting to keep other professionals from intruding. For example, psychologists seem to view assessment procedures as their particular domain, and some show significant disgruntlement when other professionals attempt to use certain assessment materials and procedures. The social worker appears to believe the family is one of his territories and views with some disdain research psychologists moving into the area. Psychiatrists often view people's problems as a result of physical illness. Psychiatrists are criticized for using their conceptions of mental illness partly in order to keep other professionals from becoming centrally involved. For example, the alcoholic is seen as having mental illness. Other professionals, from some psychiatrists' viewpoint, may be somewhat useful in helping alcoholics. However, since alcoholism is a mental illness it is really the special domain of psychiatry. To the educated person these territorial imperatives in mental health are quite irrational, selfish, and narrow-minded.

From our viewpoint, the new mental health generalist has technical skills from training and has acquired the ability to serve in all the areas of human problems. His territory is the entirety of human behavvioral disturbances and impairment. He has been and will be the recipient of negative perceptions and comments from the traditional professionals, even though these may be very subtly expressed.

Two major viewpoints of traditional professionals exist. First, there is the belief that the new generalist is their colleague who will be very helpful to them in performing their work. Second, and at the other extreme, there exists a belief that the new generalist will replace them in their current job and the traditional professional will have to find another position. Conflict and anger have arisen in regard to the latter, primarily in regard to nurses in mental hospitals, social workers in community mental health centers of various types, and educators in some public and private school settings. The new mental health technicians are often perceived as a threat to employment.

Psychologists and psychiatrists apparently feel much more secure in their professions, for they often develop and direct training programs for the new generalists and seem to accept them much more readily. However, perhaps largely because of their original medical training, more psychiatrists seem to be more resistant to them, although not bothered, than do psychologists. Furthermore, many psychologists tend to view themselves as researchers, scholars, teachers, and supervisors, rather than direct service practitioners, which is the situation for most psychiatrists.

It should be emphasized that there are many different perceptions and ideas within each profession in regard to accepting the new mental health generalist, and it may be that these differences are more diverse within professional groups than among them. Nevertheless, research in mental hospitals has indicated more feelings of threat and negativism from professionals with less status, and this is usually professional nurses. Social workers are also now showing some signs of discomfort. It is believed that the stress being felt by some professional individuals and groups will become less intense as they learn that the new generalist is meant to be a colleague with them, rather than a replacement for them in their positions. Roles and functions of traditional professionals may change, but this does not mean they are eliminated.

It is becoming apparent that in some job functions the new mental health worker can perform as well or better, in terms of direct service, than the traditional professionals, particularly when working with lower socioeconomic status clients who have characteristics more in common with them and who may well reside in their own neighborhood. The middle-class, highly educated professional sometimes has difficulty working with clients significantly different from him. The analogy may be stated as follows: If one is driving down the rugged Baja Peninsula, he may reach his destination more quickly, safely, and reliably in a Volkswagen than in a Rolls Royce.

CHARACTERISTICS OF THE NEW MENTAL HEALTH TECHNICIAN
Personality characteristics

Research is being done on the psychological characteristics of the new mental health workers. Students enrolled in the mental health technology program at Maricopa Technical College were given a standard psychological assessment instrument, the 16 Personality Factor Questionnaire, or 16PF, which indicated that these particular students, in comparison to the general population, were very quick to grasp ideas and were generally more abstractly intelligent and alert. They were more mature and able to face reality calmly and maintain solid group morale. They tended to be more spontaneous and capable of facing the wear and tear of dealing with people and difficult emotional situations without fatigue. They were uninhibited, venturesome, socially bold, and talkative. However, there were indications of carelessness and a somewhat pushy style of social interaction. They were somewhat impatient, dependent, impractical, and sensitive to human feelings. They tended to dislike insensitive people and the stereotyped masculine occupations. There was little doubt of their tender-minded and helpful orientation to people. They felt very confident about their abilities and were interested in intellectual matters. Although somewhat skeptical, they were rather conservative and task-oriented. These students tended to be realistic and personally satisfied, sometimes to the extent of having low achievement motivation. They were also more relaxed and tranquil than the general population.

These students and a second group in this program were given another personality inventory, the California Psychological Inventory. The findings regarding the seventeen male and thirty-three female students follow.

Description of male students. More than the general population, the males are enthusiastic, quick, informal, spontaneous, talkative, and active. They have a high sense of personal worth, are self-accepting and self-confident, but are somewhat demanding. However, they are not very dependable and conscientious, and they are slightly more undercontrolled, impulsive, and moody. Their general level of socialization is lower than the population, and they tend to be more stubborn, resentful, and given to excess. They are more oriented to personal pleasure and self-gain; that is, they are more self-centered. Excitability and impulsivity run high. Their egocentricity is expressed by a lack of concern regarding how others perceive them. Basically, they are somewhat distant and not motivated to create a favorable impression on others.

Description of female students. In many respects the women had characteristics in common with the men. They also tended to be more spontaneous, enthusiastic, talkative, and informal than the general population. However, they did not think so highly of themselves as did the men. Like the men, in comparison with the general population they are not highly dependable and conscientious, and they have a low level of socialization. They are also somewhat stubborn, demanding, and resentful. However, they tend to be less self-centered and impulsive, which primarily may be related to their learned female sexual role. Unlike the men, they are slightly more concerned about how others react to them and somewhat more interested in favorably impressing others.

Women tended to be more achievement-oriented in settings requiring autonomy and independence as positive behaviors than the general population. The women are more flexible, adventurous, and adaptable in their thinking and social behavior.

Other trends. Several profile trends on this instrument are worthy of notation, although statistical significance was not obtained. The students are clearly not conforming, scholarly persons, but they are somewhat rebelliously striving toward achievement through their own actions. This is suggested by the upward slope for both males and females on achievement via conformity in conjunction with achievement via independence. Both males and females are somewhat higher on the measures of psychological mindedness and flexibility, which indicates an orientation toward understanding people and ability to adapt to reality factors to be of service to them.

Discussion. The California Psychological Inventory profiles show we have selected students who are quite boisterous and have high energy levels. They think rather highly of themselves. However, their socialization level, ability to control impulses, and acceptance of responsibility for their own behavior is less than would be desired. Interestingly, it should be noted these last characteristics are consistent with those of psychologists and psychiatrists, as suggested by other research. This is considered an important finding indicating that mental health technician students are similar to traditional mental health workers in some respects, but all of these groups are below the mean in comparison to the general population. Like psychologists but different from psychiatrists, the students are not impressed with getting people to think highly of them, to say the least. Their striving for independence, nonconformance in standard educational settings, and orientation toward people are believed in general to be positive qualities. The somewhat negative characteristics of these new mental health generalists are probably less debilitating than those found in aides and attendants in many mental health agencies. There is a noticable quality of adolescent acting out, a striving for identity, and push for relevance and meaning by the students. The CPI basically is in agreement with our observations derived from working with the students and reports by their instructors and practicum supervisors.

Personality characteristics and job performance

Another study attempted to ascertain characteristics related to expected and actual job performance. The 16 Personality Factor Questionnaire was given to mental health workers in a mental hospital working with the entire range of mentally disturbed patients. In comparison with results from a previous study (Cattell and Shotwell, 1954), this Arizona State Hospital group was more liberal, analytical, free thinking, well informed, and inclined to experiment with problem solutions than were mental health workers noted as being successful in other institutions. It was found that being a successful mental health worker is in part a result of matters of time, place, and characteristics of the client. Successful mental health workers 20 years ago would not necessarily be successful today. Successful mental health workers in a rural southeastern state institution would not necessarily be successful in Phoenix, Arizona. Successful mental health workers with retarded children would not necessarily be successful with bright, college-educated drug abusers having a crisis with their families.

The entire orientation to disturbed and impaired people appears to be changing from a custodial and maintenance function to psychosocial therapeutic treatment and rehabilitation. More intellectual and emotional demands exist for the new mental health worker, which means selection, training, and performance standards require careful study.

However, it should not be expected that all mental health workers will exhibit comparable characteristics, for individual differences exist, will always exist, and must be not only expected and tolerated but encouraged. It appears to

Fig. 13. I'm me; you're you; I like myself. (Harold M. Lambert.)

be a truism that strength resides in diversity and stagnation results from in-breeding and demands for conformity. People have a right to be different, and we should never attempt to make them identical robots.

A LOOK TOWARD THE FUTURE

The future of the new mental health worker in the United States is very bright. There is an obvious demand for his services, and the adequacy of his compensation and status is increasing. Recent reports regarding traditional professionals directly and primarily engaged in mental health work clearly show the lack of sufficient numbers. Manpower research has noted that those actually engaged in mental health work in the United States number approximately 20,000 psychiatrists, 18,000 psychologists, 12,000 M.S.W. social workers, and 30,000 nurses. Educators, rehabilitation therapists, and others are in short supply, and the training programs have not shown that the manpower shortage will be meaningfully reduced in the near future, if ever. Therefore, the preparation of the new mental health generalist and technician should be understood as the major way in which more adequate services ultimately will be provided to the millions of people in need of improved behavioral effectiveness.

REFERENCES AND SUGGESTED READINGS

Albee, G. W. 1959. Mental health manpower trends. New York, Basic Books, Inc., Publishers.

Arizona Society of Mental Health Technology. 1972. Journal of Mental Health Technology, vol. 1.

Arnhoff, F. N., Rubinstein, E. A., and Speisman, J. C., editors. 1969. Manpower for mental health. Chicago, Aldine-Atherton, Inc.

Bower, W. H. 1968. Choices to be made in psychiatric technology. Presented at psychiatric technicians' meeting, Pueblo, Colorado.

Bower, W. H. 1968. Psychiatric technology and mental health manpower problems. Presented at National Association of Psychiatric Technology, California Society of Psychiatric Technicians, San Francisco.

Bower, W. H. 1970. Emergence of the mental health worker. Presented at National Association of Psychiatric Technology, Topeka.

Bower, W. II. 1970. Recent developments in mental health manpower. Hospital and community psychiatry 21:11-17.

Cattell, R. B., and Shotwell, A. 1954. Personality profiles of more successful and less successful psychiatric technicians. American Journal of Mental Deficiency 58:496-499.

Gartner, A. 1971. Paraprofessionals and their performance: a survey of education, health and social service programs. New York, Praeger Publishers, Inc.

Grosser, C., Henry, W. E., and Kelly, J. G., editors. 1969. Nonprofessionals in the human services. San Francisco, Jossey-Bass, Inc., Publishers.

Guerney, B. G., Jr., editor. 1969. Psychotherapeutic agents: new roles for nonprofessionals, parents, and teachers. New York, Holt, Rinehart and Winston, Inc.

Holler, R. F. 1971. Selecting and training associate of arts degree mental health workers. Presented at Western Psychological Association, San Francisco.

National Association of Psychiatric Technology and Colorado Psychiatric Technicians Association. 1969. New frontiers in psychiatric technology. Sacramento, National Association of Psychiatric Technology and the Colorado Psychiatric Technicians Association.

National Association of Psychiatric Technology and California Society of Psychiatric Technicians. 1970. Major psycho-social problems and the psychiatric technician. Sacramento, National Association of Psychiatric Technology and the California Society of Psychiatric Technicians.

Rioch, M. J., and others. 1963. National Institute of Mental Health pilot study in training mental health counselors. American Journal of Orthopsychiatry 33:678-689.

Roesch, R. 1971. The status and potential of the new mental health worker. Presented at National Association of Human Services Technologies, Dallas.

Sobey, F. 1970. The nonprofessional revolution in mental health. New York, Columbia University Press.

Southern Regional Education Board. 1971. 1970 status report: community college mental health worker programs in the South. Atlanta, Southern Regional Education Board.

Southern Regional Education Board. 1971. Plans for teaching mental health workers: community college curriculum objectives. Atlanta, Southern Regional Education Board.

Southern Regional Education Board. 1971. Proceedings of national faculty development conference: community college mental health worker programs (Louisville). Atlanta, Southern Regional Education Board.

U. S. Department of Health, Education, and Welfare, Public Health Service, National

Institutes of Mental Health. 1971. Experiments in mental health training (Publ. No. 2157). Washington, D. C., U. S. Government Printing Office.

Western Interstate Commission for Higher Education. 1971. Community college mental health worker program: a reference resource. Boulder, Colorado, Western Interstate Commission for Higher Education.

GLOSSARY

꽃

achievement Accomplishment in an area or on a test of knowledge or skill; a personal motive.

acting out Exhibiting problems in overt behavior, rather than controlling them via suppression or other defenses.

addiction Physical dependence upon drugs or alcohol.

adjustment Relationship that exists between an individual and his coping with the environment.

adjustment reaction In children, minor and transistory negative reactions to immediate situational conflicts.

adrenal glands Pair of endocrine glands located on the top of the kidneys.

ambivalence Having both positive and negative feelings toward some object or individual at the same time.

amnesia Loss of memory with no known physiological cause.

anal stage In psychoanalytic theory, the period during which the child's interest and gratifications center on anal activities.

antisocial reactions Deviant behaviors of an illegal type that are often damaging to other people. The person may have a marked degree of hostility and in the long run is damaging to himself. He does not develop meaningful relations with other people.

anxiety Vague tenseness or fear without a clear referent.

anxiety reaction One of the major psychoneuroses, characterized by intense apprehension.

arithmetic mean One measure of central tendency, commonly called the average, that is computed by summing all the scores in a frequency distribution and then dividing by the number of scores.

assertive training Method of treatment to help highly aggressive or highly submissive clients acquire responses of a normally assertive type.

attitude Tendency to respond with emotion either positively or negatively to certain persons, objects, or situations.

authoritarian personality Individual who finds security in authority and wants a social hierarchy in which everybody has and knows his place.

autistic Thoughts that do not correspond to external reality and that are strongly determined by a person's internal thought processes.

avoidance learning Learning to avoid a noxious stimulus such as shock by responding appropriately to a warning signal.

bedlam Popular contraction of the name of the early London asylum of St. Mary of Bethlehem; refers to chaotic conditions.

behavior Any observable action or set of responses of a person or animal.

behavior disorder General term referring to psychoneurotic reactions, psychotic reactions, character and personality disorders, and chronic brain syndromes. This means about the same as mental illness, although the logic is clearer.

behavior therapy Form of psychotherapy focusing on changing the problem behavior by using techniques of respondent, operant, and observational learning. It means about the same thing as behavior modification.

behavioral sciences Sciences most concerned with human and animal behavior. The principal behavior sciences are psychology,

241

sociology, and social anthropology, but they also include certain aspects of history, economics, political science, and zoology.

behaviorism Point of view that psychology is limited to the study of observable behavior.

belief Acceptance of the validity of a statement; the thought portion of an attitude.

bibliotherapy Reading by client of assigned material in a topic area relating to the client's problems.

castration anxiety In psychoanalytic theory, fears centering around injury or loss of the genitals as punishment for forbidden sexual desires. Men who are fearful and unable to adequately achieve are described as castrated. A woman who dominates her husband or male supervisor might be referred to as a castrating woman.

catatonia State of muscular rigidity that is sometimes seen in certain cases of schizophrenic reactions. There may be alternations between stupor and excitement.

central nervous system Structure included in the brain and the spinal cord.

cerebral cortex Gray matter covering the cerebrum.

cerebellum Structure in the hindbrain concerned with the coordination of movements and balance.

cerebral hemispheres Symmetrical halves of the cerebrum.

cerebrum Largest structure of the forebrain, consisting of white matter and deeper structures and covered by the cerebral cortex or gray matter.

ceremonies Celebrations and other events noting important changes in the lives of a cultural group's members. These include initiations, rites of passage, graduations, and weddings.

chaining Learning of a series of responses in which the stimulus arising from one response is associated with the next response in the series.

character disorders Behavior deviations not marked by a high degree of anxiety but that are ineffective and bothersome to others.

chemotherapy Treatment of a psychoneurotic or a psychotic reaction with a drug or chemical substance.

childhood psychosis More severe form of childhood behavior disorders, which are usually differentiated into childhood autism and childhood schizophrenia. They involve a substantial loss of contact with reality.

chromosomes Structures in the body and germ cells containing genes.

chronic brain syndrome Behavior disorders caused by long-lasting disturbances in brain function.

chronological age (CA) Age in years.

classical conditioning Learning that takes place when a conditioned stimulus is paired with an unconditioned stimulus.

client-centered therapy A nondirective therapy developed by Carl Rogers that typically is neither as intensive nor as prolonged as psychoanalysis.

clinical psychology A branch of psychology concerned with recognizing and treating severe disorders.

coefficient or correlation Number between +1.00 and −1.00 expressing the degree of relationship between two sets of measurements arranged in pairs. A coefficient of +1.00 (or −1.00) represents perfect correlation, and a coefficient of .00 represents no correlation at all.

cognitive dissonance Condition produced by inconsistencies between simultaneously held beliefs or between a belief and behavior.

compensation Defense mechanism in which an individual substitutes one activity for another in an attempt to satisfy frustrated motives.

compulsion Irrational act or set of behaviors that constantly intrude into a person's behavior.

compulsive reaction Behavior disorder in which a person finds ambiguity and uncertainty extremely uncomfortable. It is characterized by rigidity of habits and excessive conscientiousness.

concept Internal process representing a common property of objects or events, usually represented by a word or name.

conditioned response Response elicited by a conditioned stimulus after respondent learning.

conditioned stimulus In respondent learning, the stimulus that is originally ineffective but that, after pairing with an unconditioned stimulus, evokes conditioned response very similar to the unconditioned response.

conditioning General term synonymous with learning.

conduct disturbance In children, socially disapproved behavior, such as stealing and fighting.

conformity The tendency to be influenced by group pressure and to go along with group norms.

congenital Existing at birth or before birth but not hereditary.

congruent Natural, honest, and not phony.

contingency Relationship between behavior and reinforcement, the reinforcement being given only if the behavior occurs.

continuous reinforcement Reinforcement of all correct responses each time they occur.

control The group in an experiment that is similar in all respects to the experimental group except that it does not receive the experimental treatment.

controlling stimulus Stimuli that do not elicit behavior but serve as a discrimination for indicating the presence of conditions under which the emitted behavior has previously been reinforced.

conversion reaction Psychoneurotic reaction in which psychological problems are converted into physical symptoms, so that the person appears to have various ailments that have no physical basis.

counseling Giving assistance to individuals with personal or vocational problems.

criterion In the evaluation of tests, the job or level of performance that a test is supposed to predict.

critical period A period of time in which an organism is most ready for the acquisition of certain responses.

cross-cultural method The approach that studies cultural patterns among societies.

cue Any object or event that provides information to the person and functions as a stimulus to direct the person to a reinforcer.

culture Customs, habits, traditions, and objects that characterize a people or a social group. It includes the attitudes and beliefs that the group has about important aspects of its life.

culture pattern Widely shared beliefs and ways of behaving in a society.

defense mechanisms Psychological maneuvering with which one protects himself from anxiety-arousing events.

delinquency Antisocial or illegal behavior by a minor.

delusion An irrational belief or thought, usually of grandeur or of persecution. It is characteristic of paranoid reactions.

dependency need The need to depend on other people for advice and moral support.

dependent variable The variable that changes as a result of changes in the independent variable (experimental treatment).

depressive disorder Condition characterized by anxiety, loss of self-esteem, guilt feelings, self-depreciation, or suicidal tendencies.

deprivation Withholding some object or event from a person until it acquires such reinforcing properties that it can be used to increase highly desirable responses.

descriptive statistics Statistical measures that summarize and describe the characteristics of a frequency distribution or the relationship between two or more distributions.

desensitization A method used in psychotherapy to enable a person to be comfortable in situations in which he was previously highly anxious by repeatedly

exposing him to the situation in modified form.

deviation I.Q. Intelligence quotient based on standard scores, so that I.Q.'s more nearly compare in meaning from one age to another.

deviation score Differences between the score obtained and the mean of the distribution that includes the obtained score.

diagnosis Determination of the nature and extent of a disorder.

directive therapy Therapy in which the therapist actively prescribes remedies and courses of action much as a physician prescribes medicine.

discrimination Process of learning to respond differentially to different stimuli.

disorientation Confusion with respect to time, place, or person.

displacement Transferring thought or feeling from one object to another.

dissociative reaction Neurotic reaction involving repression. Certain aspects of personality and memory are compartmentalized and function more or less independently, for example, amnesia and multiple personality.

dominant gene Gene whose hereditary characteristics are always expressed.

dream analysis Analysis of dream content to obtain information about the source of a person's emotional problems.

Durham Rule Legal interpretation of insanity that holds that the defendant will not be held criminally responsible for his behavior if he has a mental illness or defect.

dysfunction Impairment or disturbance in some functioning of an organism.

dyssocial reactions Illegal behavior damaging to other people, although the persons may have deep and meaningful emotional attachments to some others. Certain underworld groups have many dyssocial persons.

ego In psychoanalysis, a term referring to the self and to ways of behaving and thinking realistically and effectively. The ego delays satisfaction when necessary and it directs behavior into socially acceptable channels.

ego ideal In psychoanalytic theory, the optimum characteristics one envisions for himself; models toward which he strives.

Electra complex In psychoanalytic theory, the intense love of the daughter for the father.

electroconvulsive shock therapy (ECT) A form of therapy used primarily with depressed patients. It involves administering electrical shocks to the forebrain sufficient to produce convulsions.

emotion Affective states that can be experienced and have arousing and motivational properties.

emotional immaturity Failure to develop normal adult degrees of independence and self-reliance, with consequent use of immature adjustive patterns and inability to maintain equilibrium under stresses that most people can meet satisfactorily.

empathy Concern for other people; not the same as sympathy.

empirical Founded on experiments, surveys, and substantiated facts, as distinguished from that which is asserted by argument, reasoning, opinion, or armchair theorizing.

encounter groups Small groups oriented toward encountering basic psychological operations of relatively normal people (also known as T-groups).

endocrine glands Glands that secrete substances called hormones.

enuresis Bed wetting.

escape learning Learning to escape from a noxious or unpleasant situation by making an appropriate response.

etiology Causation; the systematic study of the causes of disorders.

ethnocentric personality Individual who is generally hostile or prejudiced toward groups to which he does not belong.

existential theory Philosophical viewpoint oriented to the basic aspects of life existence.

exhibitionism Public display or exposure of genitals for purpose of sexual excitement and pleasure.

experimental method Scientific method in which conditions that are likely to effect a result are controlled and manipulated by the experimenter.

extinction In respondent learning, the gradual waning and eventual disappearance of the conditioned response following repeated presentation of the conditioned stimulus in the absence of the unconditioned stimulus. In operant learning, the drop in response rate that occurs when reinforcement no longer follows a response.

factor analysis Statistical method that isolates a few common factors in a large number of tests, ratings, or other measurements.

fantasy Daydreaming and imagining.

father figure Instance of transference in which a person is regarded as though he were a father.

feedback Situation in which some aspect of the output regulates the state of the system; conceived as a form of reinforcement in learning viewpoints.

fetishism Sexual deviation in which the individual achieves sexual gratification by means of an object (hair, handkerchief, panties) that symbolizes the person to whom it belongs.

fixation Rigid habit developed by repeated reinforcement or as a consequence of frustration.

fixed-interval schedule Schedule of partial reinforcement in which responses are reinforced on a time basis.

flight of ideas Rapid succession of ideas without logical association or continuity.

forebrain Most forward of three divisions of the brain. It includes the cerebrum, thalamus, and hypothalamus.

fraternal twins (dizygotic, heterozygotic) Twins who develop from two different fertilized eggs (ova). Consequently, they may be as different in hereditary characteristics as ordinary brothers and sisters.

free association Psychoanalytic technique of having a patient say whatever comes to his mind, regardless of how irrelevant or objectionable it may seem on the surface.

frequency distribution Set of measurements arranged from lowest to highest (or highest to lowest) and accompanied by a count (frequency) of the number of times each measurement occurs.

frigidity Inability of a woman to experience sexual pleasure or gratification.

frustration Thwarting of behavior.

fugue Fleeing from unpleasant situations, often in conjunction with amnesia.

functional In reference to behavior disorders, having no demonstrable organic cause or etiology; also known as psychogenic.

generalist One who performs some work of all types, in contrast to a specialist, who performs more restricted work.

genes Elements in chromosomes that transmit hereditary characteristics.

genital stage In psychoanalytic theory, a stage in development during which the adolescent begins to display heterosexual interests.

gerontology Study of all aspects of old age.

gestalt therapy Set of techniques designed to help the person confront himself and the discrepancies in his perceptions and relations with himself and other people.

gonads Sex glands, which are the testicles in the male and the ovaries in the female.

group norm A widely shared expectation of behavior among members of a group.

group therapy Discussion of personal problems by a group of patients under the guidance of a therapist. This may take a variety of forms depending on the theoretical orientation of the therapist.

guilt Unpleasant feeling of sinfulness arising from behavior contrary to one's ethical principles. It involves both self-devaluation and apprehension about fears of punishment.

habituation In respondent learning, the tendency of an unconditioned response to weaken with repeated presentation of the unconditioned stimulus.

habit disturbances In children, annoying behavior problems, such as nail biting and thumb sucking.

hallucination Sensory experience in the absence of external stimulation. Hallucinations are often present in schizophrenic disorders.

halo effect Tendency to perceive an individual in generally positive terms because of one positive characteristic, and, conversely, the tendency to perceive a person generally negatively as a result of one negative characteristic.

Hawthorne effect Introduction of anything into group functioning that subsequently increases group effectiveness and performance.

hebephrenic type Schizophrenic disorder characterized by childish behavior.

homosexuality Sexual interest in or overt sexual activity with members of one's own sex.

hypnosis State in which a person is extremely susceptible to the suggestion of the hypnotist.

hypochondriasis Neurotic reaction characterized by excessive concern about one's health in the absence of related physical illness.

hypomania Manic excitement in manic-depressive reactions.

hypothalamus Region of the forebrain that contains centers for the regulation of sleep, temperature, thirst, sex, hunger, and emotion.

id In psychoanalytic theory, the aspect of personality concerned with bodily instinctual demands. The id seeks immediate gratification with little regard for the consequences or for the realities of life.

identical (monozygotic) twins Twins who develop from the same fertilized egg (ovum). They have exactly the same kinds of chromosomes and genes and hence the same hereditary characteristics.

identification Tendency to model behavior after that of others; also a defense mechanism.

imitation Copying the behavior of another.

immature personality Characterized by behavior problems indicative of mild retardation in social development.

implosive therapy In contrast to desensitization, intentional overloading of the person with intense discomfort until he habituates to the anxiety-arousing object or event.

impotence Inability of male to achieve orgasm.

imprinting Concept that there is an optimal time for practice and behavioral expression. It also involves the idea that there

may be critical periods during which specific types of learning or behavior change take place.

inadequate personality Individual who is neither physically nor mentally grossly deficient but who manifests inadequate responses to intellectual, emotional, social, and physical demands. He shows ineptness, poor judgment, and a lack of adaptability.

incest Sexual relations between close relatives such as father and daughter or brother and sister.

incompetent Legal designation of individual as incapable of managing his affairs with ordinary prudence because of mental illness or deficiency.

independent variable Variable that may be selected or changed by the experimenter and that is responsible for changes in the dependent variable.

inference Conclusion or judgment that is at least one step removed from objective data.

inferential statistics Statistical methods for inferring population characteristics from an obtained sample.

inferiority complex According to Alfred Adler, an attitude developed out of frustration in striving for superiority.

inhibition Decreasing tendency to respond with repetition of a response.

insanity Legal term for mental disorder, implying lack of responsibility for one's behavior and an inability to manage one's affairs.

insight In psychotherapy, the understanding of one's own motives and their origins.

insight therapy Treatment of a behavior disorder by attempting to uncover the deep emotional causes of the patient's difficulty. It represents an attempt to guide the patient to self-understanding.

instinct Pattern of behavior that is genetically determined and operative without the benefit of experience or learning.

instrumental learning Learning situations in which the responses of the subject are instrumental in producing reinforcement; also known as operant learning.

intellectualization Defense mechanism by which the individual achieves some insulation from emotional hurt by reducing or distorting the emotional charge associated with particular thoughts or events.

intelligence General term covering a person's abilities on a wide range of tasks involving a vocabulary, numbers, problem solving, and various other concepts.

intelligence quotient (I.Q.) Number obtained for children by dividing chronological age into mental age and multiplying by 100. Deviation I.Q.'s are used for adults.

internal environment Environment within the

body, including the temperature of the body, oxygen, food supplies, minerals, hormones, and related substances.

intoxication psychosis (alcohol) Psychosis developed as a result of prolonged alcoholism. It is characterized by defects of memory, disorientation, and delusions.

involutional reaction Agitated depression or paranoid reactions in women at menopause, considerably influenced by psychological factors.

learning General term referring to a relatively permanent change in behavior that is the result of past experience or practice. It includes observational learning, respondent learning, and operant learning and excludes behavior changes resulting from drugs and fatigue.

learning disabilities Term used to describe the behavior of children who are not retarded or disturbed but who nevertheless exhibit developmental problems, particularly in learning situations. The child may be normal in all other respects but be unusually hyperactive or have an exceptional difficulty learning arithmetic or some other content area.

lesbianism Homosexuality in women.

libido In psychoanalytic theory, the driving force for behavior.

lobotomy Surgical procedure involving separation of neurofibers between the frontal and other regions of the brain. In the past it was believed that the operation led to a decrease in abnormal behavior. The procedure is less commonly used today because it is of doubtful benefit.

lunacy Legal term roughly synonymous with insanity. The term originates from the Latin word "luna" (moon). The moon was presumably the cause of certain types of mental illness.

maladjustment Broad term covering all problems of behavioral ineffectiveness.

malingering Conscious falsification of illness or disability.

masochism Achievement of sexual gratification through the experience of pain.

masturbation Self-stimulation of genitals for sexual pleasure.

maturation Completion of developmental processes in the body. Maturation is governed by heredity and environment.

McNaghten Rule Legal interpretation of insanity that basically asks whether the person is able to distinguish between right and wrong.

measurement Assignment of numbers to objects or events according to specified rules.

median Middle score in a frequency distribution when all scores are ranked from

highest to lowest (or lowest to highest). It is one measure of central tendency.

mental age (M.A.) Norm indicating the age level at which the child is performing. For example, if a 10-year-old child does as well on an intelligence test as the average child of 12, his mental age is 12.

mental health General term referring to state relatively free of psychoneurotic and psychotic behavior problems.

mental health technologies Methods and techniques used to improve the behavioral condition of disturbed people. These include individual and group counseling or therapy, chemotherapy, education, remotivation, and numerous others.

mental health worker Term that may pertain to any of the traditional mental health professionals, although it is more commonly used in reference to individuals with less formal education, including those who have Associate in Arts degrees in mental health technology and related areas.

mental retardation Condition marked by a significant deficiency in general intellectual ability.

mild retardation Degree of mental retardation characterized by an I.Q. of 53 to 69.

Minnesota Multiphasic Personality Inventory (MMPI) Widely used pencil and paper personality questionnaire particularly applicable to assessment of severe behavior disorders.

mode Most common or frequent score in a distribution of measurements.

modeling Performing some behavior for the purpose of allowing an observing person to learn the behavior; similar to imitation.

moderate retardation Degree of mental retardation characterized by an I.Q. of 36 to 52.

mongolism Genetically determined form of mental retardation generally characterized by slanting eyes, stubby fingers, and a variety of other physical abnormalities; also known as Down's syndrome.

mores Customs that enforce social values having ethical or moral significance. Violation brings strong social disapproval.

multiple personality Existence of two or more rather distinct behavior patterns that are intermittently expressed by one person.

mutism Refusal or inability to speak.

narcoanalysis Analysis of a person's traumatic memories under the influence of a sleep-inducing drug, for example, sodium amytal.

nervous system Brain, spinal cord, and nerves serving the various sense organs, endocrine glands, and muscles of the body.

neurasthenia General nervousness, fatigue, and insomnia often accompanied by depression, feelings of inadequacy, and inability to work.

neurotic traits In children, irrational fears, sleepwalking, and other behaviors indicative of rather serious problems.

nondirective therapy Therapy in which the patient is dominant and given the greatest possible opportunity to express himself and solve his own problems.

normal curve Bell-shaped frequency distribution often approximated by measures from behavior science.

norms An average or standard, or a distribution of measurements, obtained from a large number of people. It permits the comparison of an individual score with the scores of comparable individuals.

nurse Professional person with basic education in the applied biological science areas; may have advanced training in psychiatric nursing.

observational learning Learning that occurs as a result of an organism observing the behavior of another organism and the conditions that ensue following the behavior; similar to imitation.

obsession Seemingly irrational idea that constantly intrudes into a person's thoughts.

obsessive-compulsive reaction Psychoneurotic reaction characterized by obsessions and/or compulsions.

Oedipus complex In psychoanalytic theory, child's direction of intense affectionate response toward the parent of the opposite sex.

operant learning Emitted rather than elicited behavior, with the responses performing some instrumental operation on the environment.

oral stage In psychoanalytic theory, the period during which an infant's satisfactions center around his mouth and sucking.

organic viewpoint View that all behavior disorders have an organic basis; similar to medical model.

overcompensation Overreaction to feelings of inferiority so that a person becomes superior in things in which he otherwise would not be.

pancreas Organ in which the islets of Langerhans are located. The islets are part of the endocrine system, secreting a hormone known as insulin, which controls blood sugar level.

paranoid reaction Behavior disorder marked by extreme suspiciousness and elaborate beliefs that others are plotting against the person. Delusions of persecution sometimes appear to have a grain of truth.

parathyroid glands Two pairs of endocrine glands located on the thyroid glands of the neck. They secrete hormones concerned in the regulation of calcium and phosphorus levels in the body.

partial reinforcement Reinforcement that does not occur after every response but intermittently on the basis of time or number of responses.

passive-aggressive personality Person who expresses hostility by excessive aggression, stubborn childlike pouting, extreme dependency, or passive resistance.

penis envy In psychoanalytic theory, the jealousy females feel toward males because of their obvious sexual organs. During development the jealousy regarding physical differences is expressed in psychological terms in regard to status, roles, and power.

peripheral nervous system Part of the nervous system lying outside the skull and the backbone.

personality All aspects of the person that characterize his individuality and his relationships to others.

personality disorders See **character disorders.**

perversion Deviation from the norm.

pervert Sexual deviate.

phallic stage In psychoanalytic theory, the period during which the child first becomes interested in his sexual organs and forms sexual desires for the parent of the opposite sex; also known as Oedipal stage.

phobic reaction Psychoneurotic reaction characterized by intense irrational fear.

pituitary gland Gland located beneath the hypothalamus that secretes hormones that stimulate or inhibit other glands of the body. It also secretes a growth hormone that controls general rate of growth of the body.

placebo Application of substances and procedures that have no demonstrable effect other than the patient or subject's belief that they do. The placebo effect is an improvement in the patient's condition or a change in the subject's behavior that occurs even though there has been no valid medication or therapy.

play therapy Use of play activities in psychotherapy with children. The counterpart for adults is recreational therapy.

prejudice Judgment prior to obtaining knowledge. It is usually an emotionally toned attitude for or against an object, person, or group of persons, often placing a person or group at a disadvantage.

Premack principle For any pair of responses use of the more highly probable one to positively reinforce and increase the less probable one.

primary gain Direct and obvious function served by disability, such a the hallucinating soldier being removed from combat.

probability Relative frequency of occurrence of an event expected over the long run.

profound retardation Degree of mental retardation characterized by an I.Q. of 20 or below.

projection Defense common in paranoid reactions involving disguising a source of conflict by ascribing one's motives to someone else.

projective methods Methods used in the study of personality. A subject is presented with a relatively ambiguous stimulus and asked to describe it in a meaningful way or to tell a story about it.

psychiatry Branch of medicine specializing in the diagnosis and treatment of behavior disorders.

psychoanalysis Theory of behavioral development and a method of psychotherapy developed by Sigmund Freud.

psychodrama Specializing technique of psychotherapy in which patients act out the roles, situations, and fantasies relevant to their personal problems; similar to role playing.

psychology Behavioral science that studies people and animals.

psychoneurotic reaction Behavior disorder, less severe than a psychotic reaction, in which a person is unusually anxious and incapacitated in his work and his relations with other people. He often attempts to ward off anxiety by using exaggerated defense mechanisms.

psychopathic deviate Individual characterized by antisocial, amoral conduct; old term for sociopathic personality

psychopharmacology Study of the effects of drugs on behavior and psychological functions.

psychotic reaction Behavior disorder more severe than a psychoneurotic reaction and often requiring institutionalization.

psychosomatic illness Bodily disorder precipitated or aggravated by psychological problems.

psychotropic drug Medication that can affect behavior. Many psychotropic drugs are useful in the treatment of behavior disorders.

psychotherapy Treatment of behavior disorders and mild adjustment problems through the application of personality theories and learning principles.

punishment Application of a stimulus for the purpose of eliminating undesirable behavior. When response rate decreases following presentation of a stimulus, that stimulus is said to be a punishment.

race Group of human beings having common and distinctive innate physical characteristics.

racism Viewpoint regarding superiority and inferiority on the basis of racial origin.

random sampling Selecting samples of individuals, objects, or measurements solely by chance, usually for describing a certain population.

range Difference between the highest score and the lowest score in a frequency distribution.

rating General term for the method in which an observer rates some characteristic that an individual is considered to have.

rational emotive theory Theory by Ellis emphasizing the rational rather than merely the emotional aspects of one's behavior.

rationalization Interpretation of one's own behavior so as to conceal the motive it expresses and to assign the behavior to some other motive.

reaction formation Disguising of a motive so completely that it is expressed in a form that is directly opposite to its original intent.

reality principle In psychoanalysis, the function of the ego, consisting of setting and achieving attainable goals.

reality testing Individual's behavior aimed at determining and dealing with the nature of his social and physical environment.

recessive gene Gene whose hereditary characteristics are not expressed when it is paired with a dominant gene but are expressed when paired with another recessive gene of like characteristics.

recidivism Recurrence of behavior disorder following apparently successful treatment.

reinforcement Any object or event following a response that tends to influence the probability of that response occurring again.

reinforcing stimuli In operant learning, stimuli that follow a response and influence the probability that the response will reoccur.

regression Behavior of an earlier or more primitive form, frequently encountered in children and adults faced with stress.

relaxation Method of releasing muscle tension either by itself or in conjunction with other techniques to achieve positive effects on a client.

reliability Indication of the degree to which observed results are consistently obtained.

replacement therapy Compensation for the effects of gland removal or deficiency by administration of the gland's hormone.

representative sampling Sampling to obtain a cross section of a population and a reduction of those biases that make the sample unrepresentative.

repression Defense in which memories and motives are not permitted to enter consciousness but are operative at an unconscious level.

resistance Blocking of important memories and associations as a result of personal conflicts. It is typical in counseling and therapy.

response Any action or behavior that may or may not be readily observed to be associated with a stimulus.

response generalization Eliciting of similar responses by the same stimulus, the probability depending upon the similarity of the responses to each other.

respondent learning Eliciting reflex responses, previously elicited only by the unconditioned stimuli, to the conditioned stimuli through pairing of unconditioned and conditioned stimuli.

role playing Technique used in simulation of real situations to promote understanding of personal problems and practice new patterns of adaptive behavior.

roles Set of behaviors expected of a person holding a certain status.

Rorschach test Projective method using relatively ambiguous inkblots as stimuli.

sadism Sexual deviation in which an individual obtains sexual gratification by inflicting pain upon others.

sampling Selecting a set of individuals or measurements from a large population of possible individuals or measurements according to some specified rule.

sampling error Error resulting from chance differences in selecting a sample from a population.

satiation Giving the person all the objects or events he desires on a noncontingent basis until he wants no more. It is used in cases for which the reinforcement is considered inappropriate, such as the collection and hoarding of hundreds of spoons by a mental hospital resident.

schedule of reinforcement Some specified sequence of partial reinforcement, such as a ratio schedule or an interval schedule.

schizophrenic reactions One of the psychotic reactions characterized by fantasy, regression, hallucinations, delusions, and general withdrawal from contact with the person's environment.

school phobia Irrational fear of schools that may involve absolute refusals to attend school.

secondary gain More subtle benefits obtained from having a disability, such as the care and sympathy given to hypochondriacs.

self-actualization According to Maslow, the highest need in man's hierarchy of needs.

senile psychosis Psychotic behavior pattern that appears in some individuals with advancing age and characterized by defects of memory, general disorientation, and delusions.

severe retardation Degree of mental retardation characterized by an I.Q. of 20 to 35.

sexual deviation Obtaining sexual excitement and satisfaction from unusual objects and behavior.

shaping Teaching a desired response through a series of successive steps that lead the learner to the final response. Each small step leading to the final response is reinforced. This is also known as the method of successive approximations.

shock therapy Treatment of behavior disorders by some agent causing convulsion and/or coma. Such agents include insulin, metrazol, and electric shock to the brain.

significance Probability statement of the likelihood of obtaining a given difference or correlation between two sets of measurements by chance. Often stated by giving P values, for example, $P < .001$. This example means the probability of obtaining such a statistical result is less than one out of a thousand. Therefore, it is not believed to be a chance finding.

sibling Brother or sister.

social approval Social reinforcement strongly influencing human behavior.

social attitude Attitude held in common with a number of other persons, as distinguished from personal attitudes that may be unique to a single individual.

social class Grouping of people on a scale of prestige in a society according to their social status. It is determined by many factors, such as nature of occupation, amount and kind of income, moral standing, family genealogy, social relationships and organizations, and area of residence.

social group Any group of people, formal or informal, who share some common interest or attachment and characterized by face to face interaction. Large dispersed groups such as unions are defined as social organizations or institutions rather than social groups.

social institution Collection of objects, customary methods of behavior, and techniques of enforcing such behavior on individuals; for example, a union, a mental hospital, an army, a political party, and schools.

social maturity Degree of development of social and vocational abilities.

social needs Needs, usually learned, that require the presence or reaction of other people for their satisfaction.

social pathology Abnormal patterns of social organization, attitudes, or behavior; undesirable social conditions that tend to produce individual pathology.

social structure General term referring to the fact that each society typically assigns ranks to its members, expects them to do certain kinds of work, have certain attitudes and beliefs, and otherwise behave in accordance with their status.

social worker Person with advanced training who investigates the family and social background of persons with behavior problems and who assists the psychotherapist by maintaining contact with a patient and his family. The social worker is often a member of a team consisting of psychiatrists, psychologists, and mental health workers.

socialization Process by which the family and culture teaches the child behaviors they consider appropriate.

society Group of individuals with a distinguishable culture.

sociopathic personality Type of behavior disorder characterized by little anxiety. It may take several forms: antisocial reaction, dyssocial reaction, sexual deviation, or an addiction.

somatic Pertaining to the body; organic as distinct from psychological.

somnambulism Walking during the sleeping state without indications of verbal awareness.

spinal cord Part of the nervous system encased in the backbone. It is a reflex center and a pathway for impulses to and from the brain.

staff approach (team approach) An approach to the understanding, treatment, and prevention of abnormal behavior, involving the team work of psychiatrists, psychologists, social workers, mental health workers, and others.

standard deviation Measure of the variability of a frequency distribution, computed by squaring the deviation of each score from the arithmetic mean, summing the resulting squares, dividing by the number of scores, and finally taking the square root of the resulting quantity.

standard score The z score; the score obtained by multiplying a z score by an arbitrary constant (for example, 10 or 20) and adding the result to an arbitrary mean (such as 50 or 100).

standardization Establishment of uniform conditions for administering a test and interpreting test results. A large number of individuals are tested in the same way to provide norms with which to compare any particular test score.

standardization group Group of people on which a test is standardized. To interpret individual scores on a test, one should know the characteristics of the standardization group.

statistics Collection of mathematical techniques used in the quantitative analysis of data and used to facilitate evaluation of the data; numbers used to describe distributions and to estimate errors of measurement.

status Position representing differences important in the exchange of goods and services and in the satisfaction of needs in a society.

stereotype Fixed set of greatly oversimplified beliefs that are held generally by members of a group. They may not be totally false.

stimulus Any object or event that regularly precedes a response.

stimulus generalization Eliciting of same response by similar stimuli, the probability of response depending upon the degree of similarity of other stimuli to the original stimulus.

subcultural delinquency Behavior patterns reinforced by the neighborhood or small group but condemned by the larger society.

sublimation In psychoanalysis, the use of a substitute activity to gratify a frustrated motive.

successive approximations Reinforcing relatively small components of the final complex response in an effort to lead the learner to this final response; same as shaping.

suggestion Uncritical acceptance of an idea. Suggestion is used to effect temporary relief of neurotic problems, particularly hysterical ones. It is also used by propagandists and advertisers to change or maintain attitudes and beliefs.

superego In psychoanalytic theory, that which functions largely as a conscience and restrains the activity of the ego and the id.

superiority According to Adler, a major striving of the person. Failure to achieve superiority may generate an inferiority complex.

supportive therapy Treatment of a personality problem by listening to a person's problems, suggesting courses of action, and reassuring him about what he has done or proposes to do. Such therapy may be effective in mild or transient disturbances.

symbolization Process of one object or event coming to signify another. Symbolization occurs in dreams, during which an angry mother may be represented by an angry cow.

syndrome Generally, a collection of symptoms; in psychology, a pattern of behavioral characteristics and their underlying causes; similar to abnormal behavior pattern.

t score A particular standard score, obtained by multiplying the z score by 10 and adding 50 to the result.

taboos The do's and don't's of a particular

society, strongly inculcated into members of that society.

technician One who works at a practical level. He is generally not a scientist or developer of knowledge.

test Standardized sample of the performance of a person on a task or set of tasks.

thematic apperception test (TAT) A frequently used projective method consisting of relatively ambiguous pictures about which a person tells stories.

theory In science, a principle or set of principles that explains a number of facts and predicts future events and outcomes of experiments.

thyroid gland Endocrine gland in the neck that produces the hormone thyroxin.

thyroxin Hormone secreted by the thyroid gland. It controls the general rate at which energy is produced in the body; it is a regulator of metabolism.

tic Intermittent twitching or jerking, usually of facial muscles.

token economy Behavior modification technique used with groups. It is similar to the capitalistic form of economics, with tokens serving the function of money.

trait Aspect of personality that is generally characteristic of a person and that distinguishes him in some way from many other people.

transference Identification of some person in the individual's immediate environment with some important person in his past life. Usually the identification is made unconsciously. In therapy, the person in the individual's past life with whom he identifies the therapist is typically his father or mother.

transient personality reactions Transient behavior problems in the face of special or acute stress.

trauma Wound or injury that may be either biological or psychological.

unconditional positive regard True and full acceptance of another person, but not necessarily of his behavior.

unconditioned response (UR) Reflexive response elicited by an unconditioned stimulus (US).

unconditioned stimulus (US) Stimulus that consistently elicits a reflexive response.

unconscious motivation Motivation that can be inferred from the person's behavior but that cannot be verbalized by the person himself.

unconscious processes Psychological processes or events of which a person is unaware; he does not verbalize the process.

validity Extent to which a method of measurement does what it is supposed to do. Validity often is expressed in terms of a coefficient of correlation representing the relationship between a set of measurements and some criterion.

variability Spread of scores in a frequency distribution.

variable One of the conditions measured or controlled in an experiment.

variable interval schedule Program used in operant learning in which subjects are reinforced after an interval of time varying around a specified average.

variable ratio schedule Program used in operant learning in which subjects are reinforced after a number of responses varying around a specified average.

voyeurism Sexual deviation in which the individual obtains sexual gratification through looking, particularly at the nude bodies or erotic activities of others.

Wechsler Adult Intelligence Scale (WAIS) Individual intelligence test for adults.

Wechsler Intelligence Scale for Children (WISC) Individual intelligence test for children.

z score Score obtained by dividing the standard deviation into the deviation of an obtained score from the arithmetic mean of the frequency distribution. It is convenient for the comparison of scores without regard to the units of measurement employed.

zygote Product of the union of a sperm cell from the father and an egg cell from the mother.

REFERENCES
and
SUGGESTED READINGS

Adorno, T. W., Frenkel-Brunswik, E., Levinson, D. J., and Sanford, R. N. 1950. The authoritarian personality. New York, Harper & Row, Publishers.

Albee, G. W. 1959. Mental health manpower trends. New York, Basic Books, Inc., Publishers.

American National Red Cross. 1957. First aid textbook. New York, Doubleday & Company, Inc.

American Psychiatric Association. 1968. Diagnostic and statistical manual of mental disorders, ed. 2 (DSM-II). Washington, D. C., American Psychiatric Association.

Anastasi, A. 1968. Psychological testing. New York, The Macmillan Company.

Arizona Society of Mental Health Technology. 1972. Journal of Mental Health Technology, Vol. 1.

Arnhoff, R. N., Rubinstein, E. A., and Speisman, J. C., editors. 1969. Manpower for mental health. Chicago, Aldine-Atherton, Inc.

Asch, S. E., 1956. Studies of independence and submission to group presence: I. A minority of one against a unamious majority. Psychological Monographs, Vol. 7, Series No. 416.

Association of Hospital and Institution Libraries. 1971. Bibliotherapy methods and materials. Chicago, American Library Association.

Ayllon, T., and Azrin, N. 1968. The token economy: a motivational system for therapy and rehabilitation. New York, Meredith Corporation.

Bandura, A. 1969. Principles of behavior modification. New York, Holt, Rinehart and Winston, Inc.

Bandura, A., and Walters, R. H. 1963. Social learning and personality development. New York, Holt, Rinehart and Winston, Inc.

Becker, W. C., and Krug, R. S. 1964. A circumplex model for social behavior in children. Child Development 35:371-396.

Berne, E. 1964. Games people play: the psychology of human relationships. New York, Grove Press, Inc.

Binet, A., and Simon, T. 1905-1908. The development of intelligence in children. In Jenkins, J., and Patterson, D., editors. 1961. Studies in individual differences. New York, Appleton-Century-Crofts.

Blake, R. R., and Mouton, J. 1964. The managerial grid. Houston, Gulf Publishing Company, Book Division.

Bower, W. H. 1968a. Choices to be made in psychiatric technology. Presented at psychiatric technicians' meeting, Pueblo, Colorado.

Bower, W. H. 1968b. Psychiatric technology and mental health manpower problems. Presented at National Association of Psychiatric Technology, California Society of Psychiatric Technicians, San Francisco.

Bower, W. H. 1970a. Emergence of the mental health worker. Presented at National Association of Psychiatric Technology, Topeka.

Bower, W. H. 1970b. Recent developments in

mental health manpower. Hospital and Community Psychiatry **21**:11-17.

Boyd, W. 1971. An introduction to the study of disease. Philadelphia, Lea and Febiger.

Braun, J. 1966. Clinical psychology in transition. New York, World Publishing Company.

Cameron, N. 1963. Personality development and psychopathology: a dynamic approach. Boston, Houghton Mifflin Company.

Carkhuff, R. 1972. The art of helping: a guide for developing helping skills for parents, teachers and counselors. Amherst, Mass., Human Resource Development Press.

Cattell, R. B. 1957. Personality and motivation structure and measurement. New York, Harcourt, Brace, and World.

Cattell, R. B., and Shotwell, A. 1954. Personality profiles of more successful and less successful psychiatric technicians. American Journal of Mental Deficiency **58**:496-499.

Coleman, J. C. 1964. Abnormal psychology and modern life, ed. 3. Chicago, Scott, Foresman and Company.

Crane, S. 1962. The red badge of courage. New York, P. F. Collier, Inc.

Cronbach, L. 1960. Essentials of psychological testing. New York, Harper & Row, Publishers.

Dollard, J., and Miller, N. 1950. Personality and psychotherapy: an analysis in terms of learning, thinking, and culture. New York, McGraw-Hill Book Company.

Douban, E., and Adelson, J. B. 1966. The adolescent experience. New York, John Wiley & Sons, Inc.

Ellis, A. 1962. Reason and emotion in psychotherapy. New York, Lyle Stuart, Inc.

Eysenck, H. J., editor. 1961. Handbook of abnormal psychology. New York, Basic Books, Inc., Publishers.

Eysenck, H. J. 1966. The effects of psychotherapy. New York, International Science Press.

Festinger, L. 1957. A theory of cognitive dissonance. New York, Harper & Row, Publishers.

Freud, S. 1943. A general introduction to psychoanalysis, ed. 3. Garden City, N. Y., Garden City Publishing Co.

Freud, S. 1953. Complete psychological works of Sigmund Freud (translated and edited by James Strackey). London, Hogarth Press and Institute of Psychoanalysis.

Freund, J. 1960. Modern elementary statistics. Englewood Cliffs, N. J., Prentice-Hall, Inc.

Galton, F. 1869. Classification of men according to their natural gifts. In Jenkins, J., and Patterson, D., editors. 1961. Studies in individual differences. New York, Appleton-Century-Crofts, pp. 1-16.

Gartner, A. 1971. Paraprofessionals and their performance: a survey of education, health and social service programs. New York, Praeger Publishers, Inc.

Greenspoon, J. 1955. The reinforcing effect of two spoken words on the frequency of two responses. American Journal of Psychology **68**:409-416.

Grosser, C., Henry, W. E., and Kelly, J. G., editors. 1969. Nonprofessionals in the human services. San Francisco, Jossey-Bass, Inc., Publishers.

Guerney, B. G., Jr., editor. Psychotherapeutic agents: new roles for nonprofessionals, parents, and teachers. New York, Holt, Rinehart and Winston, Inc.

Harlow, H. F., and Harlow, M. K., 1962. Social deprivation in monkeys. Scientific American **207**(5):136.

Hathaway, S. 1966. MMPI: professional use by professional people. In Braun, J., editor. Clinical psychology in transition. New York, World Publishing Co., pp. 97-103.

Hildum, D., and Brown, R. 1956. Verbal reinforcement and interviewer bias. Journal of Abnormal and Social Psychology **53**:108-111.

Hilgard, E. R., and Bower, G. H. 1966. Theories of learning. New York, Appleton-Century-Crofts.

Hill, W. F. 1963. Learning: a survey of psychological interpretations. San Francisco, Chandler Publishing Company.

Holland, J. L. 1966. Psychology of vocational choice. Boston, Ginn and Company.

Holler, R. F. 1971. Selecting and training associate of arts degree mental health workers. Presented at Western Psychological Association, San Francisco.

Hull, C. 1933. Hypnosis and suggestability: an experimental approach. New York, Appleton-Century-Crofts.

Hunziker, J. 1971. A comparison of participant modeling and vicarious extinction in the treatment of fear of the water. Unpublished Masters thesis, Arizona State University.

Isaacs, W., Thomas, J., and Goldiamond, I. 1960. Application of operant conditioning to reinstate verbal behavior of psychotics. Journal of Speech and Hearing Disorders **25**:8-12.

Jacob, S. W., and Francone, C. 1965. Structure and function in man. Philadelphia, W. B. Saunders Co.

Jahoda, M. 1958. Current concepts of mental health. New York, Basic Books, Inc., Publishers.

Jones, M. C. 1924. A laboratory study of fear: the case of Peter. Pedagogical Seminary **31**:308-315.

Kesey, K. 1962. One flew over the cuckoo's

nest. Bergenfield, N. J., New American Library.

Kessler, J. W. 1966. Psychopathology of childhood. Englewood Cliffs, N. J., Prentice-Hall, Inc.

Kimble, D. P. 1966. Physiological psychology: a unit for introductory psychology. Reading, Mass., Addison-Wesley Publishing Co., Inc.

Kinsey, A. C., Pomery, W. B., Martin, C. E., and Gebhard, P. H. 1953. Sexual behavior in the human female. Philadelphia, W. B. Saunders Co.

Knudson, A. G. 1965. Genetics and disease. New York, McGraw-Hill Book Company.

Krasner, L. 1966. Behavior control and social responsibility. In Braun, J., editor. Clinical psychology in transition. New York, World Publishing Co., pp. 140-145.

Kretch, D., Crutchfield, R. S., and Ballackey, E. L. 1962. Individual in society. New York, McGraw-Hill Book Company.

Lanyon, R. I. 1971. Mental health technology. American Psychologist 26:1071-1076.

Lorenz, K. A. 1952. King Solomon's ring. New York, Crowell Collier and Macmillan, Inc.

Lyman, H. 1963. Test scores and what they mean. Englewood Cliffs, N. J., Prentice-Hall, Inc.

McGregor, D. 1960. The human side of enterprise. New York, McGraw-Hill Book Company.

Marks, P., and Seeman, W. 1963. Actuarial description of abnormal personality: an atlas for use with the MMPI. Baltimore, The Williams & Wilkins Co.

Maslow, A. H. 1954. Motivation and personality. New York, Harper & Row, Publishers.

Masters, W., and Johnson, V. 1970. Human sexual inadequacy. Boston, Little, Brown and Company.

May, R., editor. 1961. Existential psychology. New York, Random House, Inc.

Mayes, M. E. 1970. Abdallah's nurse's aide study manual. Philadelphia, W. B. Saunders Co.

Milgram, S. 1964. Group pressure and action against a person. Journal of Abnormal and Social Psychology 69:137-143.

Moreno, J. 1959-1969. Psychodrama (3 vols.). Beacon, N. Y., Beacon House.

Morgan, C. T. 1965. Physiological psychology. New York, McGraw-Hill Book Company.

Morgan, C. T., and King, R. A. 1966. Introduction to psychology. New York, McGraw-Hill Book Company.

Morrison, T. F., Cornett, F. D., and Tether, J. E. 1959. Human physiology. New York, Holt, Rinehart and Winston, Inc.

Mowrer, O., and Mowrer, W. 1938. Enuresis: a method for its study and treatment. American Journal of Orthopsychiatry 8: 436-459.

National Association of Psychiatric Technology and California Psychiatric Technicians Association. 1969. New frontiers in psychiatric technology. Sacramento, National Association of Psychiatric Technology and the California Psychiatric Technicians Association.

National Association of Psychiatric Technology and California Society of Psychiatric Technicians. 1970. Major psycho-social problems and the psychiatric technician. Sacramento, National Association of Psychiatric Technology and the California Society of Psychiatric Technicians.

National Commission on Mental Health Manpower. 1968. Careers in psychiatry. New York, The Macmillan Company.

Perls, F. 1951. Gestalt therapy: excitement and growth in the human personality. New York, Julian Press, Inc.

Peterson, D. R. 1961. Behavior problems of middle childhood. Journal of Consulting Psychology 25:205-209.

Premack, D. 1959. Toward empirical behavior laws: I. Positive reinforcement. Psychological Review 66:219-223.

Quay, H. C., and Quay, L. 1965. Behavior problems in early adolescence. Child Development 36:215-220.

Rapaport, D., Gill, M., and Schaefer, R. 1968. Diagnostic psychological testing. New York, International Universities Press.

Reynolds, G. S. 1968. A primer of operant conditioning. Chicago, Scott, Foresman and Co.

Rioch, M. H., and others. 1963. National Institute of Mental Health pilot study in training mental health counselors. American Journal of Orthopsychiatry 33:678-679.

Roesch, R. 1971. The status and potential of the new mental health worker. Presented at National Association of Human Services Technologies, Dallas.

Rogers, C. 1951. Client-centered therapy: its current practice, implications and theory. Boston, Houghton Mifflin Company.

Rogers, C. 1961. On becoming a person: a therapist's view of psychotherapy. Boston, Houghton Mifflin Company.

Rokeach, M. 1964. The three Christs of Ypsilanti. New York, Alfred A. Knopf, Inc.

Rosenthal, D. 1955. Changes in some moral values following psychotherapy. Journal of Consulting Psychology 19:431-436.

Secord, P. F., and Backman, C. W. 1964. Social psychology. New York, McGraw-Hill Book Company.

Sheldon, W. H. 1954. Atlas of men. New York, Harper & Row, Publishers.

Skinner, B. F. 1953. Science and human behavior. New York, The Macmillan Company.

Skinner, B. F. 1960. Pigeons in a pelican. American Psychologist **15**:28-37.

Skinner, B. F. 1969. Contingencies of reinforcement: a theoretical analysis. New York, Appleton-Century-Crofts.

Skinner, B. F. 1971. Beyond freedom and dignity. New York, Alfred A. Knopf, Inc.

Sobey, F. 1970. The nonprofessional revolution in mental health. New York, Columbia University Press.

Southern Regional Education Board. 1971a. 1970 status report: community college mental health worker programs in the South. Atlanta, Southern Regional Education Board.

Southern Regional Education Board. 1971b. Plans for teaching mental health workers: community college curriculum objectives. Atlanta, Southern Regional Education Board.

Southern Regional Education Board. 1971c. Proceedings national faculty development conference: community college mental health worker programs (Louisville). Atlanta, Southern Regional Education Board.

Stampfl, T., and Levis, D. 1967. Essentials of implosive therapy: a learning theory based psychodynamic behavioral therapy. Journal of Abnormal Psychology **71**:496-503.

Szasz, T. S. 1970. The manufacture of madness: a comparative study of the inquisition and the mental health movement. New York, Harper & Row, Publishers.

Telford, C. W., and Sawrey, T. M. 1967. The exceptional individual: psychological and education aspects. Englewood Cliffs, N. J., Prentice-Hall, Inc.

Thigpen, C. H., and Cleckley, H. M. 1957. The three faces of Eve. New York, McGraw-Hill Book Company.

Ullmann, L., and Krasner, L. 1965. Case studies in behavior modification. New York, Holt, Rinehart and Winston, Inc.

Ullmann, L., and Krasner, L. 1969. A psychological approach to abnormal behavior. Englewood Cliffs, N. J., Prentice-Hall, Inc.

U. S. Department of Health, Education, and Welfare, Public Health Service, National Institutes of Mental Health. 1971. Experiments in mental health training (Publ. No. 2157). Washington, D. C., U. S. Government Printing Office.

Watson, J. B., and Rayner, R. 1920. Conditioned emotional reactions. Journal of Experimental Psychology **3**:1-14.

Way, L. 1962. Adler's place in psychology: an exposition of individual psychology. New York, P. F. Collier, Inc.

Western Interstate Commission for Higher Education. 1971. Community college mental health worker program: a reference resource. Boulder, Colo., Western Interstate Commission for Higher Education.

Winchester, A. M. 1965. Modern biological principles. Princeton, N. J., D. Van Nostrand Co.

Wolberg, L. 1967. The technique of psychotherapy, ed. 2. New York, Grune & Stratton, Inc.

Wolf, M., Risley, T., and Mees, H. 1964. Application of operant conditioning procedures to the behavior problems of an autistic child. Behavior Research and Therapy **1**:305-312.

Wolman, B. B., editor. 1965. Handbook of clinical psychology. New York, McGraw-Hill Book Company.

Wolpe, J., and Lazarus, A. 1966. Behavior therapy techniques: a guide to the treatment of neuroses. London, Pergamon Press Ltd.

Woodworth, R. S., and Sheehan, M. R. 1964. Contemporary schools of psychology, ed. 3. New York, The Ronald Press Company.

Zilboorg, F., and Henry, G. W. 1941. A history of medical psychology. New York, W. W. Norton & Company, Inc.

Appendix

A

PRINCIPLES OF BEHAVIOR ASSESSMENT

SCIENCE, OBSERVATION, SAMPLES, AND INFERENCES

The assessment procedures currently used by behavioral scientists are based on much broader knowledge than was available to Galton, Binet, and those who developed the Army Alpha Test. Modern procedures are scientific methods based on the observation of samples of behavior from which inferences and/or predictions can be made about other behaviors.

Science and observation

Modern behavior assessment procedures are scientific. It is believed necessary for anyone working with people to understand the terms "science," "behavioral science," and "behavior assessment" prior to instituting behavior change methodologies.

Science is a way of looking at the world. It is characterized by empiricism, which is a school of thought that holds that the only true knowledge one can gain is founded on events that can be verified through observational sensory experience. When we speak of a scientific fact we are talking about an event or relationship that can be observed or experienced. Scientific fact must be distinguished from philosophical and metaphysical fact. Either of these may be based only upon argument, armchair theorizing, or opinion, all in the absence of observation. The aim of science is the prediction and control of the phenomena under study. The methods of science are limited to the study of those objects or events that can be observed and/or altered through the use of physical procedures. If we are to be scientific in our studies of behavior, we are limited to discussion of those aspects of behavior that can be observed. This does not deny the existence of minds or souls but places them outside the realm of science. Neither the mind nor the soul is a tangible, physical entity. These are usually defined in metaphysical or philosophical terms and as such cannot be observed.

The ability of man to observe events in his environment and the behavior of others is the cornerstone of science. Individual differences in this ability have necessitated the development of standard observational methods. If one wished to ascertain the length of an object, he could ask several other people to observe it and give him an estimate of its length. The probable result of this effort would be the production of several differing estimates of length, none of which was exact. If one were to repeat this experiment and introduce some standard observational method, such as a ruler or measuring stick, the result would likely be quite different. If each of the individuals observed the length of the object using some sort of standard measuring device, it is likely that each estimate of length would be more accurate and that the individuals would be in greater agreement. Therefore, when we speak of scientific observation we are talking about the use of a standard measuring instrument and its application to some observable phenomenon.

The sciences are differentiated not so much in terms of their methods but in terms of what they measure and the predictions that they make. For example, physics and psychology are sciences, both being systematic and empirical. They are distinguished by the fact that physics is concerned with the physical realm and psychology with the behavioral.

Psychologists take the viewpoint of Thorndike (Cronbach, 1960) in behavioral science and assessment. "If a thing exists, it exists in some amount." "If it exists in some amount, it can be measured." Conceptions of behavior based on notions that defy measurement are of no use to the behavioral scientist.

Samples and inferences

We have said that man's observational ability is the cornerstone of science. However, the limitations inherent in the human biological organism and the extreme complexity of the many phenomena that man has attempted to observe have necessitated the development of methods of measuring objects or events that cannot be directly observed and those that are so numerous as to make direct observation of each impossible. For example, it is impossible for man to directly observe certain frequencies of light or sound because neither can be sensed by man physiologically. Similarly, it is impossible for man to observe and study all of the grains of sand on a beach because the millions of particles of sand would require such an enormous expenditure of time as to make such a venture impossible for a man to complete in his lifetime. These same problems are present when one attempts to measure behavior. If it were desirable to know how soldiers would behave in a particular combat situation, it would be impractical to attempt observation of each individual in that situation.

Limitations of the observational capabilities of man have necessitated the development of indirect methods of measurement and the concepts of samples and inferences. Indirect observation refers to the use of a procedure that allows the measurement of a phenomenon, such as an extremely high-frequency sound or an inner emotional state, which cannot be observed without the aid of an instrument. Many psychological tests involve indirect observation, for they are intended to measure some hypothetical inner state or process within an individual, such as his present emotional condition or thought processes. Because man is limited in terms of the number of things he can observe within his lifetime, scientists often base their predictions on the study of a sample of the events they are studying. If one can obtain a representative sample of a given event, it is possible to make conclusions about all of the events.

A representative sample means that all of the events about which a prediction is to be made had an equal chance of being included in the sample. If we wish to make predictions or draw conclusions about the characteristics of all the grains of sand on a beach, we would select at random a number of these particles of sand for study and analysis. If we wanted to predict the behavior of all soldiers in a particular combat situation, we would select at random a group of soldiers and study their behavior in that situation. If our sample is truly representative, we can make inferences about the general nature of the phenomena we are studying. That is, we could infer from the characteristics of the sample particles of sand the characteristics of all the particles of sand on the beach (Freund, 1960) or we could infer that all soldiers will behave like those we studied in the combat situation.

STATISTICS AND MEASUREMENT

We can never be absolutely certain that the inferences we make will be totally accurate. All measurement, whether direct or indirect, includes a component of error. Fortunately, the amount of error can be estimated with the use of statistics. When we make scientific observations we must evaluate our inferences in order to determine the amount of error involved in our measurement.

Variability and error

One of the characteristics of measurement is variability. The word "variability" refers to the fact that when we make repeated measurements of the same event or group of events, many of the results that we obtain will differ from one another. In the physical sciences these differences are more likely to be small. However, in the behavioral sciences the measuring instruments used are often much less precise and consequently show greater variability.

Let us assume that a man wishes to weigh himself on his bathroom scale at home. He is interested in finding out his weight at the end of the day for 30 consecutive days. Each day he records his weight on a chart. The chart will show that he recorded differing weights many times during this 30-day period. Variability is evident in the results of his measurement of weight.

There are three factors that contribute to this variability, which are common to variability in measurement of any kind. The first of these is actual change in what is measured. The man's weight may have truly varied during the time that he was recording it, which could be the result of diet or exercise. The second factor is the measuring instrument itself. Continued use of the scale may have resulted in a lessening of accuracy of the instrument. The third factor contributing to variability is the individual who utilizes the measuring instrument. The man may have not perceived the numbers on the scale accurately every time he weighed himself.

Changes in the measuring instrument and differences in the individual using the instrument are commonly referred to as sources or origins of error. Error refers to the influence of some uncontrolled or unspecified factor on our measurement. Some of the differences in the man's weight over the 30-day period could be attributed to changes in the measuring instrument and changes in the man's use of that instrument, rather than actual changes in his weight.

Fig. 14 illustrates the data acquired by the man in his study of his own weight in chronological order. This is one method of presenting measurement data, but it gives us very little information about the characteristics of the thing measured. Another method of illustrating the results of a measurement procedure is shown in Fig. 14 in the form of a frequency distribution. The numbers on the horizontal line indicate an observed weight. The numbers on the vertical line indicate how many times the man observed a particular weight (that is, the frequency of observation of that weight).

Plotting the results of measurement in the form of a frequency distribution enables us to observe both the central tendency and the variability of the measurements. Central tendency refers to measured values that indicate where the center of the distribution lies. The most commonly used measure of central tendency is the arithmetic mean or average (Freund, 1960). It is computed by adding up all of the observed scores and dividing by the number of observations. This computation is illustrated in Fig. 14 for the distribution of weights.

While the average of the scores gives us an idea of where the center of the distribution lies, it tells us little about the variability present in our measurement. The average is very susceptible to the presence of extreme scores and may give an inaccurate picture of where the center of distribution lies if our measurements include very extreme scores. For example, if we substituted an extreme score such as 195 in the calculation of the average shown in Fig. 14, the result of this computation would be quite different and not give us a clear picture of the distribution of scores.

Therefore, when evaluating a distribution of measurements it is also important to use a measure of variability, one such measure being the range. This statistic is computed by subtracting the smallest score from the largest score. The number resulting from this computation indicates the extent of differences between our various measurements in a rather crude fashion. The measure of variability most often employed in describing a distribution of observations is

Day	Weight	Weight squared
1	120	14,440
2	121	14,641
3	121	14,641
4	120	14,440
5	119	14,161
6	119	14,161
7	118	13,924
8	121	14,641
9	120	14,440
10	121	14,641
11	119	14,161
12	120	14,440
13	122	14,884
14	120	14,440
15	122	14,884
16	120	14,400
17	121	14,641
18	123	15,129
19	117	13,689
20	120	14,400
21	121	14,641
22	119	14,161
23	120	14,400
24	122	14,884
25	120	14,400
26	118	13,924
27	119	14,161
28	118	13,924
29	119	14,161
30	120	14,400

Sum of weights—3,600.0

Sum of weights squared—12,960,000.0

Sum of squared weights—432,054.0

The average ($\bar{x}$) is calculated with the following formula:

$$\bar{x} = \frac{\Sigma x}{n}$$

For the distribution of weights, where

Σx = Sum of scores
n = Number of observations

$\bar{x}$ would be computed as follows:

$$\bar{x} = \frac{3600.0}{30.0}$$
$$\bar{x} = 120$$

Range = Highest score – Lowest score
Range (observed weights) = 123 – 117
Range = 6.0

The standard deviation (σ) is calculated with the following formula:

$$\sigma = \sqrt{\frac{\Sigma x^2 - \frac{(\Sigma x)^2}{n}}{n-1}}$$

For the distribution of weights, where

Σx^2 = Sum of squared weights
$(\Sigma x)^2$ = Sum of weights squared
n = Number of observations

σ would be calculated as follows:

$$\sigma = \sqrt{\frac{432,054. - \frac{12,960,000.}{30}}{30-1}}$$

$$\sigma = \sqrt{\frac{432,054 - 432,000}{29}}$$

$$\sigma = \sqrt{\frac{54}{29}}$$

$$\sigma = \sqrt{1.86}$$

$$\sigma = 1.36$$

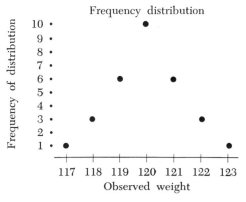

Frequency distribution

Fig. 14. Construction of a frequency distribution and calculation of the average, range, and standard deviation in a hypothetical case.

the standard deviation. It is computed by finding the square root of the average of the squared deviations of the observed scores from the mean. The calculation of this statistic for the distribution of weights is illustrated in Fig. 14. This statistic provides a number that enables us to examine how closely the mean actually corresponds with the true distribution of scores. For example, the standard deviation that we calculate for the distribution of weights is small. This tells us that very few of our observations differ a great deal from the mean. However, if the standard deviation were larger, it would tell us that many of our measurements differed considerably from the mean and would indicate that the mean was not giving us a very clear picture of the true distribution of our observations.

A large standard deviation may indicate the presence of considerable error in our measurements. We have seen that when making a physical measurement, such as the weight of the man on the scale, the resulting standard deviation was small. This indicates not only that our measurements differ very slightly from the average but also that there may be little error in our measurements. However, when measuring behavioral phenomena, especially when using a psychological test or other assessment procedure, the standard deviation is likely to be rather large.

Confidence and error

For evaluating the results of a group of measurements, we need a procedure that can tell us just how much confidence we can place in our measurement. Confidence in this context means the degree to which we can be certain that the variability that we observe in our measurement is actually the result of changes in the thing measured, rather than errors of measurement. Thus, when we speak of the degree of confidence that we have in the accuracy of our measurements, we are referring to the probability that we would obtain a similar measurement as a result of error or chance alone. For example, an evaluation of the confidence that we have in a specific measurement might be expressed in the following terms: This score will occur by chance once in 100 times. This means that if we performed the measurement 100 times we would find this result only once as the result of chance. The other 99 times we obtained this measurement, it would reflect an actual change in whatever we were measuring.

Measurement procedures in the behavioral sciences are used not only for individual assessment but also for evaluating the effects of different treatments, such as psychotherapy, drug effects, or rehabilitation activities. An experimental group—that is, a group of patients or clients who have received a specific treatment—and a control group—one that has not received that treatment or is receiving no treatment at all—are often compared. If we wished to assess the effectiveness of a particular form of psychotherapy in a mental hospital, we might first select at random a group of at least sixty patients. We would divide this group randomly into two equal parts, one of which will be the experimental

	Experimental Group			Control Group	
Patient	Score	Score squared	Patient	Score	Score squared
1	9	81	31	11	121
2	5	25	32	11	121
3	9	81	33	11	121
4	9	81	34	7	49
5	5	25	35	13	169
6	5	25	36	13	169
7	9	81	37	11	121
8	11	121	38	7	49
9	9	81	39	5	25
10	5	25	40	5	25
11	11	121	41	13	169
12	9	81	42	5	25
13	3	9	43	7	49
14	3	9	44	11	121
15	9	81	45	5	25
16	1	1	46	7	49
17	5	25	47	11	121
18	5	25	48	13	169
19	3	9	49	11	121
20	3	9	50	15	225
21	5	25	51	11	121
22	13	169	52	7	49
23	9	81	53	7	49
24	9	81	54	11	121
25	5	25	55	7	49
26	5	25	56	7	49
27	11	121	57	11	121
28	9	81	58	7	49
29	11	121	59	7	49
30	5	25	60	3	9

Sum of scores—210.0

Sum of scores squared—44,200.0

Average—7.0

Sum of squared scores—1,750.0

Standard deviation—3.11

Sum of scores—270.0

Sum of scores squared—72,900.0

Average—9.0

Sum of squared scores—2,710.0

Standard deviation—3.11

Fig. 15. Behavior rating scale scores, mean, and standard deviation of experimental and control group at the end of a hypothetical experiment.

group and the other the control group. Each person would have an equal chance of being placed in either the experimental group, which will receive our treatment of psychotherapy, or the control group, which will not receive our treatment.

The easiest way of dividing the two groups randomly is to place the names of all the individuals on slips of paper, shuffle them as one would a deck of cards, and place the first half (thirty) of the names drawn in the experimental group and the second half (thirty) in the control group. The next step in this experiment would be to evaluate the level of functioning of all of the members of both groups with some assessment procedure, such as a behavior rating scale. We would then have an initial measurement against which we could compare the change resulting from treatment or nontreatment. After a specified period of time, perhaps 2 months, we would again evaluate the behavior of both groups using the same behavior rating scale. An example of the measurements that we might obtain from following a procedure such as this is illustrated in Fig. 15.

In order to compare the effectiveness of treatment versus nontreatment, we compare the average score on the behavior rating scale of the experimental group with the average score of the control group at the end of the experiment. The average score for the experimental group is lower than the average score of the control group, as shown in Fig. 15. However, the standard deviation is rather large. The hypothesis is that error is involved in our measurement. Therefore, we need a method that will tell us how much confidence we can have that the difference between the average of the experimental group and the average of the control group is indicative of a true difference, rather than the result of errors in measurement.

A measure of differences: the z statistic

One of the methods most commonly used to evaluate the difference between two averages is known as the z statistic. It is based on the concept of deviation from the average and the characteristics of a hypothetical frequency distribution known as the normal curve. This distribution is illustrated in Fig. 16. It is a perfectly symmetrical, bell-shaped figure. The average or mean lies in the exact center of the distribution, and the standard deviation is used to divide the area under the curve into meaningful parts (Freund, 1960). The curve is divided into sections in terms of the probability of observing a specific score. To determine the probability of a particular score, we must examine the notation under the curve in Fig. 16. This curve is divided into standard deviation units. The number +1.0 indicates the point on the curve that is one standard deviation above the average. The number +2.0 indicates that point that is two standard deviations above the average. Similarly, the number –1.0 indicates that point that is one standard deviation below the average and the number –2.0 denotes that point which is two standard deviation units below the average.

The numbers shown in the area between the various standard deviation units indicate the percentage of observations that will fall between these two points. For example, the number 34 is between 0 and +1.0 This indicates that 34% of our observations will fall between the mean and one standard deviation above the mean. The number 34 also is shown in the space between 0 and –1.0, indicating that 34% of our observations will fall in this area. On this basis, we can hypothesize that 68 out of 100 times that we make a specific measurement the score we obtain will lie somewhere between one standard deviation below and one standard deviation above the average. Further, we can see that only 2% of

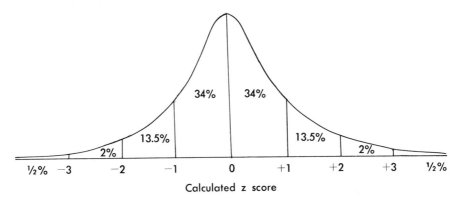

Calculated z score

For determining the confidence we can have in the accuracy of the difference between two means, the following formula for z may be used:

$$z = \frac{\bar{x}_1 - \bar{x}_2}{\sqrt{\dfrac{\sigma_1^2}{n_1} + \dfrac{\sigma_2^2}{n_2}}}$$

For the data in Fig. 15, where

$\bar{x}_1$ = Mean of control group
$\bar{x}_2$ = Mean of experimental group
σ_1^2 = Standard deviation of control group squared
σ_2^2 = Standard deviation of experimental group squared
n_1 = Number of patients in control group
n_2 = Number of patients in experimental group

z would be computed as follows:

$$z = \frac{9.0 - 7.0}{\sqrt{\dfrac{3.11^2}{30} + \dfrac{3.11^2}{30}}}$$

$$z = \frac{2.0}{\sqrt{.32 + .32}}$$

$$z = \frac{2.0}{\sqrt{.64}}$$

$$z = \frac{2.0}{.80}$$

$$z = 2.50$$

Fig. 16. Standard normal curve and the calculation of z in a hypothetical case.

the time would we expect to find a score lying at a point between two and three standard deviations above the mean.

When enough measurements are taken of a given phenomenon, these measurements displayed in the form of a frequency distribution will take the form of the curve shown in Fig. 16. This curve has been found to accurately describe not only a number of physical dimensions of man but also such abstract concepts as intelligence and personality. If we were to administer the behavior rating scale from our hypothetical experiment to hundreds of patients, we would find that their scores would eventually be distributed in the form of a normal curve.

Similarly, if we divided hundreds of patients into two groups of thirty and did not give any group our therapy, we would find that the differences between the average score of each pair of groups would also be distributed in the form of the normal curve. In using the z statistic to test the difference between the average of our experimental group and the average of our control group, we are comparing this observed difference with the distribution of differences that would be obtained from groups of patients who had received no therapy.

The letter z stands for standard deviation units on the normal curve. When we calculate this statistic, the resulting number tells us in standard deviation units how much our observed difference deviates from the average. The greater this deviation tends to be, the more confidence we can have that our result is indicative of a true difference between the things measured rather than a manifestation of errors of measurement or lack of treatment effect. For example, we have said that computation of the z statistic, in the case of our hypothetical experiment, compares the observed difference between the average of our experimental and control groups with the distribution of differences that would be obtained in the absence of therapeutic effects. Fig. 15 shows the scores that we might obtain if we carried out this hypothetical experiment, and Fig. 16 illustrates the computation of z from these scores. We can see that z in this case is a rather large 2.5. This indicates that there is a difference of 2.5 standard deviation units between the mean of the experimental group and the mean of the control group. We would expect to find a difference of this magnitude in only 2% of the cases in the absence of therapy. In other words, this result would only occur 2 times in 100 as a result of chance errors of measurement. Hence, the z statistic indicates that we can have a good deal of confidence that our therapy is effective, for the behavior problems measured by the rating scale decreased.

A measure of relationship: the correlation coefficient

Another purpose of using assessment procedures is prediction. We want to know to what extent we can predict future behavior on the basis of past behavior. We might wish to know how well we can predict a person's grade point average in college on the basis of his score on a college entrance examination. In the case of our hypothetical therapy experiment, we may wish to find out to what extent we can predict changes on our behavioral rating scale from the amount of

Patient	Rating scale score	Rating scale score squared	Number of hours of therapy	Hours of therapy squared	Product of hours in therapy and rating scale score
1	9	81	6	36	54
2	5	25	6	36	30
3	9	81	6	36	54
4	9	81	6	36	54
5	5	25	6	36	30
6	5	25	6	36	30
7	9	81	6	36	54
8	11	121	4	16	44
9	9	81	6	36	54
10	5	25	6	36	30
11	11	121	4	16	44
12	9	81	6	36	54
13	3	9	8	64	24
14	3	9	8	64	24
15	9	81	6	36	54
16	1	1	10	100	10
17	5	25	6	36	30
18	5	25	6	36	30
19	3	9	8	64	24
20	3	9	8	64	24
21	5	25	6	36	30
22	13	169	2	4	26
23	9	81	6	36	54
24	9	81	6	36	54
25	5	25	6	36	30
26	5	25	6	36	30
27	11	121	4	16	44
28	9	81	6	36	54
29	11	121	4	16	44
30	5	25	6	36	30

Sum of rating scale scores—210.0

Sum of rating scale scores squared—44,100.0

Sum of squared rating scale scores—1,750.0

Sum of hours of therapy—180.0

Sum of hours of therapy squared—32,400.0

Sum of squared hours of therapy—1,144.0

Sum of products of rating scale score and hours of therapy—1,148.0

Fig. 17. Correlation coefficient and its calculation in a hypothetical case.

therapy a person has received. One statistic used in determining the relationship between two measures or variables is the correlation coefficient. Fig. 17 shows a distribution of measurements that we might have obtained in our hypothetical experiment had different individuals received different amounts of therapy. This figure also shows how the correlation coefficient, which is represented by the letter r, is computed (Freund, 1960). The result of computing

The Pearson product moment correlation coefficient is computed with the following formula:

$$r \text{ (correlation coefficient)} = \frac{(n)(\Sigma xy) - (\Sigma x)(\Sigma y)}{\left(\sqrt{n \cdot \Sigma x^2 - (\Sigma x)^2}\right)\left(\sqrt{n \cdot \Sigma y^2 - (\Sigma y)^2}\right)}$$

For the data from the hypothetical experiment, where

$$
\begin{aligned}
n &= \text{Number of pairs of observations} \\
\Sigma xy &= \text{Sum of the products of rating scale score and hours of therapy} \\
\Sigma x &= \text{Sum of rating scale scores} \\
\Sigma y &= \text{Sum of hours of therapy} \\
\Sigma x^2 &= \text{Sum of the squared rating scale scores} \\
(\Sigma x)^2 &= \text{Sum of the rating scale scores squared} \\
\Sigma y^2 &= \text{Sum of the squared hours of therapy} \\
(\Sigma y)^2 &= \text{Sum of the hours of therapy squared}
\end{aligned}
$$

r would be computed as follows:

$$r = \frac{(30)(1148) - (210)(180)}{\left(\sqrt{(30)(1750.) - 44,100}\right)\left(\sqrt{(30)(1144.) - (32,400)}\right)}$$

$$r = \frac{34,440 - 37,800}{\left(\sqrt{52,500 - 44,100}\right)\left(\sqrt{34,320 - 32,400}\right)}$$

$$r = \frac{-3360}{\left(\sqrt{8400}\right)\left(\sqrt{1920}\right)}$$

$$r = \frac{-3360}{(91.65)(43.82)}$$

$$r = \frac{-3360}{4016.10}$$

$$r = -.84$$

This indicates that as the number of hours of therapy increases, the score of the patient on the rating scale tends to decrease. Therapy, in this hypothetical case, is highly related to behavior change.

Fig. 17, cont'd. For legend see opposite page.

this statistic is always a number between –1.0 and +1.0. If we obtain a correlation coefficient that is either +1.0 or –1.0, it indicates the presence of absolutely perfect predictability. For example, if we had obtained an r of +1.0 in our hypothetical experiment, we would be able to predict a person's score on the behavioral rating scale perfectly from the amount of therapy he received. An important point to remember, however, is that the correlation coefficient is a measure of relationship and not of causality. The correlation coefficient only tells us how well we can predict one thing from another. It does not tell us that the changes in one thing are causing changes in another. For example, it could be shown that daytime temperature in India is highly correlated with ice cream sales in New York. That is, if we knew the temperature on a specific day in New Delhi, we could predict the amount of ice cream sold in New York City on that date. This does not mean that the temperature in India is causing ice cream sales in New York to increase or decrease. All the correlation coefficient can tell us is the degree to which two things are related. If we wish to examine causality, which is to determine whether or not changes in one are the cause of changes in another, we must employ a measure of difference, such as the z statistic in an experimental design.

Reliability

We have noted that one of the sources of errors in measurement is the measurement instrument itself. We discussed how deterioration of a scale could contribute to errors of the measurement of a man's weight. The most common method of assessing error of the measurement instrument is to measure the same variable a number of times in the absence of change in the variable measured. For example, we might obtain a standard weight, such as those used in a physics laboratory, and weigh it several times on our scale. In the case of behavioral assessment we might give the same person the same test on 2 consecutive days. In both of these cases it would be highly probable that any change in our measurement would be the result of error in the measurement instrument. In carrying out these procedures we would be evaluating the reliability of our measurement instrument. Reliability refers to the degree to which the results of our measurements are consistent with one another (Cronbach, 1960).

The most frequent method of evaluating reliability is the correlational method, which involved the computation of r for successive measurements of the same variable. In behavioral assessment this is known as test-retest reliability (Lyman, 1963). The test-retest reliability of a particular assessment procedure is determined by finding the correlation coefficient between the scores obtained on one administration of the test and the scores obtained on a following administration of the test. The time interval between the administration of the test is variable and may range from a few days to several months or years.

It is of utmost importance that the reliability of a test be high. That is, the correlation coefficient between successive administrations of the test should be as close to 1.0 as possible and hopefully no lower than 0.7. The reason high reliability is so important is that the results of behavioral assessment procedures are used to predict future behavior or in helping a person make important decisions in his life. If the assessment procedure is unreliable, we can have little confidence that the information we obtain from this procedure is accurate. If we administered the test again it may give us results that would lead us to a different prediction or to a different decision. Thus, an unreliable assessment procedure not only limits the confidence we can have in our prediction but increases the likelihood that we will make errors in our decisions.

Validity

If we have determined that an assessment procedure is reliable, we have only attended to one of the problems associated with the use of behavioral assessment procedures. Another that we need to ascertain is the degree to which the test is valid. Validity refers to the extent to which an assessment instrument measures what it is supposed to measure. Does it actually predict future behavior? Does it accurately describe present behavior? Does it accurately indicate causal relationships?

There are several types of validity. One of the most common is predictive validity. This can be determined through the use of either a measure of relationship or a measure of differences. If we were using a test to predict the effectiveness of psychotherapy, we would compute a correlation coefficient between scores on our tests prior to therapy and ratings of improvement at the end of therapy. If the test has predictive validity the correlation coefficient that we obtain should be relatively high. We might also be interested in whether or not a test accurately discriminated between those people who will succeed in school and those who will fail. In this case we would use the z statistic to compare the average score on our test of people who were successful in school with the average score of people who failed. If the z statistic indicated we could place a good deal of confidence in the difference of these two averages, we could also say that our tests had predictive validity.

The other most common form of validity is known as content validity. This refers to the extent to which the behaviors a person is required to perform when taking a test are representative of the behaviors that the test is supposed to measure. School achievement tests, such as might be used by a mathematics teacher, usually are content valid. A test may have good predictive validity in the absence of apparent content validity. For example, scores on a personality test may be very useful in predicting job performance in a factory, even though none of the questions on the test is clearly related to the specific type of work performed in the factory. Thus, it is important to ask ourselves just what we want the test to tell us. If we wish to know how well a person has learned something, such as the parts of an automobile or the content of a course in college, we would want to use a test that has a high degree of content validity. On the other hand, if we want to predict future behavior in some situations, we will choose a test that enables us to predict most accurately (Hathaway, 1966). The test we choose may assess behaviors that appear to be logically unrelated to the behaviors we are trying to predict. Since we are interested in maximizing the effectiveness of our prediction, we will use a test that is most highly related statistically to the change we wish to predict, regardless of the apparent irrelevance of the content of the test.

There is no one perfect indication of validity. Rather, validity must be determined in terms of the purpose for which we wish to use the assessment procedure. A test is valid to the extent that it enables us to predict, to describe, or to accurately examine the phenomenon in which we are interested (Lyman, 1963).

REFERENCES

Cronbach, L. 1960. Essentials of psychological testing. New York, Harper & Row, Publishers.

Freund, J. 1960. Modern elementary statistics. Englewood Cliffs, N. J., Prentice-Hall, Inc.

Hathaway, S. 1966. MMPI: professional use by professional people. In Braun, J., editor. 1966. Clinical psychology in transition. New York, World Publishing Company.

Lyman, H. 1963. Test scores and what they mean. Englewood Cliffs, N. J., Prentice-Hall, Inc.

Appendix

B

COLLEGE PROGRAMS IN MENTAL
HEALTH TECHNOLOGY*

ALABAMA

Dr. Francis X. Lynch
Gadsden State Junior College
George Wallace Drive
Gadsden, Alabama 35903
  (205) 546-0484, Ext. 41

Dr. Max Joiner
Mental Health Technology Program
Jefferson State Junior College
2601 Carson Road
Birmingham, Alabama 35215
  (205) 853-1200, Ext. 57

Mr. James Seymour
Mental Health Technology Program
John C. Calhoun State Technical Junior College
P.O. Box 548
Decatur, Alabama 35601
  (205) 353-3102

ARIZONA

Dr. Ronald F. Holler
Mental Health Technology Program
Maricopa Technical College
2500 East Van Buren Street
Phoenix, Arizona 85008
  (60) 275-3611, Ext. 271

Dr. Donna Hawxhurst
Mental Health Technologies Program
Mesa Community College
1833 West Southern Avenue

Mesa, Arizona 85201
  (602) 969-5521

Mr. Keith Leafdale
Navajo Community College
Many Farms Rural Post Office
Chinle, Arizona 86503
  (602) 721-6302

CALIFORNIA

Mr. Max Burdick
Health Science Department
Bakersfield College
Bakersfield, California 93305
  (805) 871-7120

Dr. Nicholas A. Cummings
Associate of Arts Program
California School of Professional Psychology
2150 Judah Street
San Francisco, California 94122
  (415) 661-5450

Dr. Paul F. Stegner
Canada College
4200 Farm Hill Boulevard
Redwood City, California 94061
  (415) 364-1212

Mr. Gerald Amada
State Health Services
City College of San Francisco
50 Phelan Avenue
San Francisco, California 94112
  (415) 587-7272

*The information in this Appendix has been provided by the Center for Human Services Research, The Johns Hopkins Hospital, Baltimore, Maryland.

Ms. Esther W. Komanti
Cuesta College
Drawer A
Atascadero, California 93422
  (805) 466-2200, Ext. 33

Ms. Mary Lorene Steckler
Psychiatric Technician Program
Cypress College
9200 Valley View
Cypress, California 90630
  (714) 545-9331, Ext. 248

Dr. Rolf Bruckner
Volunteer Administration Program
Gavilan College
P.O. Box 126
Gilroy, California 95020
  (408) 842-8411

Ms. Rayda Parker
Psychiatric Technician Program
Golden West College
15744 Golden West Street
Huntington Beach, California 92647
  (714) 892-7711, Ext. 462

Dr. Max Sheanin
Psychological Services Curriculum
Los Angeles City College
855 North Vermont Avenue
Los Angeles, California 90029
  (213) 663-9141, Ext. 330

Ms. Ann Spadone
Los Angeles Harbor College
1111 Figueroa Place
Wilmington, California 90744
  (213) 835-0161

Ms. Margaret M. Shurgot
Psychiatric Technician Program
Los Angeles Trade Technical College
400 W. Washington Boulevard
Los Angeles, California 90015
  (213) 746-0800, Ext. 450

Ms. Ruth Cline
Psychological Services Curriculum
Los Angeles Valley College
5800 Fulton Avenue
Van Nuys, California 91401
  (213) 781-1200, Ext. 267

Mr. Irvin Colt
Occupational Education
Psychiatric Technician Program
Mount San Antonio College
1100 North Grand Avenue
Walnut, California 91789
  (714) 595-2211, Ext. 339

Mr. Inice Chirco
Psychiatric Technician Program
Rio Hondo College
3600 Workman Mill Road
Whittier, California 90608
  (213) 692-0921, Ext. 240

Mr. Jack L. Harwell
San Bernardino Valley College
701 South Mt. Vernon Avenue
San Bernardino, California 92403
  (714) 885-0231, Ext. 380

Ms. Clara Dieter
Psychiatric Technician Training
Santa Rosa Junior College
1501 Mendocino Avenue
Santa Rosa, California 95401
  (707) 996-1011, Ext. 206

Mr. Jack Connelly
Southwestern College
900 Otay Lakes Road
Chula Vista, California 92010
  (714) 420-1080

Dr. Gary S. Felton
Human Services Worker Training Program
Allied Health Education
  (530/152C)
VAH (Brentwood) (Psychosocial Medicine)
Wilshire and Sawtelle Boulevards
Los Angeles, California 90073
  (213) 478-3711, Ext. 2295 or 6173

Ms. Margaret E. McCann
Department of Nursing Education
Ventura College
4667 Telegraph Road
Ventura, California 93003
  (805) 642-3211

COLORADO

Mr. James G. Dugger
Mental Health Workers Program
Metropolitan State College
250 West 14th Avenue
Denver, Colorado 80204
  (303) 292-5190, Ext. 259

Mr. Paul M. Pantleo
Department of Mental Health
Mental Health Technology Program
Southern Colorado State College
Pueblo, Colorado 81105
  (303) 543-1170, Ext. 2385

CONNECTICUT

Mr. Edward E. McGinnis
Middle Level Mental Health Workers Training
Junior College of Connecticut
University of Bridgeport
Bridgeport, Connecticut 06602
  (203) 384-0711, Ext. 559

Mr. Thomas P. Connors
Public Service Career Program
Manchester Community College
P.O. Box 1046
Manchester, Connecticut 06040
  (203) 646-4900, Ext. 361

Dr. Thomas Houle
Psychology Department

Mattatuck Community College
640 Chase Parkway
Waterbury, Connecticut 06702
(203) 757-9661

Ms. Amy B. Slade
Mental Health Workers Program
Middlesex Community College
425 Hunting Hill Avenue
Middletown, Connecticut 06457
(203) 347-7411, Ext. 47

FLORIDA

Mr. Lyman B. Harris
Mental Retardation Professional Associate
    Program
Chipola Junior College
Marianna, Florida 32446
(904) 482-4935, Ext. 151

Ms. Louise Atty
Mental Health Technology Program
Daytona Beach Junior College
P.O. Box 1111
Daytona Beach, Florida 32015
(904) 252-9671, Ext. 348

Mr. F. Robert Stuckey
Hillsborough Junior College
P.O. Box 22127 Airport Collegium
Tampa, Florida 33622
(813) 872-4851, Ext. 257

Mr. Kenneth H. Orkin
Mental Health Technology Program
Miami-Dade Junior College
11350 S. W. 27th Avenue, Bldg. 900
Miami, Florida 33167
(305) 685-4485

Ms. Eleanor Salisbury
Mental Health Technology Program
Palm Beach Junior College
3400 Congress Avenue
Lake Worth, Florida 33460
(305) 965-8000

Mr. Robert W. North
Human Service Associate Program
Santa Fe Junior College
723 West University Avenue
Gainesville, Florida 32601
(904) 378-5311, Ext. 55

Mr. Gordon W. Denham
Mental Retardation Program
St. Petersburg Junior College
St. Petersburg Campus
P.O. Box 13489
St. Petersburg, Florida 33733
(813) 544-2551, Ext. 267

GEORGIA

Mr. Elliot Palefsky
Mental Health Work Program
Armstrong State College
Savannah, Georgia 31406
(912) 354-9715, Ext. 284

Dr. Melvin B. Drucker
Mental Health Assistants Program
Georgia State University
33 Gilmer Street
Atlanta, Georgia 30303
(404) 658-3039 or 658-3088

Dr. John Daniel
DeKalb College
Clarkston, Georgia 30341
(404) 292-1520, Ext. 214

IDAHO

Mr. David M. Cohen
Mental Health Technician/Social Worker Aide
    Program
North Idaho College
1000 West Garden Avenue
Coeur d'Alene, Idaho 83814
(208) 667-7422, Ext. 251

ILLINOIS

Dr. Hershel Statham
Mental Health Assistants Program
Carl Sandburg College
Box 1407, South Lake Storey Road
Galesburg, Illinois 61401
(309) 342-4141

Ms. Joyce Burnett
Coordinator of Community Services
Central YMCA Community College
211 West Wacker Drive
Chicago, Illinois 60606
(312) 222-8279

Dr. Raymond W. Olson
Human Service Program
College of DuPage
22d Lambert Road
Glen Ellyn, Illinois 60137
(312) 858-2800, Ext. 505

Dr. G. Edward Stormer
Human Service Program
Kankakee Community College and Governors
    State University
Park Forest South, Illinois 60466
(312) 563-2211, Ext. 334

Mr. Orell R. Vanderwater
Mental Health Aide Program
Lincoln Land Community College
3865 South Sixth Street/Frontage Road
Springfield, Illinois 62703
(217) 529-6661, Ext. 260

Mr. Gary Prouty
Mental Health Aide Program
Department of Human Service
Prairie State College
P.O. Box 487
Chicago Heights, Illinois 60411
(312) 756-3110

Dr. Ron Hollstrom
Mental Health Technician Program
Rock Valley College

3301 North Mufford Road
Rockford, Illinois 61107
(815) 226-2600

Ms. Sharon Rise
Thornton Community College
50 West 162nd Street
South Holland, Illinois 60473
(312) 331-8820

Mr. Don Green
Elgin Community College
1700 Spartan Drive
Elgin, Illinois 60120
(312) 697-1000

Dr. Frances McCann
Triton College
2000 Fifth Avenue
River Grove, Illinois 60171
(312) 456-0300

INDIANA

Dr. Sherwin Kepes
Community Mental Health Training
Purdue University
2101 East U. S. 30
Fort Wayne, Indiana 46805
(219) 483-8121, Ext. 328

Vincennes University
Vincennes, Indiana 47591
(812) 882-3350

IOWA

Mr. Thomas Hunt
Des Moines Area Community College
Ankeny Boulevard
Ankeny, Iowa 50021
(515) 964-0651

Dr. Harold H. Anderson
Community Service Associate Program
Iowa Western Community College
923 East Washington
Clarinda, Iowa 51632
(712) 542-5117, Ext. 243

Ms. Judy Parker
Psychology Instructor
Grand View College
East 9th & Grandview
Des Moines, Iowa 50316
(515) 265-4232

KANSAS

Mr. T. Clarence Brown
Mental Health Workers Program
Allen County Community Junior College
1801 North Cottonwood
Iola, Kansas 66749
(316) 365-5116

Mr. Jimmie L. Downing
Barton County Community College
Great Bend, Kansas 67530
(316) 792-2701

Mr. Charles Kerr
Mental Health Worker Training
Cowley County Community College
Arkansas City, Kansas 67005
(316) 221-1200, Ext. 305

KENTUCKY

Ms. Claudia B. Watson
Mental Health Assistants Program
Henderson Community College
University of Kentucky
Highway 60 West
Henderson, Kentucky 42420
(502) 827-1867

Mr. Thomas L. Riley
Middle Level Mental Health Workers Training Program
Hopkinsville Community College
North Drive
Hopkinsville, Kentucky 42240
(502) 886-3921

Mr. James Mahanes
Jefferson Community College
P.O. Box 1036
Louisville, Kentucky 40201
(502) 584-0181

Ms. Doris Schmidt
Mental Health Technology Program
Morehead State University
Box 856
Morehead, Kentucky 40351
(606) 783-3271

Ms. Mary K. Bailey
Mental Health Associate Program
Somerset Community College
Montecello Road
Somerset, Kentucky 42501
(606) 678-8174, Ext. 26

Ms. Joan Angelone
Department of Allied Health
Southeast Community College
Cumberland, Kentucky 40823
(606) 589-2145

Dr. Robert E. Hall
Alice Lloyd College
Pippa Passes, Kentucky 41844
(606) 368-2101

LOUISIANA

Mr. Sterling Smith
Delgado Junior College
615 City Park Avenue
New Orleans, Louisiana 70019
(504) 486-5403

MAINE

Dr. Arthur L. Benton
University of Maine
Bangor, Maine 04474
(207) 945-9446

MARYLAND

Dr. Enno K. Lohrmann
Human Service Program
Anne Arundel Community College
Arnold, Maryland 21012
(301) 647-7100, Ext. 285

Dr. Shabse H. Kurland
Mental Health Associate Program
Catonsville Community College
800 South Rolling Road
Catonsville, Maryland 21228
(301) 752-5640

Dr. Eveline D. Schulman
Community College of Baltimore
2901 Liberty Heights Avenue
Baltimore, Maryland 21215
(301) 462-5800, Ext. 245

Mr. Patrick J. Sherry
Mental Health Associate Program
Essex Community College
Baltimore, Maryland 21237
(301) 682-6000, Ext. 350

Ms. Constance L. Moerman
Mental Health Associate Program
Montgomery College
Takoma Avenue & Fenton Street
Takoma Park, Maryland 20012
(301) 587-0415, Ext. 67

Dr. Shanti Tayal
Mental Health Clinician Program
Prince Georges Community College
301 Largo Road
Largo, Maryland 20870
(301) 336-6000, Ext. 385 or 235

Dr. Robert Grooms
Department of Psychology
Frostburg State College
Frostburg, Maryland 21532
(301) 689-6621

Garrett County Community College
McHenry, Maryland 21541
(301) 387-6666 or 245-2181

Dr. John J. Connolly
Harford Junior College
401 Thomas Run Road
Bel Air, Maryland 21014
(301) 734-7171

MASSACHUSETTS

Dr. Salah A. Batrawi
Mental Health Assistants Program
Bay Path Junior College
588 Longmeadow Street
Longmeadow, Massachusetts 01160
(413) 567-0621, Ext. 43

Dr. Daniel J. O'Neill
Mental Health Technology Program
Bristol Community College

64 Durfee Street
Fall River, Massachusetts 02720
(617) 678-2811, Ext. 41

Ms. Betsy Woodacre
Training for Teaching Careers in Early Childhood Education Program
Dean Junior College
99 Main Street
Franklin, Massachusetts 02038
(617) 528-9100, Ext. 386

Mr. Bernard F. Prescott
Community Mental Health Technology Program
Greenfield Community College
125 Federal Street
Greenfield, Massachusetts 01301
(413) 774-3131, Ext. 54

Ms. Joy Heaker
Massasoit Community College
290 Thatcher Street
Brockton, Massachusetts 02402
(617) 588-9100

Mr. Frederic B. Viaux
Mental Health Technology Program
Middlesex Community College
Springs Road
Bedford, Massachusetts 01730
(617) 275-8910, Ext. 42

Dr. Peter J. Trainor
Community Mental Health Technology Program
Mount Wachusett Community College
130 Elm Street
Gardner, Massachusetts 01440
(617) 632-1280, Ext. 35

Ms. Mary T. Killeen
Mental Health Technology Program
Springfield Technical Community College
Armory Square
Springfield, Massachusetts 01105
(413) 781-6470, Ext. 71 or 22

Ms. Glorida Carritte
Laboure Junior College
2100 Dorchester Avenue
Boston, Massachusetts 02124
(617) 296-8300

Ms. Lyda S. Peters
New Careers Program
Metropolitan College
Boston University
720 Harrison Avenue, 6th Floor
Boston, Massachusetts 02218
(617) 262-4200, Ext. 5875 or 262-0571

Mr. Donald W. Beattie
North Shore Community College
3 Essex Street
Beverly, Massachusetts 01915
(617) 927-4850

MICHIGAN

Mr. Craig Berke
Ferris State College
Starr 105
Big Rapids, Michigan 49307
　(616) 796-9971, Ext. 227

Ms. Shirley Lampky
Associate of Arts in Mental Health Program
Mid Michigan Community College
Harrison, Michigan 48625
　(517) 386-7792, Ext. 25

Mr. Darrol E. Robinson
Mental Health Associate Program
Oakland Community College
Auburn Hills Campus
2900 Featherstone Road
Pontiac, Michigan 48057
　(313) 852-1000, Ext. 261

Ms. Carol Watson
Director of Community and Social Services
Human Services Department
Wayne County Community College
Detroit, Michigan 48202
　(313) 832-5500

Mr. Kenneth F. Light
Vice President for Academic Affairs
Lake Superior State College
Sault Ste. Marie, Michigan 49783
　(906) 632-6841

Dr. Ralph A. Austermiller
Muskegon Community College
221 South Quarterline Road
Muskegon, Michigan 49443
　(616) 773-9131, Ext. 284

Oakland Community College
Bloomfield Hills, Michigan 48013
　(313) 647-6200

Ms. Lillian Kelmenson
Oakland Community College
Highland Lakes Campus
Union Lake, Michigan 48085
　(313) 363-7191

Ms. Mary Smith
Schoolcraft College
18600 Haggerty Road
Livonia, Michigan 48151
　(313) 591-6400

Mr. Mehran Thomson, Jr.
Washtenaw Community College
P.O. Box 345
Ann Arbor, Michigan 48107
　(313) 971-6300

MINNESOTA

Mr. Roger C. Betz
Mental Health Workers Program
Inver Hills State Junior College
8445 College Trail
Inver Grove Heights, Minnesota 55075
　(612) 455-9621

Dr. Walter J. Cullen
Metropolitan State Junior College
Minneapolis, Minnesota 55406
　(612) 335-8944

Dr. Grace Ramseyer
Child Development Technician Program
St. Mary's Junior College
2600 South 6th Street
Minneapolis, Minnesota 55406
　(612) 332-5521, Ext. 65

Mr. David Foat
Human Service Program
University of Minnesota
Box 393, Mayo Memorial Building
Minneapolis, Minnesota 55455
　(612) 373-9139

Veterans Administration Hospital
St. Cloud, Minnesota
　(612) 252-1670

MISSISSIPPI

Ms. Louise Jones
Health Occupations
Gulf Coast Junior College
Perkinston, Mississippi 39573
　(601) 928-7211

Mr. James Baddley
Allied Health Programs
Hinds Junior College
Raymond, Mississippi 39154
　(601) 857-5261

Mr. David H. Wicks
Saints Junior College
Lexington, Mississippi 39095
　(601) 834-1246

MISSOURI

Ms. Yvette Dubinsky
Forest Park Community College
5600 Oakland
St. Louis, Missouri 63110
　(314) MI4-3300

Dr. Florence Brown
Meramec Community College
Kirkwood, Missouri 63122
　(314) 966-3402

Mr. Dwight W. Rieman
University of Missouri-Columbia
Columbia, Missouri 65201
　(314) 449-0531

MONTANA

Dr. Larry J. Blake
Human Services Technology Program
Flathead Valley Community College
P.O. Box 1174
Kalispell, Montana 59901
　(406) 752-3411

NEBRASKA

Mr. Charles L. Pratt
Mental Health in Community Service Program

Nebraska Western College
1601 East 27th Street, N.E.
Scottsbluff, Nebraska 69361
(308) 635-3606, Ext. 41

Ms. Locada Bruce
Health Division
Central Nebraska Technical College
Box 1024
Hastings, Nebraska 68901
(402) 463-9811

NEW HAMPSHIRE
Ms. Shirley L. Kransner
White Pines College
Chester, New Hampshire 03036
(603) 887-4401

NEW JERSEY
Dr. Harry Sherer
Brookdale Community College
765 Newman Springs Road
Lincroft, New Jersey 07738
(201) 842-1900

Dr. Karoly Nagy
Rehabilitation Assistant Education Program
Middlesex County College
Edison, New Jersey 08817
(201) 548-6000, Ext. 278

NEW MEXICO
Mr. Joseph Lucero
Community Mental Health Training Program
College of Santa Fe
St. Michael's Drive
Santa Fe, New Mexico 87501
(505) 982-6384

Associate Degree Human Resource Aide Program
Eastern New Mexico University-Roswell Campus
P.O. Box 6761
Roswell, New Mexico 88201
(505) 347-5441, Ext. 252

Dr. Stephen R. Perls
Associate of Arts in Community Services Program
University of New Mexico School of Medicine
930 Stanford, N. E.
Albuquerque, New Mexico 87106
(505) 277-5428

NEW YORK
Dr. Norman E. Farber
Community Mental Health Assistant Program
Borough of Manhattan Community College
799 Seventh Avenue
New York, New York 10020
(21) 262-5431 or 262-5380

Ms. Audrey Cohen
College for Human Services
201 Barick Street

New York, New York 11218
(212) 989-2002

Mr. Dale White
Human Service Program
Corning Community College
Corning, New York 14830
(607) 962-9213

Mr. Raymond Cagan
Community Mental Health Assistant Program
Dutchess Community College
Pendell Road
Poughkeepsie, New York 12601
(914) 471-4500, Ext. 24

Ms. Arline Lyle
Human Service Program
Hudson Valley Community College
Vandenburgh Avenue
Troy, New York 12180
(518) 283-1100

Dr. Martin E. Danzig
Kingsborough Community College of The City University of New York
2101 Oriental Boulevard
Manhattan Beach
Brooklyn, New York 11235
(212) 769-9200

Ms. Barbara Merrill
Human Service Program
Monroe Community College
1000 East Henrietta Road
Rochester, New York 14623
(716) 442-9950, Ext. 341

Mr. J. Peter Martin
Community Mental Health Assistant Program
North Country Community College
20 Winona Avenue
Saranac Lake, New York 12983
(518) 891-2915, Ext. 50

Dr. Lawrence L. Barrell
Human Service Program
Rockland Community College
145 College Road
Suffern, New York 10901
(914) 356-4650, Ext. 288

Bernard Schwartzberg
Community Service Assistant Program
State University Agricultural and Technical College
Conklin Hall, Room 4
Melville Road
Farmingdale, New York 11735
(516) 420-2043

Mr. C. Nacker
Mental Health Assisting Program
Sullivan Community College
South Fallsburg, New York 12779
(914) 434-5750

Human Services Training Program
Tompkins/Cortland Community College
175 Main Street

Groton, New York 13073
(607) 898-5825

Mr. Robert A. Kurland
Community Service Assistant Program
Ulster County Community College
Stone Ridge, New York 12484
(914) 687-7621, Ext. 27

Ms. Dorothy Kelly
Human Services Program
Onondaga Community College
700 East Water Street
Syracuse, New York 13210
(315) 492-9548

NORTH CAROLINA

Mr. Bradford Reynolds
Human Service Associate Program
Central Piedmont Community College
P.O. Box 4009 Kings Drive at Elizabeth
Avenue
Charlotte, North Carolina 28204
(704) 372-2590, Ext. 282

Mr. Everette D. Allen
Mental Health Associate Program
Lenoir Community College
P.O. Box 188
Kinston, North Carolina 28501
(919) 527-6223, Ext. 41

Ms. Margaret French
Mental Health Associate Program
Pitt Technical Institute
P.O. Drawer 7007
Greenville, North Carolina 27834
(919) 756-3130, Ext. 41

Ms. Elizabeth Alexander Kelly
Sandhills Community College
P.O. Box 1379
Southern Pines, North Carolina 28387
(919) 692-6185, Ext. 42

Mr. Dan Cowley
Mental Health Associate Program
Wayne Community College
Box 1878
Goldsboro, North Carolina 27530
(919) 735-5152, Ext. 32

Mr. Larry Whitlock
Mental Health Associate Program
Western Piedmont Community College
Morganton, North Carolina 28655
(704) 437-8688, Ext. 64

Mr. Frank L. Eagles
Wilson County Technical Institute
P.O. Box 4305
Wilson, North Carolina 27893
(919) 237-1195

Dr. Robert G. Brock
Edgecombe County Technical Institute
P.O. Box 550
Tarboro, North Carolina 27886
(919) 823-5166

OHIO

Mr. Thurston L. Cosner
Mental Health Technology Program
Cuyahoga Community College
2900 Community College Avenue
Cleveland, Ohio 44115
(216) 241-5966, Ext. 361

Ms. Jane G. White
Mental Health Technology Program
Muskingum Area Technical Institute
400 Richards Road
Zanesville, Ohio 43701
(614) 454-0101, Ext. 209

Ms. Helen Worstell
Mental Health Technology Program
Ohio University/Athens Mental Health Center
Mental Health Technology Department
212 Gordy Hall
Athens, Ohio 45701
(614) 594-3976

Mr. Robert J. Buehler
Mental Health Technology Program
Sinclair Community College
140 South Perry Street
Dayton, Ohio 45402
(513) 252-6501, Ext. 289

Dr. Theodore H. Wohl
Hamilton County Diagnostic Clinic
University of Cincinnati
295 Erkenbrecher Avenue
Cincinnati, Ohio 45229
(513) 221-8282

Mr. Thomas F. Graham
Walsh College
Canton, Ohio 44720
(216) 499-7090

OKLAHOMA

Mr. Dan B. Gottsch
Community Mental Health Program
Northern Oklahoma College
12220 East Grand
Tonkawa, Oklahoma 74653
(405) 628-2581, Ext. 50

Fr. Paul Zohler
Saint Gregory's College
Shawnee, Oklahoma 74801
(405) 273-9870

OREGON

Mr. George Buttles
Mental Health Technology Program
Chemeketa Community College
4389 Satter Drive N.E.
Salem, Oregon 97303
(503) 585-7900, Ext. 84

Ms. Patricia L. Lantz
Community Mental Health Worker Program
Clackamas Community College
19600 South Molalla Avenue

Oregon City, Oregon 97045
(503) 656-2631, Ext. 264

Mr. Willotta Asbjornsen
Mental Health Worker Training Program
Mt. Hood Community College
26000 S. E. Stark Street
Gresham, Oregon 97030
(503) 666-1561, Ext. 124

PENNSYLVANIA

Mr. Douglas A. Whyte
Mental Health Work Program
Community College of Philadelphia
34 South 11th Street
Philadelphia, Pennsylvania 19107
(215) 569-3680, Ext. 281

Ms. Katherine B. O'Neil
Harcum Junior College
Bryn Mawr, Pennsylvania 19010
(215) 525-4100

Ms. Ann Lyon
Mental Health Technology Program
Harrisburg Area Community College
3300 Cameron Street Road
Harrisburg, Pennsylvania 17110
(717) 236-9533, Ext. 278

RHODE ISLAND

Ms. Elizabeth P. Carollo
Department of Education and Social Services
Rhode Island Junior College
199 Promenade Street
Providence, Rhode Island 02908
(401) 331-5500, Ext. 40

Mr. John W. Stout
Community and Social Services Program
Roger Williams College
Bristol, Rhode Island 02809
(401) 255-2341

SOUTH CAROLINA

Mr. Roy T. Denton
Mental Health Technology Program
Greenville Technical Education Center
Box 5616, Station B
Greenville, South Carolina 29606
(803) 242-3170, Ext. 307

Mr. George Panos
Community and Mental Health Technology
 Program
Midlands Technical Education Center
316 Beltline Boulevard
P.O. Drawer Q
Columbia, South Carolina 29205
(803) 782-5471, Ext. 260

Ms. Moseley
Human Service Program
Palmer Junior College
125 Bull Street
Charleston, South Carolina 29401
(803) 722-0531

SOUTH DAKOTA

Sister Alicia Dunphy
Academic Dean
Presentation College
Aberdeen, South Dakota 57401
(605) 225-0420

TENNESSEE

Dr. Jack N. Forsythe
Mental Health Technology Program
Columbia State Community College
Columbia, Tennessee 38401
(615) 388-0120, Ext. 287

Mr. James C. Moore
Human Services Career Education
Volunteer State Community College
Nashville Pike
Gallatin, Tennessee 37066
(615) 452-8600

Mr. J. Pritchett
Cleveland State Community College
Cleveland, Tennessee 37311
(615) 472-7141

Dr. John E. Pate
Vanderbilt University
Nashville, Tennessee 37203
(615) 254-5411

Dr. James Coburn
Walters State Community College
Morristown, Tennessee 37814
(615) 581-2121

TEXAS

Mr. James L. Moncrief
Human Service Program
Amarillo College
P.O. Box 447
Amarillo, Texas 79105
(806) 376-5641, Ext. 297 or 352

Mr. Perry Carter
Human Service Program
Angelina College
P.O. Box 1768
Lufkin, Texas 75901
(713) 634-7744, Ext. 55

Dr. C. William Day
Mental Retardation Program
Cooke County Junior College
P.O. Box 815
Gainesville, Texas 76240
(817) 665-3476, Ext. 24

Dr. Ruby H. Herd
El Centro College
Main & Lamar
Dallas, Texas 75202
(214) 746-2312

Mr. J. Lawrence Cantwell
Community Health Worker Program
Galveston College
School of Allied Health Sciences

University of Texas Medical Branch
Galveston, Texas 77550
   (713) 765-2695, Ext. 20

Mr. Dexter L. Betts
Director of Program Development
Dallas County Community College District
200 Main Bank Building
Main and Lamar
Dallas, Texas 75202
   (214) 746-2149

Dr. Aaron Seamster
Del Mar College
Corpus Christi, Texas 78404
   (512) 882-6231

Dr. Chester R. Hastings
McLennan Community College
Waco, Texas 76703
   (817) 756-6551

Mr. Harold F. Layhee
Inter-Institutional Programs
Midwestern University
3400 Taft
Wichita Falls, Texas 76308
   (817) 692-6611

Dr. William Sproull
Tarrant County Junior College District
Fort Worth, Texas 76102
   (817) 336-7851

UTAH

Mr. Richard Bolton
Human Service Psychiatric Technology Program
Utah Technical College at Provo
1395 North 150 East
P.O. Box 1009
Provo, Utah 84601
   (801) 373-4400, Ext. 252

VERMONT

Ms. Lenore McNeer
Mental Health Technology Program
Vermont College
College Street
Montpelier, Vermont 05602
   (802) 223-2135

VIRGINIA

Mr. Marvin Glenn Weber
Mental Health Technology Program
Blue Ridge Community College
P.O. Box 80
Weyers Cave, Virginia 24486
   (703) 234-2461, Ext. 23

Dr. Ben F. Wheless
Mental Health Program
Sullins College
Virginia Park
Bristol, Virginia 24201
   (703) 669-6112, Ext. 25

Mr. W. M. Houchins
Mental Health Technology Program
Virginia Western Community College
3095 Colonial Avenue, S.W.
Roanoke, Virginia 24015
   (703) 344-2031, Ext. 359

Dr. Douglas M. Montgomery
Tidewater Community College
Portsmouth, Virginia 23702
   (703) 484-2121

WASHINGTON

Ms. A. Laverne Phillips
Social Services Program
Bellevue Community College
3000 145th Place, S. E.
Bellevue, Washington 98007
   (206) 641-2331

Dr. Robert Heaberlin
Mental Health Program
Ft. Steilacoom Community College
P.O. Box 3186
Tacoma, Washington 98499
   (206) 588-3623

Pat Rivest
Human Service Program
Spokane Falls Community College
W3410 Ft. Wright Drive
Spokane, Washington 99204
   (509) 456-2810

Seattle Central Community College
Seattle, Washington 98122
   (206) 587-4100

Tacoma Community College
Tacoma, Washington 98465
   (206) 752-6641

WEST VIRGINIA

Mr. James T. Handlen
Potomac State College of the University of West Virginia
Keyser, West Virginia 26726
   (304) 788-3011

WISCONSIN

Ms. Mary Ann Johnson
Waukesha Technical Institute
800 Main
Pewaukee, Wisconsin 53072
   (414) 691-3200, Ext. 256

INDEX